"A Hard Saying"

The Gospel and Culture

Francis J. Moloney, S.D.B.

D0838796

A Michael Glazier Book
THE LITURGICAL PRESS
Collegeville, Minnesota
www.litpress.org

A Michael Glazier Book published by The Liturgical Press

Cover design by Greg Becker. Illustration: *Mañana de Pascua,* 1833, by Caspar David Friedrich. © Museo Thyssen-Bornemisza, Madrid. Used with permission.

1   2   3   4   5   6   7   8

Library of Congress Cataloging-in-Publication Data

Moloney, Francis J.
      A hard saying : the Gospel and culture / Francis J. Moloney.
            p.   cm.
      Includes bibliographical references and index.
      ISBN 0-8146-5953-5 (alk. paper)
      1. Bible. N.T.—Criticism, interpretation, etc.   2. Bible. N.T. Gospels—Criticism, interpretation, etc.   3. Christianity and culture.   I. Title.

      BS2361.3 .M65   2001
      226'.06—dc21
                                                                00-047791

For
The Redemptorists
of
Holy Redeemer College
Washington, D.C.

Contents

PREFACE

My adult life has been lived in many places, and as a result my shorter writings have often appeared in geographically or culturally restricted contexts. I am grateful to have the opportunity to reproduce a number of my articles, judged by my colleagues as important, to a wider reading public. The collection that follows contains studies I have published from 1979 to the recent past, some appearing here for the first time. Each piece betrays its "origins." I am proud to be an Australian, and the bulk of the articles that follow were originally published in *Pacifica. Australian Theological Studies, Australian Biblical Review,* or *The Australasian Catholic Record.* I am also proud to be a Salesian of Don Bosco, and thus other articles in this volume first appeared in the official journal of the Salesian Pontifical University in Rome, *Salesianum,* or as studies honoring my colleagues at that university. My other point of "origin" was the University of Oxford, where I completed my doctoral studies in 1975. I had a close association with the Benedictine Sisters at St. Mary's Priory, Fernham, in those years, and through them established contact with *The Downside Review,* which first produced several of the essays that follow.

I have a deep respect for the careful and painstaking historical and philological work that supports all quality biblical scholarship. However, from my first encounter with Jules Cambier, S.D.B., who taught a course on Paul's letter to the Romans at the Salesian Pontifical University in 1967, I have been aware that a critical reading of our sacred texts challenges established cultures, both secular and religious. One place in the New Testament where this is stated is in John 6:60. The disciples have witnessed the bread miracle (6:1-15), experienced Jesus' self-revelation as "I AM" on the sea (vv. 16-21), and heard the discourse on the bread from heaven (vv. 25-59), but some decide they can no longer follow Jesus. They look back across all that Jesus has said, and assert:

"This is a hard saying; who can listen to it?" (6:60). Unable to accept Jesus' radical reinterpretation of their traditions, they "drew back and no longer went about with him" (v. 66).[1] The Christian Church, inevitably caught in a culture and history of its own making, will always find the Gospel "a hard saying."

Apart from my publications in the area of Johannine studies much of my research and occasional writing reflects upon the interface between the New Testament and "contemporary cultures." Some of it appears here: women, divorce, and celibacy, a fragile Church and its sinful members, health care and the importance of human life, the shame of an exclusive eucharistic table, sacraments, the Spirit, and postmodern literary criticism. Although the studies had their own original setting they were chosen and rewritten for this publication to create a unity around the theme of the book's subtitle: "The Gospel and Culture." Not one of them appears exactly as it was first published. Each study has seen some rewriting, and references to contemporary literature have been added to older articles.

Everything I teach or write is guided by words written a number of years ago by Professor Morna D. Hooker, whom I was privileged to have as the supervisor of my doctoral research at the University of Oxford from 1972 to 1975. Morna set the agenda for my teaching and writing when she wrote of the need for scholars to face "the problems of relating the givenness of the past with the exhilarating experience of the present."[2] In preparing these papers for further publication I have been struck by the immense influence that the work of Raymond E. Brown, s.s., has had on me over the three decades of my professional life as a biblical scholar. Ray's passing in August 1998 was an immense loss to contemporary biblical scholarship, but it was the achievement of his own dearest wish, to come to grips with "The Resurrection of the Messiah" in his sharing of that resurrection experience "face to face."[3] In publicly recognizing all I have received from him and thanking God for the gift of Ray Brown I express the sentiments of many scholars of my generation who have had the good fortune to learn so much from him in so many ways. He was not only the premier biblical scholar of

---

[1] On John 6:60-66 see Francis J. Moloney, *The Gospel of John*, SP 4 (Collegeville: The Liturgical Press, 1998) 226–29.

[2] Morna D. Hooker, "In His Own Image," in Colin Hickling and Morna D. Hooker, *What about the New Testament? Studies in Honour of Christopher Evans* (London: SCM, 1975) 41.

[3] For Ray's tongue-in-cheek expression of this hope see his *The Death of the Messiah. From Gethsemane to the Grave. A Commentary on the Passion Narratives in the Four Gospels.* ABRL (New York: Doubleday, 1994) xii.

our time but also a consummate gentleman and a wonderful Catholic priest.

I am grateful to The Liturgical Press and to its Academic Editor, Dr. Linda Maloney, for making this work possible. One of the reasons for its existence is my recent shift from Australian Catholic University to The Catholic University of America, Washington, D.C. My students from the United States ask why these pieces are not more readily available. Theresa Thanh-Tuyen Nguyen, M.T.G., an enthusiastic M.A. graduate of The Catholic University of America, supported me in the preparation of material not available in electronic form. I am also grateful to my colleague at The Catholic University, Bill Loewe, and my dear friend and long-standing critic, Nerina Zanardo, F.S.P., who read many of these rewritten essays. Between them they read everything!

I am using the publication of this volume as a means to thank publicly the Redemptorists of the Baltimore Province, with whom I share the Christian and the religious life at Holy Redeemer College in Washington, D.C. Without their support and companionship my presence in Washington might have been very brief.

Francis J. Moloney, S.D.B., A.M., F.A.H.A.
Department of Biblical Studies
The Catholic University of America
Washington, D.C.

ACKNOWLEDGMENTS

Thanks are due to the following for permission to reproduce the essays in this volume. Some rewriting of the original essay has taken place in every case, but the argument of each contribution remains the same.

"Jesus and Women" first appeared in Mario Cimosa and Ferdinando Bergamelli, eds., *Virgo Fidelis. Miscellanea di studi mariani in onore di Don Domenico Bertetto, S.D.B.* Bibliotheca "Ephemerides Liturgicae Subsidia" 43. Rome: Edizioni Liturgiche, 1988, 53–80.

"Matthew 19:3-12 and Celibacy: A Redactional and Form-Critical Study," *JSNT* 2 (1979) 42–60.

"The Vocation of the Disciples in the Gospel of Mark," *Sal* 43 (1981) 487–516.

"Narrative Criticism of the Gospels," *Pac* 4 (1991) 181–201.

"When is John Talking about Sacraments?" *AusBR* 30 (1982) 10–33.

"John 18:15-27: A Johannine View of the Church," *DRev* 112 (1994) 231–48.

"The Fourth Gospel: A Tale of Two Paracletes," was published in an earlier form as "The Johannine Paraclete and Jesus," in A. Strus and R. Blatniky, eds., *Dummodo Christus annuntietur. Studi in Onore di Prof. Jozef Heriban.* BibScRel 146. Rome: LAS, 1998, 213–28. It was presented in its present form at the annual general meeting of the Australian Catholic Biblical Association in June 1998 at Melbourne University, Victoria, Australia.

"'God so loved the world.' The Jesus of John's Gospel," *ACR* 75 (1998) 195–205.

"Jesus Christ: The Question to Cultures," *Pac* 1 (1988) 15–43.

"The Eucharist as Jesus' Presence to the Broken," *Pac* 2 (1989) 152–75.

"Life, Healing and the Bible: A Christian Challenge," *Pac* 8 (1995) 315–34.

"Adventure with Nicodemus. An Exercise in Hermeneutics," appeared in an earlier form as "To Teach the Text: The New Testament in a New Age," *Pac* 11 (1998) 159–80. It was delivered in its present form at the annual meeting of the Catholic Biblical Association of America in August 1998, at the University of Scranton, Pennsylvania, U.S.A.

ABBREVIATIONS

AB	Anchor Bible
ABR	*Australian Biblical Review*
ABRL	Anchor Bible Reference Library
ACR	*Australasian Catholic Record*
AGJU	Arbeiten zur Geschichte des Antiken Judentums und des Urchristentums
AnBib	Analecta Biblica
ANRW	Wolfgang Haase and Hildegard Temporini, eds., *Aufstieg und Niedergang der Römischen Welt: Teil II: Principat – Religion.* Berlin: Walter de Gruyter, 1972–
AThR	*Anglican Theological Review*
ATLA	American Theological Library Association
BBB	Bonner biblische Beiträge
BDF	Blass, F., A. Debrunner, and R. W. Funk. *A Greek Grammar of the New Testament and Other Early Christian Literature.* Chicago: University of Chicago Press, 1961.
BeO	*Bibbia e oriente*
BETL	Bibliotheca ephemeridum theologicarum lovaniensium
BGBE	Beiträge zur Geschichte der biblischen Exegese
BHT	Beiträge zur historischen Theologie
Bib	*Biblica*
BJRL	*Bulletin of the John Rylands University Library of Manchester*
BK	*Bibel und Kirche*
BSRel	Biblioteca di Scienze Religiose
BTB	*Biblical Theology Bulletin*
BThSt	Biblisch-theologische Studien
BVC	*Bible et vie chrétienne*
BZ	*Biblische Zeitschrift*

BZNW	Beihefte zur *Zeitschrift für die neutestamentliche Wissenschaft*
CBQ	*Catholic Biblical Quarterly*
DRev	*Downside Review*
EBib	Etudes bibliques
EstEcl	*Estudios eclesiásticos*
ETL	Ephemerides theologicae lovanienses
ExpTim	*Expository Times*
FB	Forschung zur Bibel
FRLANT	Forschungen zur Religion und Literatur des Alten und Neuen Testaments
FTS	Frankfurter theologische Studien
Greg	*Gregorianum*
HeyJ	*Heythrop Journal*
HKNT	Handkommentar zum Neuen Testament
HTCNT	Herder's Theological Commentary on the New Testament
HTKNT	Herders theologischer Kommentar zum Neuen Testament
ICC	International Critical Commentary
Int	*Interpretation*
IRT	Issues in Religion and Theology
JAAR	*Journal of the American Academy of Religion*
JBL	*Journal of Biblical Literature*
JR	*Journal of Religion*
JSNT	*Journal for the Study of the New Testament*
JSNTSup	Journal for the Study of the New Testament: Supplement Series
JSOT	Journal for the Study of the Old Testament
JSOTSup	Journal for the Study of the Old Testament: Supplement Series
JTS	*Journal of Theological Studies*
LAS	Libreria Ateneo Salesiano
Laur	*Laurentianum*
LD	Lectio divina
LV	*Lumen vitae*
LXX	Septuagint
NCB	New Century Bible
NJBC	*The New Jerome Biblical Commentary.* Edited by R. E. Brown, et al. Englewood Cliffs, N.J.: Prentice Hall, 1990.
NovT	*Novum Testamentum*
NovTSup	Novum Testamentum Supplements
NRTh	*La nouvelle revue théologique*
NTD	Das Neue Testament Deutsch
ÖTK	Ökumenischer Taschenbuch-Kommentar
Pac	*Pacifica. Australian Theological Studies*

PG	Patrologia graeca [= Patrologiae cursus completus: Series graeca]. Edited by J.-P. Migne. 162 vols. Paris, 1857–1886
PL	Patrologia latina [= Patrologiae cursus completus: Series latina]. Edited by J.-P. Migne. 217 vols. Paris, 1844–1864
RB	*Revue biblique*
RSV	Revised Standard Version
Sal	*Salesianum*
SANT	Studien zum Alten und Neuen Testaments
SBB	Stuttgarter biblische Beiträge
SBFA	Studii Biblici Franciscani Analecta
SBL	Society of Biblical Literature
SBLDS	Society of Biblical Literature Dissertation Series
SBM	Stuttgarter biblische Monographien
SBS	Stuttgarter Bibelstudien
SBT	Studies in Biblical Theology
ScrB	*Scripture Bulletin*
SNT	Studien zum Neuen Testament
SNTSMS	Society for New Testament Studies Monograph Series
Str-B	Strack, H. L., and Paul Billerbeck, *Kommentar zum Neuen Testament aus Talmud und Midrasch.* 6 vols. Munich: C. H. Beck, 1922–1961.
SUNT	Studien zur Umwelt des Neuen Testaments
TD	*Theology Digest*
TDNT	*Theological Dictionary of the New Testament.* Edited by Gerhard Kittel and Gerhard Friedrich. Translated by G. W. Bromiley. 10 vols. Grand Rapids: Eerdmans, 1964–1976.
TGl	*Theologie und Glaube*
ThQ	*Theologische Quartalschrift*
ThV	*Theologische Versuche*
TS	*Theological Studies*
TThSt	Trierer theologische Studien
TTZ	*Trierer theologische Zeitschrift*
TZ	Theologische Zeitschrift
WBC	Word Biblical Commentary
WMANT	Wissenschaftliche Monographien zum Alten und Neuen Testament
WUNT	Wissenschaftliche Untersuchungen zum Neuen Testament
ZKT	*Zeitschrift für Katholische Theologie*
ZNW	*Zeitschrift für die neutestamentliche Wissenschaft und die Kunde der älteren Kirche*
ZTK	*Zeitschrift für Theologie und Kirche*

PART 1

THE SYNOPTIC GOSPELS

CHAPTER 1

JESUS AND WOMEN

Any attempt to interpret Jesus' personal relationships and psychological attitudes involves significant difficulties. There have been several recent and varied attempts to pursue studies in the area of Jesus' sexuality,[1] but it is widely admitted that the evidence is scarce, and that care must be taken not to make too many decisions on the basis of scant material. The accounts of the life of Jesus as we have them in our four canonical gospels are heavily conditioned by each evangelist's theological point of view. Many would, in fact, claim that it is simply impossible to glean any portrait of Jesus that could provide us with an idea of his attitudes to and relationships with women.

---

[1] See especially William E. Phipps, *The Sexuality of Jesus* (New York: Harper & Row, 1973). Phipps infers that Jesus had a positive attitude to his own sexuality because of his commendations of marriage and his considerate treatment of women. See the review of the book by J. H. Rhys in *ATR* 56 (1974) 363–65. For a recent interpretation of Jesus as the founder of a homosexual secret sect see Morton Smith, *The Secret Gospel. The Discovery and Interpretation of the Secret Gospel According to Mark* (New York: Harper & Row, 1973). See the convincing rebuttal of Smith's argument in Quentin Quesnell, "The Mar Saba Clementine: A Question of Evidence," *CBQ* 37 (1975) 48–67, and Helmut Merkel, "Auf dem Spüren des Urmarkus. Ein neuer Fund und seine Beurteilung," *ZTK* 71 (1974) 123–44. Smith has since published a further work, *Jesus the Magician* (London: Victor Gollancz, 1978). Here he argues that the available anti-Jesus material from antiquity (generally suppressed by the Christian Church) shows that some of Jesus' contemporaries understood him as a *goēs* (a magician, a fraud). One of the aspects of such characters was that they gave themselves freely to irregular sexual activities. The study is not good history. It suffers from a subjective and tendentious interpretation of both biblical and secular texts.

3

In my opinion this oft-repeated skepticism is too rapidly assumed. It is remarkable how much material in the gospels touches on such attitudes and relationships. I will attempt, in the pages that follow, to delve into some of the material available to us in the gospels that indicates Jesus' attitude to, and relationships with, the women in his story. This is *not* a study of New Testament women characters, but a study of *Jesus*. I have been greatly enlightened by contemporary feminist readings of biblical texts, but the following study uses more traditional methods to ask questions about Jesus, not about the women.[2] It is with great pleasure that I dedicate this study to one of my own esteemed teachers during my years at the Salesian Pontifical University, Don Domenico Bertetto, a man who devoted much of his scholarly life to studying and teaching the mysteries of God's ways in "the woman" *par excellence* of the New Testament: Mary of Nazareth.[3]

It is of value to see how much material, coming from a wide variety of traditions and literary forms, is dedicated to the issue of Jesus' ways with and on behalf of women. It is possible that much of the material, which I will now list, reaches back, in one form or another, to the life and experience of Jesus of Nazareth.[4]

---

[2] I have neither the skills nor the experience of a woman to develop a feminist hermeneutic. I thus ask more historical questions that may provide data for that hermeneutic. Since this paper was first published (1988) much has happened in feminist biblical scholarship. Joining a broader consensus of audience-focused interpretative processes, some contemporary feminist scholars would reject my attempt to establish some historical elements that might serve a feminist reading of the New Testament. They would suggest that I am still working from a male perspective within male-determined historiography. See, for example, The Bible and Culture Collective, *The Postmodern Bible* (New Haven: Yale University Press, 1995) 225–71. For a presentation of contemporary feminist scholarship see the issue "Feminist Theology: The Next Stage," *Pac* 10 (1997). See also the bibliography collected by Maryanne Confoy in "Annotated Bibliography: Christian Feminist Writing," in Maryanne P. Confoy, Dorothy A. Lee, and Joan Nowotny, eds., *Freedom & Entrapment. Women Thinking Theology* (Melbourne: Harper Collins, 1995) 223–34.

[3] Domenico Bertetto s.d.b. died, fittingly, while delivering a series of lectures at the Marian shrine in Loreto in August 1988.

[4] For surveys of this material see Josef Blank, "Frauen in den Jesusüberlieferungen," in Gerhard Dautzenberg, Helmut Merklein, and Karlheinz Müller, eds., *Die Frau im Urchristentum*. QD 95 (Freiburg: Herder, 1983) 9–91; Evelyn and Frank Stagg, *Woman in the World of Jesus* (Philadelphia: Westminster, 1978) 101–60; Karl-Hermann Schelkle, *The Spirit and the Bride. Woman in the Bible* (Collegeville: The Liturgical Press, 1979) 67–90. Most important, however, is Elisabeth Schüssler Fiorenza, *In Memory of Her. A Feminist Reconstruction of Christian Origins* (New York: Crossroad, 1983) 99–159. Schüssler Fiorenza, as

The texts can be grouped in the following fashion:[5]

1. Women feature as the main protagonists in a series of miracle stories, all of which have their literary origins in the Gospel of Mark and have generally been retold by Matthew and Luke.[6]

---

the subtitle of her book indicates, asks an important historical question: "Were women as well as men the initiators of the Christian movement?" (p. xviii). She, like all scholars asking that question, is faced with the difficult task of first developing a hermeneutical approach and then applying that approach to 'he androcentric and patriarchal texts of the early Church. She does it well (see *In Memory of Her* 3–95). I believe that she comes close to proving her contention that "regardless of how androcentric texts may erase women from historiography, they do not prove the actual absence of women from the center of patriarchal history and biblical revelation" (p. 29). She seeks a method to "[transform] androcentric historiography into our common history" (p. 70). Rosemary Radford Ruether, *Sexism and God-Talk. Towards a Feminist Theology* (Boston: Beacon, 1983) 18, also writes of the need for such an approach: "To look back to some original base of meaning and truth before corruption is to know that truth is more basic than falsehood. . . . To find glimmers of this truth in submerged and alternative traditions through history is to assure oneself that one is not mad or duped. Only by finding an alternative historical community and tradition more deeply rooted than those that have become corrupted can one feel sure that in criticizing the dominant tradition one is not just subjectively criticizing the dominant tradition but is, rather, touching a deeper bedrock of authentic Being upon which to ground oneself. One cannot wield the lever of criticism without a place to stand." See also Elisabeth Moltmann-Wendel, *The Women Around Jesus. Reflections on Authentic Personhood* (New York: Crossroad, 1982) 1–12. This position opposes the work of such scholars as Mary Daly, who argue that we must now abandon the Christian tradition as a source for theology and look to the experience of women. On this, with all relevant references to Daly, see Schüssler Fiorenza, *In Memory of Her* 22–26. For a study of the gospel material see Ben Witherington III, *Women in the Ministry of Jesus*, SNTSMS 51 (Cambridge: Cambridge University Press, 1984). Witherington's study is a careful and somewhat over-optimistic historical approach to the gospels. He traces the uniqueness of Jesus' ways: "Jesus' teaching relating to women and their roles is sometimes radical, sometimes reformational, and usually controversial in its original setting" (p. 52).

[5] Some readers will be aware that the classifications used here for the gospel material come from form criticism. However, for the purposes of this study they are self-evident and need no further theoretical explanation.

[6] I am accepting that Mark was the first gospel to be written, and that it was one of the sources used by both Matthew and Luke. I am well aware that this presupposition, which had almost become a new dogma in New Testament source criticism, is now being questioned by William R. Farmer, Bernard Orchard, Hans-Herbert Stoldt, and others. While this criticism of Markan priority is healthy,

a. The healing of Peter's mother-in-law (Mark 5:24-34; Matt 8:14-15; Luke 4:38-39);

b. The healing of the woman with a hemorrhage (Mark 5:24-34; Matt 9:20-22; Luke 8:43-48);

c. The raising of the daughter of Jairus (Mark 5:21-24, 35-43; Matt 9:18-19, 23-26; Luke 8:40-42, 49-55);

d. The Syrophoenician (Canaanite) woman (Mark 7:24-30 [Syrophoenician]; Matt 15:21-26 [Canaanite]).

2. In two important passages women characters are used in a polemical situation with the religiously respectable. One of the passages is from Mark and is repeated by Luke, while the other, probably after a long, independent history in the growing traditions, has found its way into the Fourth Gospel.

a. The attack on the Pharisees, followed by the example of the poor widow who gives her all (Mark 12:38-44; Luke 20:45–21:4);

b. Jesus and the woman caught in adultery (John 7:53–8:11).

3. Women are also prominent in a series of parables found in the "Q" material or only in the Matthean tradition.

a. The parable of the leaven (Matt 13:33);

b. The parable of the two sons (Matt 21:28-32);

c. The parable of the wise and foolish virgins (Matt 25:1-13).

4. The narrative of the anointing of Jesus at Bethany can be found, in a variety of forms, in all four gospel traditions (Mark 14:3-9; Matt 26:6-13; John 12:1-8; see also Luke 7:36-50).

5. The presence of women at the cross, at the burial, and at the empty tomb of Jesus is again found, in a variety of forms, in all four gospel traditions (Mark 15:42–16:8; Matt 27:57–28:10; Luke 23:50–24:11; John 20:1-2, 11-18).

The *quantity* of the material is impressive. Even so, I have omitted the specifically Lukan material (e.g., Mary in the Lukan infancy narrative: Luke 1–2; the widow of Nain: 7:11-17; Martha and Mary: 10:38-42; the cure of the crippled woman: 13:10-17),[7] and the Johannine woman

---

I would still stand by the statement of the position I have adopted, as articulated by Joseph A. Fitzmyer, "The Priority of Mark and the 'Q' Source in Luke," in *To Advance the Gospel. New Testament Studies* (New York: Crossroad, 1981) 3–40.

[7] As well as the commentaries, for an analysis of this material see Francis J. Moloney, *Woman: First among the Faithful. A New Testament Study* (Melbourne: Collins Dove, 1984) 40–64, and Blank, "Frauen," 39–68.

characters (the mother of Jesus: John 2:1-11; 19:25-27; the Samaritan woman: 4:1-42; Martha and Mary in ch. 11; Mary Magdalene: 20:1-2, 11-18, 25).[8] It has been my experience that a study of the Lukan and Johannine passages increases one's understanding of Jesus' way with women. Indeed, it is unnecessarily skeptical to suggest that the use of this material by the Lukan or Johannine author to serve an individual theological agenda necessarily renders it "unhistorical." It cannot be denied that these materials play an important role from the evangelists' theological point of view, and for that reason alone we will leave them to one side for the limited purposes of this study.[9] The above selection, therefore, leaves us with material that has good possibilities of coming into the storytelling traditions of the early Church from authentic memories reaching back to the time of the pre-Easter Jesus.

There is, however, more material from the synoptic tradition that merits our attention. Although female characters may not be actively involved in certain narratives, there are indications in them that throw further light on Jesus' attitude to women:[10]

  a. Looking upon a woman lustfully (Matt 5:28);
  b. The divorce material (Mark 10:1-12; Matt 5:31-32 and 19:1-12; Luke 16:8);
  c. Jesus' true family (Mark 3:31-35; Matt 12:46-50; Luke 8:19-21).

A full-scale study of all this material would lead to a large volume in its own right. I intend to comment as concisely as possible on each text. Similar themes emerge consistently. A short word on my "method" is necessary at this point. I have already indicated that there is general

---

[8] For an analysis of this material see Moloney, *Woman: First among the Faithful* 74–92, and Blank, "Frauen," 68–88.

[9] I must again insist that the aim of this study is not a *feminist* reading of gospel texts, but an attempt to use the narratives to discover something about Jesus of Nazareth. However each evangelist may have told the story, the *traditions* they received say something about Jesus and women. Recent *feminist* studies of both the Lukan and the Johannine material indicate that one must read *against the grain* of the texts as we find them in the Lukan and Johannine redaction to give them contemporary relevance for women. See Turid Karlsen Seim, *The Double Message: Patterns of Gender in Luke and Acts* (Nashville: Abingdon, 1994), Barbara Reid, *Choosing the Better Part? Women in the Gospel of Luke* (Collegeville: The Liturgical Press, 1996), and Adeline Fehribach, *The Women in the Life of the Bridegroom. A Feminist Historical-Literary Analysis of the Female Characters in the Fourth Gospel* (Collegeville: The Liturgical Press, 1998).

[10] For a useful analysis of this material see Evelyn and Frank Stagg, *Woman in the World of Jesus* 126–43.

skepticism about our ability to recover Jesus' attitudes and the nature of his personal relationships. I am in total agreement with the majority of critical scholars who refuse any attempt to develop a "psychology of Jesus," yet I have listed a large amount of material from the gospels that touches upon how he related to women. The material, as we have it now, is found in the gospels. This means, inevitably, that we are using sources for our interpretation that are themselves interpretations.

Since this is the case, the reader must be aware of what I am trying to do with this reflection. Most (but not all) of the material has its origins in Mark and has been used by Matthew and/or Luke. Thus in many cases I will study the passage within the context of the Markan (or Matthean, Lukan, or Johannine) theological and literary structure. From this I hope to show that across the various gospel *traditions* there seems to be a core of solid *tradition*. I am well aware that the passages have been retold, remodeled, and rewritten in the developing traditions of the earliest Church. New Testament authors sometimes present the Jews, their leadership, and Jewish thought and practice in a negative fashion. This harshness often reflects the tensions between two children from the same household as they drifted apart. It may not have been the experience of Jesus. This must be recalled at those places in the following analysis where Jesus' attitudes are sharply contrasted with those of the Jews, their leaders, and their religious thought and practice. I am not arguing here that I am rediscovering the *ipsissima verba* or the *ipsissima facta* of Jesus of Nazareth. Nor should we think that we have an accurate record of the Jewish world of Jesus. However, I believe that there is reason to be confident that we are able to come into close contact with the *ipsissima locutio* of Jesus through the analysis that follows.[11]

---

[11] I trust that this commonly used distinction is not confusing, as it is important. When one refers to the *"locutio"* one evades the necessity to pin down and prove every historical word and deed (an extremely difficult task), yet one is able to indicate an attitude or a way of life that shines through the various reports, no matter how far they may be from an accurate description of actual words and events. On this issue see Joachim Jeremias, *New Testament Theology* (London: SCM, 1971) 15–33; Norman Perrin, *Rediscovering the Teaching of Jesus* (New York: Harper & Row, 1967) 15–33. Much of the material to be examined, however, would respond to the testing of the "criteria" developed for research into the historical Jesus. Particularly useful are the criteria of dissimilarity, multiple attestation, coherence, and embarrassment. For a good discussion of these criteria see John P. Meier, *A Marginal Jew. Rethinking the Historical Jesus.* 2 vols. ABRL (New York: Doubleday, 1991–93) 1:167–95. It is beyond the scope of this study to pursue the issue here, but some general remarks will be made below in my "initial conclusions."

1. MIRACLE STORIES

1.1. The cure of Simon's mother-in-law: Mark 1:29-30
(see also Matt 8:14-15; Luke 4:38-39)

In Mark's gospel Jesus' first public actions take place on a Sabbath (see the indications of 1:21). In fact, he heals a man (1:21-28) and a woman (1:29-31) in immediate succession. In this way his public ministry opens with evidence of his rejection of any taboos that might inhibit his ability to help those in need. This impression is further strengthened when one looks closely at just what it meant *for Jesus* to heal Simon's mother-in-law through touch. As she lay sick with a fever Jesus went to her and *touched* her. The fever departed, and she *served* them. There are two important details to be noticed if we want fully to appreciate all the implications of this passage. First, Jesus touches a woman by taking her by the hand, showing internal freedom. Then, as perhaps even today, a respected religious leader would not take any woman by the hand. It is useless to speculate on his prior knowledge of Simon's mother-in-law. Such questions go beyond anything indicated in the text itself.

Though there were precedents for a rabbi taking the hand of another man and miraculously healing him, there are no examples of rabbis doing so for a woman, and certainly not on the Sabbath when the act could wait until after sundown. Indeed, a man could be suspected of evil desires if he touched any woman other than his wife. This was true even if she was a cousin, and more true if the woman was no relation at all. At the very least Jesus could be accused of contracting uncleanness and violating the Sabbath.[12] Consequently he opens himself to further accusation by allowing himself to be served by this woman. This may appear normal enough to us, but there were some, at least in later centuries, who contended that no self-respecting rabbi would allow such a thing. As Rabbi Samuel (d. 254 C.E.) said: "One must under no circumstances be served by a woman, be she adult or child."[13]

---

[12] Witherington, *Women in the Ministry of Jesus* 67.

[13] For detail and further Jewish texts see Str-B 1:480. See further the comments of Witherington, *Women in the Ministry of Jesus* 67: "What is interesting about her act is that women, according to some rabbis, were not allowed to serve meals to men. It also appears that this may be a violation by the woman of the prohibition against her on the Sabbath. Perhaps she realizes that if Jesus was free to heal her on the Sabbath, then she was free from the Sabbath restrictions preventing her from serving and helping others." The issue of "touching" is important to my study. Unfortunately the texts given in Strack-Billerbeck are late, but the ritual purity issues surrounding a woman's monthly period (the

In the Markan version of the life of Jesus the first day of Jesus' public ministry (see Mark 1:21-34)[14] is highlighted by this new approach to a woman. In fact, the episode of the curing of Simon's mother-in-law forms the center of the day's activities: he cures the possessed man in the synagogue (1:21-28), raises the fever-stricken woman (1:29-31), and then cures all who come to him (1:32-34). The evangelist deliberately places the "woman" episode at the center of the day's activities. He thus highlights Jesus' attitude and approach to a woman in the midst of the miraculous presence of the overpowering reign of God, vanquishing the reign of evil, which is symbolized by devil possession and physical illness.

1.2. The healing of the woman with the hemorrhage and the raising of Jairus' daughter: Mark 5:21-43 (see also Matt 9:18-26; Luke 8:40-56)

Although I listed these two stories separately in my overall classification, it is obvious that in all three synoptic gospels the story of the daugh-

---

unstated problem in all "touching" [and the "serving"]) deserve further investigation. See Lev 15:19-24; 18:19; 20:18; Isa 30:22; Ezek 7:19-20; 18:6; 22:10; 36:17; and the tractate *Niddah* in both the Mishnah and the Talmudim.

More recent scholarship has shown that the traditions that come to us reflect something of a closing down on the more relaxed relationships that may have been in place in everyday life before the loss of the nation and the Temple. On this see Tal Ilan, *Jewish Women in Greco-Roman Palestine* (Peabody, Mass.: Hendrickson, 1996) 176–84. However, a recent study of the presence of women at meals within the Greco-Roman context of early Christianity only accentuates the problem. The presence of women at meals in a Greco-Roman society was extremely complex (see Kathleen E. Corley, *Private Women, Public Meals: Social Conflict in the Synoptic Tradition* [Peabody, Mass.: Hendrickson, 1993] 24–79). With reference to Mark 1:29-31 Corley affirms that the serving of Simon Peter's mother-in-law "could carry scandalous overtones when performed by a woman within the context of a meal" (p. 88). Corley responds to those who wish to associate the idea of "serving" with the early Christian idea of diaconate as "certainly incorrect" (see p. 88 and the references in n. 20).

[14] Commentators often point to this section of the opening "day" of Mark's gospel as a literary construction around a typical day in which God's power breaks into the lives of the afflicted through the presence and the power of Jesus. See, for example, Vincent Taylor, *The Gospel according to St. Mark* (London: Macmillan, 1966) 170–85; Rudolf Pesch, *Das Markusevangelium.* 2 vols. HTKNT II/1-2 (Freiburg: Herder, 1976–77) 1:116–36; Ernst Lohmeyer, *Das Evangelium des Markus.* Meyers Kommentar 1/2 (Göttingen: Vandenhoeck & Ruprecht, 1967) 34–40; Dennis E. Nineham, *Saint Mark.* The Pelican Gospel Commentaries (Harmondsworth: Penguin, 1969) 73–83.

ter of Jairus is used as a "frame" around the account of the woman with the flow of blood. The technique of "pairing" and "framing" stories is a very common feature of Mark's gospel,[15] and it is important to interpret the two accounts together. They have been put together by Mark (or by the tradition before Mark) because one throws light on the other. It is a recognition of this principle that must direct our interpretation.[16]

However, it is also important to look at the wider context of these passages, since we find that they play an important role in a deliberate gathering of "woman stories" to form the conclusion of a section of Mark's gospel that has been dominated by Jesus' miraculous activity. From Mark 5:35 onward there has been a gradual crescendo of increasingly significant miracles:

- 4:35-41: a nature miracle as Jesus calms the storm and the waters: "even the wind and the sea obey him" (4:41);
- 5:1-20: a spectacular victory over the demons, as he drives out a legion of unclean spirits from the Gerasene demoniac;
- 5:21-24: the request from Jairus;
- 5:25-34: a victory over human illness as he cures the woman with the hemorrhage;
- 5:35-42: a victory over death itself in the raising of Jairus' daughter.[17]

[15] This is a widely recognized feature of Markan style, and the current climate of rhetorical studies of the gospels is giving increasing consideration to these features. See, for example, David Rhoads and Donald Michie, *Mark as Story. An Introduction to the Narrative of a Gospel* (Philadelphia: Fortress, 1982) 51; John R. Donahue, *Are You the Christ? The Trial Narrative in the Gospel of Mark.* SBLDS 10 (Missoula: Scholars, 1973) 57–63; Howard Clark Kee, *Community of the New Age. Studies in Mark's Gospel* (Philadelphia: Westminster, 1977) 45–56; Joanna Dewey, *Markan Public Debate. Literary Technique and Concentric Structure in Mark 2:1–3:6.* SBLDS 48 (Chico: Scholars, 1980) 21–22. Donahue (*Are You the Christ?* 58–59) offers a comprehensive list.

[16] This point is missed by Witherington, *Women in the Ministry of Jesus* 71–72, because of an unreasonable attempt to show the "historicity" of the basic sequence of events as we have them reported in Mark 5:21-34. An appreciation of the evangelist's literary use of the tradition can be a help, and not a hindrance, in our recovery of Jesus' way with women. It is also largely disregarded in the important essay of Mary Rose D'Angelo, "Gender and Power in the Gospel of Mark: The Daughter of Jairus and the Woman with the Flow of Blood," in John C. Cavadini, ed., *Miracles in Jewish and Christian Antiquity. Imagining Truth.* Notre Dame Studies in Theology 3 (Notre Dame, Ind.: Notre Dame University Press, 1999) 83–109.

[17] This Markan literary scheme of a series of miracle stories is not taken into account by D'Angelo, "Gender and Power," 96–102, in her discussion of the function of the two stories in Mark.

Notice the progression from the calming of a natural disturbance, through the demonic, into human illness, and finally to a victory over death. Once we have seen this logic at work it is significant to notice that both people involved in the final miracles are women.

Part of the purpose of these accounts is to throw into relief the limitations of the faith of the disciples over against the complete self-abandon of the woman with the hemorrhage and the ruler of the synagogue. This is especially clear in the "good sense" of the disciples who almost mock Jesus' question: "Who touched my clothes?" with their reply: "You see the crowd pressing in on you; how can you say, 'Who touched me?'" (v. 31). The mockery and laughter surrounding Jesus' statement that the girl is only asleep (vv. 39-40) carry a similar message. But why did Mark, or perhaps a tradition before Mark, join the story of the woman with the hemorrhage with the raising of the daughter of Jairus? The message about faith may have been one of the reasons, but some commentators point to the appearance of the number "twelve" in both stories: the illness had lasted twelve years (v. 25) and Jairus' daughter was twelve years old (v. 42).[18] The commentators do not make enough of the repetition of "twelve years." For example, Vincent Taylor, followed by many other scholars, regards the reference to the twelve years in the case of the flow of blood as a "round number to describe an affliction of long standing,"[19] and the indication that the girl was twelve years old as "added to explain the walking" so that it would be clear that she could walk![20] Marie-Joseph Lagrange simply dismisses the whole issue by claiming: "Cette femme est malade depuis que la fille de Jaïre est au monde: simple coincidence."[21] I wonder.

In addition to the unifying theme of faith there are two further elements that link the stories. We have already seen in the analysis of the healing of Simon's mother-in-law that Jesus' touching her was important. This theme emerges again in the miracle of the woman with the flow of blood:

> "If I but *touch* his clothes, I will be made well" (5:28). "Who *touched* my clothes?" (v. 30). "You see the crowd pressing in on you; how can you say, 'Who *touched* me?'" (v. 31).

[18] For a survey of the suggestions that have been made, as well as his own hypothesis regarding the "pairing" of these originally independent accounts see Pesch, *Das Markusevangelium* 1:312–14, and the literature cited there.

[19] Taylor, *St Mark* 290.

[20] Ibid. 294.

[21] "The woman has been ill as long as the daughter of Jairus has been alive: a simple coincidence." Marie-Joseph Lagrange, *Evangile selon Saint Marc*. EBib (Paris: Gabalda, 1920) 135.

Once we see the centrality of the theme of "touching," that same theme emerges in the raising of Jairus' daughter as Jesus is described as taking her by the hand—but here it is further linked with the unexpected indication that the girl was twelve years old:

> He took her by the hand and said to her, *"Talitha cum,"* which means, "Little girl, get up!" And immediately the girl got up and began to walk about (she was twelve years of age). (vv. 41-42)[22]

Given Mark's consistent reporting of Jesus' easy readiness to touch women of any state or condition, and given further the precise indication that the young girl was, in fact, a young woman of twelve years of age, this may have been told in order to increase the shock created by Jesus' action. She was of marriageable age. As Raymond E. Brown has explained in reference to Jewish marriage practices:

> The consent, usually entered into when the girl was between twelve and thirteen years old, would constitute a legally ratified marriage in our times, since it gave the young man rights over the girl. She was henceforth his wife.[23]

In such a situation Jesus' "taking her by the hand" is an ambiguous gesture for a religious leader. There is a hint in the text that she may not have been dead (v. 39), and this would excuse Jesus from the impurity he would incur by touching a dead body (according to Num 19:11-13). Whatever that situation might have been, she was "twelve years old." She was a woman. Yet Jesus is portrayed as unconcerned about the possibility of incurring ritual impurity. He is prepared to take a twelve-year-old girl by the hand. Mark's point is that Jesus is prepared to cut through any danger of ritual impurity or taboo when it is a case of giving life.

The affectionate gesture of touching is further enriched by the tender Aramaic expression *talitha cum.* It could well be translated as "My dearest little one, stand up," and has been retained in the Greek version of Mark because of its powerful eloquence and its impact. Now the encounter between Jesus and this young woman takes on a special significance, and a

[22] The RSV accepted the textual variant *cumi,* which would be the proper Aramaic form of the feminine imperative; underlying the NRSV is the more difficult masculine form, *cum.* See Bruce M. Metzger, *A Textual Commentary on the Greek New Testament* (Stuttgart: German Bible Society, 1994) 74–75.

[23] Raymond E. Brown, *The Birth of the Messiah. A Commentary on the Infancy Narratives of Matthew and Luke* (New York: Doubleday, 1977) 123. See further Joachim Jeremias, *Jerusalem in the Time of Jesus. An Investigation into Economic and Social Conditions during the New Testament Period* (London: SCM, 1969) 364–68. See the summary of rabbinic opinion on this question in Witherington, *Women in the Ministry of Jesus* 2–6.

link between the two miracle stories, so entwined in the gospel tradition, becomes more obvious. In both stories Jesus touches the unclean.[24] He touches a woman in a pathological condition that excludes her from the ritual life of Israel (see Lev 15:25; *Zabim* 5:1.6),[25] and he touches the dead body (see Num 19:11-13) of a young woman (see *Ber.* 5b).[26] Both touchings tell us that Jesus brings a new concept of wholeness and holiness.[27] The power of the reigning presence of God, which he was convinced had arrived in the human story in his person, in his word, and in his touch, breaks through all barriers of cultic and ritual observance.[28]

---

[24] D'Angelo, "Gender and Power," 87–91, grants that the woman's flow of blood renders her impure, but rejects the suggestion that Mark is interested in the issue of purity.

[25] See John J. Pilch, *Healing in the New Testament. Insights from Medical and Mediterranean Anthropology* (Minneapolis: Fortress, 2000) 45–53, 64–66, especially 49–51. D'Angelo, "Gender and Power," 95, on the basis of ancient medical therapies, comes to a parallel conclusion: "The woman with a flow of blood for twelve years suffers from a womb that is inappropriately open. The twelve-year-old girl may well represent the young girl who dies because her womb is closed; at twelve, she is at the age for marriage in Roman law." D'Angelo is correct in her insistence that Mark 5:21-43 is not "a critique of purity codes" (p. 102). But her claim to a fresh interpretation by relocating them "in the context of miraculous and medical healing in antiquity and the literary and theological project of the gospel of Mark" (p. 85) is unconvincing. I find the links with the medical healing traditions contrived, and her attention to the literary and theological project of the gospel of Mark too sketchy.

[26] Recent scholarship, however, suggests that the rabbinic legislation on the relationship between a woman's period and her right to participate in Israel's everyday life and practice may have been more prescriptive than descriptive. While laws were made, women and men got on with daily life.

[27] For D'Angelo, "Gender and Power," 98, the touching is to be located "in the context of ancient medical therapies." She rejects any relationship between touching the impure and uncleanliness (see p. 87).

[28] D'Angelo, "Gender and Power," 87, locates the final composition of Mark some 10–20 years after 70 C.E., noting that "some" date it about 70, while "many" including herself look to the subsequent two decades for its compilation. On p. 106 n. 27, in her note attached to this affirmation, she only cites two scholars (Achtemeier and Collins), both of whom date Mark about 70 C.E. Who are the "many"? In her interpretation of the Markan use of the traditions she claims, on the basis of evidence from Plutarch (late first and early second century C.E.) and Philostratus (late second and early third century C.E.), that Mark's message is christological in another sense: "power is active through the participation of others" (p. 101; see also pp. 103–104). *The Oxford Classical Dictionary*, edited by N.G.L. Hammond and H. H. Scullion (Oxford: Clarendon Press, 1970) describes Plutarch as "tantalizing and treacherous to the historian (p. 849) and the work of Philostratus as having "mystical and orientalizing tendencies," possibly "a counter blast to Christian propaganda" (p. 825). Why is this evidence given priority in her discussion?

The girl twelve years of age—now marriageable—gets up and walks. She rises to womanhood. The young woman, who now begins to pour forth her life in menstruation, and the older woman who experiences menstruation as a pathological condition, are both restored. They are "given" new life. Here we find that the life-giving powers of women, manifested in the flow of blood, are not "bad" or "impure" (the older woman), nor are they the cause of problems for Jesus as he touches the younger woman. They are not to be cut off in death (the younger woman). They are "restored" so that the women can go and live in *shalom,* in the well-being and happiness of God's reigning presence, which has "touched" their lives in Jesus of Nazareth.[29]

1.3. The Syrophoenician woman: Mark 7:24-30
(see also Matt 15:21-26)[30]

This section of Mark's gospel deals most obviously with the question of the Gentile mission (see 7:24–8:10). This is made clear in Mark's geographical indications in 7:24 and 31:

> From there he set out and went away to the region of Tyre (v. 24). . . .
> Then he returned from the region of Tyre, and went by way of Sidon towards the Sea of Galilee, in the region of the Decapolis (v. 31).

This would be a roundabout way of going from Tyre to the Lake of Galilee, but Mark constructs this circuitous route to keep Jesus in Gentile territory. Further, there are several references to Gentile themes in the second multiplication of the bread, especially in 8:3:

> "If I send them away hungry to their homes, they will faint on the way—and some of them have come from a great distance."

A similar hint is given through the use of the number "seven" in 8:5 and 8, in contrast to the use of the number "twelve" in the first multiplication (see 6:43).[31]

---

[29] See, for this suggestion, Schüssler Fiorenza, *In Memory of Her* 122–24. See also Rachel Conrad Wahlberg, *Jesus According to a Woman* (New York: Paulist, 1975) 31–41.

[30] For a detailed comparative study of the Markan and Matthean versions of this account see Witherington, *Women in the Ministry of Jesus* 63–66. For stimulating readings of the passage from a number of feminist perspectives, including her own, see Elisabeth Schüssler Fiorenza, *But She Said. Feminist Practices of Biblical Interpretation* (Boston: Beacon, 1992) 11–15, 96–101, 160–63.

[31] The double use of a multiplication of bread and fish in Mark 6 and 8 has been read as the same basic message aimed at a Jewish (6:31-44) and then a

At the head of this section stands the vivid story of the faith of the Syrophoenician woman. However, the shock this narrative can create for the reader is eased when one gives due attention to the severe encounter between Jesus and certain traditional, but hypocritical, ways of Judaism in 7:1-23 (see particularly the punishing use of Isa 29:13 in vv. 6-7). Equally important is the virtual denial of one of the basic criteria for ritual cleanliness, addressed to his misunderstanding disciples in v. 18: "Then do you also fail to understand? Do you not see that whatever goes into a person from outside cannot defile . . . ?"[32] It is immediately after this episode that a Gentile woman comes to petition Jesus on behalf of her daughter (another woman!). The point of the story as we now have it is to show (with considerable effect!) that she has no human rights, and that she can lay no claim to Jesus' power and authority. It is Jesus himself who tells her so (v. 27). Her answer, "Sir, even the dogs under the table eat the children's crumbs" (v. 28), shows her deep recognition of her nothingness. Hugh Anderson has commented well:

> She comes making no legal claims and pleading no special merits, but just as she is, empty-handed and in need, and daring only to accept God's gift in Jesus. Thereby is exemplified the contrast between Jewish legalism and the faith that waits on God.[33]

It is equally obvious that the faith of the woman is to be contrasted not only with the self-righteousness of certain forms of Judaism as portrayed in the gospels, but also with the hard-headed misunderstanding of the disciples. What must be further noticed is that *a woman* is

---

Gentile (8:1-10) audience since the time of Augustine. However, it has recently been strongly challenged by Morna D. Hooker, *The Message of Mark* (London: Epworth Press, 1983) 45–50. See also eadem, *The Gospel According to St Mark* (London: A. & C. Black, 1991) 187–89. Robert M. Fowler, *Loaves and Fishes. The Function of the Feeding Stories in the Gospel of Mark*. SBLDS 54 (Chico: Scholars, 1981), reasserts the importance of the need for the disciples to see more widely than their Jewish roots, and claims that the function of the double narrative in the gospel is to show the reader that he/she must not fail to understand such a message, as the disciples in the narrative did. He suggests that this message hinges around the ironic question of 8:4: "How can one feed these people with bread here in the desert?" (see especially 91–148).

[32] See, on this, the remarks of Eduard Schweizer, *The Good News According to Mark* (London: S.P.C.K., 1971) 146–47: "Vss. 17-18a, which are clearly Markan both in language and in content, show that what Mark considers the real point of the passage is the disciples' lack of understanding in spite of the clarity of Jesus' statement (vs. 15). Accordingly he has to conclude the controversy with that lack of understanding and with Jesus' reprimand."

[33] Hugh Anderson, *The Gospel of Mark*. NCB (London: Oliphants, 1976) 191–92.

used to indicate this first step of a non-Jew and a non-disciple into true faith as she pleads that *her daughter* be cured.

Already, from this rapid analysis of four Markan miracle stories where women play a leading role, we can see some common themes emerging:

(a) There was a freedom in Jesus of Nazareth that shows he was ultimately free from culturally, historically, and even religiously conditioned constraints and prejudices. This has been made particularly clear by Jesus' allowing himself to both touch and be touched by women of all conditions. It is also to be found in his allowing himself to be served by Simon's mother-in-law.

(b) There is the repeated use of a woman and a woman's faith in contrast to the lack of faith demonstrated by Jesus' Jewish opposition, as Mark presents it (Jairus' daughter, the Syrophoenician woman) and by his own disciples (the woman with the hemorrhage, the Syrophoenician woman).

(c) Women are set in positions of primacy, at least in Mark's gospel. The first Gentile to come to faith is the Syrophoenician woman, and the culminating demonstration of the irresistible presence of the active reign of God made present in Jesus is shown in two great miracles that involve women who are deliberately portrayed as having an intimate personal contact with Jesus: the woman with the hemorrhage and Jairus' daughter.

2. CONFLICT STORIES

2.1. The widow's mite: Mark 12:38-44
(see also Luke 20:45–21:4)[34]

After the biting attack on Jewish leadership (the group indicated in 11:27) through the parable about the false keepers of the vineyard (12:1-11), the rest of Mark 12 is dominated by a series of conflicts between Jesus and these same leaders. The Pharisees challenge him on taxes paid to a foreign power (vv. 13-17); the Sadducees debate the resurrection of the dead (vv. 18-27); the scribes raise the issue of the first of all the commandments (vv. 28-34). These conflicts lead Jesus into a direct attack on the hypocrisy of the scribes, who have the correct garb and the places of honor but "devour widows' houses and for the sake of appearance say long prayers" (v. 40).

We are dealing with a key issue in the teaching and the way of Jesus. He has no desire for pomp and ceremony; he wants his disciples, both

---

[34] See the well-documented analysis of Witherington, *Women in the Ministry of Jesus* 16–18.

women and men, to give their all. The scribes, the Pharisees, and the
Sadducees, with whom Jesus has argued up to this point, are only
pretending to be "God-people." This section of the gospel therefore
rounds off the condemnation of such a form of faith and religiosity
with the other side of the medal: the story of the widow's mite. The
widow—so despised and, above all, abused by the so-called "righteous ones" (see v. 40)—gives her all: "she . . . has put in everything
she had" (v. 44). She has lived out in practice the ideals expressed in
the vocation of the first disciples, where Jesus has called them to leave
all and "follow" him (see 1:16-20; 2:13-14; 3:13-19).[35] After our study of
the miracle stories, where we found that women were used quite regularly *over against* the recognized Jewish authorities, and also over
against a lack of faith in Jesus' own disciples, it is interesting—and important—to see that this concluding section of Jesus' encounter with
official Judaism is rounded off with the use of a further woman character to show what it really means to be a disciple.[36]

Mark makes it very clear in vv. 43-44 that the issue at stake is discipleship: "Then he called his *disciples* and said to them . . . 'she . . . has put
in everything she had.'" The passage is certainly an attack on the legalism of the Jewish authorities, but it is more than that. Mark is not happy
to leave the teaching of Jesus merely in a negative key. It is to be a challenge to disciples. The evangelist, therefore, tells his story for his own
disciples, and for the disciples of all time. All are capable of thinking that
faith and its practice can be controlled and measured by one's own performance. The message of the Markan Jesus, correcting such false views,
comes to us through the example of a woman, one who gave her all.

2.2. The woman taken in adultery: John 7:53–8:11

This beautifully written passage breaks unexpectedly into the section of the Fourth Gospel devoted to the Feast of Tabernacles (John
7:1–10:21), and is universally recognized as a foreign insertion into the

---

[35] On these vocation stories, and their implications for an understanding of
Mark's gospel, see my essay, "The Vocation of the Disciples in the Gospel of
Mark," in this volume, pp. 53–84.

[36] Werner Kelber, *Mark's Story of Jesus* (Philadelphia: Fortress, 1979) 64–66,
perceptively links the attitude of the woman to the incipient faith of the scribe
in 12:32-34. He concludes his study of ch. 12 with the following remarks: "The
Kingdom of God and the temple are irreconcilably opposed to each other.
Only two persons, a male and a female, have endorsed Jesus' temple teaching—a scribe who adopts Jesus' fundamental article of faith and the widow
who lives according to it. The acceptance of male and female into the new
community bids defiance to the old all-male power structure of the chief
priests, scribes, elders, Herodians, Pharisees and Sadducces" (p. 66).

Johannine text at a late stage. This is shown by the history of the text as we now have it. It is absent from all important early manuscripts, and when it does begin to appear it can be found in a variety of places throughout the gospels.[37] We cannot hope to examine all the historical and textual complexities of this passage. It is a synoptic-type passage and, as should be clear from what we have already seen, it may well reflect an experience of the historical Jesus kept alive in the tradition until it finally found its way into the text of the Fourth Gospel. We must examine the story in its own right, and there are several features that merit our particular attention.

Jesus is presented in a situation of conflict. After setting the scene of Jesus' teaching "all the people" in the Temple (7:53–8:2), the author presents the scribes and Pharisees, who lead in a woman who has been caught in adultery.

> In order to have the proof required by the rabbis for this crime the woman must be caught *in coitu.* Thus, the evangelist depicts a highly suspicious situation: Where is her partner in crime? Did the husband hire spies to trap his wife? Did he wish to set aside his wife without giving her the *ketubah,* or did he want certain proof of her infidelity?[38]

A woman in considerable disarray is dragged before Jesus for a series of reasons, all of which are somewhat suspicious.

The Jewish leaders publicly accuse the woman and then challenge Jesus.[39] They know what Moses would think of such a situation, and what he would do, but they ask Jesus: "What do you say?" (v. 5). There is an obviously contrived use of the woman to pit Jesus against the teaching of Moses. To clarify this the author adds an explanatory note: "They said this to test him, so that they might have some charge to bring against him" (v. 6). The polemic is very strong and very public— and the confused, half-clad woman is a mere trapping in the conflict! In the "game" being played by the scribes and Pharisees the woman, as such, has no place except as an excuse to debate the Law. She will serve ideally as someone for them to instrumentalize for their own purposes: to teach Jesus of Nazareth a point or two about the Law of Moses.

---

[37] See, for a full discussion of the evidence, Metzger, *Textual Commentary* 187–90. For analyses of the passage, as well as the usual commentaries, see Blank, "Frauen," 82–88; Gail R. O'Day, "John 7:53–8:11: A Study in Misreading," *JBL* 111 (1992) 631–40. See also Francis J. Moloney, *The Gospel of John.* SP 4 (Collegeville: The Liturgical Press, 1998) 258–65.

[38] Witherington, *Women in the Ministry of Jesus* 21–22.

[39] The Scribes and Pharisees are caricatured by whoever was the author of this passage. For the alarm many Christian interpreters have shown regarding Jesus' lack of concern over the sin of adultery see O'Day, "John 7:53–8:11," 633–40.

In a first move Jesus simply turns away from the discussion, as ashamed of them as they are pretending to be of her. Then he issues his challenge: that the one without sin cast the first stone (v. 7). The "sin" referred to by Jesus probably touches the same area of sinfulness of which they accuse the woman, and thus they drift away. At the end of the account only Jesus and the woman remain on the scene. She is now no longer an object, a necessary evil for the purposes of a discussion. Jesus neither condones nor condemns her sin. No one condemns her (v. 11); hence she can take up the challenge to sin no more, the challenge to look squarely at a new self-understanding and thus to the possibilities of a new life that "the men" in the earlier part of the story would never have allowed for her. They would not have dreamt of such a possibility, because they had the Law of Moses on their side. Jesus is not threatened or shocked by a sinner, as he is not "bound" by any tradition or law that kills. He is challenged by the need to lead that sinner, woman or man, into a newness of life, something the men in the story would not allow for this particular woman.

The background to this story is the inner security that appears to have marked the life-style of Jesus of Nazareth. It can be sensed as he shows his readiness to turn traditional values upside down if their observance means that a woman thereby becomes a "thing," in this case a necessary evil in a debate over a point of law. The challenge is that all be given the chance for life, and in this Jesus succeeds, while the scribes and Pharisees disappear into failure.

> The Pharisees are tense, but he is calm and relaxed throughout; he accepts the woman openly and lovingly, as an adult and as a person. He has a sureness of touch; he can handle the situation and the relationship with her because he has nothing to be afraid of in himself. Not only had he no sin, but he must have completely accepted and integrated his own sexuality. Only a man who has done so, or at least begun to do so, can relate properly to women.[40]

3. Parables

It is generally recognized that the parables of Jesus put us into close contact with his preaching, and there are three very short parables from the "Q" material, or in Matthew alone, where women characters are used.

---

[40] Daniel Rees et al., *Consider your Call. A Theology of Monastic Life Today* (London: S.P.C.K., 1979) 169. This volume, edited by Dom Daniel Rees, o.s.b., of Downside Abbey, is a collection of essays on the theme of the title. The chapter on celibacy, from which the above citation was taken, was written by Dame Maria Boulding, o.s.b., of Stanbrook Abbey.

3.1. The parable of the leaven: Matt 13:33 // Luke 13:20-21

This very brief parable is widely accepted as an excellent illustration of Jesus' authentic preaching on the kingdom of God.[41] It stresses the initiative of God in the kingdom: the remarkable, rapid, unexpected, and inevitable inbreaking of God's active reigning presence, which can give life and vitality to all that it touches:

> The kingdom of heaven is like [leaven] that a woman took and mixed in with three measures of flour until all of it was leavened.

The use of the woman here probably reflects the simple fact that women were usually responsible for the baking. Still, as Jesus preaches the kingdom we find that a woman is at the center of the parable.

There may be more to it. Three measures of flour could feed one hundred people, so there may be a hint that this leavening is associated with some special sort of meal. It has been suggested that this hint (and it is no more than a hint) indicates that the parable points to more than the surprising and bountiful inbreaking of the kingdom. Is it significant that it is a woman who takes the place of the priest who would normally bake the unleavened cakes for the special offerings of a solemn festal occasion? It may be that what we have here is not only a message of urgency but also of the reversal of cultural criteria associated with the coming of the kingdom.[42]

3.2. The parable of the two sons: Matt 21:28-32

There is some discussion over the original form of this parable, but it may go back to Jesus himself, almost in the form in which Matthew has found it in his own traditions.[43] Its contents are well known. One son refuses to work in the vineyard, but repents and does what he was asked, while another is full of good words but does nothing (vv. 28-30). The parable of the two sons leads Jesus to his point: it is the tax collectors and the prostitutes who will enter the kingdom of heaven before the chief priests and the elders of the people (v. 31; see v. 23).

---

[41] See Joachim Jeremias, *The Parables of Jesus* (London: SCM, 1963) 146–49. This parable is also found in *GThom* 20. The material the woman mixes with the flour is more properly translated "leaven" than the NRSV's "yeast."

[42] For a more fully detailed exegesis of this passage, from which I have taken the above suggestion, see Witherington, *Women in the Ministry of Jesus* 40–41, 156–57.

[43] See Blank, "Frauen," 33; Eduard Schweizer, *The Good News According to Matthew* (London: S.P.C.K., 1976) 410–11; Jeremias, *The Parables of Jesus* 80–81.

As the passage runs further one of our ever-present themes reappears: it is not the righteous in the eyes of the world who are the "God-people," but those who are receptive to the challenge of Jesus of Nazareth. Already with John the Baptizer the prostitutes had shown the way to the hard-headed and self-righteous religious leaders of Israel (v. 32). This is the case because the latter were not prepared to *repent*, to turn away from their current way of life. They worked from the mistaken presupposition that there was no need for any radical reassessment of their situation and their style of life. Only the sinner, aware of his or her nothingness yet *receptive* to the life-giving power of God's reign offered in Jesus, can ever hope to enter the kingdom that he proclaimed and lived. Tax collectors and prostitutes are those elected by Jesus as the sort of people who have such openness and receptivity.

3.3. The parable of the wise and foolish virgins: Matt 25:1-13

In this famous parable we are dealing with what was originally a parable of Jesus calling all to be ready to respond to the invitation offered by God to humankind in the coming of Jesus and his preaching of the kingdom. The Matthean tradition and the evangelist's use of the parable have shifted its sense slightly to make stronger reference to the end-time and to the final coming of the Son of Man (see especially vv. 5-6 and 13, and Matthew's situating of this parable within the overall context of teaching on the end-time in ch. 25).[44] Yet the challenge issued by Jesus is still clearly present. The parable urges disciples of all times to be ready, open, and receptive to the appearance of the kingdom of God.

Revelation 19:6-7, 9, again using marriage symbolism, has reinterpreted Jesus' original teaching very well:

> ". . . the Lord our God the Almighty reigns.
> Let us rejoice and exult
> and give him the glory,
> for the marriage of the Lamb has come . . .
> Blessed are those who are invited to the marriage supper of the Lamb."

[44] On this see Schweizer, *Matthew* 465–66; Jeremias, *The Parables of Jesus* 51–53, and especially 171–75 for Jeremias' reconstruction of the *situation in the life of Jesus* that may have given birth to the original parable. For a full discussion of the possible tradition history of the parable see Witherington, *Women in the Ministry of Jesus* 41–44. See the fine recent study of Matt 25:1-13 in Vicky Balabanski, *Eschatology in the Making. Mark, Matthew and the Didache.* SNTSMS 97 (Cambridge: Cambridge University Press, 1997) 24–54.

This is not a future invitation. It is a present reality.[45]

It is interesting to see Jesus' adoption of women characters to make his point. Here, however, the women show both possibilities. Some are open, receptive, and prepared for the coming of the kingdom, and they are wise. Some are not prepared, and they are judged as foolish. The parable is linked to the way weddings were celebrated in the time of Jesus, but the women's reported behavior shows the possibility of success or failure in discipleship. This theme appears very strongly in some later texts in the New Testament where woman symbolism is used, especially in John 16:21-24 and Rev 12:17 and 21:11.[46]

4. THE ANOINTING OF JESUS

This account is found, in a variety of forms, in all four gospel traditions (see Mark 14:3-9; Matt 26:6-13; John 12:1-8). Somewhat different, but clearly related, is Luke 7:36-50. The Matthean version (Matt 26:6-13) is a rewriting of Mark 14:3-9, but both Luke (7:36-50) and John (12:1-8) report a similar story that may have come to them via their own independent traditions.[47] There is, therefore, every possibility that we are dealing with an event that happened during Jesus' ministry and was passed down through a variety of traditions. This "history" produced at least the three versions of an anointing story that we have in the canonical gospels. Such a variety of ways through which the same story is told and retold is generally a good guide to the historicity of the basic event.[48]

It is clear, nevertheless, that Mark, and Matthew following Mark, have rewritten the story as a preparation for the death and burial of Jesus in a way that suited their purposes, given the lack of anointing in the urgent burial scenes of both gospels. Through the anointing at Bethany Mark and Matthew show that the manner of Jesus' burial was already foreseen and that the body of Jesus had already received its due reverence despite

[45] See especially the interpretation of Eugenio Corsini, *The Apocalypse. The Perennial Revelation of Jesus Christ.* Good News Studies 5 (Wilmington: Michael Glazier, 1983) 341–44.

[46] For my further reflections on these passages see Moloney, *Woman: First Among the Faithful* 65–73, 82–87.

[47] For a comparative study see Blank, "Frauen," 22–28. On the complicated Lukan version see Witherington, *Women in the Ministry of Jesus* 53–57. See also the reflective commentary of Elisabeth Moltmann-Wendel, *The Women Around Jesus* 93–104, especially her important remarks on corporeity and touching on pp. 101–104.

[48] Such reports respond well to the test of the criterion of multiple attestation and coherence. In this case dissimilarity and embarrassment also apply.

the violent death and rushed burial. In Luke the theme of forgiveness is uppermost (see especially Luke 7:41-50).[49] In John we again find the theme of the preparation of the body for burial (see especially John 12:7), although from a slightly different perspective given the fact that in the Fourth Gospel Jesus is buried with a regal anointing (John 19:38-42).[50]

Thus each evangelist has used an event taken from their living traditions about Jesus and has told it in his own way to express a particular "point of view." Through all this, however, is it possible to discover what the event tells us about Jesus and his attitude to and relationship with women? Through the retelling of the story a series of features comes through clearly:

(1) The event takes place in the presence of either Pharisees (Mark, Matthew, and Luke) or disciples (John). Possibly both groups were present: the Jewish and the future Christian religious leaders form the public for the scene.

(2) The gesture is marked by a superabundance of both the quality and the quantity of the oils used. This is an indication of affection, trust, and abandon to the person of Jesus.

(3) Jesus has allowed himself to be touched intimately by a woman. In Mark and Matthew it is his head that is anointed, while in both Luke and John the feet are anointed. Luke goes even further into the intimacy of the woman's tears, her hair used to towel him, and her kissing of Jesus. It is against this background of the intimacy of touch that the Lukan motif of the sinner has been developed. The remarkable freedom of Jesus is again found, this time in a quite spectacular fashion.

(4) The event creates difficulty for "the righteous ones," be they Pharisees (synoptic gospels) or disciples (Fourth Gospel). Whether it was because of Jesus' intimacy with a woman (Luke) or the problem of the excessive waste of the precious ointment (Matthew, Mark, and John) need not concern us. They regarded both Jesus and the woman as being in the wrong.[51]

---

[49] The Lukan account of this event is best understood when read within the context of the overarching Lukan use of the theme of Jesus and women, one example of Luke's broader interest in Jesus' presence to the marginalized. For a study of the Lukan material see Moloney, *Woman: First Among the Faithful* 40–64.

[50] For a more detailed study of this scene in the Fourth Gospel see Francis J. Moloney, *Signs and Shadows. Reading John 5–12* (Minneapolis: Fortress, 1996) 180–83; idem, *The Gospel of John* 348–50. See also Moltmann-Wendel, *The Women around Jesus* 51–58.

[51] This is especially clear for Luke 7:36-50. See Witherington, *Women in the Ministry of Jesus* 55–56.

(5) Turning their values upside down, Jesus insists upon the woman's "beautiful deed" (Mark and Matthew) and her love (Luke). Ultimately what matters above all is the recognition of Jesus and an all-encompassing love for him. She demonstrates both of these, and for that reason:

". . . wherever the good news is proclaimed in the whole world, what she has done will be told in remembrance of her" (Mark 14:9).

Our brief survey of this account as it is reported across all four gospels shows that many themes discovered in our earlier analysis of the gospel material reappear:

(a) The superior quality of the faith of a woman is portrayed over against the well-measured reactions of Jewish leaders and disciples.
(b) Jesus' internal freedom and the absence of ambiguity in the intimacy of touch is again present throughout this encounter.
(c) The woman is presented as a model, a person whose faith in Jesus and deeply felt affection for him are a challenge to disciples of all times as "what she has done will be told in remembrance of her."[52]

5. WOMEN AT THE TOMB OF JESUS

An outstanding feature of the gospels' treatment of women characters is the presence of women at the empty tomb and their being the first to proclaim the Easter message. It is found in all four gospels (see Mark 15:42–16:8 [although, for his own reasons, Mark does not have the women proclaim the Easter message]; Matt 27:57–28:10; Luke 23:50–24:11; John 20:1-2, 11-18). We do not have the space to discuss all the historical and theological issues that surround the scholarly assessment of these texts. I would like simply to attempt an indication of what stands behind the four different versions of these crucial events as they are reported by the four evangelists.[53] I am again presupposing

---

[52] Several scholars, beginning with Clement of Alexandria (*Paedagogus* 2,8; PG 8:466-80), have suggested that the spread of the fragrance of the perfume through the whole house as reported in John 12:3 is the johannisation of the Markan theme about the universal preaching of this quality of discipleship. This interesting argument has a long history but probably attempts too much. It seems to me that it offsets Martha's words on the evil odor that will come from the open tomb of Lazarus (see 11:39) and is therefore a sign of a profligate abundance of Mary's commitment to Jesus (see Moloney, *The Gospel of John* 349).

[53] The magisterial study of the *events* surrounding the empty tomb is still that of Hans von Campenhausen, "The Events of Easter and the Empty Tomb,"

that the Markan version of these narratives is the ultimate source for both Matthew and Luke.[54]

On those presuppositions one can list the following events as reasonably probable and common to all accounts:

(1) Women remain close to the cross of Jesus despite the absence of the male disciples. This is found in all three synoptic gospels. The Fourth Evangelist has transformed this into a highly symbolic scene centered on the mother-son relationship established between the mother of Jesus and the Beloved Disciple (John 19:25-27).[55] The women observe from afar and know where Jesus is buried. All three synoptics make this point.

(2) On the morning of the third day some women, or maybe only one woman (most probably Mary Magdalene) come to visit the tomb. The motivation for this visit is difficult to ascertain. The question of whether or not they came to anoint the body (see Mark 16:1, where this is given as the motive for the visit although it is never mentioned again) is somewhat confused, and may well be secondary.

(3) The women (woman) find the tomb empty; they receive there some form of revelation explaining that Jesus has been raised, and an instruction that they are the ones who must announce this to the disciples.

(4) Although Mark closes his gospel by leaving the women in silence, this is a uniquely Markan twist. The women (woman) almost certainly did proclaim something like Luke 24:34: "The Lord has risen indeed" (see also 1 Cor 15:4-5).[56] This stands be-

---

in idem, *Tradition and Life in the Church. Essays and Lectures in Church History* (London: Collins, 1968) 42–89. For an excellent synthesis of ongoing discussions see Raymond E. Brown, *The Virginal Birth and the Bodily Resurrection of Jesus* (New York: Paulist, 1973) 69–133 and, more recently (although a trifle angry) William L. Craig, "The Historicity of the Empty Tomb of Jesus," *NTS* 31 (1985) 39–67. For a perceptive study of Mark's use of women in his theology of discipleship see Schüssler Fiorenza, *In Memory of Her* 316–23. See also Winsome Munro, "Women Disciples in Mark?" *CBQ* 44 (1982) 225–41. A useful study of each evangelist's presentation of the events at the empty tomb can be found in Edward L. Bode, *The First Easter Morning. The Gospel Accounts of the Women's Visit to the Tomb of Jesus.* AnBib 45 (Rome: Biblical Institute Press, 1970). See also Witherington, *Women in the Ministry of Jesus* 118–23.

[54] The Pauline "narrative" found in 1 Cor 15:3-7 will be considered below.

[55] On this passage see Francis J. Moloney, *Mary: Woman and Mother* (Homebush: St Paul Publications, 1988) 41–50.

[56] The words of the confession the women might have made are, of course, impossible to rediscover. However, the passive form, the brevity of the expression,

hind the accounts of Matthew and Luke as they rewrote Mark's version in the light of their own traditions, and it is also behind John's use of his Mary Magdalene tradition.

(5) The proclamation of the women is not believed by the disciples. The gospels, including Mark (especially Mark!) are remarkable in their consistent presentation of the doubt and unfaith of the disciples, both at the proclamation of the resurrection and at the appearances (see Mark 16:8; Matt 28:16-17; Luke 24:10-12, 13-35; John 20:2-10).

The above list could be regarded as a minimum, and would be widely accepted. The interpretation of this minimum, of course, would be another matter! Nevertheless, it appears that several of our now-familiar themes return.

(a) The women's faith and loyalty to Jesus sees them through the trauma of his death and burial and eventually leads them to proclaim: "The Lord has risen indeed!" There is a *primacy* both in the quality of the women's faith and in their being the first to come to faith in the risen Lord.

(b) This takes place within the context of a group of disciples who have fled in fear (see especially Mark 14:50 and the parabolic commentary on their flight in vv. 51-52: the young man who "followed" but, when confronted with danger, ran away *naked in his nothingness*).[57] The same disciples are universally presented as refusing to accept the Easter proclamation of the women. The faith of women stands out in strong contrast to the lack of faith among the male disciples, including the "pillars" of the discipleship group.

The consistency of this theme across all gospel traditions is a fair indication that there was a recollection in the earliest Church that women

---

the reference to Jesus as *Kyrios,* a term that may well have been common among the disciples during his ministry but took on a more exalted significance in the post-resurrection Church, all indicate that it may have been something like what we now find in Luke 23:34. The passage is widely recognized as "confessional" and (at least) pre-Lukan. See, on this, Reginald H. Fuller, *The Formation of the Resurrection Narratives* (New York: Macmillan, 1971) 111–12; I. Howard Marshall, *The Gospel of Luke. A Commentary on the Greek Text* (Exeter: Paternoster; Grand Rapids: Eerdmans, 1978) 899–900; Pheme Perkins, *Resurrection: New Testament Witness and Contemporary Reflection* (New York: Doubleday, 1984) 222–23.

[57] See Harry Fleddermann, "The Flight of the Naked Young Man (Mark 14:51-52)," *CBQ* 41 (1979) 412–17; Donald Senior, *The Passion of Jesus in the Gospel of Mark.* The Passion Series 2 (Wilmington: Michael Glazier, 1984) 83–85.

were the first to witness the empty tomb and that they were the primary witnesses to the resurrection. There is no reason why such an account would have been invented by Mark and then followed by the subsequent traditions.

The fact that the experience of the women is not found in what is most probably the earliest written account of the Easter events—the confession of faith in 1 Cor 15:3-7—does not destroy the evidence of the gospels. We are dealing with two different forms of literature. Paul was not writing a "gospel" in the strict literary sense of that word. He was making use of a confession of faith that had come to him from pre-Pauline tradition and adapting it both to his context and his purpose.[58] One of those purposes (perhaps the most important in the Corinthian situation?) was to include himself, "one untimely born" (15:8), among "the apostles," a uniquely masculine group in the gospel traditions. It also appears to me that the reference to "the third day" in 15:4 may take us back to the experience of the women at the tomb, as that expression appears to have come to birth in the language of the early Church in the first moments of its resurrection experience. Then, in fact, some women found an empty tomb "on the third day."[59]

6. Initial Conclusions

Some initial conclusions can be drawn from the material surveyed. There are good reasons to argue that behind this material from the gospels where women play an active role stands an authentic memory from the life of Jesus, no matter how much it has been remodeled by the evangelists or the traditions before them.[60] As this is the case, we

---

[58] See the discussion by Evelyn and Frank Stagg, *Woman in the World of Jesus* 144–60. Also excellent, and theologically perceptive, is Hubert Ritt, "Die Frauen und die Osterbotschaft. Synopse der Grabesgeschichten (Mk 16:1-8; Mt 27:62–28:15; Lk 24:1-12; John 20:1-18)," in Dautzenberg, Merklein, and Müller, eds., *Die Frau im Urchristentum* 117–33. For a survey of 1 Cor 15:3-8 see Fuller, *The Formation of the Resurrection Narratives* 8–49.

[59] On the origins of the "third day" language see especially von Campenhausen, "The Events of Easter and the Empty Tomb," 77–87.

[60] Most commentators would claim that this "woman" material plays no part in Mark's overall theological argument. If this is the case, then Mark used it as it came to him in this way in his traditions. See, for example, Taylor, *St Mark* 178, 347, etc. Witherington's informative and helpful book, *Women in the Ministry of Jesus,* suffers from a desire to prove too much on this score. He strikes an excellent balance in his commentary on the story of the widow's mite: "It is irrelevant whether this is a story once told by Jesus and now transformed, or an actual incident in His life. In either case, it will reveal to us something of His

can conclude that Jesus' contact with women, his openness to them, his preparedness to share his life with them—even those considered least important and least worthy by the culture and the religious practice of his contemporaries—was revolutionary. It is yet another indication that the reigning presence of God that broke into history in the person and teaching of Jesus of Nazareth could not be held within the bonds of human traditions and cultural expectations.

It is always possible, of course, that Mark did develop this use of women characters as a sophisticated literary technique to communicate a particular point of view, and that the later traditions merely picked up this tendency from his work. It could be claimed that he used women characters as a foil to show the weakness of the supposedly strong, be they Jewish religious leaders (see Mark 12:41-43) or disciples of Jesus (see Mark 5:24-34 and 14:3-9). This appears most unlikely to me. Given the insignificant role of women in first-century Jewish society,[61] Mark has taken over (i.e., he did not invent) something unique from the life of Jesus. We have seen that he is capable of using this material for his own purposes within literary contexts he has constructed. The present "location" of the women stories in the Markan narrative is surely the result of Mark's literary and theological activity, but this in no way detracts from the impact that Jesus' attitudes to women leaves on the careful reader of these passages, and one can only ask where Mark received this tradition. If everything began with Mark, how are we to explain an equally rich tradition dealing with Jesus' approach to the women in his life that we find in Luke and John, traditions that do not depend on Mark?

It should be further pointed out that the theme of a reversal of values, exemplified by this continual use of women to show the strength of the

---

attitude about widows" (p. 18; see also his similar remarks on John 8:1-11 on p. 21). It is possible that the accounts were invented entirely by the earliest (pre-Markan) Church. But even if this were the case for one or other (or even all) of the "women" pericopes, what generated these stories? Schüssler Fiorenza, *In Memory of Her* 316–23, has shown that *despite* the powerful "patriarchalization" of the late-first-century Church the Gospel of Mark could still use women as "paradigms of true discipleship." I would suggest that this is closely linked to the historical development of the gospel "form." A part of this development was deeply-felt loyalty to the authentic memory of Jesus and his ways. See also Moltmann-Wendel, *The Women around Jesus* 107–17.

[61] For a good general survey see Evelyn and Frank Stagg, *Woman in the World of Jesus* 15–54. For a brief but concise analysis of relevant rabbinic material see Witherington, *Women in the Ministry of Jesus* 1–10. A bibliography of studies in this area (now somewhat dated) can be found in ibid. 198–99.

weak and the weakness of the supposedly strong, is not a Markan importation into the biblical story. However important it may be for his theology it is something Mark and his community received from Jesus of Nazareth, and that Jesus received from his involvement in God's plan as demonstrated to him through the sacred history of his people.[62]

From these narratives with women as their protagonists it appears that we can reasonably claim that Jesus of Nazareth began a new era in the history of women. The later preaching of the Christian Church would go its various ways in the interpretation and application of the place and function of women within a Christian community. Already in the first two centuries we find that sometimes it will be positive (see, for example, a certain reading of the Lukan and Johannine "woman" material),[63] and sometimes it will be negative (see, for example, 1 Tim 2:11-12; 3:9-11; Titus 2:4-6; 5:5, and especially the Gnostic *Gospel of Thomas,* Logion 114). Whatever the outcome, it is important to appreciate that "modern Christianity" did not initiate the movement toward a "discipleship of equals." As a marginal Jew of the first century Jesus suffered from some of the limitations of his time and place, but a discipleship of equals had its *beginnings* in the person, the behavior, and the attitude of Jesus of Nazareth.

7. SOME FURTHER TEXTS

There are other texts that merit some brief consideration before we conclude this reflection, texts from the gospels where women do not actually appear in the narrative but where the teaching of Jesus further shows a change of attitude to women.

Within the context of Jewish law and practice all sins in the area of adultery were sins against a man.[64] A man who had sexual relations

---

[62] The theme of "reversal" runs through the First Testament. One need mention only some of the outstanding examples: the choice of David (1 Sam 16:1-13), the vocation of some of the prophets (Jeremiah: see Jer 1:6-8, and Amos: see Amos 7:14-15), the message to abandon the criteria of military and political power (e.g., Isaiah 7 and Daniel 7). The great woman characters in the First Testament can be seen in the same light, especially Ruth and Esther. The life and teaching of Jesus, at least as we have them recorded in the Gospel of Mark, seem to be strongly marked by this idea (see, for example, Mark 8:34–9:1; 9:35-37; 10:42-45). For a helpful reflection on this see Michael T. Winstanley, *Come and See. An Exploration into Christian Discipleship* (London: Darton, Longman & Todd, 1985) 74–82.

[63] I say "a certain reading" because some contemporary feminist readings of this material do not trace a positive portrait. For details see above, n. 9.

[64] For a survey see Evelyn and Frank Stagg, *Woman in the World of Jesus* 15–32. See also Moshe Greenberg, "Crimes and Punishments," *IDB* 1:739–40 on sexual

with another man's wife committed adultery, but it was not adultery for an unmarried woman to have sexual relations with a married man. Judah was not regarded as guilty for taking Tamar, who he thought was a prostitute. On the contrary, it was the already pregnant Tamar who was almost stoned to death (see Gen 38:12-26). David was seen and judged as sinning against Uriah when he took Bathsheba. The woman and her experience are not even mentioned in the account of those events in 2 Samuel 11–12. When Nathan castigates David he says:

> "Why have you despised the word of the LORD, to do what is evil in his sight? You have struck down Uriah the Hittite with the sword, and have taken his wife to be your wife, and have killed him with the sword of the Ammonites" (2 Sam 12:9).

What Bathsheba made of all this is in no way indicated by the text, and would not have been regarded by the author of 2 Samuel as significant enough to record.

Although prostitution was regarded as a sin, it was not penalized (see Lev 19:29; 21:7; Deut 23:17). The sinfulness was only on the part of the woman. A man who visited a prostitute was not regarded in the same way as a woman who gave herself to prostitution. The same male-oriented legislation stands behind the law on rape. Rape was primarily a crime against the father whose daughter was raped (see Exod 22:16-17; Deut 22:28-29), just as adultery was a crime against the husband of the woman involved (see, on all this, the indications of Deut 22:13-30 and Prov 6:26-35). Into this situation Jesus speaks boldly:

> "You have heard that it was said, 'You shall not commit adultery.' But I say to you that everyone who looks at a woman so that she shall become desirous has already committed adultery with her in his heart" (Matt 5:27-28*).[65]

The rabbis warned men against looking at a woman lest she lead them astray,[66] but Jesus reverses this position, if the translation proposed above is correct. "What is being treated in our passage is not male instability in the face of the temptress, but male aggression that leads to sin."[67] The woman is no longer a "thing" that somehow is caught up in

---

sins. The article runs from pp. 733–44. For a brief but succinct presentation of the early rabbinic material see Witherington, *Women in the Ministry of Jesus* 2–6.

[65] This translation is based on the interpretation of Klaus Haacker, "Der Rechtssatz Jesu zum Thema Ehebruch (Mt 5:28)," *BZ* 21 (1977) 113–16.

[66] See Str-B 1:299–301.

[67] Witherington, *Women in the Ministry of Jesus* 20.

a series of male-oriented rights and pleasures. A woman is a person to whom all respect and honor are due. There is to be no more aggressive male leering and joking about possible pleasures. They are to be replaced with relationships of mutual love and respect, where a man and a woman can be one—at all levels.

The discussions over divorce were also male-oriented.[68] In the time of Jesus the divorce laws were discussed on the basis of Deut 24:1:

> Suppose a man enters into marriage with a woman, but she does not please him because he finds *something objectionable* about her, and so he writes her a certificate of divorce, puts it in her hand, and sends her out of his house . . . .

In the interpretation of this law there were two schools of thought. Rabbi Shammai took a hard line, insisting that the all-important expression "something objectionable" had to refer to a serious moral defect *on the part of the woman.* In that case the bill of divorce could be written, and she could be dismissed from the home. An easier line (for the man) was argued by Rabbi Hillel. He claimed that any cause was good enough to fulfill the requirements of "something objectionable." The two examples given in the Mishnah for Hillel's persuasion are: if there is a more attractive woman available, or if the cooking is burnt (*m. Gittin* 9.10). Notice, yet again, that the giving of the bill of divorce depends entirely upon defects *on the part of the woman.*

Once one is aware of this debate, which was going on at the time of Jesus, the question of the Pharisees in the following discussion leads Jesus to speak out boldly against such a situation:

> Some Pharisees came to him, and to test him they asked, "Is it lawful for a man to divorce his wife *for any cause*?"[69] He answered, "Have you not read that the one who made them at the beginning 'made them male and female,' and said, 'For this reason a man shall leave his father and mother and be joined to his wife, and the two shall become one flesh'? So they are

---

[68] For a fuller discussion see my essay, "Matthew 19:1-12 and Celibacy. A Redactional and Form-Critical Study," in this volume, pp. 35–52. See, since then, William A. Heth and Gordon J. Wenham, *Jesus and Divorce. Towards an Evangelical Understanding of New Testament Teaching* (London: Hodder & Stoughton, 1984); Raymond F. Collins, *Divorce in the New Testament* (Collegeville: The Liturgical Press, 1995).

[69] Rabbi Hillel's interpretation of Deut 24:1 is reflected in this question. As in many rabbinic debates, Jesus is asked to take a position and his interlocutors will then make the opposite argument. Jesus, however, transcends the discussion.

no longer two, but one flesh. Therefore what God has joined together, let no one separate" (Matt 19:3-6).

This revolutionary teaching of Jesus is as countercultural today as it was then.[70] Here we have an explicit contrast drawn between the ways of men, society, custom, and culture: the bill of divorce versus God's ways "from the beginning"—a quality of mutuality and love that is so intense that man and woman become one. The sexual situation must not be the imposition of the will and the body of a man upon the will and the body of a woman. God did not create men and women to live in this way. Any legislation on divorce that made the woman a "tennis ball" that could be struck from partner to partner had to be wrong. At least at the level of some current interpretations of Deut 24:1 this was possible in the world of Jesus. Such a situation could not pass the critical presence of God's reign in the person of Jesus. We again sense the extraordinary freedom of Jesus of Nazareth as he takes on an interpretation of the Law of Moses to assert that "the two shall become one flesh" and that no man must dare to interfere in this oneness created by mutual respect and love. Such a oneness is God-given: what right has any man to interfere?[71]

---

[70] Witherington, *Women in the Ministry of Jesus* 125: "Jesus' rejection of divorce would have offended practically everyone of his day."

[71] This message runs across the New Testament (see Mark 10:1-12; Matt 5:31-32; 19:3-12; Luke 16:18; 1 Cor 7:10-16). Even the "exception clauses," found only in Matthew (Matt 5:32 and 19:9), are probably to be explained in terms of a need to dissolve an illegitimate marriage union (contracted while the couple were still pagans?) when a couple entered the largely Jewish-Christian Matthean community. See the fuller study of this issue in "Matthew 19:3-12 and Celibacy," pp. 35–52 of this volume. A due recognition for this is vital for a well-founded and healthy renewal of our "discipleship of equals" (Schüssler Fiorenza). While I can understand some of the anger, it pains me to read the half-truths published by Ruether, *Sexism and God-Talk* 260–61: "The Christian Church teaches that birth is shameful, that from the sexual libido the corruption of the human race is passed on from generation to generation. Only through the second birth of baptism, administered by the male clergy, is the filth of the mother's birth remedied and the offspring of the woman's womb made fit to be a child of God. . . . She must obediently accept the effects of these holy male acts upon her body, must not seek to control their effects, must not become a conscious decision maker about the destiny of her own body." As a male, committed to the Christian Church, I object to the continual use of the present tense in this emotional passage. Whatever women's experiences may have been and perhaps still are in some cases where the "Christian" Church is not what it was called to be, we are on a journey *together*. It is the only Christian way to go, even though the light at the end of the tunnel may only be a faint glimmer.

8. CONCLUSION

What was it in Jesus of Nazareth that created such a revolutionary newness? As was suggested at the beginning of this essay, one can only formulate a hypothesis. Given the nature of gospel material and the impossibility of developing a coherent "psychology of Jesus" I suggest, on the basis of the analysis just completed, that Jesus was motivated by the conviction that in his presence a new "Kingdom" was breaking into the human story.[72] In this "Kingdom" God was allowed to be God, and men and women—children of the same God, Jesus' Father (see John 20:17)—were allowed to be men and women, brothers and sisters equally. Jesus announced that he came to establish such a situation:

> "Who are my mother and my brothers?" And looking at those who sat around him, he said, "Here are my mother and my brothers! Whoever does the will of God is my brother and sister and mother" (Mark 3:33-34; see also Matt 12:46-50; Luke 8:19-21).

A new set of criteria has entered history in the person and message of Jesus of Nazareth. I am aware that I am writing from my Christian context, but perhaps nowhere in the history of humankind has any man been to women what Jesus was to women. As in so many aspects of our Christian lives, supposedly modeled on the life-style of Jesus, the challenge of Jesus' relationships with women stands largely unrealized:

> [Women have] never known a man like this Man—there never has been such another. A prophet and teacher who never nagged at them, never flattered or coaxed or patronized; who never made arch jokes about them . . . who rebuked without querulousness and praised without condescension . . . who never mapped out their sphere for them, never urged them to be feminine or jeered at them for being female; who had no axe to grind and no uneasy male dignity to defend; who took them as he found them, and was completely unself-conscious. There is no act, no sermon, no parable in the whole Gospel that borrows its pungency from female perversity; nobody could possibly guess from the words and deeds of Jesus that there was anything "funny" about women's nature.[73]

---

[72] For a detailed presentation of the gospel evidence showing Jesus' teaching on the incipient presence of the Kingdom see Meier, *A Marginal Jew* 2:398–506.

[73] Dorothy L. Sayers, "The Human-not-quite-Human," in *Unpopular Opinions* (London: Victor Gollancz, 1946) 121–22.

CHAPTER 2

MATTHEW 19:3-12 AND CELIBACY: A REDACTIONAL AND FORM-CRITICAL STUDY

It is generally taken as a fact that Jesus of Nazareth was celibate,[1] despite some recent suggestions to the contrary,[2] and there are but few contemporary discussions of the marital status of Jesus.[3] The most probable reason for this comparative lack of scholarly interest in a subject that stands at the center of so many current cultural and religious questions[4] is that there appears to be no New Testament evidence

[1] See, for example, the remarks of Marco Adinolfi, "Il celibato di Gesù," *BeO* 13 (1971) 145: "Unless the exegete wishes to become a novelist, there is nothing clearer than the celibacy of Jesus." As this is the very first remark of an article devoted to the celibacy of Jesus, it rather forecloses the historical investigation.

[2] See above, p. 3, n. 1 to the study "Jesus and Women."

[3] See Marco Adinolfi, "Il celibato di Gesù," 145–58; Jean Galot, "The Celibacy of Jesus," *Emmanuel* 76 (1970) 151–59; Jacques Guillet, "La chasteté de Jésus-Christ," *Christus* 17 (1970) 163–76; José Ignacio González Faus, "Notas marginales sobre el celibado de Jésus," in Antonio Vargas-Machuca, ed., *Teología y mundo contemporaneo: Homenaje a K. Rahner en su 70 cumpleaños* (Madrid: Ediciones Christiandad, 1975) 213–39; Bruno Proietti, "La scelta celibataria alla luce della S. Scrittura," in idem, ed., *Il Celibato per il Regno*. Studi a cura dell'Istituto di Teologia della vita religiosa "Claretianum" (Milan: Ancora, 1977) 23–25. The article (extremely well documented) runs from pp. 9–75.

[4] This remark simply refers to the ongoing conflicts the Christian, and especially the Roman Catholic, tradition has in matters of human sexuality: birth

either for or against the celibacy of Jesus. Most recently Bruno Proietti has written: "The Gospels do not affirm whether he was celibate or married. However, in this case their silence must be interpreted as an affirmation of his celibate state."[5] This last statement is a little too strong. Certainly there are indications within the gospels that hint that he did not have a wife: his family is mentioned (Mark 3:31-32; 6:3; John 6:42; 7:3) but a wife never appears. He is presented as a wandering preacher dominated only by the urgency of his mission (see Matt 8:19-20). Nevertheless, these indications *prove* nothing.[6] We must be careful not to take as proven something that remains one (the more likely in this case) of two possibilities. The problem exists, it seems, because we have no definitive evidence in either direction.

Perhaps some contemporary exegesis of Matt 19:12 could yield such evidence. A redactional consideration of the famous "eunuch saying" within the context of Matt 19:3-12 may provide radical teaching on divorce that must be judged, in the light of the rest of the New Testament evidence, as an *ipsissima locutio Jesu*. A form-critical study of Matt 19:12 may take us back to *ipsissima verba Jesu* used by Matthew or his source. Jesus speaks of the purpose and function of his celibate life-style.[7]

---

control, celibacy of the clergy, homosexuality, women in ministry, admission of the remarried to the eucharistic table. The list could be longer, but these few indications already make the point.

[5] Proietti, "La scelta celibataria," 23.

[6] See ibid. 23–24. On p. 23, n. 47, Proietti remarks: "Over the centuries there have always been attempts to show that Jesus was married." This should warn us that the traditional interpretation is *not the only one possible.* Much more objective is the remark of Jacques Guillet, "La chasteté du Jésus-Christ," 163: "Le Christ ne parle guère de la chasteté. Le mot lui-même ne figure pas dans les évangiles et ne fait pas partie de la langage de Jésus. Le Christ a proposé aux siens la douceur, la pauvreté, le pardon, la foi, il ne paraît les avoir appelés à la chasteté, ni leur donné en exemple sa chasteté" [Christ hardly spoke about chastity. The word itself does not figure in the gospels and is not part of the language of Jesus. Christ called his own to kindness, poverty, forgiveness, faith; he does not appear to have called them to chastity or given them an example of his own chastity]. As the reader will discover, on the basis of my study of Matt 19:12 I will not agree with Guillet's final remark.

[7] There is a large bibliography on this passage. I will refer only to specialized works here, sending the reader to the footnotes of those works for full bibliographical details. For an up-to-date and well-documented recent discussion of the question see Raymond F. Collins, *Divorce in the New Testament* (Collegeville: The Liturgical Press, 1992).

THE SIGNIFICANCE OF MATTHEW 19:12
WITHIN THE CONTEXT OF MATTHEW 19:3-12:
A REDACTIONAL STUDY

The passage is introduced by a typically Matthean expression (see 7:26; 11:1; 13:53; 26:1) and some rather obscure geographical indications.[8] This is followed by a further stereotyped Matthean reference to Jesus' teaching and healing (see 12:15; 14:13-14). Having introduced the passage by setting the scene, Matthew describes an encounter between Jesus and the Pharisees (vv. 3-9). There seem to be two factors in the discussion. In the first place there is an attempt by the Pharisees to lure Jesus into taking sides in the famous discussion between Rabbi Hillel and Rabbi Shammai over the divorce clause in Deut 24:1, which permits divorce when a man "finds something objectionable (*ʿerwat dābār)*" about his wife. Both rabbis referred to the עֶרְוַת דָּבָר (*ʿerwat dābār,* literally "a shame of a thing"), but Hillel stressed the *dābār.* This led him to argue that any *thing* was sufficient for divorce, e.g., burnt food or another woman who was more attractive. This interpretation is reflected in the Pharisees' asking whether one could put away one's wife κατὰ πᾶσαν αἰτίαν in Matt 19:3. Shammai on the other hand stressed the *ʿerwat* and insisted that the cause for divorce must be something shameful.[9] The Shammaites, therefore, kept the grounds for divorce within the area of impurity or immodesty, while the Hillelites used any grounds.

The second factor that must be noticed for a correct interpretation of the text is the use of the verb πειράζω in v. 3. The attitude of the Pharisees is one of hostility. They are not merely asking Jesus, as a known authority, what he thinks about that particular discussion. They obviously wish to trap him by disagreeing with whatever side he takes. This reflects a situation in Matthew's community, where a radical prohibition of divorce was being implemented.[10] Such a radical prohibition

---

[8] It is difficult to identify "the region of Judea on the other side of the Jordan," but it probably means *toward* the region of Judea by *means of* a journey along the other side of the Jordan, thus avoiding Samaria. There is some confusion in Mark 10:1 that Matthew has attempted to clarify.

[9] See, on this discussion, Str-B. 1:312–19. See also the treatment of the question in John P. Meier, *Law and History in Matthew's Gospel.* AnBib 71 (Rome: Biblical Institute Press, 1976) 143–47.

[10] Meier, *Law and History* 145–46, shows the importance of this hostility for Matthew's context: "We should realize that we have in Mt 19:3-12 not a word for word report of how Jesus disputed with some Jews c. A.D. 30, but a Christian composition drawn up with the final pronouncement of Jesus in mind from the beginning. The *Streitgespräch* as it stands in Mt reflects the Christian

cuts across both the permission given in Torah in Deut 24:1 and the subsequent rabbinical interpretations of that passage, with the position that there is to be no separation of spouses at all except for one very specific situation (vv. 4-6, 8-9). Matthew, writing for a largely Jewish community, still sets his discussion within the context of the well-known legal debate but, as is his custom, he shows that a follower of Jesus is called to go beyond the Law. The followers of Jesus have been called to a righteousness that is more radical than the righteousness that could be had from the observance of the Law. Jesus Christ has introduced a new situation in which the Christian is called to live the τελείωσις of the Law (5:17,48; 19:21).[11]

There is little need here to enter into the details of the discussion with the Pharisees. It follows a good rabbinic form in which the Pharisees pose the question (v. 3) and Jesus answers by citing from the Torah (v. 4: Gen. 1:27; 5:2; v. 5: Gen. 2:24), concluding with his own comment on those texts in v. 6: "So they are no longer two but one flesh. What therefore God has joined together, let not man put asunder." The reply of Jesus comes as a shock. It is nothing short of an absolute prohibition of divorce (see Mark 10:6-7).[12] The Pharisees, not to be outdone, reply in their turn with a further quotation from Torah (v. 7: Deut 24:1), but Jesus (and thus far, although rearranging, Matthew has largely followed his source: Mark 10:2-12) explains that this came about only because of the hardness of the heart of Israel in the days of Moses (v. 8; see Mark 10:5).

In v. 9 we encounter the typically Matthean λέγω δὲ ὑμῖν ὅτι (see 5:22, 28, 32, 34, 39, 44). No longer is the discussion carried forward on the au-

---

awareness of having broken not only with a particular rabbinic opinion, but with the permission of Dt 24:1 itself."

[11] In his important insistence that Matt 19:9 is not Jesus' espousal of the Shammaite cause Meier (ibid. 146) tends to obscure the contact with the Jewish discussion. This appears unnecessary to me, as the discussion was just as significant in the '70s and '80s and would have continually troubled the members of Matthew's community in their attempt to respond to Jesus' radical prohibition of divorce probably more "historically" reported (from the 30's?) in Mark 10:2-12. Not all would agree with this last statement. See for example Bruce Vawter, "Divorce and the New Testament," *CBQ* 39 (1977) 531–35. In support of my position is the important article of Joseph A. Fitzmyer (whom Vawter takes to task), "The Matthean Divorce Texts and some New Palestinian Evidence," *TS* 37 (1976) 221–23.

[12] I am presupposing throughout that Matthew is using Mark. For a recent convincing restatement of this case for Mark 10:2-12 and Matt 19:3-12 see David R. Catchpole, "The Synoptic Divorce Material as a Traditio-Historical Problem," *BJRL* 57 (1974–75) 93–110.

thoritative word of the Torah, but on the word of Jesus himself who has not come to abolish the Law, but to bring it to its perfection (see 5:17). We must see this passage as directed to a very real situation in the Matthean church because here, unlike Mark (10:10-11) and Luke (16:18), Matthew allows that there is one specific case where a separation is to be granted: ἐπὶ πορνείᾳ. In a similar teaching about divorce in 5:31-32 (and a much closer parallel to Luke 16:18) Matthew makes the same exception: παρεκτὸς λόγου πορνείας (5:31). Thus Matthew adds these exceptive clauses to his two major sources: Mark and Q. The significance of this exception clearly lies in the meaning given to πορνεία.[13] It is outside the scope of this article to review all the possible meanings of the word, even within the New Testament (see, for example, the variety of uses in 1 Cor 5:1; 6:13; 2 Cor 12:21; Col 3:5; Eph 5:3; Acts 15:20, 29). Matthew's use of it in these passages has also been variously interpreted: adultery, fornication, prostitution, harlotry, incest, etc.[14] I believe that Matthew uses it in the sense of Acts 15:20, 29, referring to illicit marriage-unions within a degree of kinship forbidden by Lev 18:6-8.

[13] As one would imagine, the bibliography on this question is immense. For an extensive bibliography see the excellent work of E. Vallauri, "Le clausole matteane sul divorzio: tendenze esegetiche recenti," *Laur* 17 (1976) 82–112. See further Antonio Vargas-Machuca, "Los casos de divorcio admetidos por S. Mateo (5,32 y 19,9). Consecuencias para la teología actual," *EstEcl* 50 (1975) 5–54; Meier, *Law and History* 140–41 n. 38, and the notes to the articles by Fitzmyer and Vawter mentioned above (n. 11). For a recent and valuable survey of the New Testament use of πορνεία see Joseph Jensen, "Does *porneia* mean Fornication? A Critique of Bruce Malina," *NovT* 20 (1978) 161–84.

[14] The argument is that behind the word πορνεία stands the Hebrew word *zěnût* (זְנוּת) indicating the proscription of marriage within certain degrees of kinship (see Lev 18:13). Analogously to the NT use of the word πορνεία, the word *zěnût* is used with a variety of senses in the OT. It is used to speak of harlotry (Jer 3:2, 9; Ezek 23:27) and also of idolatry (Num 14:33). In the LXX it is translated by πορνεία (e.g., Jer 3:2, 9). Fitzmyer, "Matthean Divorce Texts," 197–226 argues convincingly that "in CD 4,20 and 5,8-11 we have 'missing link' evidence for a specific understanding of *zěnût* as a term for marriage within forbidden degrees of kinship or for incestuous marriage; this is a specific understanding that is found among Palestinian Jews of the first century B.C. and A.D." (p. 221). See further the well-argued position of Meier, *Law and History* 140–50. This position seems to have had its origins in the work of Francis X. Patrizi (1876). It was taken up and made popular by Joseph Bonsirven (1948) and carried further by Heinrich Baltensweiler (1959). It has a wide acceptance in current scholarship, as is evidenced by the recent work of Fitzmyer (1976), Meier (1976), and Augustine Stock, "Matthean Divorce Texts," *BTB* 8 (1978) 24–33. For full bibliographical details see the references above in n. 13 and Fitzmyer, "Matthean Divorce Texts," 208–10.

What is vital for our concern is to locate the purpose of these exceptive clauses in the Matthean version of the words of Jesus, which in both Mark and Luke allow no exception. What was the particular problem of Matthew's church that led to the insertion of these phrases into what certainly appears to have been at least the *ipsissima locutio Jesu* on the matter of divorce?[15] The Gospel of Matthew speaks to a community largely composed of Jewish Christians facing difficulties on two fronts:[16]

1. The expulsion from their ancient Jewish, Torah-centered life-style became inevitable as official Judaism gradually came to see that any sect believing that Jesus was "the Christ" could not remain in its ranks.
2. The Christian message, largely couched in Jewish terms and traditions, was now being preached to Gentiles, and they were joining the community without any Jewish background.

The major part of Matt 19:1-9, as we have seen, is addressed to the first problem. It tells the Jewish Christians that they are called to a life of "higher righteousness," but the insertion into v. 9 "was undoubtedly to handle the situation of Gentiles who were coming into [the community] and already found themselves in the material condition proscribed for Jews by Lev 18:6-18."[17] There was a danger of laxity here, just as there had been in Corinth where an incestuous relationship was being tolerated by the community until Paul expressly forbade the

[15] It is important to be aware that, with the exception of Matthew 5 and 19, the NT is absolute in its prohibition of divorce. See 1 Cor 7:10-11; Mark 10:2-12; Luke 16:18.

[16] This is not the place to argue this widely held position. See, for example, Werner Georg Kümmel, *Introduction to the New Testament* (London: SCM, 1975) 105–19; Augustin George and Pierre Grelot, eds., *Introduction critique au Nouveau Testament*. Introduction à la Bible, Édition nouvelle III. 7 vols. (Paris, Desclée, 1976) 2:88–98. See also the helpful survey of Daniel J. Harrington, "Matthean Studies Since Joachim Rohde," *HeyJ* 16 (1975) 375–88. There has been a recent revival of the theory that Matthew is directed to a Jewish audience, that the role of the Law and Jewish traditions are being defended. In this view the Gentile mission is only grudgingly accepted. For an energetic statement of this position see David C. Sim, *The Gospel of Matthew and Christian Judaism. The History and Social Setting of the Matthean Community*. Studies of the New Testament and Its World (Edinburgh: T & T Clark, 1998). See, however, Donald Senior, *The Gospel of Matthew*. Interpreting Biblical Texts (Nashville: Abingdon, 1997) 71–84.

[17] Fitzmyer, "Matthean Divorce Texts," 211.

practice as πορνεία (1 Cor 5:1). In the Pauline passage the word clearly refers to the sort of incestuous relationship forbidden by Lev 18:8.[18] Understood in this sense, the Matthean exception had an important role to play in the community's theology of marriage. It was not to allow a certain elasticity but to take a rigorous line against "the lax practice of maintaining incestuous unions in the case of proselytes."[19] It is important to notice, at this stage of our study, that the Matthean church, in dealing with the unique vocation to Christian marriage, experienced difficulties with a group of people who had not received any formation in Old Testament mores: their Gentile converts.[20]

The Pharisees suddenly disappear from the scene, and the audience now becomes οἱ μαθηταὶ αὐτοῦ. Matthew 19:10-12 has no parallel in the rest of the synoptic tradition and v. 10 shows several marks of Matthean redaction. The adverb "thus" (οὕτως) is very popular in Matthew (33x); the word ἄνθρωπος used in the indefinite sense of "a man" or "a person" is frequent in Matthew, and συμφέρειν is found only in Matthew among the synoptics.[21] This is an indication that the Matthean church and its problems are close at hand. Matthew leaves his source and introduces, by means of v. 10, an application of the law of divorce to a problem that is troubling his community. I would suggest that vv. 10-12 have been introduced from the same background as the exceptive clauses in 5:31 and 19:9. The community has a problem, and Matthew addresses himself to it. The "story" is about Jesus and his immediate disciples; the "message" is for those disciples of Jesus in the Matthean church who turn to the gospel for the words of their Master.[22]

---

[18] This contact with 1 Cor 5:1 is important, as scholars often object that the word πορνεία is not found in Lev 18:6-18. Paul, referring to an incestuous situation explicitly condemned by Lev 18:8, uses the word πορνεία.

[19] Meier, *Law and History* 150. As we will be largely following his suggestion for 19:12, it should be noted that Jacques Dupont, *Mariage et divorce dans l'évangile. Matthieu 19,3-12 et parallèles* (Bruges: Desclée de Brouwer, 1959) 110–14, refuses to accept this position. He suggests (pp. 93–157) that in the case of infidelity on the part of the woman a *separatio mensa et toro* was permitted, but not a remarriage.

[20] See also Stock, "Matthean Divorce Texts," 24–33; John Donahue, "Divorce: New Testament Perspectives," in Kevin T. Kelly, *Divorce and Second Marriage. Facing the Challenge* (new and expanded ed. Kansas City: Sheed & Ward, 1997) 212–28, especially 219–22.

[21] Pierre Benoit, Marie-Émile Boismard, and Arnaud Lamouille, *Synopse des Quatre Évangiles en Français.* 3 vols. (Paris: Cerf, 1965–77) 2:308.

[22] This technique has been shown as central for an understanding of the Fourth Gospel by J. Louis Martyn, *History and Theology in the Fourth Gospel* (New York: Harper & Row, 1968). Martyn speaks of a "two-level drama." The

The reply of the disciples in v. 10, paralleling that of the Pharisees in v. 7, is understandable and eminently reasonable from *a human and social* point of view. If Christian marriage is so sacred that divorce is completely forbidden, and even those who, in their pre-Christian days, had married illicitly in the Christian view of things must now separate, then it is better not to marry at all. The reply of Jesus to this comment takes the discussion outside these horizons: "Not everyone can accept this teaching [literally "word"], but only those to whom it is given." There is a difficulty over τὸν λόγον τοῦτον. Which "word" is Jesus referring to? Does he refer back to the discussion of vv. 3-9, and especially to v. 9, which is a restatement in more precise terms of what had already been said in v. 6, or is this in agreement with the disciples' statement in v. 10? If it is the latter, then v. 12 must be understood as Jesus' explanation of what it means not to marry.

Along with many commentators,[23] I see τὸν λόγον τοῦτον as referring back to vv. 3-9, and especially to the harsh line taken in v. 9. An important reason for this position—generally overlooked by commentators—is the parallel between vv. 9-12 and vv. 23-26. In both passages one finds a harsh word from Jesus (vv. 9 and 23-24), followed by a stunned, human reaction from the disciples (vv. 10 and 25), finally resolved by a word from Jesus, referring back to his harsh statement, on the possibility of humanly impossible things in a God-given situation (vv. 11 and 26). In vv. 23-26 Matthew reworked Mark 10:23-27 to make his point concerning marriage and divorce in the community, but Mark's discussion of divorce (10:2-12) did not make this further point. Thus Matthew added vv. 10-12 before resuming his contact with Mark in vv. 13-15 (see Mark 10:13-16). It is not enough to point out that vv. 3-9 form a unit addressed to the Pharisees, and that vv. 10-12

---

same technique plays an important role in all four gospels. Recent use of narrative-critical principles has advanced this further by applying the distinction between "story" and "discourse" developed by Seymour Chatman (*Story and Discourse: Narrative Structure in Fiction and Film* [Ithaca, N. Y.: Cornell University Press, 1978]) to the gospel narratives.

[23] See the resumé of this discussion, with bibliography, in Jacques Dupont, *Mariage et divorce* 166–70. See further Pierre Bonnard, *L'Evangile selon Saint Matthieu*. Commentaire du Nouveau Testament 1 (Neuchâtel: Delachaux et Niestlé, 1970) 284; H. Benedict Green, *The Gospel according to Matthew*. New Clarendon Bible (Oxford: Oxford University Press, 1975) 169, who support the position I have taken. See, however, W. D. Davies, *The Setting of the Sermon on the Mount* (Cambridge: Cambridge University Press, 1963) 393–95, and David Hill, *The Gospel of Matthew*. NCB (London: Oliphant, 1972) 281, who take the opposite position.

are addressed to the disciples in a section clearly introduced by Matthew in v. 10, and thus conclude that v. 11 must refer to v. 12. This is to stop short at a *formal* analysis. The fact remains that Matthew placed vv. 3-9 and 10-12 together, and we must understand the passage as a whole, even if we are able to trace the different elements used to form it.[24] For Matthew vv. 3-9 did not formulate one message (about marriage and divorce, directed to the Pharisees) followed by another separate statement in vv. 10-12 (about voluntary celibacy, directed to the disciples). On the contrary, vv. 3-9, taken from Mark and rearranged for his own purpose by Matthew, form the preface for the saying introduced by the stunned question of v. 10 and pronounced by Jesus in vv. 10-12.

The demand the Matthean Jesus makes upon his followers, that they never divorce one another, arises from the fact that they are now *Christians*. The marriage situation under discussion is not ἡ αἰτία τοῦ ἀνθρώπου μετὰ τῆς γυναικός, but a gift that we, in our theological jargon, would call "a graced situation." Jesus is speaking about the unique union of man and woman that the tradition has come to call a "Christian marriage." Not all marriages can be defined as such, and thus separations can take place, but for those to whom this gift is given there can be no possibility of breaking apart what God has put together (v. 6). As long as one judges the situation of "a man with a woman" in secular, sexual, and human terms the demands of Jesus are impossible, and divorce is a necessity. But when it is "accepted" as God-given, the position taken by Jesus (and Matthew's community) is the only one possible.[25] This is also the point made by vv. 23-25 in the discussion following the encounter with the rich young man. In the face of the radical demands of discipleship Jesus' followers complain: "Then who can be saved?" (v. 26; see v. 10). Jesus replies that in merely human terms it would indeed be impossible, but παρὰ θεῷ πάντα δυνατά (v. 26; see v. 11). The New Testament teaches that the radical demands of Christian discipleship must be met within the context of a disciple who is prepared to

---

[24] This point is well made by Quentin Quesnell, "Made Themselves Eunuchs for the Kingdom of Heaven," *CBQ* 30 (1966) 341–44. See pp. 343–44, where Quesnell shows that the "correction" technique, outlined above, is common throughout the Gospel of Matthew.

[25] The "givenness" of Christian marriage is finely illustrated by Matthew's choice of the verb χωρέω. It is correctly translated as "to accept in an intellectual sense," but it also carries the idea of "to make space for." Thus the idea of being "open" to the gift that is given is also conveyed by the verb usually translated as "accept."

lose him/herself in openness to the gifts that God alone can give. Matthew is in full agreement with this teaching.[26]

The point made by v. 12, *in its present Matthean context,* continues this line of thought. In my reading of the exceptive clause in v. 9 I concluded (along with most current scholarship) that Matthew introduced these clauses because of a given situation in his community. I then argued that the conversion of Gentiles was leading to a difficulty in the community's concept of Christian marriage as, in the Jewish-Christian view of things, some of these new converts were married incestuously. Since this was the case, the marriages had to be dissolved. I believe that we must look to the same *Sitz im Leben der Kirche* for an explanation of v. 12. For many reasons, some of which will appear below, the eunuch passage is generally held to be traditional, possibly coming from Jesus himself, while the command ὁ δυνάμενος χωρεῖν χωρείτω has been added to the older saying to apply it to its present context. Whether this happened in a pre-Matthean stage or in the actual composition of the gospel is difficult (perhaps impossible?) to determine, but it is not important for our purposes.[27] It is clear that v. 12 was not "invented" by Matthew, but what does it mean in his context? Jacques Dupont has, in my opinion, indicated the way to a satisfactory solution of this question.[28] However, I would differ from his suggestion concerning the Matthean situation that has caused the insertion of the saying here.

[26] See the reflections of Quesnell, "Made Themselves Eunuchs," 349–57. He concludes: "Such a love would be then truly a sign in the world—and worthy therefore of the name Catholic tradition has given it—the name of Sacrament, mystery" (p. 357).

[27] Only Matthew uses the verb χωρέω in the sense of being open to receive something (15:17; 19:11, 12). The only other use of the verb in the synoptic tradition is in Mark 2:2 where it has its primary sense in the phrase "there was no longer room for them" to describe the predicament of those bearing the paralytic, whom they eventually let down through the roof. Verse 12 takes up the verb used in v. 11, adding to what was a more traditional passage in v. 12abc the Matthean recommendation of v. 12d. See Josef Blinzler, "*Eisin eunouchoi.* Zur Auslegung von Mt 19:12," *ZNW* 48 (1957) 264–67; Benoit, Boismard, and Lamouille, *Synopse* 2:308–309.

[28] Dupont, *Mariage et divorce* 161–222. See Quesnell, "Made Themselves Eunuchs," for a further development of Dupont's argument. Surveys of this discussion can be found in Giuseppe Segalla, "Il testo più antico sul celibato: Mt 19,11-12," *Studia Patavina* 17 (1970) 121–39, and especially in Thadée Matura, "Le célibat dans le Nouveau Testament d'après l'exégèse récente," *NRTh* 107 (1975) 487–96. Matura accepts the argument of Blinzler on Matt. 19:12 (see below), but rejects the Dupont-Quesnell position. The whole article, rich in insight and bibliographical detail, runs from pp. 481–500; 593–604. A similar

Dupont has argued that v. 12 continues and concludes, in a very radical fashion, the argument on divorce. Here, I believe, he is correct. However, he understands the exceptive clause in v. 9 in the "classical" sense, i.e., as a permission to separate in the case of infidelity on the part of the woman. He then interprets v. 12 as a demand that when this happens there is to be no remarriage. The separation does not dissolve the marriage and the Christian who remarries in these circumstances commits adultery. The only way to avoid this situation is to accept a life similar to that of a eunuch "for the sake of the kingdom of heaven." Matthew, therefore, urges that those who have separated never remarry, because of their Christian faith. I would suggest, in the light of my different interpretation of v. 9, that the situation referred to is once again that of the Gentile converts. The members of the Matthean church would have welcomed these new elements into their midst, but the strange and different ways of the Christian community must have been difficult for the Gentile to understand and accept. This situation must have caused many defections.[29] Verse 12 reflects this situation. Some have returned to their earlier beliefs and practices, and thus to their former marital practices in paganism, while the marriage-partner has remained in the Matthean community.

That such situations existed in the earliest Church is evidenced by 1 Cor 7:12-16. How does Matthew resolve the situation? He is more radical than Paul, who allows the non-Christian party to leave the marriage, "for God has called us to peace" (v. 15). Matthew summons his separated ex-pagans to a life of celibacy for the sake of the kingdom they have recently embraced or, better, that has recently embraced them. We must recall that Matthew has made two major insertions into his source, Mark. These insertions must have been caused by a very precise situation in the Matthean church. This, I suggest, is where Dupont's suggestions fall slightly short. It is more than likely that both insertions into Matthew's Markan *Vorlage* (v. 9 and vv. 11-12) are directed to the *same* problem: the regulation of the marriage difficulties of the newly-arrived Gentile converts.

This interpretation does justice to the present tense of the third-person imperative χωρείτω, often overlooked by commentators. The

---

position has also been argued by Jerome Kodell, "The Celibacy Logion in Matthew 19:12," *BTB* 8 (1978) 19–23.

[29] The idealism of Christian morality has always been a cause of difficulty. It is not "worldly" enough. See the valid criticism of Dupont's link between v. 9 and v. 12 in Proietti, "La scelta celibataria," 34–35.

paraenesis of v. 12d is not simply a straight command: "Let him receive it" (RSV). That would require an aorist imperative. The difficult situation of an abandoned husband or wife was a fact in the community. Matthew exhorted them to remain faithful in their loneliness if they wished to remain open to the radical demands of a God with whom "all things are possible." There was a decision that had to be made, and this is expressed by the aorist εὐνούχισαν, but once the decision was made it still had to be lived. It was not just "accepted" once and for all without any further problems. It called for a continual and radical openness to the overpowering presence of God's lordship in the life of these struggling new Christians. This is the sense of the διὰ τὴν βασιλείαν τῶν οὐρανῶν. This situation can only be described by the present imperative.[30]

This leads us to two further objections to Dupont's thesis that are frequently raised.[31] The word "eunuch" means an incapacity for marriage, but Matthew's "eunuch," if Dupont is correct, would still be quite capable of marriage, and could remarry if the first partner died.[32] Another difficulty that arises is that Dupont's analysis ultimately sees the need for continence not as a charism, but as something that arose of necessity if one wished to remain in the community.[33] Both objections are overcome by a consideration of the sense of the preposition διά. The word can have both a final sense: "for the sake of the Kingdom, in order to construct or gain the Kingdom," and a causal sense: "because of the Kingdom." Josef Blinzler has shown that Matt 19:12 must be given the causal sense.[34] Matthew exhorts the abandoned spouses of his community to live their celibacy "because of" the Kingdom. They should be so taken up and swept off their feet by the overwhelming presence of God's lordship that there can be no possibility

---

[30] See BDF 172–74, §§ 335-37. Dupont, *Mariage et divorce* 188–90, argued that this was not a special charism. I disagree. Verse 11 indicates that Christian marriage is a "given" situation, and it is this "givenness" that continues, even into the state of separation because of the unfaithfulness of one of the parties. This is the significance of the verb χωρέω in v. 12d, as it was in v. 11. Dupont is here influenced by his (correct) insistence that at the Matthean stage one cannot speak of celibacy as a qualitatively superior state of life. But this has led him to ignore the qualitatively superior state of the faithful Christian over against the one who falls away. This is the point of Matt 19:12.

[31] See Kodell, "The Celibacy Logion," 21.

[32] See Jean Galot, "La motivation évangelique du célibat," *Greg* 53 (1972) 739.

[33] See above, n. 30. See also Leopold Sabourin, "The Positive Values of Consecrated Celibacy," *Supplement to the Way* 10 (1970) 52.

[34] Blinzler, "*Eisin eunouchoi*," 261–64.

(thus the *analogous* use of "eunuch") of committing themselves to a further marriage relationship. The saying in no way prohibits a further Christian marriage, but the accent must be placed on the "Christian" aspect. It would only be possible when one's former partner was dead. The second objection to Dupont's thesis is similarly resolved by my conviction that the call to celibacy is not "imposed by someone else," but is "given" as it is the result of the overpowering presence of God's lordship.

Despite these corrections to Dupont's original thesis, it appears to me that his basic argument is correct. Matthew 19:3-12 should be understood as a discussion of divorce. This was one of the many difficult situations that had to be resolved by an understanding of Jesus as the new Moses who had brought the Law to its perfection (the problem of the relation between Christian community and Synagogue) without eliminating the original demands of God, which retain their perennial importance (the problem of introducing converts into a community that still lived according to the fundamental principles of Jewish morality). The theory of this process is stated in Matt 5:17-20, but the practice is found in Matt 19:3-12.

THE SIGNIFICANCE OF MATTHEW 19:12 ON THE LIPS OF JESUS: A FORM-CRITICAL STUDY

I have already mentioned that Matthew is working with material that came to him from earlier tradition. In my survey of vv. 3-9 I was able to find parallels in both Mark and Luke indicating that this was the case. Verses 10-12, however, have no parallel in the New Testament. I argued above that v. 10 and v. 12d were from the hand of Matthew or, at least, were added in a pre-Matthean stage to a passage that is widely accepted as coming from the historical Jesus. There are several factors that lead scholars to this conclusion:

1. The harshness of the word "eunuch." This word was offensive and crude, and would never have been "invented" by the early Church and placed on the lips of Jesus. The saying must have originally been on the lips of Jesus and it has been preserved, despite the use of such a crude word, precisely because he said it.
2. The spiraling structure of the phrase is typical of the Semitic *mashal* form:[35]

---

[35] See Dupont, *Mariage et divorce* 191–96 for the Jewish background to this form and language.

> There are *eunuchs* . . .
> and there are *eunuchs* . . .
> who have been made *eunuchs* . . .
> and there are *eunuchs*
> who have made themselves *eunuchs*

This rhythmic spiraling movement, leading the reader (or the listener) to the final "punch line" ("for the sake of the Kingdom of heaven") shows all the traces of being both Semitic and easily remembered because of its rhythm.

3. Although we have no canonical parallels to this passage, both Justin Martyr and Epiphanius have it in a slightly different form from that of Matthew. This suggests that they received the saying from an independent source.[36] This does not necessarily lead us back to Jesus, but it indicates that the saying is not a Matthean creation.

4. The most influential factor, however, lies in the extreme difficulty that has to be overcome by anyone who wishes to locate this saying in the apologetic of the early Church. It is almost impossible to imagine a *Sitz im Leben der Kirche* that would have caused the creation of a saying that spoke of Christians as "eunuchs." A closer look at this question shows that we must go back to the historical Jesus to find the origin of this strange saying.

As I have already mentioned, the major issue to be solved in this saying is the origin of the use of the word "eunuch." In our own period it is an offensive enough expression, but in antiquity, where eunuchs were an estranged part of society, it seems impossible that the early Church would have Jesus say that "there are eunuchs who have made themselves eunuchs for the sake of the kingdom of heaven." The rabbinic literature speaks of two types of eunuch:[37] "the eunuch of the sun," סְרִיס חַמָּה (serîs hammāh) and "the human-made eunuch," סְרִיס אָדָם (serîs ʿādām). The "eunuch of the sun" is one whom the sun has always seen as such, and in Matt 19:12 Jesus describes such people as "eunuchs who have been so from birth." The "human-made

[36] See Josef Blinzler, "Justinus *Apol.* 1,15,4 und Mattäus 19,11-12," in Albert Descamps and André de Halleux, eds., *Mélanges bibliques en hommage au R.P. Béda Rigaux* (Gembloux: Duculot, 1970) 44–55; Benoit, Boismard, and Lamouille, *Synopse* 2:308.

[37] For a more detailed treatment of the summary that follows see Johannes Schneider, *TDNT* 2 (1964) 765–68. See also Giuseppe Segalla, "Il testo più antico," 122–24, and especially Blinzler, *"Eisin eunouchoi,"* 256–64.

eunuch" is the one who has been made a eunuch by human intervention, and in Matt 19:12 Jesus calls such people "eunuchs who have been made eunuchs by others." The third type of eunuch envisaged by the words of Jesus in 19:12 "for the sake of the kingdom" is an unheard-of category.[38]

The attitude of the ancients to eunuchs was decidedly negative, yet the "eunuch" theme is central to our passage. Despite its crudeness and its offensive implications it is used, as a noun and in a verbal form, no less than five times in this one verse. Deuteronomy 23:1 forbids the presence of a eunuch among God's chosen people, and both Jewish and pagan literature present them as sycophantish, fat, beardless, feminine—but despotically cruel.[39] It is unthinkable that the early Church would have spoken of its members with this word, or that Matthew himself would have called his Gentile converts "eunuchs." We must, therefore, ask whether there was a situation in the life of Jesus that could have led him to use the word in a way that can make sense of Matt 19:12.

There is ample evidence in the gospels that Jesus was the object of continual *ad hominem* abuse from his opponents. He and his disciples do not fast (Mark 2:18), they violate the Sabbath (Mark 2:23), and they take their meals without the ritual lustrations (Mark 7:5). Jesus himself is called "a glutton and a drunkard, a friend of tax collectors and sinners" (Matt. 11:19). "You are a Samaritan and have a demon," accuse "the Jews" in John 8:48. On another occasion we are told that "they have called the master of the household Beelzebul" (Matt 10:25). Josef Blinzler has convincingly argued that in this same type of situation Jesus was called "eunuch!" Given the importance of marriage and the production of children it appears more than probable that there was something about the life-style of Jesus of Nazareth that enabled his opponents to call him a eunuch in a derogatory and abusive sense.[40] The rabbinic evidence makes it clear that it was an unconditional duty for a rabbi to marry, in obedience to Gen 1:28. There is only one known celibate

---

[38] There is a qualitative distinction between the first two types of eunuch and the third. According to Eusebius, *Hist. Eccl.* 6,8 (PG 20, 536-537), Origen failed to make this distinction! See, however, Origen, *Comm. In Matt.* 15,1 (PG 13, 1253), where such a literal interpretation of the Matthean text is criticized by Origen himself.

[39] See Blinzler, *"Eisin eunouchoi,"* 257, n. 11, and the references and texts in Segalla, "Il testo più antico," 123.

[40] See Blinzler, *"Eisin eunouchoi,"* 254–70. See the interesting list of texts reporting derogatory statements against the unmarried and the abusive use of the word "eunuch" in Adinolfi, "Il celibato di Gesù," 146, nn. 3-6.

rabbi, Ben Azzai, but he was sharply criticized by other rabbis. In *b. Sotah* 4b it is assumed that he must have been divorced, and *b. Ketub.* 63a accuses him of having had sexual relations with the daughter of Akiba.[41] The unmarried state was obviously blameworthy. It is understandable that the gospels do not report the actual insults made by Jesus' opponents, but Matt 19:12 can certainly be understood as Jesus' reaction to attacks from people who sought excuses to hurl abuse at this troublesome character. An unmarried man was immediately open to such abuse, particularly as he was a troublesome public figure.[42]

I would suggest that Blinzler's analysis of the *Sitz im Leben Jesu* of Matt 19:12 is correct and that, for our purposes, we can draw three conclusions from this analysis:

1. That the origin of the saying, no matter how it is used in its present Matthean context, is to be found on the lips of Jesus as a calm but shattering reply to his critics. Here we are in touch with a rare insight into the thought and language of Jesus. He takes on his opponents with a calm dignity, using their language in a new way, a way that, according to Jesus, could make sense because of the presence of the Kingdom (see Mark 1:15).
2. That this saying was not merely uttered once, but was Jesus' oft-repeated response to those who abused him because of his celibate state. To a stereotyped form of abuse Jesus gave a regular answer, asking his accusers to try to understand him and his celibacy in the light of "the kingdom." In this way the saying gained a permanent place in the tradition. Even though it is not found (understandably) in Mark and Luke, it crops up again in Justin and Epiphanius, despite the harshness of the word "eunuch."
3. That Jesus was celibate. This form-critical study ultimately leads us to a more than probable conclusion that the words of Matt 19:12 on the lips of Jesus were an explanation of his celibate state. The gospels do give us evidence for the celibacy of Jesus of Nazareth.

Our study of Matthew's use of his sources to formulate a radical prohibition of divorce in Matt 19:3-12 has led us to ask further questions about those sources. We have found that 19:12 most probably comes from the lips of the celibate Jesus of Nazareth, in reply to the abusive

---

[41] See Schneider, *TDNT* 2:767.

[42] This practice has not died out over the centuries. Most cultures and languages have terms of abuse that refer to a man's sexual capacities. My own Australian "popular culture" is extremely rich in such expressions!

use of the word "eunuch" aimed at him by his opponents. Thus we have established the fact of Jesus' celibacy, but what did it mean?

There is little need to repeat here what I mentioned above concerning the use of the preposition διά. When Matthew took over this saying to use it for his own purposes he retained the original sense of the preposition. Jesus' opponents knew of two types of eunuch: the one born so and the one made so by human intervention. Like Jesus, these people were "unable" to accept a normal married situation. However, the cause of Jesus' "inability" was not physical. He was so taken over by the urgent presence of the Kingdom that he could do no other than give himself entirely to it. The celibacy of Jesus was not something that he made happen to himself by first deliberating whether it should happen and then deciding in favor of it, so that he would be able to dedicate himself entirely to the construction of the Kingdom to come. The causality ran in the opposite direction. In Jesus of Nazareth the guiding principle and overwhelming experience of his life was the presence of the lordship of the God of Israel whom he called "Father" (see Matt 11:27; Mark 13:32; 14:36; Luke 11:2, and the whole of the Fourth Gospel). It was this "lordship" that led him to his state of celibacy, to his being a "eunuch" because of the overwhelming presence of "the Kingdom" in his life. His reply to his opponents, however, is not just a defense of himself and an explanation of why he was not married. It would also have been (and still remains) an invitation to all those who heard this quiet reply to consider just what this Kingdom might hold if it so determined the life of the man Jesus.

CONCLUSION

It is sometimes argued that the use of the plural εἰσιν εὐνοῦχοι indicated that Jesus was speaking not only of himself, but also of John the Baptist, some of his disciples, or even the Essenes.[43] This is not necessarily the case. The use of the plural on the lips of Jesus here should be understood as an "allusive plural,"[44] created by the rhetorical situation of abuse and reply. In Matthew's use of the saying the plural has its full numerical sense, but there is no need to look beyond Jesus for the origin of this startlingly new life-style of men and women who can do no

---

[43] See, for example, Blinzler, *"Eisin eunouchoi,"* 263–64; H. Benedict Green, *Matthew* 169–70. Constantin Daniel, "Esséniens et eunuques (Mt 19,10-12)," *Revue de Qumran* 6 (1967–69) 353–90, argues that the second type of eunuch that Jesus refers to (those made eunuchs) indicates the Essenes, and that this phrase already refers to a *homo religiosus*, not to castration.

[44] BDF 77–78, § 141.

other except abandon the normal practice of married life. The "allusive plural" can take on a further sense as the gospel is read within the Christian community. It not only indicates others who, along with Jesus in the 30's of the first century, were also celibates "for the sake of the kingdom," but it *invites* people to a radical *sequela Christi*. This *sequela*, however, must not be based on the *fact* of the celibacy of Jesus, but on the *reason* for that state in his life. Thus Christians may be celibate not because they are deprived, deformed, or in some way "strange," but because they are so taken up by the overwhelming presence of the lordship of God that they are existentially incapable of married life. This does not make their life any easier, but like Jesus they are "eunuchs for the sake of the kingdom of heaven," and they ultimately point to a value beyond all measurable values, God's lordship in the lives of all woman and men, married and celibate.[45]

---

[45] An article that suggests a theology and practice of celibacy along these lines is Ruggero Balducelli, "The Decision for Celibacy," *TS* 36 (1975) 219–42. A theology of consecrated celibacy has much to gain from these reflections. No longer is such a life based on a dubious piece of paraenesis (i.e., Jesus' recommendation that some remain celibate to construct the Kingdom [Matt 19:12]); instead it is founded in the life and person of Jesus of Nazareth. See in this direction J. M. R. Tillard, *Devant dieu et pour le monde. Le projet des religieux.* Cogitatio Fidei 75 (Paris: Cerf, 1975) 145–52; Jean-Marie van Cangh, "Fondement évangélique de la vie religieuse," *NRTh* 105 (1973) 635–47.

CHAPTER 3

THE VOCATION OF THE DISCIPLES IN THE GOSPEL OF MARK

It could be said that, even in a secular understanding of the expression, a "sense of vocation" gives life hope and purpose. If the answer to such questions as "why am I married to this particular man or woman," "why am I involved in this particular profession, in this particular lifestyle" is merely "because it just happened that way," life loses its challenge and can degenerate into a modern-day fatalism. This almost platitudinous reflection should be noted as an introduction to a biblical consideration of vocation. When we come to analyze vocation, and particularly the Christian vocation, while the positive sciences will always have a very important role to play, we are in the realms of mystery. We are attempting to say something about the uncontrollable but powerfully important aspects of the mystery of God at work in the hearts, minds, souls, and lives of men and women. In the Christian tradition, therefore, a biblical reflection has its place.

When face to face with mystery Christians believe that they have "a word from the other side" in the biblical accounts of God's presence to the human story, especially in and through the person of Jesus Christ (see John 1:14; 2 Cor 1:20; 3:16–4:6).[1] The study that follows will focus its attention on the vocation to discipleship as it is portrayed in the Gospel of Mark. Martin Dibelius has correctly described these vocation stories as

[1] See Vatican Council II, Constitution on Divine Revelation *(Dei verbum)* 7–10.

"paradigms."[2] I am skeptical about Dibelius's claim, as a historian, that the paradigms were constructed entirely from the experience of the post-resurrectional Church, yet his term "paradigm" indicates the lasting significance of these stories. They are a biblical model that challenged the first disciples and the early Church, and continue to challenge all who claim to be responding to the call to walk behind Jesus of Nazareth.

THE CONTEMPORARY DISCUSSION OF MARKAN DISCIPLESHIP

The baffling question that must be resolved by any serious consideration of the disciples in the Gospel of Mark is that of their failure. The popular idea of a disciple of Jesus is that of a courageous and persevering follower, yet Mark's account tells a different story. There are signs of a positive theology of discipleship in the vocation stories of 1:16-20; 2:13-14; 3:13-19, in the disciples' being entrusted with "the secret [or: mystery] of the kingdom of God" in 4:11, and in the missionary success of the Twelve in 6:6b-13, 30.[3] But already in the earlier sections of the gospel an obtuseness emerges (see 4:35-41; 6:45-52; 8:14-21) and grows into a hardening lack of understanding, or even opposition, in the second half of the gospel (see 8:32-33; 9:19, 32; 10:24, 26, 32). It culminates in the flight of 14:50: "all of them deserted him and fled," and the betrayal of Peter in 14:66-72. The flight and betrayal are made even more dramatic by the oaths of Peter and the rest of the disciples in 14:29-31:

> Peter said to him, "Even though all become deserters, I will not." Jesus said to him, "Truly I tell you, this day, this very night, before the cock

[2] Martin Dibelius, *From Tradition to Gospel*. Library of Theological Translations (Cambridge and London: James Clark, 1971 [original German 1919]) 43, 111–14. See also Günther Schmahl, "Die Berufung der Zwölf im Markusevangelium, *TTZ* 81 (1972) 208, where he uses the term "paradigm" as I have used it. Rudolf Bultmann, *The History of the Synoptic Tradition* (Oxford: Basil Blackwell, 1986 [original German 1921]) 28, 61–63, 67–68 speaks of these stories as "ideal scenes," with much the same implications as Dibelius.

[3] I believe that the reasons for the failure of the disciples (who are never again associated with the mission of Jesus in Mark) are seminally present in 6:30*: "Those sent out returned to Jesus and told *him* all the things that *they* had done (πάντα ὅσα ἐποίησαν) and all the things that *they* had taught (ὅσα ἐδίδαξαν)." Mark makes his point well by inserting the account of the loss-of-self for truth on the part of the Baptist (6:14-29) between the mission of the Twelve and their triumphant but full-of-self return. Scholars have generally not seen this, and it needs further development. For some preliminary reflections see Francis J. Moloney, *Disciples and Prophets. A Biblical Model for the Religious Life* (London: Darton, Longman and Todd, 1980) 140–42.

crows twice, you will deny me three times." But he said vehemently, "Even though I must die with you, I will not deny you." And all of them said the same.

There can be little doubt that such a skillfully arranged narrative, preparing the reader for the climaxes of 14:50 and 14:66-72 through the fickle oaths of 14:29-31, is the work of an excellent storyteller, however much the details may or may not have their roots in the original historical experience of the first disciples of Jesus.[4] In writing a gospel that tells the story of a group of disciples who move inevitably toward failure Mark was speaking to his own community, proclaiming a message about *their* discipleship. We are not dealing with a history book, but with a message Mark understood as "good news" (see Mark 1:1).[5] Thus far one could say that there is general agreement among scholars. All see the growth of the failure motif through the gospel, but when it comes to the interpretation of Mark's use of this theme serious divisions arise.

Fundamental to any discussion of the failure motif in Mark's gospel is the epoch-making work of William Wrede, *Das Messiasgeheimnis in den Evangelien*, first published in 1901 and since then reappearing in four editions, the latest in 1969.[6] Wrede claimed that Jesus was a Galilean teacher and a charismatic figure who never made messianic claims for himself. However, by the time Mark came to write his gospel Jesus was being acclaimed as the Messiah. Mark had to resolve

---

[4] This steady movement toward total failure has been widely recognized, but variously interpreted. For an excellent survey see Robert C. Tannehill, "The Disciples in Mark: The Function of a Narrative Role," *JR* 57 (1977) 396–403. This important study is now available in William Telford, ed., *The Interpretation of Mark*. IRT 7 (Philadelphia: Fortress, 1985) 134–57. Tannehill's understanding of Mark's theological technique in "telling a story" is very helpful. On this aspect of Mark's gospel see also John R. Donahue, *Are You the Christ? The Trial Narrative in the Gospel of Mark*. SBLDS 10 (Missoula: Scholars, 1973) 224–35.

[5] This has also been widely recognized. It is well presented by Karl-Georg Reploh, *Markus: Lehrer der Gemeinde. Eine redaktionsgeschichtliche Studie zu den Jüngerperikopen des Markus-Evangeliums*. SBM 9 (Stuttgart: Katholisches Bibelwerk, 1969). See, for example, his programmatic analysis of 1:14-15 on pp. 13–26. This, of course, is not new. It was at the heart of the argument of Willi Marxsen's pioneering work, *Mark the Evangelist. Studies on the Redaction History of the Gospel*. Translated by James Boyce, et al. (New York and Nashville: Abingdon, 1969).

[6] William Wrede, *Das Messiasgeheimnis in den Evangelien. Zugleich ein Beitrag zum Verständnis des Markusevangeliums* (4th ed. Göttingen: Vandenhoeck & Ruprecht, 1969). English: *The Messianic Secret*. Library of Theological Translations. Translated by J. C. G. Greig (Cambridge and London: James Clark, 1971).

a tension created by the "story" of Jesus that came to him in his traditions and showed no knowledge of Jesus as the Messiah, in face of his Church's belief that Jesus was the Messiah. He solved the problem, claims Wrede, through a literary technique that has been called "the messianic secret." There is no "story" of Jesus as the Messiah because:

(a) The disciples were continually commanded by Jesus never to speak of his messianic deeds and person (see 1:25, 34; 3:12; 5:43; 7:36; 8:26, 30; 9:9, etc.).
(b) They are portrayed as failing to understand him, and thus their "story" is not the true story.

None of this took place during the lifetime of Jesus. It has been inserted into the gospel by the evangelist. In this way Wrede answers the problem of the failure of the disciples by seeing it entirely as a literary tool of Mark, answering the problems of his community. His argument continues to fascinate scholars, and many of his methods and presuppositions became fundamental principles in the systematic establishment of form criticism, which he preceded by some twenty years.[7]

Wrede's solutions have not gone unchallenged, and the major difficulties with his theory are:

(a) Wrede *presupposes* that Jesus of Nazareth had no messianic consciousness. This is asserted, but never proved.
(b) He also *presupposes* that the answer to the problem of secrecy and ignorance must be literary and not historical.
(c) He claims that all the texts that touch in some way upon the secrecy motif, including the disciples' blindness, must be explained by the *one* literary technique: the messianic secret. There is no room left for any other literary or historical solution. A blanket solution generally obscures the complexity of a problem, and this is certainly the case with Wrede's argument.

I merely indicate these difficulties, as there is no call for a detailed discussion of Wrede's thesis here.[8] I have presented a short summary of it

---

[7] Form criticism had its systematic and formal beginnings in the work of Karl Ludwig Schmidt (1919), Martin Dibelius (1919), and Rudolf Bultmann (1921).

[8] Most studies of the messianic secret cover this ground. See the useful and well-documented survey of David E. Aune, "The Problem of the Messianic Secret," *NovT* 11 (1969) 2–8. See also Georges Minette de Tillesse, *Le Secret messianique dans l'évangile de Marc.* LD 47 (Paris: Cerf, 1968) 9–34. See the collection of important studies edited by Christopher Tuckett, *The Messianic Secret.* IRT 1 (Philadelphia: Fortress, 1983).

because Wrede was the first to seek a thorough solution to the question of the failure of the disciples. All other discussions of Markan discipleship begin here. In the debate since Wrede it appears to me that one can largely divide schools of thought into three major groups. The reader will be aware that, while most scholars would be able to find themselves under one or other of the following classifications, there are many finely-nuanced solutions of detail that a full-scale survey of the discussion would have to document further. Our purposes do not call for such completeness; thus I will present three major "schools of thought," indicating a sample selection of scholarly adherents to each position.

1. Mark uses the disciples as models for people called by Jesus and appointed to a task. They are thus models for all future disciples, including the members of the Markan community.[9]

This position could be called the positive or traditional view of Mark's teaching on discipleship. In light of the many exaggerated concentrations on the failure motif it is of value that the positive aspects of Markan discipleship are well argued by these scholars. They would see the failure to understand as a part of the suffering necessarily involved in discipleship.[10] Essential to this view is a positive interpretation of the promise of the young man to the women in 16:7:

> "But go, tell his disciples and Peter that he is going ahead of you to Galilee; there you will see him, just as he told you."

All is forgiven; they will meet the risen Lord.[11]

---

[9] See, for example, Sean Freyne, *The Twelve: Disciples and Apostles. A Study in the Theology of the First Three Gospels* (London: Sheed & Ward, 1969). On Mark see pp. 106–50; James Donaldson, "'Called to Follow.' A Twofold Experience of Discipleship in Mark," *BTB* 5 (1975) 67–77; Klemens Stock, *Boten aus dem Mit-Ihm-Sein. Das Verhältnis zwischen Jesus und den Zwölf nach Markus.* AnBib 70 (Rome: Biblical Institute Press, 1975).

[10] See, for example, Freyne, *The Twelve* 129–36; Donaldson, "'Called to Follow,'" 76.

[11] There has been a long (and still unresolved) debate over the meaning of Mark 16:7. Following the lead of Ernst Lohmeyer, many (e.g., C. F. Evans, George H. Boobyer, J. B. Lightfoot, Willi Marxsen, Norman Perrin, Theodore J. Weeden, Werner Kelber) would see this as a reference to a gathering in Galilee, waiting for the parousia. Others, with Rudolf Bultmann and Vincent Taylor as the chief protagonists (e.g., Ernst Haenchen, Eduard Schweizer, T. Alec Burkill, D. E. Nineham, Hugh Anderson) would see it as the promise of a resurrection appearance. For a full discussion and bibliography see Robert H. Stein, "A Short Note on Mark 14:28 and 16:7," *NTS* 20 (1973–74) 445–52. I personally

> In this way, we are left with a picture of the little group restored again after the apparent catastrophe of death, "with Jesus" once more. . . . This was no failure for the school of Jesus in Mark's eyes. For the Twelve are reassembled around the risen Lord ready to carry out their mission as it had been originally conceived.[12]

While much of value is found in this argument, too little is made of the gradual movement to flight and betrayal. It is clearly a very important part of the Markan message. Above all, not enough attention is given to 16:8. We must interpret 16:7 in the light of the failure of the women to communicate the promise of the young man as the gospel comes to a close:[13]

> So they went out and fled from the tomb, for terror and amazement had seized them; and they said nothing to anyone, for they were afraid (16:8).

2. The disciples' failure is fully appreciated, but they remain a group that represents the reality of Christian discipleship.[14]

Scholars of this persuasion place the disciples' inability or refusal to understand Jesus' and therefore their own role and destiny at the cen-

---

believe that it refers to neither, but to the lifegiving and experienced presence of the risen Lord *in the Markan community.* This case will be argued in full in a volume being prepared for Hendrickson Publishers, entitled *The Gospel of Mark. A Commentary.* See, however, the parallel suggestions of Andreas Lindemann, "Die Osterbotschaft des Markus. Zur theologischen Interpretation von Mark 16:1-8," *NTS* 26 (1979–80) 298–317, and Henning Paulsen, "Mk XVI 1-8," *NovT* 22 (1980) 138–75.

[12] Freyne, *The Twelve* 137–38.

[13] Another "storm center" of recent Markan scholarship is involved in this debate. Did Mark's gospel end at 16:8, or have we lost an original ending that contained a resurrection appearance? For both textual and theological reasons I believe that Mark ended his gospel at 16:8. For a brief but telling presentation of this case see Norman Perrin, *The Resurrection Narratives: A New Approach* (London: SCM, 1977) 20–22. See also Pieter W. van der Horst, "Can a Book End with *gar*? A Note on Mark 16,8," *JTS* 23 (1972) 121–24. See further the comprehensive study of Joseph Hug, *La finale de l'Evangile de Marc (Mc. 16,9-20).* EB (Paris: Gabalda, 1918). See especially pp. 25–32 and 187–215.

[14] See, for example, Minette de Tillesse, *Le secret messianique* 258–76; Quentin Quesnell, *The Mind of Mark. Interpretation and Method through an Exegesis of Mark 6,52.* AnBib 38 (Rome: Biblical Institute Press, 1969) 114–25; Ralph P. Martin, *Mark: Evangelist and Theologian* (Exeter: Paternoster Press, 1972) 111–17,

ter of the discussion.[15] There is a general recognition among scholars of a Markan narrative technique in the gradually widening gap between the disciples and Jesus, leading to the final dénouement in ch. 14. However, this lack of understanding has nothing to do with a direct attack upon the disciples by the evangelist. It is a Markan technique to enhance the person of Jesus, who appears mysteriously outside *human* comprehension. Mark's use of the lack of understanding among the disciples has nothing to do with a messianic secret (*pace* Wrede and his many followers), but through this technique the evangelist calls attention to a mystery that lies at the heart of his theological perspective: human beings can never understand the cross unless *given* the power to do so. However (and here 16:7 again becomes central), despite their lack of understanding, an association with the person, message, and mission of Jesus has been entrusted to the disciples. In face of a lack of understanding Mark calls his community (and the gospel calls disciples of all times) to a deeper commitment of faith.

Ernest Best has summarized this argument well:

> If the power of Jesus is to be properly understood this can only be done in the light of the weakness of man; if Mark wishes to show Jesus' power he must show the weakness of the disciples. . . . Jesus' teaching as Mark views it was not primarily intended for the few, Peter, James, Andrew and John . . . but was intended for all who would be his followers; the role of the disciples in the gospel is there to be examples to the community. Not examples by which their own worth or failure is shown, but examples through whom teaching is given to the community and the love and power of God made known.[16]

132–33; Camille Focant, "L'incomprehension des disciples dans le deuxième évangile," *RB* 82 (1975) 161–85; Ernest Best, "The Role of the Disciples in Mark," *NTS* 23 (1976–77) 377–401; Tannehill, "The Disciples in Mark," 386–405; Reploh, *Markus: Lehrer der Gemeinde*; Heikki Räisänen, *The Messianic Secret in Mark*. Translated by Christopher Tuckett. Studies of the New Testament and Its World (Edinburgh: T & T Clark, 1990) 195–222; Howard Clark Kee, *Community of the New Age* (London: SCM, 1977) 87–100.

[15] An important distinction that should be made among the scholars listed under this general classification is that some would stress the disciples' *inability* to understand (e.g., Focant) while others stress that the disciples *refuse* to understand (e.g., Best).

[16] Best, "The Role of the Disciples," 387–88, 400–401. See also Räisänen, *Messianic Secret* 211–22; Tannehill, "The Disciples in Mark," 392–93, 395: "The more clearly the reader sees that the disciples represent himself, the more clearly the necessary rejection of the disciples' behavior becomes a negation of

Although there are matters of detail I would argue with some of the scholars who defend this view, here we are close to a narrative and theological solution to the problem of a discipleship that fails. It does justice to the two basic elements in the Markan portrait of the disciples:

(a) the considerable amount of *positive* discipleship teaching, the major part of which (the vocation stories) this paper will later analyze, and

(b) the motif of failure.

They show, correctly, that Mark is not primarily concerned with a theology of discipleship that has its own internal coherence, but with a discipleship that functions as part of Markan christology. Disciples are invited to go beyond the criteria of human success stories into the mystery of a failure that the power and love of God can heal.[17]

3. The disciples are used by Mark to represent a heretical group within his community. As such, the evangelist uses them as an anti-model for Christian discipleship. They are what disciples of Jesus should not be.[18]

The most thorough study arguing this case is Theodore J. Weeden, *Mark: Traditions in Conflict*, but the founding father of this line of thought

---

one's past self. The recognition of the disciples' failure and the search for an alternative way becomes a search for a new self who can follow Jesus faithfully as a disciple." See further Focant, "L'incompréhension," 176: "C'est à elle que Marc s'adresse à travers les disciples pour souligner à la fois les exigences d'une vie à la suite de Jésus et la confiance en Dieu qui peut tout" [It is to (the Markan community) that Mark addresses himself via the disciples, to emphasize both the demands of a life as followers of Jesus and the confidence in God that is capable of all things]. See also David J. Hawkin, "The Incomprehension of the Disciples in the Markan Redaction," *JBL* 91 (1972) 491–500, especially 496–500, and Kee, *Community of the New Age* 96.

[17] For my initial attempts to trace a Markan theology of discipleship along these lines see Moloney, *Disciples and Prophets* 133–54.

[18] See, for example, Norman Perrin, "Towards an Interpretation of the Gospel of Mark," in Hans Dieter Betz, ed., *Christology and a Modern Pilgrimage. A Discussion with Norman Perrin* (Missoula: Scholars, 1974) 1–52. Perrin could be regarded as the founder of this school of thought. His initial ideas have been developed by his students at the University of Chicago. See Theodore J. Weeden, *Mark: Traditions in Conflict* (Philadelphia: Fortress, 1971); Werner Kelber, *The Kingdom in Mark. A New Place and a New Time* (Philadelphia: Fortress, 1974); idem, ed., *The Passion in Mark. Studies on Mark 14–16* (Philadelphia: Fortress,

is Norman Perrin. He laid the basis for this discussion by attempting to show that the Gospel of Mark reflects an urgent situation in the Markan community at the time of the Jewish War (69–70 C.E.):

> In their situation a false eschatology has arisen; there are false prophets and/or false Messiahs among them and they have come to accept a mistaken expectation. In this situation Mark uses the setting of the ministry of Jesus, and allows the disciples to expose the question or express the false teaching and then puts the correct teaching on the lips of Jesus.[19]

Perrin does not seek to carry any farther than this the identification of the nature of the heresy on the lips of the disciples. Weeden will do that.

The other cornerstone of Perrin's argument that becomes central to the later developments of Weeden, Kelber, and Donahue is that Mark's gospel is *not* about the Passion leading to the vindication of the resurrection. Convinced that the original gospel ended at 16:8, Perrin argues that 16:7 is not the promise of a resurrection appearance, but about the parousia, which will take place in Galilee.[20] Jesus is leading the Markan community to the Gentiles, and it is there they will see him. Wherever the mission of the Christian community is carried on (see Isa 9:1; 1 Macc 5:15; Matt 4:15: "Galilee of the Gentiles"), there they will meet Christ in the parousia. In 16:8 the disciples are finally dismissed from the scene, as they are not even told of the promise, but Mark is speaking to his own community involved in the mission to the Gentiles. The disciples' role is a negative one, but a message is proclaimed to the Markan community:

> He [Mark] intends to lead his readers firmly to the situation in which they will gladly accept the travail and the tribulation of the present and remain firm in the conviction that it will demise eventually in the coming of Jesus as Son of Man, and they can endure what must be between now and then, as Jesus endures his passion.[21]

Theodore J. Weeden carries Perrin's argument farther, into an explicit identification of the heresy portrayed by the Markan use of the disciples. He argues that there are three stages in the disciples' relationship with Jesus:

1976); John R. Donahue, *Are You the Christ?* An earlier independent study came to similar conclusions: Joseph B. Tyson, "The Blindness of the Disciples in Mark," *JBL* 80 (1961) 261–68.

[19] Perrin, "Towards an Interpretation," 25.

[20] See n. 13 above.

[21] Perrin, "Towards an Interpretation," 26.

(a) *Unperceptiveness:* they are unable to perceive who Jesus is (1:16–8:26).
(b) *Misconception:* they will not see Jesus as the suffering Son of Man because they want a "Christ."
(c) *Rejection:* made especially clear in Peter's betrayal and the reaction of the women in 16:8.

This process takes place because the disciples are committed to a *theios aner* ("divine man") christology. Even the more positive vocation stories show them understanding their vocation as a call to a *theios aner* discipleship, i.e., they respond to a call to follow a miracle worker (3:13-14); they share in his secrets and his esoteric message (4:11), and they are exclusive, cut off from both crowd and family (1:16-20). In the end Peter confesses Jesus as the *theios aner* "Christ" (8:29).

> The evidence points unmistakably to the conclusion that the Markan disciples not only viewed Jesus as a *theios aner* Christ but also display all the traits of a *theios aner* discipleship.[22]

The gospel was written to correct the heresy portrayed through the characterization of the disciples, and they represent a heresy present in Mark's community. Mark has no Easter theology, as that would play into the hands of the heretics. The evangelist insists that the members of the Markan community will not meet Jesus till the end-time. Anyone who claims that Jesus is already present eliminates suffering and expectation from Christian life, and beguiles the community. The gospel ends at 16:7-8 with the dismissal of the disciples and a promise that "the time of Jesus' exaltation is not Easter but the *parousia*."[23] Mark attempts to defeat his opponents by telling the *real* story of Jesus, which is about the Passion and the parousia, in sharp contrast to the ecstatic, charismatic message of the heretics.

> I conclude that Mark is assiduously involved in a vendetta against the disciples. He paints them as obtuse, obdurate, recalcitrant men who are at first unperceptive of Jesus' messiahship, then oppose its style and character, and finally reject it. As a *coup de grace*, Mark closes his Gospel without rehabilitating the disciples.[24]

Many difficulties are raised by this analysis. The rest of this study will be devoted to one of them. What are we to make of the positive

---

[22] Weeden, *Mark: Traditions in Conflict* 64.
[23] Ibid. 137.
[24] Ibid. 50–51.

discipleship material in the early sections of the Gospel of Mark? Do the vocation stories indicate that the disciples understood themselves as being called to a *theios aner* discipleship? Can we find in the Markan vocation stories a genuine biblical model for the deep need in women and men of all times and persuasions to respond to the power and love of the God who created them?[25]

THE MARKAN VOCATION STORIES

Three vocation stories appear in the early chapters of Mark's gospel: the calling of Simon, Andrew, James, and John (1:16-20), the calling of Levi (2:13-14), and the calling and appointing of the Twelve (3:13-19). They are what one might call *positive* vocation stories, as there is a wholly positive response in each case. These three accounts will occupy our attention throughout the remainder of this study. However, there are two other vocation stories in Mark that could receive more attention: the Gerasene demoniac (see especially 5:14-20) and the story of the rich man (10:17-22). We might call these accounts *negative* vocation stories, as we find in them a differently structured invitation to discipleship, and the response is not quite as simple as that of the earlier accounts. We will use these narratives to throw light on the overall Markan theology of vocation. Despite our inability to provide a detailed analysis of these two passages, they have

---

[25] Apart from the literary and exegetical problems that arise from a careful analysis of the text of the Gospel of Mark, a further—and even more serious—problem is found in Weeden's identification of the *theios aner* christology in Mark. He nowhere proves the existence of this heresy in the first-century Church, yet he identifies it with considerable precision. He does draw a parallel with the enthusiasts of the Corinthian community, but as C. K. Barrett, *A Commentary on the Second Letter to the Corinthians.* Black's New Testament Commentaries (London: A & C Black, 1973) 42, comments: "There was no clear cut line of demarcation between orthodoxy and heresy." There is a growing consensus of opinion that the *theios aner* category should not be used to describe New Testament christologies. See David L. Tiede, *The Charismatic Figure as a Miracle Worker.* SBLDS 1 (Missoula: Scholars, 1972), and especially Carl R. Holladay, *THEIOS ANER in Hellenistic Judaism. A Critique of the Use of this Category in New Testament Christology.* SBLDS 40 (Missoula: Scholars, 1977). Holladay concludes: "Its usefulness, therefore is extremely questionable, for using it in christological discussions merely introduces into an already confused field of study yet another ill-defined, if not undefinable, category, at a time where precision and clarity of thought should be sought, not sacrificed" (p. 237).

much to offer a study of the theme of discipleship in the Gospel of Mark.[26]

Mark 1:16-20

A glance at the immediate context of this passage shows that we are dealing with a literary unit. In vv. 14-15 we have an important summary of the activity of Jesus, announcing the coming of the kingdom and the call to repentance. It is placed generically in Galilee, a region (v. 14). In vv. 21-28, immediately following our passage, there is a change of place, as the action happens in the synagogue at Capernaum, and there is a change of action and the people involved: Jesus teaches and drives out an unclean spirit. Thus vv. 16-20, placed at the side of the lake, and entirely taken up with the vocation of four disciples, two sets of brothers, is a literary unity used deliberately by Mark to link the later witnesses to the Gospel with its first appearance.[27] There is a further feature that must be noticed. In typically Markan fashion, each of these originally independent pericopes are closely linked together by the continual use of καί (see vv. 9, 10, 11, 12, 13, 14, 15 [textually doubtful], 16, 17, 18, 19, 20, 21, 22, 23). These passages may have had diverse historical and literary origins, but Mark wants them to be read as a whole. We shall see below the importance of this factor for a correct understanding of vv. 16-20.

Despite the skepticism of some of the earlier form critics[28] there is now a growing consensus that the story has come to Mark from his traditions. In a detailed article Rudolf Pesch has indicated that the only clearly Markan additions are τῆς Γαλιλαίας in v. 16, added to make the link with vv. 14-15 even clearer (see the reference to Galilee in v. 14),

---

[26] For an analysis of the story of the rich man see Moloney, *Disciples and Prophets* 9–12, 93–95, and Simon Légasse, *L'appel du riche (Marc 10,17-31 et parallèles). Contribution à l'étude des fondements de l'état religieux*. Verbum Salutis 1 (Paris: Beauchesne, 1966). On the Gerasene demoniac see Rudolf Pesch, *Der Besessene von Gerasa. Entstehung und Überlieferung einer Wundergeschichte*. SBS 56 (Stuttgart: Katholisches Bibelwerk, 1972), and Franz Annen, *Heil für die Heiden. Zur Bedeutung und Geschichte der Tradition der bessessenen Gerasener (Mk 5,1-20 parr.)*. FTS 20 (Frankfurt: Joseph Knecht, 1976).

[27] See, for a comprehensive treatment, Rudolf Pesch, *Das Markusevangelium*. 2 vols. HTKNT II/1-2 (Freiburg: Herder, 1976–77) 1:108.

[28] See, for example, Bultmann, *History* 28: "There is no need to agrue that this is in no sense an historical record, but a description of an 'ideal scene.'"

and the typically Markan εὐθύς in v. 20.[29] The form of the passage is, however, highly stylized, clearly based on the model of the prophetic vocation of Elisha in 1 Kings 19:19-21.[30] In fact there are two vocation stories here, not one. A slightly structured presentation of the text will make this clear.

(a) As Jesus *passed along* the Sea of Galilee,

> *he saw*
> Simon and his brother Andrew
> casting a net into the sea . . . . *And Jesus said* to them,
> *"Follow* me and *I will make you*
> fish for people."
> And immediately *they left* their nets
> and *followed* him.

(b) *As he went* a little farther,

> *he saw*
> James son of Zebedee and his brother John,
> who were in their boat mending the nets.

---

[29] Rudolf Pesch, "Berufung und Sendung. Nachfolge und Mission. Eine Studie zu Mk 1,16-20," *ZKT* 91 (1969) 7–8. See also his *Markusevangelium* 108–116; Dennis E. Nineham, *The Gospel of St Mark*. The Pelican New Testament Commentaries (Harmondsworth: Penguin, 1969) 70. More recently, in defense of the traditional nature of the scene, see Josef Ernst, "Die Petrustradition im Markusevangelium—ein altes Problem neu angegangen," in Josef Zmijewski and Ernst Nellessen, eds., *Begegnung mit dem Wort: Festschrift für Heinrich Zimmermann*. BBB 53 (Bonn: Peter Hanstein, 1979) 36–38.

[30] See Pesch, "Berufung und Sendung," 9–12 for a detailed comparison of the two passages. See also Martin Hengel, *The Charismatic Leader and His Followers*. Translated by James Greig. Studies of the New Testament and Its World (New York: Crossroad, 1981) 16–18; Anselm Schulz, *Nachfolgen und Nachahmen. Studien über das Verhältnis der Neutestamentlichen Jüngerschaft zur Urchristlichen Vorbildethik*. SANT 6 (Munich: Kösel, 1962) 100–103; Minette de Tillesse, *Le secret messianique* 258–61. See, however, Hans Dieter Betz, *Nachfolge und Nachahmung Jesu Christi im Neuen Testament*. BHT 39 (Tübingen: J.C.B. Mohr [Paul Siebeck], 1967) 43–47. Betz sees no direct connection. His study argues that the "following" motif has little or no contact with early tradition (see pp. 27–43) and that Mark's idea of discipleship and imitation comes from Hellenistic mystery circles (see p. 33). Hengel's study, *Charismatic Leader*, is a convincing contrary argument. See his concluding remarks on pp. 84–88.

> Immediately *he called* them;
> and *they left* their father Zebedee
> in the boat with the hired men,
> and *followed him.*

Both stories, besides being identically structured, make the same points.[31] On both occasions the call comes from a Jesus who is in motion. In v. 16 he is "passing along," while in v. 19 he is "going on a little farther." This is an important theme in Mark's theology of discipleship. Jesus never rests. He seems to be relentlessly moving somewhere, a fact the disciples, as yet, do not grasp. A rapid glance at the first few chapters of Mark's gospel will show how true this is.

1:9:   Jesus came from Nazareth.
1:12:   The Spirit drove him out.
1:14:   Jesus came into Galilee.
1:16:   He passed along the sea.
1:19:   He went a little farther.
1:21:   They went to Capernaum.
1:29:   Immediately he left the synagogue.
1:35:   He got up and went out.
1:39:   And he went throughout Galilee.
2:1:   He returned to Capernaum.
2:13:   He went out again.

So it goes breathlessly on. All these indications of movement come from the hand of the evangelist and show that the Markan Jesus is endlessly on the move, urged on by some—as yet unclear—sense of mission. It is within this context, carefully constructed by the evangelist, •
that the first disciples are asked to "walk behind him."

The careful selection of verbs in 1:17: δεῦτε ὀπίσω μου, and in v. 18: ἠκολούθησαν, followed by a combination of the movement and the place behind Jesus in v. 20: ἀπῆλθον ὀπίσω αὐτοῦ, shows that it is important for Mark that the reader see the disciple as involved in a physical "walking behind" Jesus. The itinerant Jesus, going along the way of a suffering Son of Man, as the disciples will later learn, much to their amazement (see especially 8:22–10:52),[32] calls disciples to go along the same path. However, the physical "walking behind" also involves a certain spiritual attitude. Anyone who has walked down an unknown track through a wilderness

---

[31] See Schulz, *Nachfolge und Nachahmen* 98–99, 104–105.

[32] On 8:22–10:52 see the treatment of Reploh, *Markus: Lehrer der Gemeinde* 89–231, and Moloney, *Disciples and Prophets* 142–47.

behind the shoulders of a skilled and trustworthy guide will know that it is only faith in the guide that keeps one persevering along that path. So must it be for the one who is walking behind Jesus of Nazareth.[33]

Jesus is not like a rabbi, who gathered his disciples around him in a school so that they might learn bookishly.[34] The disciples of Jesus will learn from sharing the same way and the same destiny as the one calling them to come behind him. Because of this the plural verb in v. 21 is very important: "*They* went to Capernaum." As we have already seen, Mark has joined a long series of originally independent passages by means of a deliberate and continual repetition of καί. He does this to show that there is a close logical and theological link between

(a) Jesus' bursting onto the scene, announcing the proximity and the urgency of the kingdom (1:14-15), and

(b) his immediate calling of "followers" (vv. 16-20).

(c) *Together* Jesus and these followers go forth to initiate the active presence of the kingdom (vv. 21-28).

The second common feature that appears to be central to both accounts is Jesus' taking the initiative. In the first story we find: *he* saw (v. 14); *Jesus* said to them (v. 17); *I* will make you (v. 17). In the second account we find: *he* saw (v. 19); *he* called them (v. 20). This feature will grow as Mark's narrative unfolds. It will become clearer in 3:14 that anything the Twelve can do is possible only because of their association with him, but perhaps the most powerful indication of the significance of this aspect is found in our two so-called *negative* vocation stories: the Gerasene demoniac and the rich man. In both accounts the prospective disciple attempts to wrest the initiative from Jesus (see 5:18; 10:17), but each is denied discipleship under those conditions. It is only when Jesus takes the initiative from them (see 5:19 and 10:21) that he can call the ex-demoniac and the rich man to discipleship (5:19-21; 10:21). In the case of the ex-demoniac all earlier pretensions fall away, and he obediently and joyfully goes on his mission (5:20), while the contrary is the case with the rich man, who "went away grieving," a lost vocation to discipleship (10:22).[35]

---

[33] See Donaldson, "'Called to Follow,'" 67–77. For a thorough study of the growth and understanding of the use of ἀκολουθεῖν in the New Testament and the early Church see Schulz, *Nachfolge und Nachahmen*.

[34] See Hengel, *Charismatic Leader* 42–66.

[35] Stock, *Boten aus dem Mit-Ihm-Sein* 18, commenting on 5:18, puts it well: "Nicht menschlicher Wunsch entscheidet über dieses Mit-ihm-Sein, sondern allein sein auswählender Wille" [It is not human desire that decides the matter of being-with-him, but solely his elective will].

The use of the very strong expression "I will make" (ποιήσω) has sometimes been understood as coming from the LXX version of the creation story (see LXX Gen 1:1, 7, 16, 21, 25, 26, 27, 31; 2:2, 3, 4), with the implication that there is something of a new creation taking place. This is perhaps too subtle at this stage of the narrative. The new-creation idea does not seem to play an important part in Markan theology. Mark's choice of a strong, active verb with Jesus as its subject excellently conveys this author's idea: all that will become of the disciple will take place because of the initiative of Jesus, what he will do for them and make of them, and their association with him. If there is any Old Testament background it is to be found in such passages as LXX 1 Sam 12:6, where Moses and Aaron are described as "appointed" (ποιήσας) by YHWH, and 1 Kings 13:33 or 2 Chron 2:18, where the same strong verb is used for the intervention of YHWH for the appointment/institution of priests.[36] It is already clear from the context that the powerful intervention and presence of Jesus is shaping their lives, and this point will become clearer as the story of the disciples unfolds. It will be a major issue in 3:13-19, and it is, in my opinion, the key to the strange, peculiarly Markan account of the boy who "followed" Jesus (14:51) until danger threatened in 14:51-52. He too fled (v. 52), as the disciples had fled in v. 50. In their separation from Jesus both the disciples and the "young man" are naked in their nothingness. The story of the boy who fled away "naked" is thus a parabolic commentary on the situation of the disciples after their flight in 14:50.[37]

The vocation to mission is given in terms of the disciples' being made into those who "fish for people." This indication of the nature of the mission of the first followers of Jesus goes back to an original, pre-

---

[36] See, for example, Karl Hermann Schelkle, *Discipleship and Priesthood*. Rev ed. translated by Joseph Disselhorst (New York: Herder and Herder, 1965) 12–13. Better is the suggestion of Lucien Cerfaux, "La mission de Galilée dans la tradition synoptique," in *Receuil Lucien Cerfaux*. 2 vols. (Gembloux: Duculot, 1954) 1:446. Cerfaux looks to 1 Sam 12:6 as possible background for the expression in Mark (see also 3:14-16). Beda Rigaux, "Die Zwölf in Geschichte und Kerygma," in Helmut Ristow and Karl Matthiae, eds., *Der historische Jesus und der kerygmatische Christus. Beiträge zum Christusverständnis in Forschung und Verkündigung* (Berlin: Evangelische Verlagsanstalt, 1962) 474–75, also looks to Old Testament background: 1 Kings 13:33; 2 Chron 2:18, as well as 1 Sam 12:6.

[37] For some initial suggestions along these lines see Moloney, *Disciples and Prophets* 149–50. See also Harry Fleddermann, "The Flight of a Naked Young Man (Mark 14:51-52)," *CBQ* 41 (1979) 412–18.

Easter vocation to mission.[38] Most commentators claim that there is little Old Testament background for the metaphor, although some contact can be found with Jer 16:16 and Prov 6:26. Vincent Taylor suggests that the most likely reason for the expression is that they were, in fact, fishermen.[39] William L. Lane has pointed to the fact that several Old Testament passages use the image of fishers and fishing to speak of God's use of human instruments to seek out the evildoers and punish them (especially Jer 16:16-17; see also the use of fishing language to convey the same idea in Amos 4:2; Ezek 19:4-5; 1QH 5.7-8). When one reads Mark 1:16-20 in close proximity with the message of the urgently decisive presence of the kingdom and the need for conversion in vv. 14-15 the use of such language to speak of the followers of Jesus may be significant.

> The immediate function of those called to be fishers of men is to accompany Jesus as witnesses to the proclamation of the nearness of the kingdom and the necessity for men to turn to God through radical repentance. Their ultimate function will be to confront men with God's decisive action.[40]

There may be an element of truth in this interpretation, but as yet we must see it as a hint that will be further developed in 2:13-14, where the calling of Levi will radically question the "accepted" value system, and especially in 3:14-15 where the Twelve will be intimately associated with Jesus' person and task. Although outside the reach of this study, the same theme returns again in the conditions of the mission and the function of the missionary in 6:6b-13, especially in the eschatologically significant "If any place will not welcome you and they refuse to hear you, as you leave, shake off the dust that is on your feet as a testimony against them" (6:11).

---

[38] Dibelius, *From Tradition to Gospel* 112–13, regards it as traditional, while Bultmann, *History* 27–28, gives it no place in the pre-Markan tradition. See also Nineham, *St Mark* 71–72; but also Pesch, *Markusevangelium* 1:111, and "Berufung und Sendung," 18–24; and see Reploh, *Markus: Lehrer der Gemeinde* 31.

[39] Vincent Taylor, *The Gospel According to St Mark* (2nd ed. London: Macmillan, 1966) 169. Jindrich Manek, "Fishers of Men," *NovT* 2 (1957–58) 138–41 attempts to link the fishing image with the practice of baptism. It is certainly linked in early Christian art, but there is little support for this speculation in the New Testament.

[40] William L. Lane, *The Gospel According to Mark*. NICNT (Grand Rapids: Eerdmans, 1974) 68. See also Pesch, *Markusevangelium* 1:111. Pesch (ibid. 112) points out that the use of καί in v. 19 to open the second vocation story (vv. 19-20) shows that the sons of Zebedee are also called to fish for people.

As Jesus has come to create an entirely new situation in which the urgent need for the kingdom must be seen by human beings, leading them to conversion, so must it also be for the disciples. They too have been called to be "with Jesus" in bringing that new situation to pass. If contemporary scholarship is correct in seeing this call of the first disciples to fish for people as a part of the original experience of the vocation of the disciples, then from the very start disciples were called not only to follow Jesus along his way but also to repeat in their lives and teaching the urgent presence of the reign of God.

There is one further element in Mark 1:16-20 that needs attention: both vocation stories speak of a spontaneous leaving of nets, boats, father, and hired servant to walk behind Jesus (vv. 18, 20). Mark makes two points on the Christian vocation. First we see the power of Jesus. His call cannot be resisted. The response is "immediate." Although the word εὐθύς is a favorite of Mark's (he uses it forty-one times, while the rest of the New Testament together uses it only ten times!), its insertion here must not be understood as merely stylistic, or a Markan eccentricity. It has been inserted deliberately into a pre-Markan tradition, to stress the spontaneity and immediate nature of the response. As Bultmann has pointed out, the passage is above all about the Master who calls rather than the disciple who follows.[41] The possessions that were "left behind" are explicitly listed.[42] They leave nets, boats, hired servants, and father. This means that all the criteria that would normally be used by their contemporary peer group to judge their success or failure in life are abandoned: tools of trade (nets and boats) and servants, a major sign of their success because they control a work force.[43] For a first-century Galilean fisherman it would have been suicidal to leave the tools of the trade one had learned to use through long experience, to abandon all authority over a set of servants who depended on one-

[41] Bultmann, *History* 69.

[42] The deliberate repetition of the verb ἀφίημι in vv. 18 and 20 shows that Mark wants his readers to see the importance of this action. The use of this strong verb may well have had its origins in the radical preaching of the early missionaries. See, for this suggestion, C. E. B. Cranfield, *The Gospel According to Saint Mark.* Cambridge Greek Testament Commentary (Cambridge: Cambridge University Press, 1959) 69.

[43] It has been suggested that the hired servants are mentioned to contrast the generosity of the disciples with the mercenary concerns of others. It is better to see them as part of the "power structure" the disciples abandon. See Nineham, *St Mark* 73. This element in Markan theology has recently been strongly developed by Ched Myers, *Binding the Strong Man. A Political Reading of Mark's Story of Jesus* (Maryknoll, N.Y.: Orbis, 1988). On 1:16-20 see pp. 132–33.

self, one's fishing, and one's commercial skill. But the most radical break would be the abandoning of what was probably the source of all that one knew: belonging to a family and a family tradition.[44]

Some scholars see the reference to all the detail—fishermen, nets, hired hands, boats, and family—as clear indications of the basic historicity of the scene,[45] while Ernst Lohmeyer has argued that we have here a typical "epiphany story" arising from an oral tradition about the appearance of the Son of Man: the Godly Master appears.[46] Our analysis has indicated that there is a careful literary structure and a profound theological message, but that these should not be divorced from the experience of the first disciples. No doubt the immediacy of the response is idealized,[47] and the use of the expression "they left" may have come from the exhortations of the earliest preachers.[48] Mark nevertheless looks back to the genuine historical reminiscence of the impact Jesus made upon the first disciples. He reports the story along the lines of a traditional prophetic vocation account, to which an all-important newness has been added: the person of Jesus of Nazareth who calls. In doing this he announces that

> the call of God in Christ comes with a divine power which does not need to wait upon accidental circumstances; it can create the response it demands. And that response must be one of unconditional obedience, even to the point of sacrificing livelihood and the closest natural ties, as many of St. Mark's contemporaries must have known from experience.[49]

Mark 1:16-20 is so rich in pastoral and theological implications that one is forced to ask how such an episode could have happened. The

[44] In this regard see the claim of some scholars that behind Matt 11:27/Luke 10:22 and John 5:19-20 stands a well-used Jewish parable that all the son knows and can do he has from his father. On Matt 11:27 see Joachim Jeremias, *New Testament Theology. The Proclamation of Jesus* (London: SCM, 1971) 56–61. On John 5:19-20 see Francis J. Moloney, *The Johannine Son of Man*. BibScRel 14 (2nd ed. Rome: LAS, 1978) 72–73 and the notes on those pages, especially the references to the works of C. H. Dodd and Paul Gächter.

[45] See, for example, Taylor, *St Mark* 167–68; Cranfield, *Saint Mark* 68.

[46] Ernst Lohmeyer, *Das Evangelium des Markus*. Meyers Kommentar (Göttingen: Vandenhoeck & Ruprecht, 1957) 33.

[47] See, for example, Simon Peter's more gradual movement to discipleship in Luke 5:1-11, but even this passage betrays some favorite Lukan themes. See Moloney, *Disciples and Prophets* 137–38; Taylor, *St Mark* 170. In defense of the originality of the Markan scheme see Bennett H. Branscomb, *The Gospel of Mark*. Moffatt New Testament Commentary (London: Hodder & Stoughton, 1937) 27.

[48] See Cranfield, *Saint Mark* 69.

[49] Nineham, *St Mark* 71.

story as Mark tells it (quite differently from Luke 4:38-39; 5:1-11 and John 1:35-51) has the spontaneous response of two sets of brothers who leave all to follow a man they have never seen before. They follow without a word, leaving what would be regarded as the essential elements for human success. Mark is fashioning traditional material to make an important theological point, but we will only fully understand his message if we look to the wider context of our passage.[50] Mark's gospel opens with a prologue that proclaims Jesus as the Christ, the Son of God (v. 1),[51] full of the Holy Spirit (v. 8), the beloved Son (v. 11), driven by the Spirit (v. 12), and ministered to by the angels (v. 13). These are serious claims, and Lightfoot has paralleled this christological prologue to John 1:1-18.[52] The storyteller has established *for the reader* (the characters involved in Mark's account of Jesus' life-story have not read Mark 1:1-13!) who Jesus is. The account of Jesus' activity opens with his breaking into human events with the urgent message of the presence of a kingdom of God and the need for repentance (vv. 14-15). The scene changes and Jesus calls four fishermen to come behind him as fishers of people (vv. 16-20). Only after these first vocation stories do his encounters with the powers of evil begin in the synagogue at Capernaum, where his authoritative preaching makes everyone wonder (vv. 21-22) as he drives out an unclean spirit (vv. 23-26). However, it was not only Jesus who went to Capernaum, as v. 21 runs: "And *they* went into Capernaum." As yet he is the only one who teaches and acts (vv. 21 and 25), but the disciples are already on their journey "with him."

Jesus, the Christ, the Son of God, full of and driven by the Spirit (vv. 1-13), has an urgent task to perform (vv. 14-15). He must overcome evil by means of the power of the kingdom that already has its beginnings in his word and activity (vv. 21-28). However, he does not go alone. As he begins his relentless, restless journey he calls others to

---

[50] See the valuable analysis of the logic behind this section of the gospel in Robert Henry Lightfoot, *The Gospel Message of St Mark* (Oxford: Clarendon Press, 1950) 15–30. See also Pesch, *Markusevangelium* 112–14.

[51] There is a textual difficulty over the reading "Son of God" in Mark 1:1. For a thorough analysis of the whole question, with a full bibliography, see Carl R. Kazmierski, *Jesus, the Son of God. A Study of the Markan Tradition and Its Redaction by the Evangelist.* FB 33 (Würzburg: Echter, 1979) 1–9. He argues for the inclusion of the christological title. For the contrary position see Pesch, *Markusevangelium* 74, 77.

[52] Lightfoot, *The Gospel Message* 18–19. See also Morna D. Hooker, *The Message of Mark* (London: Epworth Press, 1983) 1–16.

walk behind him: "The good news has come forth and is immediately accompanied by the call to follow."[53]

All we have seen so far concerning the disciples is positive. We can find in Mark 1:1-16 the basic structure of the vocation to discipleship: Jesus calls people to follow him; they are to be associated in the critical, eschatological inbreaking of the kingdom of God; there is no place for a conditional response; it will cost no less than everything. Here we have a deliberately designed narrative that establishes a paradigm for the Christian vocation. The first disciples have been used as the model to present that vocation. However, as we have already noted, this is only one side of the Markan story of discipleship. The disciples eventually fail, and it is Peter, James, and John, disciples who have responded so generously in 1:16-20, that Jesus leads into Gethsemane. There they abandon him (14:50) and Peter will subsequently deny him (14:66-72). As a conclusion to our study of this first vocation story I would suggest that, even though the message of Mark 1:16-20 is wholly positive, the reason for the subsequent failures can already be traced here. These first vocation stories are *not* about disciples and their virtue. They are about Jesus of Nazareth, the Christ and the Son of God, full of the Spirit, urgently pressing on to his assigned task (1:1-13, 16, 19). Only insofar as *he* has the initiative (1:17, 20) and the response of discipleship is in accordance with *his* world-questioning criteria (1:18, 20) can discipleship hope to succeed.

Mark 2:13-14

When one reads Mark 2:13-14 in the shadow of 1:16-20 the similarities of structure and message are obvious. Again a slightly structured text will make it clear for the reader:[54]

---

[53] Hugh Anderson, *The Gospel of Mark.* NCB (London: Oliphants, 1976) 86.

[54] There are several textual difficulties in this passage, created by the name of the unknown Levi. For a detailed evaluation see Giuseppe G. Gamba, "Considerazioni in margine alla redazione di Mc 2,13-17," *Divus Thomas* 72 (1969) 203–204. Most scholars point to the identical structure of 1:16-20 and 2:14. See, for example, Schulz, *Nachfolge und Nachahmen* 104–105. It is often argued that 2:14 is entirely Markan, structured by the evangelist along the model of 1:16-20, which is traditional. See, for example, Rudolf Pesch, "Levi–Mattäus (Mk 2,14/ Mt 9,9; 10,3). Ein Beitrag zur Lösung eines alten Problems," *ZNW* 59 (1968) 43–45. For the contrary argument see Bas M. F. van Iersel, "La vocation de Lévi (Mc. II, 13-17, Mt. IX, 9-13, Lc. IV, 27-32)," in Ignace de la Potterie, ed., *De Jesus aux évangiles. Tradition et Rédaction dans les Evangiles Synoptiques.* 2 vols. BETL 24 (Gembloux: Duculot, 1967) 2:215–16. See also Best, "The Role of the Disciples in Mark," 384–87. Best argues that all the vocation stories are traditional.

He went out again beside the sea;
   the whole crowd gathered around him,
and *he taught them.*
As he was walking along,
he saw
   Levi son of Alphaeus sitting at the tax booth,
and *he said* to him,
"Follow me."
   And he got up and followed him.

In v. 13 we find Jesus on the move (see 1:16, 19) and there is again an indication of the urgent need for the preaching of the word (see 1:15). Within this context Jesus calls Levi, following the same model of the prophetic call we found in 1:16-20. Jesus is on the move; he sees Levi, and the future disciple's worldly occupation is given: tax collector. On his own initiative Jesus speaks and calls to follow; the response is immediate. The major element from 1:16-20 that is not found here is the indication of what the disciple has left behind (see 1:18, 20), but it is implicit, especially in the subtle use of the word καθήμενον (sitting) at the start of the narrative, changing into ἀναστάς (getting up) after the vocation. In the first instance he is firmly entrenched behind his money-bench, but after the call he stands and moves away from it.[55]

Most scholars point out that Mark 2:13-17 is a literary unit developed by the evangelist from several originally different pre-Markan traditions, but there is little agreement on the precise identification of the limits and origin of the various elements.[56] These discussions need not detain us here. I would insist, however, that vv. 13-14 need to be given more attention *in their own right.* Most commentators and critics pass quickly over these two Markan passages, claiming they are there merely to set the scene for the pronouncement story of vv. 15-17.[57] This

[55] See Paul Lamarche, "L'appel à la conversion et à la foi. La vocation de Lévi (Mc. 2,13-17)," *LV* 25 (1970) 127–28.

[56] For a detailed literary analysis see Gamba, "Considerazioni in margine," 201–12. Gamba argues that Mark created a unit out of four different passages: v. 13; v. 14; v. 15abc; vv. 15d-17. See also Pesch, *Markusevangelium* 162–63 for a slightly different suggestion. For further discussion and analysis of the passages see the articles by Pesch, van Iersel, and Lamarche mentioned above in nn. 56-57.

[57] A "pronouncement story" is a pericope that leads to a final pungent word from Jesus (in this case v. 17). The form critics are generally skeptical about the historicity of the major part of the pericope, even though generally the actual "pronouncements" are given serious consideration as historical words of Jesus. Form critics claim that the primitive community or the evangelist started with Jesus' pungent saying and constructed a scene to lead up to it. See,

is no doubt the case. But, given the strong possibility of the independent pre-Markan origins of these passages, vv. 13-14 can be approached as a literary unit. There is a complete break from 2:1-12 in terms of persons, place, time, and action. The clearly Markan v. 13 indicates that the evangelist is initiating something new. This is widely recognized,[58] but the same could be said for the break between v. 14 and vv. 15-17. There is a change of place (the walk of vv. 13-14 becomes a sitting at table "in his house" in v. 15). It is necessarily at a later time, and the action is no longer that of the itinerant Jesus calling a disciple, the proclamation of the universality of his mission. There is, of course, a clear link between the proclamation of this final theme, "to call sinners" (v. 17), and the paradigm of that proclamation in v. 14. Scholars are correct in seeing the passage as belonging to a closely argued Markan theological unit.[59] Nevertheless, whatever the historical and literary background to vv. 13-14 might be, there is a particular theological message involved in the vocation of a tax collector to discipleship at this stage of the gospel. The Markan theology of discipleship takes a new turn here, but it is generally obscured because commentators are fascinated by the form-critical classification of vv. 13-17 as a pronouncement story, and they thus read quickly through the passage to arrive at the important "pronouncement" in v. 17.

As is clear, the structural major elements of the first vocation story (1:16-20) are repeated. But we also see that Mark, in deliberately retelling the story of the vocation of a tax collector with the same literary form, wishes to repeat his theological message on discipleship, but also to carry it further. Our study of 1:16-20 showed that an itinerant

---

for example, Rudolf Bultmann, *History* 61–69. Bultmann called these pericopes "apophthegms," but they are better named "pronouncement stories." For this terminology and a criticism of the excessive historical skepticism of some of the earlier form critics see Vincent Taylor, *The Formation of the Gospel Tradition* (London: Macmillan, 1960) 63–87. For a good example of the little attention paid to vv. 13-14 in their own right as a vocation story see the generally exhaustive comments of Taylor and Pesch. Taylor (*St Mark* 202–203) notes the similarity to 1:16-20 and then discusses the Levi/Matthew problem at length. Pesch (*Markusevangelium* 164) directs all his attention to what is to follow: "Jesu erwählender Blick trifft Levi; dem Nachfolgeruf gehorcht Levi aufs Wort. Markus hat vorweg illustriert, daß Jesus gekommen ist, Sünder (= Zöllner) zu berufen" [Jesus' electing look touches Levi; Levi follows the call to follow after him to the letter. Mark has illustrated, in anticipation, that Jesus has come to call sinners (= tax collectors)].

[58] See above, n. 57, but the scholars mentioned there would differ in detail.

[59] See Gamba, "Considerazioni in margine," 212–15.

Jesus calls people to follow him; they are to be associated in the critical, eschatological inbreaking of the reign of God; there are to be no conditional responses; it will cost no less than everything. This is repeated in 2:13-14, but Levi is not a fisherman. He is a tax collector. By indicating that he is sitting in the tax office Mark shows that he is a lesser official, the one who actually took the money from the people. These were the most despised agents of an unjust system in the eyes of the Jews.[60] This is important for Mark's teaching on discipleship, and also for the situating of 2:13-14 within the Markan literary context of 2:1–3:6. This context is made up of a series of five controversies in which Jesus draws and replies to criticism from the Pharisees as he freely pushes their interpretation of the Law to its limits and claims to be bringing salvation by doing so.[61] Since this is the case it is insufficient to see 2:13-14 as a Markan repetition of 1:16-20, used as a redactional introduction to a pronouncement story in 2:13-17.

In calling Levi, Jesus summons a person who is outside the worshiping community of Judaism because his occupation is unacceptable. More than that, he is regarded as a sinner, a Jew who has sold his soul to the hated foreign power that dominated God's land. This means that in a *correct and proper* Jewish understanding of salvation Levi is *nothing*. Jesus reverses this evaluation of Levi. In calling him to discipleship he offers him *everything*. As well as using v. 14 as a paradigm for the proclamation of v. 17, we must also use v. 17 as an explanation of what Jesus has done for Levi in v. 14. What must be stressed is that discipleship cuts through all barriers of conventional religion, because Jesus of Nazareth who issues the call cannot be contained within the *correct and proper* limits of conventional religion. This is the message of the controversies in 2:1–3:6,[62] and 2:13-14 should be understood in that

---

[60] For further indications of first-century Jewish opinion on tax collectors see Taylor, *St Mark* 202–203; Lane, *Mark* 100–102.

[61] Gamba, "Considerazioni in margine," 201–26, although excessively speculative in some of the literary criteria adopted, shows how this passage plays an integral role in the overall development of Mark's argument in 2:1–3:6. Gamba, however, does not pay a great deal of attention to 2:13-14 as a vocation story, nor does he notice now Mark has used this tradition to develop his teaching on discipleship.

[62] See especially Joanna Dewey, *Markan Public Debate. Literary Technique, Concentric Structure and Theology in Mark 2:1–3:6*. SBLDS 48 (Chico: Scholars, 1980). See the summary of this study, now available as "The Literary Structure of the Controversy Stories in Mark 2:1–3:6," *JBL* 92 (1973) 394–401, reprinted in Telford, ed., *The Interpretation of Mark* 109–18. See also Gamba, "Considerazioni in margine," 324–31.

light. The immediate context of 1:16-20, especially 1:14-15 and the association of the disciples with Jesus in his teaching and work at Capernaum by means of the plural verb in 1:21, associated the *vocation* of the disciples with the *mission* of Jesus. From the beginning of the narrative the disciples are associated with Jesus' announcing and spreading the kingdom. In 2:1–3:6 a further aspect of the effects of the kingdom is being spelled out: it radically questions any humanly established criteria used to control God and religion. Therefore in 2:13-14 the *vocation* of the disciple is further associated with this additional dimension of the kingdom: the *radical reversal of values*. Discipleship is being called into the mystery of the mission of Jesus. Mark 2:13-14 does not simply repeat 1:16-20.

A growing theology of discipleship can be traced through the two vocation stories just analyzed. One is not merely the repetition of the other in a stereotyped form. This is an example of the dangers that come from an over-concentration on form. Nevertheless, despite my insistence on what is being said about discipleship in 2:13-14 it must again be pointed out that there is an all-embracing *christological* foundation to the Markan theology of discipleship that was already present in 1:16-20 but is made even clearer in 2:13-14. In the vocation stories of 1:16-20 and 2:13-14 the motifs of Jesus as an itinerant teacher who calls fishermen and sinful publicans to come behind him show that the disciple cannot be regarded simply as a virtuous and courageous "follower." The setting of 2:1–3:6 in particular shows that the important feature of the call is not the identity of the ones being summoned but the identity of the one who calls people to follow him into a radical, questioning reversal of values. It is what Jesus does for those called that will make them disciples.

"Jesus separates persons from their natural and historical setting and introduces them into an eschatological existence of communion with himself."[63] It is this *christological* principle that determines discipleship. We may already suggest that the misunderstanding and failure of the disciples, in spite of the auspicious beginnings of 1:16-20 and 2:13-14 in their respective contexts, have nothing to do with a literary trick to explain the later invention of Jesus' messiahship (Wrede) or an attack on a divine-man heresy in Mark's community (Weeden). It is the Markan way of announcing what was said more explicitly in the Fourth Gospel: "apart from me you can do nothing" (John 15:5).

[63] James M. Robinson, *The Problem of History in Mark*. SBT 21 (London: SCM, 1962) 78–79.

Mark 3:13-19

The final vocation story in Mark's gospel still has traces of the basic structure we have seen in 1:16-20 and 2:13-14. It is to be found especially in 3:13:

> *He went up* the mountain
> and *called* to him
>   those whom
> *he wanted,*
>   and *they came* to him.

Jesus is on the move. There is a heavy stress on his initiative, especially in the use of the verb θέλειν to indicate that he called only those whom he wanted. Typically, there is an immediate and wordless response. Certain elements from the earlier accounts are missing: the names of the people called (picked up in vv. 16-19), their occupations, and the abandoning of those occupations. But the same basic concept of an overpowering encounter with a Jesus who wrests all initiative from them is still present.[64] The rest of the passage, however, picks up the heavy stress on the initiative of Jesus in the appointment of the Twelve for a task, and the list of their names:

> And *he appointed twelve,*[65]
>   *to be with him,*
> and *to be sent out to proclaim the message,*
> and *to have authority to cast out demons.*
> So *he appointed* the twelve:[66]

---

[64] See Pesch, *Markusevangelium* 203 for the link with 1:16-20. Stock, *Boten aus dem Mit-Ihm-Sein* 47–49, analyzes the parallel, but notes serious differences. Stock's work is weakened by his determination to force a separation between the disciples and the Twelve. See, on this, the review by Sean Freyne in *CBQ* 39 (1977) 295–97.

[65] Many good witnesses (e.g., Sinaiticus and Vaticanus) add "whom he also named apostles," but this reading has crept into the text from Luke 6:13. See Taylor, *St Mark* 230; Bruce M. Metzger, *A Textual Commentary on the Greek New Testament* (Stuttgart: German Bible Society, 1994) 69.

[66] Verse 16a is also textually difficult. Many good witnesses have it, but it is included especially by the same textual traditions that inserted Luke 6:13 into v. 14. I am including it because of the use of the definite article in connection with *the* Twelve. It picks up v. 14, but carries farther the argument interrupted by the parenthesis created by the series of ἵνα-phrases. See for this position Marie-Joseph Lagrange, *Evangile selon Saint Marc*. EB (Paris: Gabalda, 1920) 80–81.

Simon (*to whom he gave the name* Peter);
   James son of Zebedee and
   John the brother of James
(to whom *he gave the name* Boanerges, that is, Sons of Thunder);
   and Andrew, and Philip, and Bartholomew,
   and Matthew, and Thomas, and James son of Alphaeus,
   and Thaddaeus, and Simon the Cananaean,
   and Judas Iscariot, *who betrayed him.*

There is an almost exaggerated insistence on the initiative of Jesus. Of the eleven main verbs nine are actions of Jesus, while only two refer to actions of disciples: in v. 13 "they came to him," and in v. 19 the opposite: Judas Iscariot is described as the one "who betrayed him." This needs further examination. All the subordinate verbs in the ἵνα-phrases, describing the future mission of the Twelve, depend entirely on the action of Jesus "appointing" them (ποιεῖν is again used; see vv. 14 and 16, as well as 1:17),[67] and on their "being with him" (v. 14).

We saw in our analysis of 1:16-20 and 2:13-14 that the context of each of the vocation stories played a vital role in the correct understanding of the implications of the vocation to discipleship. The same must be said here. It is universally accepted that 3:13-19 forms a literary unit. Verses 7-12 are a Markan reworking of tradition, marked by his particular theological motifs and language. Set by the sea, it presents the urgency of Jesus' preaching, and his proclamation as Son of God by the evil spirits.[68] The passage that follows the vocation narrative (vv. 20-30) is heavily dependent on pre-Markan traditions that may well have already been joined before they came to Mark. Nevertheless, Mark has reworked them into an admirable synthesis of his message: the new family of Jesus, his power as Son of God over evil, and the *culpable* refusal to accept the clear revelation of God in that power.[69] The vocation and commissioning of the Twelve, in this context, look both backward to vv. 7-12 and forward to vv. 20-30. The disciples have authority and power to continue Jesus' spreading of the kingdom, but only insofar as

---

[67] See n. 38 above.

[68] See, for example, Nineham, *St Mark* 112–13; Eduard Schweizer, *The Good News According to Mark* (London: S.P.C.K., 1971) 78–79; Pesch, *Markusevangelium* 1:198–99; Taylor, *St Mark* 225–26.

[69] This is widely recognized. See Nineham, *St Mark* 120: "It has a great deal of light to throw on the meaning of the Gospel as a whole." Schweizer, *Mark* 83, remarks: "There is scarcely any other passage where Mark's pen is as evident as it is here." See also Pesch, *Markusevangelium* 2:198–99; Taylor, *St Mark* 235, 237–38, 240–41.

they *receive* that power and belong to the new family of Jesus, associated closely with him in their "being with him" (v. 14).[70]

There can be little doubt that Mark intended to take his theology of discipleship one step further and to link the disciples more intimately with Jesus' task through the addition of this account in its present context. This is seen through the Markan insertion of "and to have authority to cast out demons" (v. 15) into a pre-Markan passage.[71] By passing this ἐξουσία on to the disciples he links them with his actions in vv. 11-12, preceding the call story, and the discussion in vv. 22-24 that followed immediately after. The wider context makes the point even clearer, as the Twelve are commissioned to be sent out, to preach, and to have authority to cast out demons (vv. 14-15). A glance back across what has gone *before* this passage reveals that this is exactly what Jesus has done up to this stage in the narrative: his incessant motion, as one "sent," his preaching (1:14, 39, 45), and his casting out of demons (1:21-28, 32-34; 3:7-12). While the missionary involvement with Jesus was already present in 1:16-20, it is the central issue in 3:13-19.

Despite the centrality of the missionary association of the Twelve with Jesus, a closer look at the passage indicates that, as in both the earlier stories, this account has nothing to do with the greatness of the disciples. We have already seen that the choosing of the Twelve, their appointment to a specific mission, and even the very names of three of them come from the initiative of Jesus. There is an added christological feature, as the Twelve are commissioned "to be with him." Some scholars make little of this aspect of the vocation of the Twelve,[72] but it appears fundamental because it gives the christological motivation for the mission of a disciple. Again we can turn to the story of the Gerasene demoniac, where the ex-demoniac asks "that he might be with him" (5:18) but is refused. He is then instructed to go and announce in his own village how much the Lord had done for him, and his obedience to this command brings wonder (vv. 19-20). Notice that the mission of the ex-demoniac is not a participation in Jesus' authoritative bringing in of the kingdom. We are not even told that his townsfolk came to believe in Jesus. The reader is told that they were amazed (v. 20). Mark's use of θαυμάζω gives us little reason to conclude that this refers to faith (see es-

---

[70] See Stock, *Boten aus dem Mit-Ihm-Sein* 53–70.

[71] Pesch, *Markusevangelium* 1:203. See especially n. 1 on that page. It appears that Mark only retouched his tradition here: the setting of the scene in v. 13, the reference to exorcism in v. 15, the giving of the extra names in vv. 16-17, and the additional comment added to the name of Judas in v. 19 (although this may also be pre-Markan). See ibid. 1:202–203.

[72] See, for example, Best, "The Role of the Disciples in Mark," 380–81.

pecially the use of the verb to speak of the wonder of Pilate in 15:5, 44; see also 6:6).[73] It has been frequently pointed out that physical presence "with" Jesus, even though not expressed in terms of εἶναι μετ᾽ αὐτοῦ, seems to be the destiny of any disciple of Jesus, and not only of the Twelve (see especially the use of κατ᾽ ἰδίαν in 4:34; 6:31-32; 9:2, 28; 13:3).[74] They are presented by Mark throughout the gospel, until the dramatic flight of 14:50, as continually by his side, with the exception of 6:12-30.[75] Given the limitations of this already over-long study, it is impossible to enter into a discussion of the relationship between the Twelve and the disciples, but it appears that the message of 3:14 must be applied to anyone called to share in Jesus' task. On their own authority they are destined to fail, but "with Jesus" they will successfully spread the kingdom.[76] The grammatical structure of the passage is

[73] Against most commentators who understand the passage in terms of a successful Gentile mission I am not denying success, but I wonder about its being a *Christian* mission. See, for an influential positive reading of the passage, Robert Henry Lightfoot, *History and Interpretation of the Gospels* (London: Hodder & Stoughton, 1931) 89–90. See subsequently Pesch, *Markusevangelium* 1:294; Nineham, *St Mark* 151; Schweizer, *Mark* 113.

[74] See Freyne, *The Twelve* 107–19. This expression, used only of the Twelve in a positive sense (see 5:18 for its other use), is one of the keys to Stock's claim that Mark separates the role of the Twelve from that of the disciples. See his *Boten aus dem Mit-Ihm-Sein* 199–203 and passim. Other discussions of the question are: Karl Kertelge, "Die Funktion der Zwölf im Markusevangelium," *TTZ* 78 (1969) 193–206; Reploh, *Markus: Lehrer der Gemeinde* 47–49; Günther Schmahl, *Die Zwölf im Markusevangelium*. TTS 30 (Trier: Paulinus Verlag, 1974). For a critical evaluation of much recent literature see Stock, *Boten aus dem Mit-Ihm-Sein* 1–5.

[75] As I indicated above (see n. 5), it appears to me that the disciples fail for the first time in their report to Jesus in 6:30, a report that shows they have understood their teaching and activity *apart from* their union with Jesus and their being sent by Jesus.

[76] I would like to note, at this stage, how the confusion over the Twelve/the disciples may have come about in Mark. Gerd Theissen, *The First Followers of Jesus. A Sociological Analysis of Earliest Christianity* (London: SCM, 1978) has pointed helpfully to two types of "disciples" in the earliest Church:
   (a) the wandering charismatics (pp. 8–16)
   (b) sympathizers in the local communities, a group of "disciples" who do not "walk behind" Jesus (pp. 17–27).
There are sections of Theissen's rapid analysis I would question, but is it possible that the *historical* group of the Twelve, chosen by Jesus, were called to a life of following their itinerant leader while many "disciples" were not itinerant? However, Mark (less so Matthew and Luke) applied the itinerant motif to discipleship as such, possibly because his traditions came from that background (Peter?). In this way the original *historical* distinction between the

clumsy, and it hints that the use of ποιεῖν in v. 14 applies strictly to the first of the ἵνα-clauses: "he appointed twelve . . . *to be with him.*" The rest of the clauses, which attend to *what* they are *to do* rather than *where* they are *to be,* are separated from the expression in v. 14 by καί.[77] It appears probable that all they are to do does not depend directly on the ποιεῖν, but on their "being with him." The passage would then run:

He appointed twelve to be with him
– so that he might send them out to preach
– and have authority to cast out demons.

If this is a correct understanding of the passage we find that the missionary character of the disciple has nothing to do with the skill, training, or virtue of the disciple, a point the disciples themselves have forgotten in 6:30; rather, it depends on Jesus' appointing them to be closely associated with his person. Only when this relationship has been firmly established can the missionary activity hope to succeed.[78]

There is a final point, generally missed by the commentators, that eloquently comments on the conclusions just drawn. This passage, set within a context of mission, shows how Jesus calls some to a physical closeness to his person so that they might do as he has done. Twelve names are given,[79] and to the final name, Judas Iscariot, a Markan note (perhaps traditional, but happily accepted by Mark?) is added: "who betrayed him." Some scholars correctly note that Mark is showing the possibility of betrayal, failure, and sin, even among the closest followers of Jesus.[80] There is more to it, however. We have seen that the appointment

---

Twelve and the non-itinerant disciples was lost. The use of εἶναι μετʼ αὐτοῦ in two places (3:14 and 5:18), which shows traces of only *some* being called to follow behind the itinerant Jesus (3:14) while another is sent back to his home and his friends (5:18-19), could be the starting point for an investigation along these lines. See further Howard Clark Kee, *Christian Origins in Sociological Perspective* (London: SCM, 1980) 54–91. On the historicity of the Twelve see John P. Meier, "The Circle of the Twelve: Did It Exist During Jesus' Public Ministry?" *JBL* 116 (1997) 635–72. See also Pesch, *Markusevangelium* 208.

[77] It would be impossible to have ἐποίησεν ἵνα ἀποστέλλῃ. See Lohmeyer, *Markus* 74; Pesch, *Markusevangelium* 203.

[78] This is the ultimate meaning of 14:28 and 16:7. This relationship will be reconstituted, despite the further failure on the part of the women (16:8). See Moloney, *Disciples and Prophets* 150–52, for some initial suggestions along these lines.

[79] There are difficulties with the names and the order of the names in the synoptic tradition. This need not detain us here. See the commentaries, especially Taylor, *St Mark* 231–34, and Pesch, "Levi-Matthäus," 40–56.

[80] See, for example, Taylor, *St Mark* 234; Pesch, *Markusevangelium* 207–208; Lagrange, *Saint Marc* 61.

of the Twelve to the mission to share in the task of Jesus is determined by a vocation to "be with him." As long as there is a physical and experienced "belonging" to Jesus, all will be well. At the close of the list of people who were called to this mission we are told of one who will fail, Judas Iscariot. It appears to me that we are also told *why* he failed. The reader of Mark's gospel knows the story, and so do the translators. Thus ὃς καὶ παρέδωκεν αὐτόν is generally rendered "who betrayed him" (NRSV). However, given the programmatic importance of εἶναι μετ᾽ αὐτοῦ in v. 14, the use of παραδίδωμι in v. 19 reflects not only the historical fact of the betrayal but also the theological tragedy of a disciple who "gave Jesus away."[81] The account of the vocation to share in the mission of Jesus begins with the *sine qua non* of belonging to Jesus, and closes with the ultimate explanation for the failure of one of those whom Jesus himself had chosen. He willfully separated himself from the source of all he could be and all he could do by handing Jesus over. Thus, through the negative example of Judas, Mark rounds off his vocation stories. It is his first explicit indication of the possibility of failure in the life of a disciple.

CONCLUSIONS

By way of conclusion I will list the facts that, it appears to me, can be drawn from our analysis of the Markan vocation stories within the context of the contemporary scholarly discussions of Markan discipleship.

1. There is a deliberate progression of the theme and theology of a vocation to discipleship in the first three chapters of the gospel. This will only be understood if 1:16-20; 2:13-14, and 3:13-19 are considered within their wider literary and theological contexts.
2. Jesus, through his initiative, sets up a new situation of obedience and service. All the accounts repeat this important aspect.
3. The disciples are not rabbinic students, learning the Law "bookishly." They are to learn by "walking after Jesus" (1:16-20; 2:14). They gain their authority and sense of mission by "being with Jesus" (3:14), and they lose it if they separate themselves from him (3:19).
4. The disciples, right from the first moment, as one can see from the link between 1:14-15 and the vocation story of 1:16-20, are not just

---

[81] The verb παραδίδωμι has a wide range of meanings, but one of its primary senses is the giving away of a possession. See H. G. Liddell-Scott, *A Greek-English Lexicon* (Oxford: Clarendon Press, 1940) 1308, where this is the first meaning given. See also Cranfield, *Saint Mark* 306. I have already noted that there are only two "actions" of disciples in this passage. One is positive: "they came to him" (v. 13), while the other is negative: "who gave him away" (v. 19).

"with Jesus." They are to be closely associated with all that he has come to do. This message is then fully developed in 3:13-19, when that passage is read in its particular context.

5. The disciples are called to move away from all standards usually judged by their peer group and "the world" to be necessary for success. This was already evident in 1:16-20, where the disciples left tools, boats, servants, and family, but it is the central issue of the call of Levi in 2:13-14. Read in its context this short passage shows that discipleship involves a radical reversal of values. Discipleship cuts across all barriers of history, custom, and culture.

6. There is always the possibility of failure. One who was "with him" and constituted "one of the Twelve" (3:14) was also the one "who handed him over" (3:19).

This adds up to a positive theology of discipleship that Mark's gospel proclaims as a paradigm for members of his own community and that retains its value for any follower of Jesus. To understand the discipleship texts in Mark's gospel as a literary technique to explain the messianic secret (Wrede) or as a vehicle to attack a false christology in the Markan church (Perrin, Weeden, etc.) is to do an injustice to *all* the data of the gospel. The failure motif looms large in the latter half of the gospel and must be given its full importance (the shortcoming of Freyne, Donaldson, etc.), but we have already seen the reason for the failure in these accounts of the vocation of the disciples. The failure of the disciples is not *primarily* a message on discipleship, but a message about the overpowering need for an uncompromised dependence on the person of Jesus. The disciple may *never* succeed in responding to the call to lose oneself in turning the values of the world upside down as one struggles to follow the way of Jesus (see 10:32 and especially 16:7-8). Nevertheless, the disciple's vocation to live through the mystery of failure, depending only on the even greater mystery of the love and power of God, stands at the heart of the message of the Gospel of Mark.[82]

---

[82] Focant, "L'incompréhension des disciples," 185, puts it well: "Il y voit l'incapacité de l'homme à saisir par ses seules forces certains mystères. Il y faut l'assistance de Dieu. . . . Marc exprime dans son évangile la tension vers une perfection jamais atteinte" [Here one sees the human incapacity to capture certain mysteries through one's own power. Divine assistance is required. . . . Mark, in his gospel, expresses the tension toward a perfection that is never attained]. See also Tannehill, "The Disciples in Mark," 392–93, 395–96, 404.

CHAPTER 4

NARRATIVE CRITICISM OF THE GOSPELS

The growing interest in the Bible as literature[1] and an awareness of the narrative nature of much biblical material[2] are producing an increasing number of studies that focus their attention on the impact of the biblical text on the reader.[3] One of the pioneering studies in this

---

[1] See, for example, Northrop Frye, *The Great Code: The Bible and Literature* (New York: Harcourt Brace Jovanovich, 1982), and Stephen Prickett, *Words and the Word: Language, Poetics and Biblical Interpretation* (Cambridge: Cambridge University Press, 1986). See also Robert Alter and Frank Kermode, eds., *The Literary Guide to the Bible* (London: Collins, 1987).

[2] See especially Robert Alter, *The Art of Biblical Narrative* (New York: Basic Books, 1981); Adele Berlin, *Poetics and Interpretation of Biblical Narrative* (Sheffield: Almond, 1983); Meir Sternberg, *The Poetics of Biblical Narrative: Ideological Literature and the Drama of Reading*. Indiana Literary Biblical Series (Bloomington, Ind.: Indiana University Press, 1985); Shimeon Bar-Efrat, *Narrative Art in the Bible*. JSOTSup 70; Bible and Literature Series 17 (Sheffield: Almond, 1989). For a survey see Mary Gerhart, "The Restoration of Biblical Narrative," *Semeia* 46 (1989) 13–29. For some initial suggestions for New Testament narratives see Norman R. Petersen, *Literary Criticism for New Testament Critics*. Guides to Biblical Scholarship, New Testament Series (Philadelphia: Fortress, 1978).

[3] For surveys see Edgar V. McKnight, *The Bible and the Reader: An Introduction to Literary Criticism* (Philadelphia: Fortress, 1985) and idem, *Post-Modern Use of the Bible: The Emergence of Reader-Oriented Criticism* (Nashville: Abingdon, 1988). See especially Stephen D. Moore, *Literary Criticism and the Gospels: The Theoretical Challenge* (New Haven: Yale University Press, 1989) and Robert M. Fowler, "Postmodern Biblical Criticism," *Forum* 5,3 (1989) 3–30.

area was that of R. Alan Culpepper on the literary design of the Fourth Gospel,[4] but this work is not a systematic reading of the text itself. After a section devoted to narrative theory Culpepper tests the text of the Fourth Gospel as narrative in the light of the major elements of such theory (narrator, point of view, time, plot, characters, implicit commentary, implied reader). Charles H. Talbert has already produced two volumes that "read" a text,[5] and Robert C. Tannehill has completed a similar approach to the Lukan corpus.[6] Jean-Noel Aletti has written an elegant narrative study of Luke,[7] and a Dutch reading of the Gospel of Mark by Bas van Iersel has appeared in English.[8]

However, we cannot approach an ancient narrative text without acknowledging a serious debt to all that one hundred and fifty years of critical scholarship have given us. There is a danger that narrative criticism will be used by the world *in front of the text* to manipulate the world *in the text* in a return to fundamentalism. The "strangeness" and "otherness" of the biblical text is explained, in part, by its being the product of a number of cultures and languages foreign to our own. An uncritical reading of biblical passages that suit a certain readership must be avoided through a close contact with traditional scholarship, which has devoted so much attention to the world *behind the text*.[9]

SYNCHRONIC OR DIACHRONIC?

The narrative-critical approach to the gospels attempts to make sense of the text as we have received it. Such a reading is sometimes called *synchronic*. The text is read from word to word, verse to verse, chapter to chapter, allowing the gospel *as it now stands* to force the interpreter to

[4] R. Alan Culpepper, *Anatomy of the Fourth Gospel: A Study in Literary Design.* Foundations and Facets (Philadelphia: Fortress, 1983). See the critical summary of this work in Stephen D. Moore, *Literary Criticism* 45–51.

[5] Charles H. Talbert, *Reading Luke. A Literary and Theological Commentary on the Third Gospel* (New York: Crossroad, 1982), and idem, *Reading Corinthians: A Literary and Theological Commentary on 1 and 2 Corinthians* (New York: Crossroad, 1987).

[6] Robert C. Tannehill, *The Narrative Unity of Luke-Acts. A Literary Interpretation.* 2 vols. Foundations and Facets (Philadelphia and Minneapolis: Fortress, 1986–1990).

[7] Jean-Noel Aletti, *L'art de raconter Jésus Christ* (Paris: Editions du Seuil, 1989).

[8] Bas van Iersel, *Reading Mark.* Translated by W. H. Bisscheroux (Edinburgh: T & T Clark, 1989).

[9] See below, pp. 91–92, for a more detailed description of what I mean by the world "in front of the text," "in the text," and "behind the text."

understand it in its own right.[10] The major commentaries and scholarly studies of the gospels produced in this century have not followed this method. They have been marked by what can be called a *diachronic* approach to the text. To take the Fourth Gospel as an example, as far back as 1928 Archbishop John Henry Bernard decided that our present text did not reflect the original state of that gospel. He commented on a reconstructed gospel.[11] In 1933 Walter Bauer published a brief but suggestive commentary that showed his allegiance to the History of Religions school and its methods. Most of the Johannine theology and language was traced back to Gnostic and other syncretistic sources.[12]

These approaches were further refined by Rudolf Bultmann in his commentary of 1941. Bultmann presupposed identifiable major sources behind the text: a synoptic-like source that provided the miracle narratives, a christianized Gnostic source that stood behind the discourses, and the original work of a creative evangelist. The gospel as a whole finally came down to us as the result of the work of an ecclesiastical redactor who added further elements to make it conform more readily to the faith and practice of the larger Church, especially its sacramental teaching and its eschatology.[13] On the basis of his identification of sources Bultmann also reorganized the text of the gospel into a logic that he claimed reflected its original order. In this method the gospel must be rediscovered by tracing its original sources and by reconstructing its original order. It is not the text itself that dictates terms to the interpreter (synchronic); it is the history of what happened *in the formation of the text* that determines the issue (diachronic).

---

[10] Such reading must not ignore difficulties that arise from textual uncertainty. One must determine in each case what the original text might have been. Similarly, while I speak of "verse to verse, chapter to chapter," such divisions are only used as helpful guides. They were not part of the original Greek manuscripts. Our present system of chapters is the work of Stephen Langton early in the thirteenth century, and the verses were arranged by Robert Stephanus in 1551.

[11] John Henry Bernard, *A Critical and Exegetical Commentary on the Gospel according to St John.* ICC (Edinburgh: T & T Clark, 1928). See especially 1:xvi–xxx. I have placed this essay in the section dedicated to "The Synoptic Gospels," as the issues concern all biblical narratives. However, to exemplify some of the theory discussed I will generally look to the narrative of the Fourth Gospel.

[12] Walter Bauer, *Das Johannesevangelium erklärt.* Handkommentar zum Neuen Testament 6 (Tübingen: J. C. B. Mohr [Paul Siebeck], 1933).

[13] Rudolf Bultmann, *Das Evangelium des Johannes.* Meyers Kommentar (Göttingen: Vandenhoeck and Ruprecht, 1941) [English: *The Gospel of John: A Commentary* (Oxford: Blackwell, 1971)].

A continued interest in the diachronic approach to the gospel texts is both understandable and necessary. Each gospel had a long and complicated literary history, and we must continue to trace that history, reflecting the history of the community itself, through careful analysis. Still, whoever may have been responsible for the final shape of a gospel consciously took stories from the recorded memory of his community and laid them side by side to form a gospel.[14] This process may have been repeated many times until our gospels were eventually produced. The practice of telling stories, handing them down from generation to generation, is not unique to the early Christian communities.

However, the repeated telling of other peoples' stories eventually leads to their becoming the storyteller's own. C. H. Dodd once wrote of the Fourth Gospel that we must respect the text as it is and not try to improve on it because the text "was devised by somebody—even if he were only a scribe doing his best."[15] Facing the same issue, Meir Sternberg notes more vigorously:

> Traditional speculations about documents and sources and twice-told tales have now piled up so high on the altar of genesis as to obscure the one remarkable fact in sight, which bears on poetics. Granting the confusion of variants that went into the making of the Bible, the fact remains that the finished discourse never introduces them as variants, but rather strings them together into continuous action.[16]

A synchronic approach to the gospels is an attempt to uncover the literary skills and theological vision of Dodd's "scribe doing his best." Such an interpretation of an ancient text, however, is immediately open to the criticism of subjectivism. Diachronic approaches attempt to discover factors that are *outside* the text itself and can in some way render our interpretations more objective. The history of modern exegesis

---

[14] When unavoidable, I will use male pronouns to speak of gospel authors but alternate "he" and "she" to speak of the reader. I recognize that authors and readers included women. I am not prepared to use the neologism s/he.

[15] C. H. Dodd, *The Interpretation of the Fourth Gospel* (Cambridge: Cambridge University Press, 1953) 309.

[16] Sternberg, *The Poetics of Biblical Narrative* 127. See also Berlin, *Poetics and Interpretation* 20–21: "Knowledge of poetics can, at the very least, provide some limit and control on diachronic study. It prevents the mistaking of certain features in the present text's discourse for evidence of earlier sources." See also her more systematic treatment of "Poetic Interpretation and Historical-Critical Methods," 111–34.

shows that such objectivity has never really been achieved,[17] but the accusation can still be made: if the only authority is the text itself, then interpretation will be largely the result of personal reaction to the text.

Narrative texts were written for readers. What follows is an attempt to describe how a real author who commits a narrative to a written form communicates a point of view through the gradual construction of an implied author to tell a story, often through the agency of a narrator speaking to a narratee. The author creates an implied reader within the unfolding narrative itself, and the whole of this dynamic—however consciously or unconsciously organized by the real author—is read by a real reader.[18] Once a narrative text has a life and a history of its own, the reader in the text and the many possible readers of the text must play a determining role in the interpretation of that text and in establishing its lasting value.

Even in a synchronic reading of a narrative, where so much attention is devoted to the impact a text makes on a reader, there are objective controls that guide the interpreter. The real author tells the story by following certain literary conventions. The situation in time, the arrangement of scenes to form a plot, the use of space, and the delineation of both character and setting, all part of the narrator's craft, come into play.[19] One of the features of contemporary literary readings of the gospels has been the increased attention given to these characteristics of the storyteller's trade.

A real author must make important choices in assembling a narrative. This is the case for any narrative, and the redaction critics have devoted a great deal of attention to the discovery of the conscious choices each of the evangelists made in composing a particular version of the Jesus story. We know from the story of Jesus as it has been told in the synoptic gospels that there were many traditions about the life and

---

[17] The issue is well put by Robert Morgan and John Barton, *Biblical Interpretation.* Oxford Bible Series (Oxford: Oxford University Press, 1988) 286: "Historical study is a valuable control against the chaos of arbitrary interpretations, but its passion for the single correct answer, were it attainable, would leave the Bible looking more fragmented than ever. It would offer from the distant past various pieces of information with little relation to the present."

[18] For a brief description of the principles of narrative I have just sketched see Seymour B. Chatman, *Story and Discourse: Narrative Structure in Fiction and Film* (Ithaca: Cornell University Press, 1978) 146–51. See also Culpepper, *Anatomy of the Fourth Gospel* 3–11.

[19] On the use of time and plot as the "events" of a story, and a space and characters and setting as the "existents" of a story see Chatman, *Story and Discourse* 43–145.

teaching of Jesus available to the early Church. Even though he may have overstated his case Werner Kelber has shown the importance of the paradigm shift that took place when oral tradition became written gospel in Mark, and the Pauline diatribe became the Pauline letters.[20]

The evangelists shaped narrative texts according to particular criteria; they decided to include some narratives that came to them from their storytelling tradition and to exclude others; the elements they chose to include have been ordered and framed within the narrative as they wished to tell it. At times the gospels give hints of dislocation, marked by clumsy seams. The interpreter, however, must also admit the possibility that such seams are deliberately intended and attempt to read the narrative in the light of this possibility.[21] Written over forty years ago within the context of Bultmann's provocative approach to the Fourth Gospel, Edwin Hoskyns' words retain their significance within the contemporary debate: "We must not rest from exegesis until the apparent gaps have been filled up so completely that each discourse moves step by step as an ordered, a theologically ordered, whole."[22]

The real author of a gospel made decisions, and chose to tell the result of these decisions in a certain way to address a real reader. What the real author desired to communicate can only be rediscovered through a careful investigation of the story as a finished and carefully constructed narrative. But even when this has been done with care one must humbly accept that no definitive interpretation of any text can be established, by whatever method. All interpreters must face the fact that no single interpretation can claim to have said the last word on the passage. One of the attractions of the historical-critical method was the

---

[20] Werner Kelber, *The Oral and the Written Gospel: The Hermeneutics of Speaking and Writing in the Synoptic Tradition, Mark, Paul, and Q* (Philadelphia: Fortress, 1983). For a more positive appreciation of the process from orality to textuality, see Paul Ricoeur, "The Hermeneutical Function of Distanciation," in John B. Thompson, ed., *Hermeneutics and the Human Sciences: Essays on Language, Action and Interpretation* (Cambridge: Cambridge University Press, 1981) 131–44.

[21] One is faced with a choice. Either the author has lost control of his sources and the interpreter has the duty to make sense out of the resulting confusion, or the author deliberately created passages that we find difficult and the interpreter must seek the author's reason for doing so. See Gérard Genette, *Narrative Discourse: An Essay in Method.* Translated by Jane E. Lewin (Ithaca: Cornell University Press, 1980) 143–55. See also Werner Kelber, "Narrative as Interpretation and Interpretation of Narrative: Hermeneutical Reflections on the Gospels," *Semeia* 39 (1987) 107–33.

[22] Edwin C. Hoskyns (ed. Francis N. Davey), *The Fourth Gospel* (2nd ed. London: Faber & Faber, 1961) 201.

hope that we would have greater control over the objective meaning of the biblical text. This has not happened, nor will it happen with the use of the more synchronic, reader-oriented methods. Contemporary literary criticism is teaching us that "we read by the only light we possess, 'our own,' a light not really distinguishable from the surrounding 'green night;' and it teaches 'a fusky alphabet.'"[23]

No single interpretation of any narrative should ever claim to have produced the final word. As Edgar V. McKnight has said: "The meaning of a text is inexhaustible because no context can provide all the keys to all of its possibilities."[24] The hermeneutical questions that any narrative text poses to an interpreter arise from a possible clash of worlds. Each gospel is the product of a world that is *behind the text*. The text can be approached as a window through which one looks in an attempt to catch sight of that world behind the text. Such has been the task of traditional historical-critical scholarship. There is a further world created by the narrative itself. This is the world *in the narrative:* its characters, its time line, the geographical background, the cultural and religious values embodied there, to mention but a few of the elements that form this world. The text can be approached as a portrait, presenting its own world. The interpreter, however, belongs to the world *in front of the text*, which may or may not be reflected or called into question by a text that can be viewed as a mirror. The interplay of these worlds cannot be ignored in a critical account of the act of reading.[25]

The interpreter must attempt to build a bridge between these worlds, to find the horizon where they merge, but the tensions and even conflicts that might exist between the worlds "behind the text," "in the text," and "in front of the text" can often result in "a fusky alphabet."[26]

---

[23] Elizabeth Freund, *The Return of the Reader: Reader-Response Criticism.* New Accents (London: Methuen, 1987) 19. See also Chatman, *Story and Discourse* 28.

[24] McKnight, *Post-Modern Use of the Bible* 241. See also Nigel Watson, "Reception Theory and Biblical Exegesis," *AusBR* 36 (1988) 55–66; Stephen Prickett, "The Status of Biblical Narrative," *Pac* 2 (1989) 26–46; Jonathan D. Culler, *On Deconstruction: Theory and Criticism after Structuralism* (London: Routledge and Kegan Paul, 1983) 110–34, 175–79.

[25] This terminology has been used by Murray Krieger, *A Window to Criticism: Shakespeare's Sonnets and Modern Poetics* (Princeton: Princeton University Press, 1964) 3–70, and further discussed by Norman R. Petersen, *Literary Criticism* 24–48. See Paul Ricoeur, "Hermeneutics and the Critique of Ideology," in *Hermeneutics and the Human Sciences* 93: "The sense of the work is its internal organization, whereas the reference is the mode of being unfolded in front of the text."

[26] See especially Paul Ricoeur, "The Task of Hermeneutics," in *Hermeneutics and the Human Sciences* 43–62. It is important to insist that no interpretation can have the "final word," but we do have a traditional text to interpret. Radical

"We live neither within closed horizons nor within one unique horizon. Insofar as the fusion of horizons excludes the idea of a total and unique knowledge, this concept implies a tension between what is one's own and what is alien, between the near and the far; hence the play of difference is included in the process of convergence."[27]

WHICH AUTHOR?

There were probably many authors of the traditions behind the four gospels. These various traditions, mostly oral, were forged into the literary units by a real author. This historical person is traditionally called Matthew, Mark, Luke, or John respectively, whoever these authors may have been in fact. But each of these four narratives is held together by the point of view of an omniscient and omnipresent implied author who is part of the narrative itself. Wayne Booth describes this phenomenon as "the intuitive apprehension of a completed artistic whole; the chief value to which *this* implied author is committed, regardless of what party his creator belongs to in real life, is that which is expressed by the total form."[28]

---

reader-response criticism would seem to deny this. See the programmatic collection of essays written from 1970–1980 by Stanley E. Fish, *Is There a Text in This Class? The Authority of Interpretive Communities* (Cambridge: Harvard University Press, 1980). For a description of these recent directions see Peter J. Rabinowitz, "Whirl without End: Audience-Oriented Criticism," in G. Douglas Atkins and Laura Morrow, eds., *Contemporary Literary Theory* (London: Macmillan, 1989) 94: "Once you take seriously the notion that readers 'construct' (even partially) the texts that they read, then the canon (any canon) is not (or not only) the product of the inherent qualities in the texts; it is also (at least partly) the product of particular choices of the arbiters of taste who create it—choices always grounded in ideological and cultural values." For a consideration of this theory and its future importance for biblical criticism see Stephen D. Moore, "Negative Hermeneutics, Insubstantial Text: Stanley Fish and the Biblical Interpreter," *JAAR* 54 (1986) 401–13, and idem, *Literary Criticism* 108–30.

[27] Paul Ricoeur, "The Task of Hermeneutics," 62; "Hermeneutics and the Critique of Ideology," 75–78, and "The World of the Text and the World of the Reader," in idem, *Time and Narrative.* 3 vols. (Chicago: The University of Chicago Press, 1988) 3:157–79.

[28] Wayne C. Booth, *The Rhetoric of Fiction* (2nd ed. Chicago: University of Chicago Press, 1983) 73–74. See pp. 70–77 on the implied author and pp. 160–63 on omniscience. See also Chatman, *Story and Discourse* 148. Sternberg, in *The Poetics of Biblical Narrative* 99–128, insists on the presence of divine omnipotence in the biblical narratives, which makes the biblical narrator different from the narrator of fiction. The biblical narrator is a shaper, never a maker of

A recent book written by four real authors has said it well:

> Four people, with very different scholarly backgrounds in the history of
> science and the philosophy of science, contributed to this study and to the
> writing of the book. However, for a number of good stylistic reasons, it
> was decided not to use the royal "we" but the more modest "I" instead.
> Henceforth, then, "we" will speak with one voice.[29]

The "one voice" is the implied author. The "person" of the real author
cannot be found within the narrative, but the real author's "persona"
is all-pervading in the implied author.

The implied author speaks through a narrator, who can be hidden
in the narrative (a covert narrator) or an obvious presence (an overt
narrator).[30] In some modern narratives the narrator may be unreliable,
and may temporarily lead the reader down wrong paths. This is not
the case with any biblical narrator. It can be said of the four gospels,
for example, that their implied authors and narrators act as one. The
reader can be sure that the real author, the implied author, and the
narrator are at one in their attempt to tell the story of God's action in
the world in the person of Jesus of Nazareth.[31] Culpepper has written:
"Although the implied author and the real author may be distinguished from the narrator in theory, in John the narrator is the voice of
the author and the vocal expression of the choices and perspectives of
the implied author."[32] The author uses the choices and perspectives of
the implied author to direct the point of view, or the several points of
view, expressed throughout the work. Through the voice of the implied author created within the text itself by the real author that point
of view is made clear. "Discovering the point of view of the implied

---

plot. This feature of biblical narrative is still present, but needs to be differently
appreciated for the narratives of the New Testament. See Erich Auerbach, *Mimesis: The Representation of Reality in Western Literature* (Princeton: Princeton University Press, 1953) 40–49.

[29] Max Charlesworth, et al., *Life Among the Scientists: An Anthropological Study
of an Australian Scientific Community* (Melbourne and New York: Oxford University Press, 1989) vii. Wayne C. Booth, *The Rhetoric of Fiction* 264–66 writes of
"The Implied Author as Friend and Guide."

[30] On this see Chatman, *Story and Discourse* 196–262; Gerald Prince, *Narratol-
ogy: The Form and Functioning of Narrative.* Janua Linguarum. Series Maior 108
(Berlin, New York, and Amsterdam: Mouton, 1982) 7–16; Bar-Efrat, *Narrative
Art in the Bible.* 13–45.

[31] Sternberg, *The Poetics of Biblical Narrative* 58–83, argues that such is the case
for all biblical narrative.

[32] Culpepper, *Anatomy of the Fourth Gospel* 232.

author . . . is the first step in discovering the meaning and purpose of the story."[33]

The attempt to identify the point of view of the real author and the implied author may presuppose too much. It is here that traditional redaction criticism fails to appreciate fully the complexities of the way narrative works. For several decades we have perhaps spoken and written too confidently of the identifiable theological perspective of each evangelist. We can never finally discover the point of view of the real author. The gospels are comparatively simple narratives, not given to the modern sophistications of unreliable relationships among author, narrator, and reader. Thus the desires of the real author are reflected in the point of view of the implied author, yet the former lies outside our scientific control. We can only work with the text itself, and that limits us to the rediscovery of the point of view of the implied author[34] even though, in the case of the gospels, one senses that the real author's intention is not far distant.

WHICH READER?

It is self-evident that an evangelist could not and did not compose the final version of a gospel with the modern reader in mind. The contemporary person who takes up the gospel and reads it is the real reader. The impact the text makes on the real reader elicits a response that may vary, even in the same reader, according to a variety of circumstances that may accompany the act of reading.[35] Similarly, while

---

[33] Berlin, *Poetics and Interpretation of Biblical Narrative* 82. On the question of point of view in biblical narratives see pp. 43–82. See also Meyer H. Abrams, *A Glossary of Literary Terms* (New York: Holt, Rinehart and Winston, 1988) 144: "Point of view signifies the way a story gets told—the mode or perspective established by an author by means of which the reader is presented with the characters, actions, setting, and events which constitute the narrative in a work of fiction." The implied author is crucial in "the way a story gets told." For a somewhat different view see Shlomith Rimmon-Kenan, *Narrative Fiction: Contemporary Poetics*. New Accents (Methuen: London, 1983) 71–85.

[34] On this see Gérard Genette, *Narrative Discourse* 26–29, and idem, *Narrative Discourse Revisited*. Translated by Jane E. Lewin (Ithaca, N.Y.: Cornell University Press, 1988) 135–54; George Steiner, *Real Presences: Is There Anything in What We Say?* (London: Faber & Faber, 1989) 169.

[35] For a survey of the real reader, with further references to contemporary literary criticism, see Jeffrey L. Staley, *The Print's First Kiss: A Rhetorical Investigation of the Implied Reader in the Fourth Gospel*. SBLDS 82 (Atlanta: Scholars, 1988) 24–27. Booth, *The Rhetoric of Fiction* 147, puts it well: "To pretend that we read

the evangelist would have been writing a gospel narrative for the members of a given community, he had no control over how they would respond to the narrative. *Within the text itself* we can sense the presence of yet another reader who emerges as the tale is told. This so-called implied reader can be called an *intratextual* phenomenon.[36]

The implied reader is recognized in the gradual unfolding of the plot through the narrative's time span and the interaction of the characters. She only knows what has already been read: the words, sentences, paragraphs, and pages. She must wait for the next word, sentence, paragraph, and page to discover what the narrator has to tell.[37]

The basis of this method is a consideration of the *temporal* flow of the reading experience, and it is assumed that the reader responds in terms of that flow and not to the whole utterance. That is, in an utterance of any length there is a point at which the reader has taken in only the first word, and then the second, and then the third, and so on, and the report of what happens to the reader is always a report of what happened *up to that point*.[38]

The implied reader, therefore, is not a person but a heuristic device used to trace the temporal flow of the narrative. However, what is not said in Stanley E. Fish's description (in his 1980 book, *Is There a Text in This Class? The Authority of Interpretive Communities*) is that the implied reader is able to look back over what has already been told. He not only emerges as forward-looking textual effect; he also knows and recalls what has happened and has been revealed in the story so far.

This is not the case for the intended reader or the real reader. The original intended readers and the contemporary real readers of a gospel lived and live in a Christian community founded on the death and

---

otherwise, to claim that we can make ourselves into objective, dispassionate, thoroughly tolerant readers is in the final analysis nonsense."

[36] As the implied reader is a textual effect, "it" is not a person, a "he" or a "she," yet the author composes a narrative in such a way that the implied reader emerges from the narrative as if she or he were a person. The telling of the story creates situations that evoke responses from the evolving textual effect of the implied reader, even though this reader is not a historical figure. For a good summary of the implied reader in contemporary literary theory see Willem S. Vorster, "The Reader in the Text: Narrative Material," *Semeia* 48 (1989) 22–7. For the application of this literary theory to New Testament narratives see pp. 28–36.

[37] See the previous note in explanation of my use of the verbs "to know," "to read," "to wait," "to discover" to speak of the "experience" of the implied reader.

[38] Fish, *Is There a Text in This Class?* 26–27. See also p. 43.

resurrection of Jesus. Some real readers may not do so, but most who have read the gospels for nearly two thousand years have done so on the basis of their belief in Jesus' death and resurrection. However, the reporting of the events of the death and resurrection of Jesus come at the end of the narrative. In the Fourth Gospel, for example, although several puzzling statements about "the hour" of Jesus (2:4; 7:30; 8:20; 12:23; 13:1; 17:1; 19:27), his being "lifted up" (3:14; 8:28; 12:32), his glorification (7:39; 12:16), and even his resurrection (2:21-22) point toward it, the implied reader does not know the end of the story. Such enigmatic references puzzle the implied reader, but the intended reader and the real reader understand them.[39]

The implied reader, an intratextual phenomenon, and the early Christian community (the intended reader), and a real reader are not the same. The members of the early Christian community and the modern readers are historical people who can take the narrative in hand to read it. They would remain a part of history even if there were no gospels. They are, therefore, *extratextual* phenomena.

The reading process is essentially temporal and the implied reader is a heuristic device one can trace to discover the temporal aspect of the reading process.[40] All critics are agreed that the implied reader is a product of the narrative itself. The name or situation of the reader is never explicitly mentioned in the text, but it is clear that a reader emerges from the evolving narrative. I am adopting the term "implied reader" to speak of that effect within the narrative, but the terminology itself can admittedly be confusing. Beyond the common belief that the implied reader is a product of the text itself and can be discerned in it,

---

[39] As Rimmon-Kenan puts it: "Placing an item at the beginning or at the end may radically change the process of reading as well as the final product" (*Narrative Fiction* 120). See, however, Sternberg, *The Poetics of Biblical Narrative* 258–63. Sternberg claims that the tensions created by the gaps and closures in a narrative text are forever new, even for a reader who has read them many times, as also for those who know the facts of the story.

[40] For the communication theory of narrative that follows I am dependent on Chatman, *Story and Discourse*. This theory has been summarized, applied to the Johannine narrative, and further developed in light of subsequent reaction to it by Staley, *The Print's First Kiss* 20–49. See also Watson, "Reception Theory and Biblical Exegesis," 45–56. Watson's terminology differs slightly, as he summarizes Hannelore Link, *Rezeptionsforschung: Eine Einführung in Methoden und Probleme*. Urban-Taschenbücher 215 (Stuttgart, Berlin, Cologne, and Mainz: Kohlhammer, 1976). The principles, however, remain the same. See also the summary of Bernard C. Lategan, "Coming to Grips with the Reader in Biblical Literature," *Semeia* 48 (1989) 3–17.

there are several understandings of what might be described as the implied reader.[41] Basic, it appears to me, is the need to maintain the distinction, made above, between a reader who is *intratextual,* a textual effect, and all other readers, who are extratextual.

The implied reader is part of the spatial gaps and temporal flow of the narrative itself.[42] She is not the original intended reader or any real reader today, yet the eventual response of intended and real readers results from the relationship established between them and the narrative's implied reader. Indeed, the Christian tradition of reading, and the community of readers through the ages that the Bible presupposes, would be rendered impossible if such were not the case. The relationship may sometimes be uncomfortable. The text may produce pleasure, pain, ambiguity, and even hostility, but some form of relationship must be there. If it is not there, the text will disappear in the dust of the shelves.[43]

This reference to the Bible leads to a further reservation. The structures and terminology detected and defined in recent times in literary circles come from scholars who are working with narrative *fiction.*[44]

---

[41] For a survey see Staley, *The Print's First Kiss* 30–37. See also Wolfgang Iser, *The Act of Reading: A Theory of Aesthetic Response* (Baltimore: Johns Hopkins University Press, 1978) 32–34, and Bas van Iersel, *Reading Mark* 12. Rimmon-Kenan, *Narrative Fiction* 86–105 argues, against Booth and Chatman, that only real author, narrator-narratee, and real reader are "participants in the narrative communication situation." She appears, however, to reintroduce my implied reader in her "extradiegetic narratee" (103–105). Berlin, in *Poetics and Interpretation* 52–53 and especially 148 n. 24, also collapses the implied reader into the narratee. See the discussion in Genette, *Narrative Discourse Revisited* 96–108.

[42] Following, among many, the indications of Robert M. Fowler, "Who is 'The Reader' in Reader Response Criticism?" *Sem* 31 (1985) 10–15. Moore, *Literary Criticism* 84–95, points out that the "reader" may best be described as a "listener." My presentation of a virginal experience of the narrative applies equally well to a listener, as Moore (87–88) acknowledges. He, among many, exaggerates the "Gutenberg galaxy" theory (95). The great patristic commentaries were pre-Gutenberg but belong more to the modern galaxy than to the aural-oral one imagined by Moore. As Steiner has (unapprovingly) commented: "Little in the business of our schooling in letters, music and the arts, in that of our lectures and seminars, would seem alien to the minds of St. Jerome or St. Augustine. The evolution of classical and medieval means of understanding into modern philology and modern hermeneutics during the seventh, eighteenth and early nineteenth centuries is one of close-knit continuity" (*Real Presences* 30–31).

[43] On this relationship see Booth, *The Rhetoric of Fiction* 137–44, 294–95. He claims: "In so far as we read this book properly, we are thus taken in by it, tricked by the narrator into playing a role in the action."

[44] See, for example, the clear description of the project by Iser, *The Act of Reading* 3–19.

The gospels are not narrative fictions in any ordinary sense. Whatever their historical value, they were not creatively invented in the same way that a novelist or a storyteller composes narratives.[45] The text of a gospel had a long history before it came to be presented in its final form. This history had its beginnings in the event of Jesus of Nazareth, however imaginatively the subsequent tradition has handled that event. Because of this, diachronic and synchronic go hand in hand in a reading of a gospel because of its witness to Jesus Christ. Adela Yarbro Collins rightly insists that we

> give more weight to the original historical context of the text. This context cannot and should not totally determine all subsequent meaning and use of the text. But if, as I am convinced, all meaning is context bound, the original context and meaning have a certain normative character. I suggest that Biblical theologians are not only mediators between genres. They are also mediators between historical periods. . . . Whatever tension there may be between literary- and historical-critical methods, the two approaches are complementary.[46]

Tracing the implied reader can justifiably be a search for a construct produced by a long storytelling tradition (synchronic) that had its beginnings in Jesus (diachronic). As Werner Kelber has warned: "Due to these intersecting worlds of narrative and tradition, the pursuit of narrative meaning is not always and inevitably compromised by explorations into tradition. Methodological purity is carried to an extreme if the genetic quest and formalist interpretation are set against each other as natural enemies."[47]

---

[45] For the classic statement of the uniqueness of biblical narrative see Auerbach, *Mimesis* 3–23. See the stimulating study of Stephen Prickett, "Poetics and Narrative: Biblical Criticism and the Nineteenth Century Novel," in Eric Osborn and Lawrence McIntosh, eds., *The Bible and European Literature: History and Hermeneutics* (Melbourne: Academia Press, 1987) 81–97. See also Werner Kelber, "Gospel Narrative and Critical Theory," *BTB* 18 (1988) 132, and idem, "Biblical Hermeneutics and the Ancient Art of Communication: A Response," *Semeia* 39 (1987) 100–101. A deconstructionist approach (see below, n. 57) would regard all writing and all figures as fiction. For a survey see Herbert N. Schneidau, "The Word against the Word: Derrida on Textuality," *Sem* 23 (1982) 23–24.

[46] Adela Yarbro Collins, "Narrative, History and Gospel," *Sem* 43 (1988) 150, 153. For a timely word of warning to both historical and literary critics see John Barton, "Reading the Bible as Literature: Two Questions for Biblical Critics," *Literature and Theology* 1 (1987) 135–53.

[47] Kelber, "Gospel Narrative and Critical Theory," 132. See, however, the deconstructionist critique of Schneidau, "The Word against the Word," 17. "If we

Paul Ricoeur has insisted that both fiction and history are narrative.[48] While it is tempting to distinguish between empirical narrative, which refers to controllable data, and fictional narrative, which does not, Ricoeur points out that both forms of narrative make referential claims and are not to be distinguished on this basis.[49] Or, as Gérard Genette has put it: "Every day we are subjects of a narrative, if not heroes of a novel."[50]

The implied reader in a narrative is always communicating with the real reader of the narrative *as the narrative unfolds*. He is like a radio station transmitting a message, but the real reader may not always receive the transmission equally well.[51] When we misread what is being transmitted, there is faulty communication. Sometimes we only receive the communication partially as a result of our careless or distracted reading. Nevertheless, there are times when we receive the transmission exactly. This happens when we are reading in tandem with the implied reader, caught up in the flow of the narrative. In these situations we sometimes may not like what the implied reader transmits to us, so we change stations or switch off. But often we are attracted by the transmission and thus go on receiving. Two thousand years of reading indicate that the Church has been attuned to the transmission of the implied reader in each of the four canonical gospels, and has thus gone on receiving.

Contemporary literary studies have taught us sensitivity to the shape of the implied reader who gradually emerges as the narrative unfolds, but historical-critical scholarship has devoted great attention to the rediscovery of the experience of the early Christian community. The very existence of four gospels as texts within the Christian tradition (and

------

sanctify this procedure ('a quest for origins') we are simply privileging one more form of the transcendental signified, the outside foundation that lets us escape the vertigo of seeing meanings resolve endlessly into other meanings."

[48] Ricoeur, "The Narrative Function," 274–96, and idem, "The Interweaving of Fiction and History," 180–92.

[49] Ricoeur, "The Interweaving of Fiction and History," 288–96. On Ricoeur's understanding of fiction as "the privileged path for the redescription of reality" see his "Metaphor and the Central Problem of Hermeneutics," 165–81. See also Prickett, *Words and the Word* 174–242. A forceful defense of the unity between fiction and history in the biblical narratives is found in Sternberg, *The Poetics of Biblical Narrative* 23–35. Sternberg, however, argues through the whole of his book for the uniqueness of biblical narrative due to the central place of God in the story and in the telling of the story.

[50] Genette, *Narrative Discourse* 230.

[51] Like all images this one limps, but it may help to clarify the textual effect of the implied reader.

elsewhere) indicates that the transmission of the implied reader was received by the intended reader of the text. Gospel criticism may well turn to narrative criticism, but it must not abandon the scholarly pursuit of traditional scholarship to rediscover the original intended readership. The interpreter's role is to "mediate between historical periods" (Adela Yarbro Collins). The *historical* intended reader was addressed by a *historical* real author through a narrative. The interpreter of that narrative is also conditioned by her *historical* context. The gospel narratives live in the Christian community today because they have been handed down, read, and interpreted in a variety of *historical* contexts for two thousand years. A neglect of history leads to the danger of a new fundamentalism as ancient texts regarded as sacred within the Christian community are extracted from the settings that gave them life and kept them alive. Such readings are, in my opinion, dishonest.

THE REAL READER

A real author, the evangelist, summons an intended readership into a deeper appreciation of Jesus as the Christ, the Son of God (see, for example, Mark 1:1; John 20:31). The "story of Jesus" as we now have it told in each gospel is the result of the journey of faith of a particular Christian community in the second half of the first century. The experience of the community and the vision it produced have been caught in a narrative directed to an implied reader via an implied author and a narrator. However slight our knowledge of the real author might be, he wrote a narrative for his intended readers so that they might face "the problem of relating the givenness of the past with the exhilarating experience of the present."[52]

Such reflections are important for our approaching a gospel as "real readers." A gospel has come down to us in its present form because it was received and handed on by the intended reader, an early Christian community. The gospels are still read as we enter the third Christian millennium. The test of the relevance of a gospel lies in its ability to speak to the faith experience of its real readers. As Seymour Chatman describes it: "When I enter the fictional contract I add another self: I become an implied reader."[53] Does the record of Jesus Christ we receive from the past in the narrative of a gospel have anything to say to the

[52] Morna D. Hooker, "In His Own Image," in Morna D. Hooker and Colin Hickling, eds., *What About the New Testament? Studies in Honor of Christopher Evans* (London: SCM, 1975) 41.

[53] Chatman, *Story and Discourse* 150.

exhilarating and sometimes frightening experience of our own time? Do we "enter the fictional contract" of this particular story of Jesus? How close are our journey and our faith experience to the journey and faith experience of the implied reader in the gospel narrative? These are the questions that will determine the ongoing relevance of the story told in a gospel. They can only be answered by a reading of the text during which a relationship between the implied reader and the experience of intended readers and the real reader is established.[54]

The reader of a gospel cannot be limited to the implied reader, to an early Christian community, or to the real reader with the text in hand today. As Robert M. Fowler has summarized: "The reader has an individual persona (mine), a communal persona (the abstracted total experience of my critical community), and a textual persona (the reader implied in the text)."[55] All must play their part in an ongoing reading of a gospel within the Christian community. Whether or not the author's construction of the implied reader speaks to the faith experience of the real reader is difficult to assess. What can confidently be claimed is that almost two thousand years of Christian readers have been able to enter the narrative contract of the four gospels. It is an objective fact that the gospels have been read and continue to be read by millions of Christian believers.

The revelance of these texts today arises from the relationship established between the implied reader and the real reader. Iser rightly claims that "the meaning of a literary text is not a definable entity but, if anything, a dynamic happening."[56] The evolving and emerging textual effect of the implied reader initiates such mutuality, not the knowledge, the doctrines, the wisdom, the faith, or the experience of the real reader.[57]

---

[54] As Steiner, *Real Presences* 210, puts it: "To read well, to take in the light of specific presentness in the painting, to hear the dynamic relations in the tonal argument, is to generate anew, to wake out of silence, out of potential absence, the proceedings of the artist." On the real reader who "assumes the role of the implied reader" see Janice Capel Anderson, "Matthew: Gender and Reading," *Semeia* 28 (1983) 23–24.

[55] Fowler, "Who is 'The Reader' in Reader-Response Criticism?" 21.

[56] Iser, *The Act of Reading* 22.

[57] A deconstructionist approach to narrative is beyond the scope of my study but could be introduced at this stage. For a stimulating example of the use of deconstruction in literary criticism see Barbara Johnson, *The Critical Difference: Essays in the Contemporary Rhetoric of Reading* (Baltimore: Johns Hopkins University Press, 1980). She claims: "If anything is destroyed in a deconstructive reading, it is not the text, but the claim to unequivocal domination of one mode of signifying over another" (p. 5). Particularly enlightening is her essay

A series of encounters links the origins of a gospel story with today's reader. The Jesus event gave birth to an early Christian community. At a given moment the real author decided to shape his narrative to meet certain needs within the community. In doing this he created an implied author, a narrator, and an implied reader, the fruit of his choices and decisions. These choices and decisions, however, were determined by his vision of the needs of the community for which the narrative was shaped. The implied reader, the heuristic device that enables us to sense the temporal flow of the narrative, is therefore shaped by, but not identical with, the intended reader. It represents not only what the in-

---

"Melville's Fist: The Execution of Billy Budd" (79–109). See also Jonathan D. Culler, *On Deconstruction* 235–42. Although generally unacceptable to biblical narrative critics (see, for example, Staley, *The Print's First Kiss* 48 n. 138; Robert Alter and Frank Kermode, *A Literary Guide* 5–6), Derrida's rejection of a metaphysics behind the words could direct narrative critics to take more seriously the "undecidability" that is so characteristic of fiction but somewhat foreign to biblical studies, which often reads narrative as a direct reference to predetermined theological truths. Derrida claims that words do not communicate prediscoursed reality. Just what is communicated can never be determined, as meaning is continually deferred. When one is attempting to talk about God this may be important. See John Dominic Crossan, "Difference and Divinity," *Semeia* 23 (1982) 29–40. For a positive assessment of Derrida's challenge to biblical interpretation see especially Moore, *Literary Criticism* 131–78, and Schneidau, "The Word against the Word," 5–28. This whole number of *Semeia* (edited by Robert Detweiler) is entitled *Derrida and Biblical Studies*. See also the important study of Kevin Hart, *The Trespass of the Sign: Deconstruction, Theology and Philosophy* (Cambridge: Cambridge University Press, 1989). For a survey of deconstructionist literary theory see D. J. Anderson, "Deconstruction: Critical Strategy/Strategic Criticism," in Atkins and Morrow, eds., *Contemporary Literary Theory* 137–57, and Vincent B. Leitch, *American Literary Criticism from the Thirties to the Eighties* (New York: Columbia University Press, 1988) 267–306. For a study of the deconstructionists at work on a text see Barbara Johnson, "The Frame of Reference: Poe, Lacan, Derrida," in eadem, *The Critical Difference* 110–46. She concludes this study (p. 146): "If we could be sure of the difference between the determinable and the undeterminable, the undeterminable would be comprehended within the determinable. What is undecidable is whether a thing is decidable or not." Literary critics themselves are deeply divided over this issue. See, for example, the elegant study of Steiner, *Real Presences*. Prickett, in "The Status of Biblical Narrative," 28, comments: "Literary criticism has perhaps been plunged into the greatest crisis of them all, radically problematized to the point where some of its most respected prophets have proclaimed the ultimate meaninglessness and futility of words themselves. That they have done so by means of words at often inordinate length is only a minor irony."

tended reader was, but especially what the real author *wanted the intended reader to become.* Thus arises the intimacy between the real author, the implied author, and the narrator. The implied reader reflects the real-author-implied author-narrator's deepest desires for a historical Christian community.

Once the narrative existed, the intended reader entered into a dialogue with the implied reader as he began to read or listen to the text. In doing this the intended reader came into contact with the desire of the narrator. This dialogue proved fruitful. The narrative transaction had its effect upon the intended reader, who judged that it was a transaction with a significance that exceeded the bounds of its own time and place. Therefore the narrative was handed on and eventually became part of the Christian canon of the New Testament. In this way later readers also entered into dialogue with the implied reader and they, in their own turn, came into contact with the narrator's desire. And so the process has continued for two thousand years. The narrative is still read today by real readers. We continue to enter into dialogue with the implied reader and we find value in it. Insofar as we continue to enter the narrative transaction and find value in it we also enter into communion with the intended reader.

Reader-oriented criticism struggles to define "the reader."[58] The experience of reading a classical text through the centuries indicates that a hard and fast definition is impossible. The intended reader both *is* and *is not* the implied reader. The real reader both *is* and *is not* the implied reader. Also, the real reader both *is* and *is not* the intended reader. At the point of *"is"* the construct of "the reader" is born.[59]

Yet, as the liberation and feminist theologians are showing, some contemporary real readers of biblical texts are unhappy with the desire of the real author, communicated through the centuries by means of the fictional contract.[60] There are an increasing number of contemporary real readers who cannot identify with many of the biblical implied readers. Nevertheless, even here the narrative may continue to be relevant because of the antipathy and ambiguity it creates. Relationships between the implied reader and the real reader need not always be

---

[58] For a critical survey see Moore, *Literary Criticism* 97–107.

[59] These four paragraphs arose from discussions with Mark Coleridge. I am grateful to him for his careful articulation of our conclusions. See, for some parallel reflections, Bernard C. Lategan, "Coming to Grips with the Reader," 9–13.

[60] For a comprehensive survey of so-called postmodern biblical readings that move increasingly away from "entering the fictional contract" see The Bible and Culture Collective, *The Postmodern Bible* (New Haven: Yale University Press, 1995). See my review of this book in *Pac* 9 (1996) 98–101.

favorable, but a relationship there must be.[61] "The insight that the Bible is not only a source of truth and revelation but also a source of violence and domination is basic for liberation theologies. This insight demands a new paradigm of biblical interpretation that does not understand the Bible as archetype but rather as prototype."[62]

CONCLUSION

In many ways the implied reader has privileges that the real reader cannot share. She is integral to the journey told through the narrative; the real reader may have a different experience. When the narrator speaks of a Jewish feast without explanation to the reader, or presupposes its liturgy, the implied reader is presumed aware of all that such a feast suggests; many real readers are not. The implied reader is assumed to know Greek and to understand double-meaning words, which many real readers do not.[63] It can be assumed that the implied reader in a gospel narrative knows the basic elements of the story of Jesus. Although it has sometimes been questioned, it is almost universally recognized that the gospels were written in and for believing Christian communities. However, the listener/reader is hearing/reading *this particular interpretation of that story* for the first time. Contemporary Christian readers have heard the voices of Matthew, Mark, Luke,

[61] This hermeneutical principle has been highlighted by liberationist and feminist readings of the New Testament. Biblical narratives often produce implied authors, narrators, narratees, and implied readers that reflect an oppressive ideology or androcentrism unacceptable to some contemporary readers. Among other things (see *The Postmodern Bible* for still more), this problem has led to the development of a specifically liberationist or feminist hermeneutic that challenges the myth of the value-free objectivity of the academy as in fact constituting an "advocacy stance." On this see the survey by Elaine Wainright, "In Search of the Lost Coin: Toward a Feminist Biblical Hermeneutic," *Pac* 2 (1989) 135–50; Jonathan Culler, *On Deconstruction* 43–64, 165–75, and the collection of essays in Letty M. Russell, *Feminist Interpretation of the Bible* (Philadelphia: Westminster, 1985). See further Juan Luis Segundo, *The Liberation of Theology.* Translated by John Drury (Maryknoll: Orbis, 1976); Elisabeth Schüssler Fiorenza, "Toward a Critical-Theological Self-Understanding of Biblical Scholarship," in eadem, *Bread not Stone* (Boston: Beacon, 1984) 136–49, and "The Function of Scripture in the Liberation Struggle: A Critical Feminist Hermeneutics and Liberation Theology," in *Bread not Stone* 43–63; Katie Geneva Cannon and Elisabeth Schüssler Fiorenza, eds., *Interpretation for Liberation* (*Semeia* 47; Atlanta: Scholars, 1989).

[62] Schüssler Fiorenza, "The Function of Scripture," 61.

[63] See Culpepper, *Anatomy of the Fourth Gospel* 212–23; Rimmon-Kenan, *Narrative Fiction* 117–19.

and John many times, and often have little or no sense of the uniqueness of *each particular story.*

Nevertheless, we real readers may find that our response, in dialogue with the experience of almost two thousand years of Christian life, often resonates with what results from the unfolding relationship between the implied author and the implied reader in a gospel. The first time we hear a good biblical story we experience a certain oneness, a wholeness we recognize, nonetheless, as unifying several currents of reality. As the experience sinks in we become aware of more than one story being told. Most will probably recognize our own story tied into the narrator's story. A few may recognize that the story's lines are tied back to a greater silent story: all of reality, which is known only through the words of the present story.[64]

On the other hand we may find (and no doubt many do find) that such a response is fatuous in our real world of mortals, money, and machines. But that is not the only thing that might happen. Sometimes we may have a further response that is independent of the implied reader and thus outside the control of the author. It is unavoidable that our response, either of empathy or antipathy, will be the result of our privileged position as the recipients of almost two thousand years of the Christian practice of reading the gospels.[65]

---

[64] Anne M. Solomon, "Story upon Story," *Semeia* 46 (1989) 3.

[65] For further reflections along the lines of this paragraph see Morgan and Barton, *Biblical Interpretation* 167–202. See also Prickett, *Words and the Word* 33–36.

PART 2

THE GOSPEL OF JOHN

CHAPTER 5

WHEN IS JOHN TALKING ABOUT SACRAMENTS?[1]

The Melbourne Scripture Seminar of 1981 was devoted to the theme: "The Sacraments: Celebrating and Creating Life." I had been invited to contribute in the area of Johannine scholarship, and the brochures advertising the Seminar stated: "Johannine literature is perhaps regarded as the most explicitly sacramental of the New Testament collection." This is true. If one were to accept the suggestions of all the scholars who have written on this issue in a positive sense one would finish with the following explicit sacramental teaching in the Fourth Gospel:[2]

Matrimony:
    The marriage feast at Cana (2:1-11)
Anointing of the Sick:
    The anointing at Bethany (12:1-8)

---

[1] I have retained this title, despite its difficulties, from the original setting of this paper, given at the Melbourne Scripture Seminar, Newman College, University of Melbourne, 24–31 August 1981. It enabled me to raise the issues of the Johannine community and its experience. See below.

[2] For the following list of possibilities see Raymond E. Brown, "The Johannine Sacramentary," in idem, *New Testament Essays* (London: Geoffrey Chapman, 1967) 75–76. Another good survey of scholarship can be found in Herbert Klos, *Die Sakramente im Johannesevangelium. Vorkommen und Bedeutung vom Taufe, Eucharistie und Busse im 4. Evangelium.* SBS 46 (Stuttgart: Katholisches Bibelwerk, 1970).

Reconciliation:
Lazarus (11:1-44)
"Whose sins you shall forgive shall be forgiven, etc." (20:23)
"He who has bathed does not need to wash, *except for his feet.*"
(13:10)[3]
Baptism:
The baptism of Jesus (1:32-33; 3:26)
The marriage feast at Cana (2:1-11)
The "cleansing" of the Temple (2:13-25)
The conversation with Nicodemus (3:1-21)
The conversation with the Samaritan woman (4:1-30)
The healing at Bethsaida (5:1-17)
The walking on the water (6:16-21)
The source of living waters (7:38)
The healing of the man born blind (9:1-38)
The Good Shepherd (10:1-18)
The raising of Lazarus (11:1-44)
The foot washing (13:1-20)
The miraculous draught of fishes (21:1-8)
Eucharist:
The marriage feast at Cana (2:1-11)
The "cleansing" of the Temple (2:13-25)
"My food is to do the will of my Father" (4:31-34)
Chapter 6, especially 6:1-15 and 6:51-58.
The foot washing (13:1-20)
The vine and the branches (15:1-11)
The meal of bread and fish (21:9-14)
Baptism and Eucharist:
Blood and water from the pierced side of Jesus (19:34)
Water and blood as witnesses (1 John 5:8).

This list is clearly "maximal." It gathers indiscriminately from the suggestions of scholars, some of them reflecting upon the text from a more systematic perspective or reading it in the light of subsequent patristic and Church thought and practice. For the contemporary biblical critic it probably comes as something of a surprise that certain events have been read as containing explicit teaching on the Christian sacra-

---

[3] The words εἰ μὴ τοὺς πόδας are textually doubtful, and may have been added by a copyist to solve the problem of sinfulness after baptism. For a discussion of this issue, with bibliographical details, see Francis J. Moloney, *The Johannine Son of Man.* BibScRel 14 (2nd ed. Rome: LAS, 1978) 192–93.

ments. One might ask, for example, how the anointing of the feet of Jesus might be linked with the Catholic sacrament of anointing, or how the cleansing of the Temple, where there is no reference to any baptismal symbols or rituals (especially water), however subtle, could refer to the fundamental Christian sacrament of baptism?

These questions could go farther, as contacts between most of the texts cited and the sacraments of the Christian tradition are tenuous at best. A further point should be raised as we begin this study. Scholars who have produced these various claims do not fall into clearly defined confessional groups. It is interesting to note that the defense of many explicit contacts between the Johannine gospel and the Christian sacramental system is not the sole preserve of conservative Catholics. Similarly, we must note that the rejection of sacramental teaching in the Fourth Gospel is not only found in schools of radical Protestant scholarship. I have no intention of discussing the details of this long and unresolved debate, of which Raymond E. Brown remarked: "Perhaps on no other point of Johannine thought is there such division among scholars."[4] Anyone interested in a fuller discussion should consult the surveys done by Brown in his *New Testament Essays*[5] and in his commentary on the Fourth Gospel,[6] and the useful survey contained in Herbert Klos's book.[7] Thinkers from all schools take up a variety of positions on the issue. A careful reading of this scholarship shows that, as always in approaching New Testament texts, what ultimately determines the answer to the question "when is John talking about sacraments?" is the set of criteria and methods adopted by each scholar in approaching the text. I will limit myself to a few contrasting positions in this debate before setting out on my own discussion. However, there are still some introductory remarks that have to be made. Indeed, the following brief discussion is partly indicative of the "criteria and methods" I adopt in my subsequent reading of the Johannine text.

1. "When Is John Talking?"

It is not accurate to ask about a single character called "John," nor are we justified in referring to "John talking." The apparently never-ending debate over the author of the gospel we call "of John" is well

---

[4] Raymond E. Brown, *The Gospel According to John*. 2 vols. AB 29, 29a (New York: Doubleday, 1966–70) 1:cxi.

[5] Brown, "The Johannine Sacramentary," 51–56

[6] Brown, *John* 1:cxi–cxiv.

[7] Klos, *Die Sakramente im Johannesevangelium*. See n. 2 above.

and widely covered in the many fine introductions to this gospel, including those of the great contemporary commentators now all available in English: Charles Kingsley Barrett, Barnabas Lindars, Rudolf Schnackenburg, and Raymond E. Brown.[8] I have also discussed this question in my own recent commentary in the Sacra Pagina series.[9] The evidence of the gospel itself, assuming that the link made between the author of the gospel and the Beloved Disciple in the secondary 21:20-24 is correct, points to an original tradition about Jesus with its source in a disciple of Jesus. This tradition deepened and developed in a Christian community that eventually established itself somewhere in Asia Minor (probably Ephesus). The development took place over a long period of time, through many trials and tribulations caused by both external and internal difficulties.

I remain convinced that the community was gathered around an all-important figure who had close contact with the historical Jesus and was most probably an ex-disciple of the Baptist (see 1:35). If this was the case we cannot ask about "John talking." We must look deeper into the life and experience of faith of a particular Christian community. The Gospel of John, like all the other gospels, is not a single person "talking" to us, but a living community of first-century Christians communicating, through their own particular Spirit-filled journey, their dynamic experience of faith that is, especially in the Fourth Gospel, a christological and an ecclesiological journey.[10]

---

[8] C. K. Barrett, *The Gospel According to St John* (2nd ed. London: S.P.C.K., 1978) 100–34; Barnabas Lindars, *The Gospel of John.* NCB (London: Oliphants, 1972) 28–34; Rudolf Schnackenburg, *The Gospel According to St. John.* 3 vols. HTCNT IV/1-3 (New York: Crossroad, 1968–82) 1:75–104; Brown, *John* 1:lxxxvii–xcviii. It should be noted that Schnackenburg, who hesitatingly opts for John, the son of Zebedee, in the first German volume of his commentary, reproduced in English, has since shifted to a position akin to the one adopted in this paper. See Rudolf Schnackenburg, "On the Origin of the Fourth Gospel," in Pittsburgh Festival on the Gospels 1970, *Jesus and Man's Hope* (Pittsburgh: Pittsburgh Theological Seminary, 1970) 233–46. Like Schnackenburg, Brown moved away from the identification of the Beloved Disciple with the son of Zebedee to a position closer to the one espoused here. See Raymond E. Brown, *The Community of the Beloved Disciple. The Life, Loves and Hates of an Individual Church in New Testament Times* (New York: Paulist, 1979) 31–34.

[9] Francis J. Moloney, *The Gospel of John.* SP 4 (Collegeville: The Liturgical Press, 1998) 6–9.

[10] See on this the contributions of Raymond E. Brown: "'And the Lord Said'? Biblical Reflections on Scripture as the Word of God," *TS* 42 (1981) 3–19; idem, "The Meaning of the Bible," *TD* 28 (1980) 305–20.

2. "ABOUT SACRAMENTS"

This is the point of greatest difficulty in all discussions of sacraments and sacramentality in the Fourth Gospel. Yet despite the fact that our various ecclesial and theological traditions have wide-reaching differences in their understanding of "sacrament," we could all gather around a general definition positing that sacraments are intimately associated with "life" and the communication of the divine life, a participation already "in the triumphant eschatological salvation promised by God through Christ as his Word, and wrought by God through Christ as the incarnate Son and mediator."[11] Obviously this notion is never explicitly spelled out in the New Testament, as a sacramental theology took centuries to evolve and is, of course, still unfolding in our pilgrim Church. The word "sacrament" comes to us from the Pauline word μυστήριον, picked up by the second-century Fathers in their attempts to forge a theology of the sacraments[12] and translated into the Latin version of the New Testament as *sacramentum*.[13]

It is difficult for us to see the New Testament, and especially the highly symbolic language of the Fourth Gospel, unburdened of our rich tradition of sign and symbol, so closely associated with our sacramental life in the Church. Yet we must be aware from the outset that for the Fourth Gospel all Jesus' activity and preaching, especially the notion of glory and glorification, so important to this gospel (see, for example, 7:39; 8:54; 11:4; 12:23, 28; 13:31-32; 14:13; 15:8; 16:14; 17:1, 4, 5, 10), is the communication of a life-giving power. Sandra Schneiders has written eloquently on this crucial feature of the Fourth Gospel.[14] Tracing "sacrament" in the

---

[11] Burkhard Neunheuser, "Sacraments," *Sacramentum Mundi. An Encyclopedia of Theology.* 6 vols. (New York: Herder & Herder, 1970) 5:378.

[12] For full details see G. W. H. Lampe, ed., *A Patristic Greek Lexicon* (Oxford: Clarendon Press, 1961) 891–93, especially section F, where reference is made to Cyril, Theodotus, Clement of Alexandria, Dionysius, and Serapion from the early centuries, who used the expression μυστήριον in the sense of *sacramentum:* "revelation of divine activity."

[13] The word *sacramentum* originally meant an oath, especially a soldier's oath of allegiance. This can still be traced in early Christian literature. See, for example, Tertullian, *Ad Martyres* 3. On this see "Sacrament," in Frank L. Cross and Elizabeth A. Livingstone, eds., *The Oxford Dictionary of the Christian Church* (2nd ed. Oxford: Oxford University Press, 1974) 1218–19.

[14] See Sandra M. Schneiders, "History and Symbolism in the Fourth Gospel," in Martinus de Jonge, ed., *L'Evangile de Jean. Sources, redaction, théologie.* BETL 44 (Gembloux: Duculot, 1977) 371–76; eadem, "Symbolism and the Sacramental Principle in the Fourth Gospel," in Pius-Ramon Tragan, ed., *Segni e Sacramenti nel Vangelo di Giovanni.* Studia Anselmiana 66; Sacramentum 3 (Rome:

Fourth Gospel in this wider sense does not call for a search for criteria: "Ultimately, the sacramental principle in the Fourth Gospel is Jesus, manifesting himself in the Church, who experiences and bears witness in and by her own history to her divine filiation in the Spirit."[15] I hope to return briefly to this issue at the end of my paper, but, as Sandra Schneiders fully appreciates,[16] this argument in no way annuls the validity of our quest. Are there descriptions of events from the story of the life of Jesus, as it is told by the Fourth Evangelist, that clearly indicate the practice and theology of a sacramental life, apart from the evangelist's seeming conviction that the very existence of the Johannine community as the continuing presence of Jesus' sonship in history made the community as such in some way sacramental?[17]

As I have already indicated, there are *many* scholars who would reply positively to that question. The departure point for a widespread understanding of sacramental references in the Fourth Gospel is found in the evidence that the early Church had practices that later tradition identified as sacramental. The synoptic tradition and Paul carry words of institution, and even though they can be reduced to two basic traditions they show that these words of Jesus, supposedly uttered on the night before he died, have had a considerable history in the life of various Christian communities before they were eventually inserted into their present contexts in the New Testament literature. The Pauline tradition (1 Cor 11:24; see also Luke 22:19) carries a command that may have come from liturgical practices: "Do this in remembrance of me," yet in other ways this tradition preserves the original setting of a meal.[18] While there is no command to repeat the action, the setting

---

Editrice Anselmiana, 1977) 221–35; eadem, "The Foot Washing (John 13:1-20): An Experiment in Hermeneutics," *CBQ* 43 (1981) 76–92.

[15] Schneiders, "Symbolism and the Sacramental Principle," 235.

[16] See especially Schneiders, "The Foot Washing (John 13:1-20)," 81–82.

[17] Xavier Léon-Dufour has argued for a deeper appreciation of two levels of understanding for a proper evaluation of the Fourth Gospel. He interprets the cleansing and the sign of the Temple, the dialogue with Nicodemus and John 6 *at the level of Jesus* in a non-sacramental way, and then argues *that the risen Lord present in the Spirit in his community* makes the *same texts* sacramental. See Xavier Léon-Dufour, "Towards a Symbolic Reading of the Fourth Gospel," *NTS* 27 (1980–81) 439–56. See especially p. 455: "The historical events call forth the mystery which sheds light upon it, but the mystery itself would peter out in pure imagination if it did not ceaselessly find its nourishment in the rich soil of time past."

[18] See further Francis J. Moloney, *A Body Broken for a Broken People. Eucharist in the New Testament.* (Revised ed. Peabody, Mass.: Hendrickson, 1997) 165–77.

within a meal has not been lost in the eucharistic practice behind the Markan tradition, repeated by Matthew (Mark 14:22-25; Matt 26:26-29).[19] The practice of baptism in the pre-Johannine churches is clearly indicated in the solemn closing words of the Matthean Jesus:

"Go therefore and make disciples of all nations, baptizing them in the name of the Father and of the Son and of the Holy Spirit" (Matt 28:19).[20]

If there is sufficient evidence to show that pre-Johannine Christianity celebrated *at least* Eucharist and baptism in its various forms of early Christian worship, it seems logical that the author of the Fourth Gospel might also show that these sacraments had their basis in the words and works of Jesus.[21] To affirm this much, it appears to me, is correct. Here I am in general agreement with those scholars who see regular references to the sacraments in John, including the celebrated but contentious claims of Oscar Cullmann. But from this starting point Cullmann's tracing hidden references to the sacramental revelation of the μυστήριον of God at every turn as the *key* to an understanding of the gospel as a whole is, in my opinion, carrying a basic truth too far.[22]

---

[19] For a lucid presentation of this case see Joachim Jeremias, "The Words of Institution," in Patrick McGoldrick, ed., *Understanding the Eucharist. Papers of the Maynooth Union Summer School 1968* (Dublin: Gill and Macmillan, 1969) 18–28. Still a classic in all these discussions is the same author's *The Eucharistic Words of Jesus* (London: SCM, 1966).

[20] There is universal agreement among contemporary scholars that Matt 28:16-20 is central to an understanding of the Matthean vision of his church and its mission. See, for example, Wolfgang Trilling, *Das Wahre Israel. Studien zur Theologie des Matthäus-Evangeliums.* SANT 10 (3rd ed. Munich: Kösel, 1964) 21–51; John P. Meier, *Law and History in Matthew's Gospel. A Redactional Study of Mt. 5,17-48.* AnBib 71 (Rome: Biblical Institute Press, 1976) 25–40; W. D. Davies and Dale C. Allison Jr., *A Critical and Exegetical Commentary on the Gospel According to Saint Matthew.* 3 vols. ICC (Edinburgh: T & T Clark, 1988–97) 3:676–91. See p. 687: "The grand denouement, so consonant with the spirit of the whole Gospel because so full of resonances with earlier passages, is, despite its terseness, almost a compendium of Matthean theology."

[21] On this see Léon-Dufour, "Towards a Symbolic Reading of the Fourth Gospel" (n. 17 above).

[22] Oscar Cullmann, *Early Christian Worship.* SBT 10 (London: SCM, 1953). For his theological and exegetical argument for the second element of his position, which does make some very valid points to which we shall eventually return, see pp. 38–59 (especially 47–50). His argument swivels around the important conclusion on p. 56: "The implicit assumption of this Gospel is that the historical events, as here presented, contain in themselves, besides what is immediately

To cite Brown's comment on Cullmann's position: "In fact, he often seems to fall back on the principle that since a passage could have been understood sacramentally, it was intended sacramentally."[23]

This position, and the various scholars who follow it (Alf Corell, Bruce Vawter, Paul Niewalda, Louis Bouyer, David M. Stanley),[24] has, as I have mentioned, a solidly-based point of departure: the positive indications of pre-Johannine literature that a variety of forms of sacramental life were part of early Christian worship.[25] We should notice, however, that the only *firmly established evidence* we have for this sacramental life relates to baptism and Eucharist.

Of course the pro-sacramentalists have not had it all their own way. The most serious opposition has come from one of the outstanding New Testament scholars of the twentieth century, Rudolf Bultmann. Bultmann's central argument is that the Fourth Gospel was originally written as an anti-sacramental document, and he can immediately point to the complete absence of words of institution and of any command to baptize in this gospel. He has a wide following among fellow German scholars (for example, Eduard Schweizer, Helmut Koester, and Eduard Lohse) and also, in subsequent years, among North American scholars. Only a minority would claim that the Fourth Gospel is "anti"-sacramental, but some would suggest that it was non-sacramental. There is an important difference between polemics and absence. For Bultmann it would be foreign to John's theological vision to present a human "cultic place" where one could have some sort of union with Christ. The Fourth Evangelist was only interested in a personal union with Jesus through a commitment based purely on a loss of self (and thus the gaining of authenticity) that comes about in a radical commitment of faith to the fact that God is made known in the scandal of the Word (the *daß* of the proclamation, and not the *was*).[26] Even Bultmann,

---

perceptible, references to further facts of salvation with which these once-for-all key events are bound up."

[23] Brown, "The Johannine Sacramentary," 55.

[24] See the references in nn. 4 and 5 above for further discussion and details.

[25] See Cullmann, *Early Christian Worship* 7–36 for his analysis of what he calls the "basic characteristics" of that worship. He is over-optimistic, and many scholars would argue against some of his firm historical conclusions because they seem to be based on fragile evidence. For a better assessment see Ferdinand Hahn, *The Worship of the Early Church.* Translated by David E. Green (Philadelphia: Fortress, 1973).

[26] See Rudolf Bultmann, *Theology of the New Testament.* 2 vols. (London: SCM, 1955) 2:70–92.

however, would admit that there are three places in the gospel where the sacraments of baptism and Eucharist are explicitly mentioned:

John 3:5: "no one can enter the kingdom of God without being born of water and Spirit."

John 6:51c-58: There are apparent eucharistic possibilities in almost every verse. The main ones are:

v. 51c: "the bread that I will give for the life of the world is my flesh."
v. 53: "unless you eat (φαγεῖν is used) the flesh of the Son of Man and drink his blood, you have no life in you."
v. 54: "Those who eat (τρώγειν is used)[27] my flesh and drink my blood have eternal life."
v. 56: "Those who eat (τρώγειν is used) my flesh and drink my blood abide in me, and I in them."

John 19:34: The blood and water flowing from the pierced side of the crucified Christ, especially in light of 1 John 5:7-8: "There are three that testify: the Spirit and the water and the blood, and these three agree."

But for Bultmann not one of these passages belongs to the original gospel as the evangelist originally compiled it. They have all been added by what Bultmann calls an "ecclesiastical redactor."[28] In simple terms, he argues that these clearly sacramental passages have been added to an anti-sacramental gospel at a later stage in order to make it conform to the life and practice of the "greater Church."

We must be careful not to ridicule these suggestions. There are internal difficulties and tensions within the Fourth Gospel that need explanation. In John 6 there appears to be a contradiction in the positive use of the word "flesh" in vv. 51, 52, 53, 54, 55, and 56 and the negative use of the word in v. 63: "It is the spirit that gives life; the flesh is useless." Bultmann's source theory and his allocation of all sacramental material to the conservative hand of an ecclesiastical redactor may not, in the

---

[27] There is a commonly used verb available to speak of the human process of eating: ἐσθίειν and its aorist form φαγεῖν. The verb τρώγειν is normally used in contexts where stress is given to the physical "munching" or "crunching" of food. It is more commonly used of animal feeding than of human. On this see Ceslas Spicq, "ΤΡΩΓΕΙΝ est-il synonyme de ΦΑΓΕΙΝ et de᾽ ΕΣΘΙΕΙΝ dans le Nouveau Testament?" *NTS* 26 (1979–80) 414–19.

[28] See Bultmann, *Theology* 2:3–14; idem, *The Gospel of John: A Commentary.* Translated by G. R. Beasley-Murray (Oxford: Blackwells, 1971) 138–40; 300; 324–25; 325–28; 677–78. For an explanation of Bultmann's source theory see Moloney, *The Gospel of John* 85–86.

end, provide a satisfactory solution to the literary and theological tensions that abound in this gospel,[29] but they do take us back to a point made earlier: this gospel was not written overnight. It had a long history within the life and faith experience of a concrete Christian community. I am prepared to accept that the sacramental passages in 3:5, 6:51c-58, and 19:34 came into the Johannine tradition late rather than early, but I see no need to omit them from an authentic interpretation of the Johannine gospel as we now have it. Raymond E. Brown again summarized my position well when he wrote:

> The recognition that some of the explicit Sacramental references belong to the final redaction does not mean any acceptance of the theory that the original Gospel was non-Sacramental or anti-Sacramental. It is a question of seeing different degrees of sacramentality in the work of the evangelist and that of the final redactor.[30]

The two opposing positions I have just outlined show different methods of approach and different criteria. From Cullmann we must learn that the gospel as a whole is the life story of Jesus, and that there is often a subtle use of that life story *from the past* to root community practice *of the present* in his life. From Bultmann, however, we must also learn that the gospel may reflect a long and perhaps troubled se-

---

[29] Two important recent books on the Fourth Gospel have their starting point in an appreciation of Bultmann's approach to literary and theological tensions in the gospel. In the end each of these scholars parts ways with Bultmann, but this contemporary recognition of his asking the right questions tells of his ongoing significance to New Testament scholarship. See John Ashton, *Understanding the Fourth Gospel* (Oxford: Oxford University Press, 1991), and Paul N. Anderson, *The Christology of the Fourth Gospel: Its Unity and Disunity in the Light of John 6*. WUNT 2nd ser. 78 (Tübingen: Mohr; Valley Forge, Pa.: Trinity Press International, 1996).

[30] And, I would add, the Spirit-filled journey of a community behind all the stages of development! For the citation see Brown, *John* 1:cxii. It is here that I would differ from the suggestions of Léon-Dufour, "Towards a Symbolic Reading." Ignoring all the recent work done on the Johannine community and its journey of faith, he insists, for example, that 3:5 and 6:53-58 would make perfect sense to a Jewish audience as they stand, and that there are no indications in the text itself (e.g., introduction of "water" into 3:5) to show a growing sacramental awareness within the Johannine community. See pp. 449–54. In the light of a more contemporary understanding of the developing theological awareness of the Johannine community I would argue for a growing awareness, reflected in a growing text. In the more than thirty years since Brown wrote his commentary and the almost twenty years since I first wrote this study both of us became less certain that we could distinguish between the evangelist and the redactor!

ries of internal and external conflicts, producing a gospel of extraordinary christological and ecclesiological complexity. I would like, now, to steer a middle course, offering four criteria for the discovery of sacramental teaching in the Fourth Gospel. The first two of these criteria are well-established and widely used. They are somewhat "external" to the material. They attempt to provide some reliable "rule of thumb" by which the exegete may work. In many ways these are rather "negative" criteria, and I suppose there is a danger that some important material will escape them. However, I believe that this is a sounder way to start an investigation, since it is possible that, once we establish a firmly based "minimum," more material might come to light because of its close contacts with that minimum.

The first criterion must be a rigorous search for elements in the text itself indicating that the author is referring to some form of sacramental ritual and symbol. For example, in John 3:5 there is the explicit reference to a "rebirth," the use of the word "water," and the idea of "entering the kingdom of God," expanding on the earlier statement in 3:3 about "seeing the kingdom of God." The same cannot be said, for example, of the curing of the paralytic in John 5:1-8. In fact, the restoration of the man (a positive element in itself) is not effected through water, but independently of it, simply at the word of Jesus: "Stand up, take your mat and walk" (v. 8). The tradition at the pool was that the water would heal (see v. 7). Jesus transcends that tradition and heals by the power of his word. The sequel to the miracle shows no further understanding or life of faith in the cured man; in fact, he appears to be extraordinarily obtuse. This lack of elements within the text itself makes a baptismal understanding of John 5 most unlikely.[31] This becomes particularly clear when one looks to the curing of the man born blind in John 9, a story in many ways parallel to the cure in 5:1-8. Here the miracle is effected by contact with water at the pool of Siloam, which the evangelist then further explains as meaning "Sent" (v. 7). The cure is followed by a gradual movement to theological sight and light as the series of interrogations of the man leads him through a journey of confessions of faith:[32]

- To his friends he says: "The man called Jesus" worked a miracle (9:11).
- To the Pharisees he says: "He is a prophet" (v. 17).

---

[31] For a study of John 5, with detailed bibliography, see Moloney, *Son of Man* 68–86.

[32] For further detail see ibid. 142–59.

- Under further interrogation from the Pharisees he retorts: "If this man were not *from God*" (v. 33).
- Finally, when Jesus seeks him out he is led to the fullness of sight: "'Do you believe in the Son of Man?' He answered, 'And who is he, *sir*? Tell me, so that I may believe in him.' Jesus said to him, 'You have seen him, and the one speaking with you is he.' He said, '*Lord*, I believe.' And he worshiped him" (vv. 35-38).[33]

The same explicit internal evidence can be found in the texts we have already mentioned several times: the eucharistic section in John 6 and the blood and water flowing from the pierced side of the cruci- fied Jesus. There may be several others (the footwashing of 13:1-20; Jesus as the source of living water in 7:38) that, when subjected to de- tailed analysis, provide internal evidence of an original sacramental meaning.[34]

This leads us to our second criterion, which must be applied in close association with the first: the use of certain passages in the liturgical practice, the literature, and the art of the early post-New Testament Church. The most significant use of this criterion has been by a Protes- tant scholar, Paul Niewalda, who argued that, given the internal diffi- culties and the never-ending disputes among scholars, we must accept that when Johannine symbolism is used by the early Church for its sacramental life and reflection we have every right to push that mean- ing back into the intention of the evangelist himself.[35] Care must be taken here. While this is a valid criterion, the argument must run in the other direction. If we find that a passage has the internal qualities of a sacramental message, and then we find that the early Church has clearly used it in this way, we have certainly made more firm the pos- sible suggestions of the text itself. Great service has been done in this investigation by the remarkable commentary of Sir Edwyn Hoskyns, especially in his investigation of the early Church's use of John 9 and

---

[33] The movement from κύριος ("sir") to Κύριος ("Lord") in v. 38 indicates a decisive step into a public confession of faith.

[34] On this see the method advocated by Rudolf Schnackenburg, "Die Sakra- mente im Johannesevangelium," in Joseph Coppens et al., eds., *Congressus Bib- licus Internationalis Catholicus de Re Biblica.* 2 vols. (Gembloux: Duculot, 1959) 2:235–54. He suggests that we first study the clearly sacramental passages and establish from them possible internal contacts with the more obscure texts. For my pursuit of this evidence in John 13 see Francis J. Moloney, "A Sacramental Interpretation of John 13:1-38," *CBQ* 53 (1991) 237–56.

[35] Paul Niewalda, *Sakramentssymbolik im Johannesevangelium? Eine exegetisch- historische Studie* (Limburg: Lahn, 1958).

13.[36] This is an area where more research is needed. It appears to me that it will be of great assistance for a deeper understanding of Johannine sacramentalism if used in close connection with the hints and indications that come to us from our close study of the text itself.

These two criteria or "rules of thumb" could be regarded as an answer to the question: why does John say these things? A careful study of the use of language and the context within which it is used leads us to some firm conclusions about the sacramental or non-sacramental nature of certain Johannine passages. When we can trace these same passages into the sacramental life and liturgy of the early Church we have a further indication that we are dealing with sacramental material. However, it is not enough to look to the words and context, asking: "why does John say these things?" We must go a step farther and ask: "why does John say these things *in this way*?" It strikes me that the most obvious sacramental material in the Fourth Gospel has been framed in a particular way. This needs to be investigated. Then one might further ask what caused the use of a consistent rhetorical pattern when referring to sacramental material.

One of the reasons given for the exclusion of the clearly sacramental passages of 3:5, 6:51c-58, and 19:34 is that the passages are powerfully anti-docetic. In simple terms, this means that the gospel as a whole tends to stress the spiritual character of the faith commitment, and the later redactors have added passages that insist upon the tangible, physical nature of the flesh and blood of Jesus and the concrete reality of the ecclesial community. An over-exaggeration of the "spiritual" message of the Fourth Gospel could lead to a position according to which the story was being read as if Jesus only "appeared" to be human. This would not do, and it had to be combated. This so-called anti-docetic tendency can be identified in all three major sacramental passages. They do read as, and must have sounded, somewhat polemical:

3:5: *No one* can enter the kingdom of God *without* being born of water and Spirit.
6:53: *Unless* you eat the flesh of the Son of Man and drink his blood, you have *no life* in you.
9:34: The telling of the flowing water and blood from the side of the pierced Jesus is followed by a powerful insistence from the evangelist: "He who saw this has testified so that you also may believe. His testimony is true, and he knows that he tells the truth" (v. 35).

---

[36] Edwyn C. Hoskyns (ed. Francis N. Davey), *The Fourth Gospel* (2nd ed. London: Faber and Faber, 1947) 363–65; 443–46. It is unfortunate that many contemporary Johannine scholars no longer consult this stimulating commentary, which sometimes reads like the poetry of the text it examines.

Contemporary Johannine scholarship has been highlighted by a growth of interest in the christological experience of this community. Unlike the great commentaries from the first half of this century, which reached their zenith in the work of Bultmann, we can no longer speak of a basic gospel into which anti-docetic elements have been inserted. These elements, lying side by side in this gospel, reflect a long history, and the fascinating studies of that history cannot delay us here.[37] However, as an example (and there are points where I would disagree),[38] I offer a summary of the contribution of a scholar whose name has appeared frequently in these pages: Raymond E. Brown.[39] His speculations are found in a book that makes full use of both the gospel and the epistles to rediscover "the Community of the Beloved Disciple."[40] This is a fascinating and easy book to read, but careful scholarship and a close contact with contemporary literature is found on every page. The book reads so well, in fact, that one could be tempted to think that scholarship, after a series of hypotheses, had at last found the answer. Brown would be unhappy if we were to fall into this temptation.[41] He argues that four stages of development can be traced: before the gospel, when the gospel was written, when the letters were written, and finally, after the letters. Through these four stages he rediscovers the following experiences of the community of the Beloved Disciple:

1. The original group, beginning within the circle of ex-disciples of John the Baptist, shows a typically early Christian "low" christology. Important at this stage is the figure of the Beloved Disciple, an ex-disciple of the Baptist, a follower of Jesus from the start, but not one of the Twelve. As I mentioned earlier, this is a change from his earlier understanding of the author of the gospel.[42] This out-

---

[37] For an earlier survey and evaluation of this direction in Johannine studies see Francis J. Moloney, "Revisiting John," *ScrB* 11 (1980) 9–15.

[38] Ibid. 11–13

[39] See my remarks on Raymond E. Brown in the Preface.

[40] Although he had already made a series of significant contributions to this discussion in scholarly journals his argument is most easily found in his book, *The Community of the Beloved Disciple.* For full details see n. 8 above. This study has been further developed in his large-scale commentary on the Johannine letters: Raymond E. Brown, *The Epistles of John.* AB 30 (New York: Doubleday, 1982) 47–115.

[41] As he remarks: "I warn the reader that my reconstruction claims at most probability; and if sixty percent of my detective work is accepted, I shall be happy indeed" (Brown, *The Community of the Beloved Disciple* 7).

[42] See above, and especially n. 8.

standing historical personality, the founding father of the community, serves as a link between the historical Jesus and the Johannine community.

2. After the admission of Samaritan and other "anti-Temple" groups, a conflict with "the Jews" begins (see 4:1-42). This leads eventually to the development of a "higher" christology, especially in the use of Εγώ εἰμι in an absolute sense and the idea of pre-existence. Both of these elements come from the Jewish literary and theological background of the community but were applied only to God and to Torah. The Johannine community applies them to Jesus.

3. As the gospel is written the community takes a final stance against those whom they would regard as nonbelievers: "the world," "the Jews," and those who still adhere to the baptism of John the Baptist. Also included in the community's list of "nonbelievers" were some groups who, in other circles, would have been regarded as believers. Brown calls them "crypto-Christians." They were Jews who believed in Jesus as the Messiah but remained in the synagogue. They were also members of Jewish Christian communities who would not confess the "high" Johannine christology. Finally, these "crypto-Christians," for the Johannine community, also came from what might be termed "the greater Church," the Christians who followed the less charismatic line of James and the Jerusalem party.[43]

The community, having taken its stance over against those "outside" their ranks, now began to experience serious internal struggles. These divisions grew from possible but conflicting interpretations of the Johannine gospel. A careful study of the letters shows that there were two groups involved, and both seemed to be using the gospel, but in different ways. In the areas of christology, ethics, eschatology, and pneumatology the letters show a historicizing, more conservative approach than the gospel. The author(s) of the letters are moving in the direction of "the greater Church," while the "opponents" are accused of de-historicizing, eliminating all the obligations that ethics, eschatology, and a true life in the Spirit must produce. They are moving in the direction of what was later known as docetic Gnosticism.[44]

---

[43] There is increasing contemporary interest in (and a growing appreciation for) James and the Jerusalem church. For a recent comprehensive study see John Painter, *Just James. The Brother of Jesus in History and Tradition.* Studies in Personalities of the New Testament (Columbia: University of South Carolina Press, 1997).

[44] See Francis J. Moloney, *James to Jude.* The Peoples' Bible Commentary (Oxford: Bible Reading Fellowship, 1999) 164-67.

4. The final moment in the history of the community is its separation and dissolution. The group behind the letters merges with the greater Church, as can be seen from Ignatius of Antioch (c.110): Johannine christology has been accepted but a Paraclete-dominated ecclesiology and ethics has been lost. The "opponents" take the gospel and their interpretation of it into Gnosticism, as can be seen from the later use of the Fourth Gospel by the Gnostic sects.

In this kind of blunt summary the skill of Brown's analysis or, as he himself describes it, his "detective work" is lost. However, I hope I have presented an accurate synthesis of the main lines of his argument, an indication of how contemporary Johannine scholarship has become sensitive to the lives, loves, and experiences of the community itself in an attempt to understand that community's gospel.

While discussing Brown's contribution I mentioned a group called "crypto-Christians," describing some of them as Jews who believed but remained in the Synagogue: Jewish Christians who would not take the step "across the street" into the Johannine community (see 12:42). Here, it appears to me, we are in touch with the reason for the polemical nature of the most obviously sacramental passages. Again I would like to dwell briefly on the situation in the life of the Johannine church that created such a situation.

Along with many contemporary scholars I see the consistent Johannine conflict with "the Jews" as the clearest indication of "when" the gospel was written, and one of the main reasons "why" it was written.[45] Until quite recent times it has been almost axiomatic to link the emergence of the Fourth Gospel with the formal expulsion of Christians from synagogue practice. Faced with the perseverance of a sect in its midst that confessed that Jesus of Nazareth was the Christ, the synagogue at Jamnia, which became the legal and intellectual center of Rabbinic Judaism after the destruction of Jerusalem in 70 C.E., called upon all faithful Jews to make a public condemnation of the followers of Jesus. To do this they inserted a "benediction" (called the *Birkat haminim*, i.e., "the blessing of the heretics") into one of their important

---

[45] The following argument, briefly presented here, has been accepted, for example, by C. K. Barrett, *St John* 127–28; Brown, *John* 1:lxxiv–lxxv; Hoskyns, *The Fourth Gospel* 360–62; Lindars, *John* 147; Siegfried Schulz, *Das Evangelium nach Johannes*. NTD 4 (Göttingen, Vandenhoeck und Ruprecht, 1972) 144–45. It has been firmly rejected by John A.T. Robinson, *Redating the New Testament* (London, SCM, 1976) 292–98. See, on this discussion, Francis J. Moloney, "The Fourth Gospel's Presentation of Jesus as 'the Christ' and J. A. T. Robinson's 'Redating,'" *DRev* 95 (1977) 239–53.

synagogue prayers, the "Eighteen Benedictions" *(shemoneh ʿesreh)*. As we have no access to the original form of the blessing, it is impossible to be certain about its exact form. According to modern reconstructions from the available sources it ran something like this: "For apostates may there be no hope, and may the Nazarenes and the heretics suddenly perish."[46] Everyone attending the Synagogue had to pray this prayer loudly, and thus it became a sort of *shibboleth.* Anyone who failed to accept this "blessing" could be identified as a follower of Jesus, the Christ, and was to be turned out of the synagogue. It is difficult to determine the exact date of the decision taken at Jamnia, but the Eighteen Benedictions, their order, and the *Birkat ha-minim* are associated with Rabbi Gamaliel II (*b. Ber.* 28b-29a); thus sometime after 85 seems to be most likely.

There has always been some difficulty in determining how rapidly this practice was implemented by the synagogues of the diaspora. This doubt has led, in the twenty years since this essay was originally written, to increasing scholarly concern regarding the relationship between the events that might have taken place at Jamnia in the mid '80s of the first Christian century and the emerging Johannine community. There are some who doubt that the events credited to Rabbi Gamaliel II ever happened, or that, if they did, they had anything to do with "the Nazarenes."[47] I am now prepared to accept that there may be no link between the formal introduction of the *Birkat ha-minim* into the Eighteen Benedictions and the emergence of the Fourth Gospel. But the text of the gospel makes it clear that *at least for the members of the Johannine community* a point of no return had been reached. They had to declare themselves for Jesus as the Christ, and in doing so lose all formal contact with Judaism. The experience of the Johannine community may have been a very local experience, but John 9:22, 12:42, and 16:2 make

[46] The original wording of this "blessing" cannot be exactly determined, as it has understandably come down to us in various corrupted forms. For the recensions (Palestinian and Babylonian), see Str-B 4:211–14. On the question of the expulsion from the synagogue see 293–333. For the history of these benedictions and the conflict the insertion of the benediction against the heretics *(Birkat ha-minim)* caused, see George Foote Moore, *Judaism in the First Centuries of the Christian Era.* 2 vols. (Cambridge: Harvard University Press, 1958) 1:289–96. For his reconstruction of the twelfth benediction, which I have followed, see p. 292 n. 8.

[47] For a good survey of this discussion see Pieter W. van der Horst, "The Birkat ha-minim in Recent Research," *ExpTim* 105 (1993–94) 363–68. Most recently see the thorough presentation by Michael Labahn, *Jesus als Lebensspender. Untersuchungen zu einer Geschichte der johanneischen Tradition anhand ihrer Wundergeschichte.* BZNW 98 (Berlin: Walter de Gruyter, 1999) 30–41.

it clear that this is no simple banning from the Synagogue (see below).[48] However local the ban may have been, the members of the Johannine community were expelled from the heritage of Israel.[49]

It is often argued that John 9 reflects the drama of the Jewish-Christian church subsequent to the decision of the Synagogue at Jamnia.[50] The parents of the man born blind refused to answer the questions of the Jewish authorities about how their son was given his sight "because they were afraid of the Jews; for the Jews had already agreed that anyone who confessed Jesus to be the Messiah would be put out of the synagogue" (9:22). It is important to notice that the Greek behind the innocuous English "be put out of the synagogue" is ἀποσυνάγωγος γένηται. This term is found only in the Fourth Gospel (see also 12:42 and 16:2). When the man himself encounters the Jews, he claims: "If this man were not from God, he could do nothing" (9:33), and he is "driven out" (v. 34: ἐξέβαλον αὐτὸν ἔξω). Once a link is made between this event reported in John 9 and a decisive break between official Judaism and Johannine Christians (however local this breakdown might have been), other passages in the gospel take on a new sense:

> 12:42: "Nevertheless many, even of the authorities, believed in him. But because of the Pharisees they did not confess it, for fear that they would be put out of the synagogue (ἀποσυνάγωγοι γένωνται)."
> 16:2: "They will put you out of the synagogues (ἀποσυναγώγους ποιήσουσιν ὑμᾶς). Indeed, an hour is coming when those who kill you will think that by doing so they are offering worship to God."

In both of these passages the term ἀποσυνάγωγος, found only in the Fourth Gospel, again appears. Barnabas Lindars has described the

---

[48] See Judith M. Lieu, *Image and Reality. The Jews in the World of the Christians in the Second Century* (Edinburgh: T & T Clark, 1996), for a positive assessment of Jewish-Christian relationships in the second century. As the author acknowledges, the book suffers from its being a study of Christian sources. What the Jewish side of the debate looked like remains untold.

[49] Bultmann, *The Gospel of John* 555, commenting on 16:2, puts it well: "The period we are concerned with is that in which the Christian community is forced to free itself from association with the Synagogues, and thus to abandon the protection of a *religio licita*. It is a period which stretches approximately from Paul to Justin, and one cannot pinpoint it any more exactly than that." The response of the Fourth Gospel to this situation is particularly clear in John 5–10. On this see Francis J. Moloney, *Signs and Shadows. Reading John 5–12* (Minneapolis: Fortress, 1996).

[50] See, for example, J. Louis Martyn, *History and Theology in the Fourth Gospel* (2nd ed. Nashville: Abingdon, 1979) 24–62; Brown, *John* 1:380; Lindars, *John* 347.

situation well when he claims that John "speaks of discipleship in terms of the conditions with which his readers were familiar."[51] Lindars accepted the link with the *Birkat ha-minim*. But however local the breakdown between the Synagogue and the Johannine Christians may have been, his words suit the situation.[52]

It appears to me that a third criterion for determining sacramental material in the Johannine gospel should be its polemical tone. The Johannine community wanted to make it clear that to believe in Jesus meant more than to believe that he was the Messiah. The members of the synagogue who had come to believe that Jesus was the Messiah (see 12:42) had to do more than rest within the comfort of their traditional customs and way of life. Belief in the Johannine Jesus called for a crossing of the road from the synagogue through a public insertion of oneself into a new community. The public gestures *par excellence* would have been the reception of baptism as an "entry" into the community (see 3:5) and public participation in the eucharistic celebrations of the Johannine community (see 6:53-54). John W. Miller, in an unpublished Princeton doctoral dissertation, has put it well:

> The observance of baptism and eucharist suggest a worshiping community sharing in a cultic life. In view of John's understanding of the unity of the Church as a visible unity and his criticism of secret disciples, it is likely that the sacraments were important as a means by which believers identified themselves with the visible community of the Church.[53]

What a generation of scholars has taken as anti-docetic because of its polemical tone is not "anti" anything. It is an aggressive affirmation of the communitarian nature of the Johannine church, and the crucial role that baptism and Eucharist played in that community.[54]

[51] Lindars, *John* 347.

[52] See David Rensberger, *Johannine Faith and Liberating Community* (Philadelphia: Westminster, 1988) 26–27.

[53] John W. Miller, *The Concept of the Church in the Gospel according to John* (Diss. Princeton, 1976) 103. See also p. 98. Miller's suggestion, which I have developed here, needs more attention in this discussion.

[54] The *opposite* suggestion has been made by Kikuo Matsunaga, "Is John's Gospel Anti-Sacramental?" *NTS* 27 (1980–81) 516–24. Matsunaga also bases his contribution on the recent suggestions of Brown and Martyn. He argues that the Fourth Evangelist has eliminated certain synoptic passages (the baptism of Jesus and the words of institution) in a spiritualizing process. He did this so that the "dropouts" from the Johannine community would see that, above all, they should have been primarily committed to the high christology developed within the community and the subsequent "Word" of Jesus. It is a question of first things first, but not of anti-sacramentalism.

We come now to our final suggestion, and I can only outline another criterion that could assume major proportions in further discussions of sacramental material in the Fourth Gospel. It was, I believe, the most important reason for the inclusion of such material in the Johannine story. We must again fix attention firmly upon the situation of the Johannine community. Through the complexities of this gospel one can trace a central, consistent christological and ecclesiological message. A God who is love (1 John 4:8, 16) loved the world so much as to send his only Son (3:16-17). This Son, Jesus Christ, has a task (ἔργον) to bring to completion (see especially 4:34 and 17:4, along with the many passages in the gospel that use words coming from τέλος). That task is to make God known, so that human beings can come to eternal life (17:2-3). Jesus performs this task in many ways, through his discourses (λόγος and ῥήματα), through his "signs" (σημεῖα), and consummately through the supreme act of love when he is "lifted up" on the cross (see 3:13-14; 8:28; 12:32; 13:1; 15:13; 19:30). Jesus not only "speaks" and "gives signs" of his oneness with a Father who is love (see 10:30, 38). He loves in a consummate fashion.[55] Because this is the case Jesus is the unique revealer of God (see especially 1:18; 3:13; 6:46; 8:38), and thus the Fourth Evangelist demands that believers "look upon" Jesus to see the revelation of the Father. This is promised in the programmatic 1:51: "you *will see* heaven opened and the angels of God ascending and descending upon the Son of Man," and repeated like an antiphon through the whole gospel (see 1:18; 4:45; 5:37; 6:2, 36; 8:38, 57; 9:37; 11:40; 14:7, 9; 15:24; 16:16, 17; 19:22, 35), climaxing in the final words of the scene at the cross: "They will *look on* the one whom they have pierced" (19:37).[56]

This is all very well, but for the Johannine community, as the first Christian century drew to a close, Jesus was no longer present! It is clear that the "absence" of the physical revelation of the glory of God in the person of Jesus posed a problem for the community. This is

[55] This is involved in John's continual use of verbs and nouns that go back to the word τέλος. Especially significant are 13:1 (εἰς τέλος) and 19:30 (τετέλεσται). Sandra Schneiders has long insisted that we should look more closely at this feature of the gospel. See especially her article, "Symbolism and the Sacramental Principle in the Fourth Gospel," 221–35. See now my study, "'God so loved the world.' The Jesus of John's Gospel," in this volume, pp. 167–80.

[56] This is made clear by the continual significant use of the verb ὁράω. On this see Cor Traets, *Voir Jésus et le Père en Lui selon l'Evangile de Saint Jean*. Analecta Gregoriana 159 (Rome: Gregorian University Press, 1967), and Moloney, *Son of Man* 155.

handled in various ways, through the teaching on the Paraclete (14:16-17, 25, 26; 15:26; 16:7-11, 13-15), [57] and Jesus' assurance of his continued presence and care throughout the last discourse (especially 13:31–14:31) and in his final prayer (especially 17:9-19). As the gospel comes to a close Jesus' final words address those who, living in the in-between time, will believe without seeing. The gospel was written to generate and support such life-giving belief (20:29-31).[58]

This theme was noticed and discussed in a fine article by Celestin Charlier over forty years ago. I would like to paraphrase the title of his article as my final criterion for tracing sacramental material in the Fourth Gospel: "The presence of the absent one."[59] It is here that the suggestions of Oscar Cullmann again become important. He too had noticed that a central issue in this gospel was to indicate that what was happening in the community's cult was a particular form of "remembering" (see 12:16; 14:26; 16:12).[60] While recognizing the value of this contribution, I would like to pursue it down a slightly different path. As one reads through the discourse of John 6:25-51b one hears again and again the theme spelled out most clearly in 6:40: "This is indeed the will of my Father, that all who see the Son and believe in him may have eternal life," and again in 6:46-48: "Not that anyone has seen the Father except the one who is from God; he has seen the Father. Very truly, I tell you, whoever believes has eternal life." One can sense an understandable reaction from an early Christian community faced with this teaching: "But where is he, that we may see him, and thus come to know the Father and possess eternal life?" The answer is given in 6:51c-58: in the broken bread and the poured wine of

---

[57] See Felix Porsch, *Pneuma und Wort. Ein exegetischer Beitrag zur Pneumatologie des Johannesevangeliums.* FTS 16 (Frankfurt: Josef Knecht, 1974). John Painter has taken up the suggestions of Brown and Martyn to show a developing understanding of the Paraclete, evidenced in the development of the farewell discourse's use of the concept. See John Painter, "Glimpses of the Johannine Community in the Farewell Discourses," *AusBR* 28 (1980) 21–38. He has developed his argument further in his "The Farewell Discourses and the History of Johannine Christianity," *NTS* 27 (1980–81) 525–43.

[58] See Francis J. Moloney, *Glory not Dishonor. Reading John 13–21* (Minneapolis: Fortress, 1998) 175–81; idem, *The Gospel of John* 536–45.

[59] Celestin Charlier, "La présence dans l'absence (Jn 13,31–14,31)," *BVC* 2 (1953) 61–75. It is interesting to note that the same title has been taken up in a further study of the discourse by Secondo Migliasso, *La presenza dell'Assente. Saggio di analisi letterario-strutturale e di sintisi teologica di Gv. 13,31–14,31* (Rome: Pontificia Università Gregoriana, 1979).

[60] See Cullmann, *Early Christian Worship* 47–50.

their eucharistic celebrations. The Eucharist, for the Johannine community, was the presence of the absent one.[61]

The same technique is used in 19:34. The Passion account has culminated with the exaltation of Jesus as King on his cross (19:17-21). There he has founded his Church (19:25-27) and brought to perfection the task his Father had given him (19:28-30). That is the Johannine understanding of a past event, but how is it to become part of the experience of the Church now? The answer is found in 19:34 as the blood and water, the life-giving sacraments of Eucharist and baptism, are described as flowing down upon the nascent Church from the King lifted up on his throne.[62] It is in the sacraments of baptism and Eucharist that the Johannine church can find the presence of the absent one.

My reflections have already been lengthy, yet they remain an initial sketch of what could and should be said. I have limited most of my testing of these last two criteria to the universally accepted sacramental passages of 3:5, 6:51c-58, and 19:34. It is better to start with established material, to test the criteria there, and then move into areas that are not quite so clear . . . but that will be a task to be faced on some other occasion.[63]

---

[61] On this see Moloney, *Son of Man* 87–107; idem, "John 6 and the Celebration of the Eucharist," *DRev* 93 (1975) 243–51.

[62] See Edward Malatesta, "Blood and Water from the Pierced Side of Christ," in Tragan, ed., *Segni e Sacramenti nel Vangelo di Giovanni* 164–81. This is a well-documented study with a fine appendix on the patristic use of John 19:34 (see our second criterion) on pp. 179–81.

[63] This is a method advocated some years ago by Schnackenburg, "Die Sakramente im Johannesevangelium," 235–54 (see n. 34 above). Since writing the above I have pursued this agenda in a number of Johannine studies. See especially *Belief in the Word. Reading John 1–4* (Minneapolis: Fortress, 1993); *Signs and Shadows* (1996); *Glory not Dishonor* (1998); *The Gospel of John* (1998).

CHAPTER 6

JOHN 18:15-27:
A JOHANNINE VIEW OF THE CHURCH

The internal logic of John 18:15-27 has long been a problem. Why are the three denials of Peter (John 18:15-18 and 25-27) separated by the report of the Jewish interrogation of Jesus by Annas (18:17-24)? Mark and Matthew both report Peter's arrival at the house of Caiaphas (Mark 14:53-54; Matt 26:57-58) before Jesus' Jewish interrogation by Caiaphas (Mark 14:55-65; Matt 26:59-68). There is no mention of Annas, who was not the high priest,[1] and once they come to the report of Peter's denials all three are told in sequence (Mark 14:66-72; Matt

---

[1] On the historical problems involved in the author's use of Annas rather than Caiaphas see C. K. Barrett, *The Gospel according to St John* (2nd ed. London: S.P.C.K., 1978) 524–25. For M. W. G. Stibbe, *John as Storyteller. Narrative Criticism and the Fourth Gospel.* SNTSMS 73 (Cambridge: Cambridge University Press, 1992) 173, the trial before Annas is historical, coming directly from the witness of Lazarus, the Beloved Disciple. Better is Barrett's conclusion: "it is difficult to resist the conclusion that the trial narratives have been rewritten by John in order to bring out what, in his opinion, were the points at issue" (*St John* 525). See also Barnabas Lindars, *The Gospel of John.* NCB (London: Oliphants, 1972) 544–47. However, on the continuing use of ἀρχιερεύς for former high priests see Raymond E. Brown, *The Gospel According to John.* 2 vols. AB 29, 29a (New York: Doubleday, 1966–70) 2:820–21. For an exhaustive overall discussion of the issue see idem, *The Death of the Messiah. From Gethsemane to the Grave. A Commentary on the Passion Narratives in the Four Gospels.* 2 vols. ABRL (New York: Doubleday, 1994) 1:404–11.

26:69-75). Luke places Peter's arrival at the high priest's house and his betrayals before Caiaphas' interrogation of Jesus (Luke 22:54-62). There are some interesting contacts between the Markan, Lukan, and Johannine traditions,[2] but none of the synoptics sandwiches the so-called "Jewish trial" between the denials by Peter.[3]

Drowned in the oceans of ink that have been spilled in an attempt to reconstruct the historical events of Jesus' trials,[4] this feature of the Johannine narrative has been given scant attention.[5] The recent mono-

---

[2] These include the female doorkeeper, and particularly the kindling of a fire and, in Luke, Peter's presence among the people who had seized Jesus. See Mark 14:54; Luke 22:54-55; John 18:18. On this see Anton Dauer, *Die Passionsgeschichte im Johannesevangelium. Eine traditionsgeschichtliche und theologische Untersuching zu Joh 18,1–19,30.* SANT 30 (Munich: Kösel, 1972) 62–63, 91–99; Kevin Quast, *Peter and the Beloved Disciple. Figures for a Community in Crisis.* JSNTSup 32 (Sheffield: JSOT Press, 1989) 71–76; Brown, *Death of the Messiah* 1:78–79 (Mark), 87–88 (Luke), 418–19 (synoptic chart); Manfred Lang, *Johannes und die Synoptiker. Eine redaktionsgeschichtliche Analyse von Joh 18–20 vor dem markinischen und lukanischen Hintergrund.* FRLANT 182 (Göttingen: Vandenhoeck & Ruprecht, 1999) 86–115.

[3] Robert M. Fowler, *Let the Reader Understand. Reader-Response Criticism and the Gospel of Mark* (Minneapolis: Fortress, 1991) 143, claims that Mark 14:53-54, 55-65, 66-72 is an intercalation of the trial of Jesus within the denial of Peter, but this is very different from the Johannine use of these events. In Mark the scene is set in vv. 53-54, but all three denials (vv. 66-72) are told in sequence after Jesus' trial before the Sanhedrin (vv. 55-65). For a comparison of the variety of ways Peter's denials are reported across the gospels see Brown, *Death of the Messiah* 1:590–91.

[4] Some major studies, listed chronologically, are: Hans Lietzmann, "Der Prozess Jesu," in idem, *Kleine Schriften.* 2 vols. (Berlin: Akademie Verlag, 1958) 2:251–63 (original publication 1934); Josef Blinzler, *The Trial of Jesus: The Jewish and Roman Proceedings against Jesus Christ Described and Assessed from the Oldest Accounts.* Translated from the 2nd revised and enlarged ed. (Westminster, Md.: Newman, 1959); Adrian N. Sherwin-White, *Roman Society and Roman Law in the New Testament* (Oxford: Clarendon Press, 1963) 1–47; S. G. F. Brandon, *The Trial of Jesus of Nazareth* (London: B. T. Batsford, 1968); Pierre Benoit, *The Passion and Resurrection of Jesus Christ.* Translated by Benet Weatherhead (New York: Herder & Herder, 1969); David R. Catchpole, *The Trial of Jesus. A Study in the Gospels and Jewish Historiography from 1770 to the Present Day.* Studia post-Biblica 18 (Leiden: E. J. Brill, 1971); Paul Winter, *On the Trial of Jesus.* Studia Judaica 1. 2nd ed. revised and edited by T. Alec Burkill and Geza Vermes (Berlin and New York: Walter de Gruyter, 1974). For a complete list see Brown, *Death of the Messiah* 1:315–27.

[5] As Alv Kragerud, *Der Lieblingsjünger im Johannesevangelium: ein exegetischer Versuch* (Oslo: Osloer Universitätsverlag, 1959) 74 n. 39, comments: "Unser Text

graph by Kevin Quast, *Peter and the Beloved Disciple. Figures for a Community in Crisis*, devotes a chapter to this section of the Fourth Gospel,[6] but little attention is given to the splitting of the story of Peter's denials into two parts framing the Jewish interrogation. Quast's study of the denials pays no attention to Jesus' witness before Annas, although he rightly concludes, without analysis: "The fourth evangelist constructed his narrative in such a way as to convey the sense that Peter's denials of association with Jesus were simultaneous with Jesus' uncompromising defence of himself and his disciples before Annas. A dramatic contrast is created wherein Jesus denies nothing and Peter denies everything."[7] This may be true, but what of the reader's involvement in the story? Jeffrey L. Staley has argued that a deliberate rhetorical strategy is found here. The reader, who only recognizes Caiaphas as the ἀρχιερεύς (see 11:47-51), is led to believe that Caiaphas conducts the interrogation in vv. 19-23, only to find in v. 24 that it was Annas. The reader has been "victimized" by a subversive narrator and thus joins both Peter and the attendant who strikes Jesus in their "violent misunderstanding and denial." In this way the reader is led away from his or her own securities into deeper faith.[8] Staley correctly concentrates on the impact this strategy makes on the reader, but I hope to

---

scheint in der bisherigen Forschung allzu leichtfertig behandelt zu sein." [Our text appears to have been treated much too superficially in scholarship to date.] Dauer, *Die Passionsgeschichte*, devotes only pp. 247–49 to the Johannine meaning of 18:19-23, and pays no attention to the surrounding vv. 15-18, 24-27. Most recently see Stibbe, *John as Storyteller* 96–105, and the fine treatment by Lang, *Johannes und die Synoptiker* 86–115.

[6] Quast, *Peter and the Beloved Disciple* 71–99.

[7] Ibid. 97–98. On p. 76 Quast lists "The construction of the narrative around the interrogation of Jesus and the lack of any references to the passing of time" as sixth in a list of "potentially significant" features of the narrative, but his study does not develop this. See also Brown, *John* 2:842. Stibbe, *John as Storyteller* 97–99, sees 18:1-27 as marked by contrasts between Jesus and Peter at a primary level and the Beloved Disciple and Peter at a secondary level. He comments, without detailed analysis: "In both instances, the conduct of Jesus and the BD is paradigmatic and exemplary, whilst that of Peter is clearly misguided and colored by pathos" (p. 99). Brown, *Death of the Messiah* 1:623–24, claims that Peter's denials serve "as a foil for the behavior of another disciple who is never deflected from his following of Jesus" (p. 623). In this way the author addresses the disciples of the Johannine community. See also Lang, *Johannes und die Synoptiker* 100–103.

[8] Jeffrey L. Staley, "Subversive Narrator/Victimized Reader: A Reader Response Assessment of a Text-Critical Problem, John 18.12-24," *JSNT* 51 (1993) 91–98.

show that the relationship between the narrator and the reader is honest, and challenging.

There is something unique about the Johannine version of this part of Jesus' story that has led to suggestions that include rearrangement of the text, changes in his source made by the evangelist, uncertainties in the source itself, and editorial additions.[9] Already in ancient Christian interpretation the Sinaitic Syriac version brought v. 24 forward to make Caiaphas the interrogating high priest, and took Peter's three denials together.[10] My reading of John 18:15-27 approaches the text in its traditional order, with respect for the theological point of view of the author. We have to "reckon with his strong and individualistic shaping of the material."[11]

THE DISCIPLES IN JOHN 18:15-18

Between the report of Jesus in a garden with his friends (18:1-11) and the Jewish interrogation (vv. 15-17) Jesus is seized (v. 12) and led to the house of Annas (v. 13a). A link is made between Annas and Caiaphas to remind the reader that Jesus' death is not for himself but for the nation, and to gather into one the dispersed children of God (vv. 13b-14; see 11:49-52). The reader is next informed that two disciples followed Jesus (v. 15: ἠκολούθει δὲ τῷ Ἰησοῦ). Simon Peter is well known as a leading disciple (see 1:41-43; 6:8, 68-69; 13:6-9, 24, 36-38), and an anonymous disciple also appeared earlier in the narrative (see 1:37-42). There is some debate over the possible identification of "another disciple" with the Beloved Disciple.[12] "The other disciple" (with the definite article) appears in ch. 20 (see 20:3, 4, 8), and the Beloved Disciple, already portrayed as an intimate disciple of Jesus in 13:23, plays an increasingly important role in the narrative from that point on (see 13:23; 19:26; 20:2). Are they one and the

---

[9] For a fully documented survey of these suggestions see Rudolf Schnackenburg, *The Gospel According to St. John.* 3 vols. HTCNT IV/1-3 (New York: Crossroad, 1966–82) 3:228–33.

[10] See the remarks of Rudolf Bultmann, *The Gospel of John. A Commentary.* Translated by G. R. Beasley-Murray (Oxford: Blackwell, 1971) 643–44.

[11] Schnackenburg, *St. John* 3:233.

[12] For the discussion see Quast, *Peter and the Beloved Disciple* 76–81; Brown, *Death of the Messiah* 1:596–98. For Stibbe, *John as Storyteller* 98–99, "the anonymous believer here is undoubtedly the BD." Stibbe identifies the Beloved Disciple with Lazarus (see pp. 78–81). The issue is further complicated by a textual difficulty. Some manuscripts add a definite article before ἄλλος μαθητής in v. 15. Others read "that disciple," while some have neither "other" nor "that." For my reading "another disciple" see Schnackenburg, *St. John* 3:234–35.

same character in the story?[13] In 20:2 it looks as if Mary Magdalene runs to a figure originally known as "the other disciple" but who is now known as "the one whom Jesus loved" (ἔχεται . . . πρὸς τὸν ἄλλον μαθητὴν ὃν ἐφίλει ὁ Ἰησοῦς). At this stage of the narrative, however, the reader is aware of the presence of two disciples in the court of the high priest, along with Jesus (v. 15).[14] Although "another disciple" may not yet be identifiable with the Beloved Disciple,[15] the figures will eventually coalesce for the reader as the Johannine narrative proceeds farther.[16] Peter gains entry to the court of the high priest through the mediation of the other disciple (v. 16). We need not discuss the various theories proposed that enable the author to call the other disciple a γνωστός of the high priest.[17] The author's point of focus is on the presence of two disciples of Jesus in the courtyard of the high priest. The introduction of the characters and the setting of the scene in vv. 15-16 has allowed the narrator to speak three times of μαθηταί and three times of Peter. The issue of Peter's being one of the μαθηταί of Jesus is immediately raised by the question of the maid who kept the door: "You are not also one of this man's disciples, are you?" Peter's first denial reverses the words of Jesus, who accepted his identity in the Garden of Gethsemane with the words ἐγώ εἰμι (see vv. 5 and 8). Peter responds οὐκ εἰμί (v. 17).[18]

The reader is aware that a lie has been told. Without comment the narrator moves on to describe the action of the ὑπηρέται and some servants who have prepared a charcoal fire against the cold. The reader recalls that the ὑπηρέται had come out to arrest Jesus, the light of the world (see 8:12; 9:5), carrying lanterns and torches (v. 2); that

---

[13] The major arguments against identification are: the lack of a definite article in 18:15, the fact that the author does not simply call him "the Beloved Disciple," as in 13:23, and the special acquaintance with the high priest. On this see Schnackenburg, *St. John* 3:235; Dauer, *Passionsgeschichte* 73–75.

[14] Only the Fourth Gospel has a session with Annas, who is not really the high priest. The author has already reminded the reader of Caiaphas' earlier words concerning the need for Jesus to die for the people (18:13-14; see 11:49-50).

[15] This problem was already recognized by Augustine, *In Johannis Evangelium* cxiii, 2 (CCSL 36:636–37). As Barrett, *St John* 525, aptly remarks: "It is quite possible to identify him as the disciple 'whom Jesus loved,' but there is no definite ground for doing so." For the case against identification see Schnackenburg, *St. John* 3:235.

[16] On this see Lang, *Johannes und die Synoptiker* 92–95.

[17] For a presentation of the earlier discussion around this issue see J. H. Bernard, *A Critical and Exegetical Commentary on the Gospel According to St John*. Edited by A. H. McNeile. 2 vols. ICC 29 (Edinburgh: T & T Clark, 1928) 2:592–97. For more recent discussion see Brown, *John* 2:822–23. On the use of the word γνωστός see Barrett, *St John* 525–26.

[18] See Brown, *Death of the Messiah* 1:602–603.

they had seized him, bound him, and taken him to Annas (18:12-13a). Peter, who has just denied that he is a disciple of Jesus, is described as μετ' αὐτῶν. He approaches the warmth and light created by characters in the story who have already sided with the powers of darkness. It is "with them" that he is standing and warming himself. This use of irony is implicit commentary on the narrative.[19] Peter is moving from light into darkness. In the story of Peter's first denial (vv. 15-18) the term "disciple" has been used four times. In addition to the technical term μαθητής the name "Peter," well known to the reader as that of an important (see 1:41-42), faithful (see 6:68-69), but misunderstanding and fragile (see 13:6-9, 24, 36-38) disciple of Jesus, appears five times. In six brief sentences the theme of "the disciple of Jesus" appears nine times, focusing the reader's attention on the larger theme of Christian discipleship. But it is a story of discipleship denied.[20]

THE WITNESS OF JESUS IN JOHN 18:19-24

There is an intimate link between vv. 15-18, with their theme of discipleship, and vv. 19-24, which open with the narrator's description of the questioning of the high priest. The reader is told that the issues at stake were Jesus' disciples and Jesus' teaching: περὶ τῶν μαθητῶν αὐτοῦ καὶ περὶ τῆς διδαχῆς αὐτοῦ (v. 19).[21] Jesus' answer reverses the order of the issues raised. He speaks first of his διδαχή (v. 20), and then of "those who have heard me" (τοὺς ἀκηκοότας): those who know what Jesus has said (v. 21). Jesus' response to the question about his "teaching" is explicit, but the same could be said for his response concerning his disciples. They have heard him; they know what he said.[22]

---

[19] So also Stibbe, *John as Storyteller* 100; Staley, "Subversive Narrator," 93–94.

[20] Augustine, *In Johannis Evangelium* cxiii, 2, comments: "Ecce columna firmissima ad unius aurae impulsum tota contremuit. . . . Negavit ergo ipsum, cum se negavit eius esse discipulum. Quid autem aliud isto modo quam se negavit esse christianum?" ["Behold, the pillar of greatest strength has at a single breath trembled to its foundations. . . . Him therefore he denied when he denied that he was his disciple. And what else did such a form of denial imply, but that of his own Christianity?"]

[21] I am arguing that the aorist ἠρώτησεν is complexive, describing an event from the past that is past, but went on for some time. See BDF 171 § 332.

[22] The link between the interrogation over the μαθηταί and the διδαχή in v. 19 and Jesus' response in vv. 20-21 is rarely noticed. See, for example, the trivial remarks of Bernard, *St John* 2:600. Barrett, *St John* 523, states that Jesus "refuses to answer." See also ibid. 527–28. I am suggesting that Jesus' words are a genuine answer both for the characters and the reader *in the text* and for the reader *of the text*. See also Lang, *Johannes und die Synoptiker* 99–104.

Jesus' public ministry came to a close in 12:36b: "After Jesus had said this, he departed and hid (ἐκρύβη) from them."[23] At this present late stage in the narrative, well after that solemn "hiding" of himself, he can only look back on that public revelation of God through word and deed, and inform Annas of two events, both in the past, but described with different forms of the past tense.

1. In v. 20b Jesus looks back on his preaching to "the Jews." It developed within the context of a steadily intensifying conflict with Jesus (see chs. 5–10), during which his total rejection, highlighted by the decision that he must die, was plotted (see 5:18; 7:1, 19, 25-26, 8:22, 37, 40). As the public ministry came to a close the leadership of "the Jews" solemnly decided that one man must die for the nation (11:50). In a final appeal Jesus associated his death with a "lifting up" to draw everyone to himself (12:32-33), but "the Jews," rightly associating the "lifting up" with the death of "the Son of Man," rejected Jesus' promise. They preferred what they already had in their own tradition (12:43).[24] After a final warning to "the Jews" that they should walk in the light while they still have the light (vv. 35-36a) the narrator solemnly concluded Jesus' public presence to "the Jews": "After Jesus has said this, he departed and hid from them" (v. 36b).[25] The reader recalls events and encounters in chs. 5–12, with their dramatic conclusion in 12:36b, when in the Passion account Jesus tells a Jewish hearing: "I have always taught in synagogues and in the temple, where all the Jews come together" (18:20b). He has taught, but he will do so no longer. There can be no going back on the definitive separation between Jesus and "the Jews" established for the reader through the narrator's comment in 12:36b. This is involved in the use of the aorist tense of the verb ἐδίδαξα. Jesus devoted himself to a period of teaching in the Temple and the synagogues, but this time of Jesus' personal teaching presence has come to an end.[26]

---

[23] The second aorist passive of κρύπτω produces an intransitive reflexive meaning: "hid himself." Severino Pancaro, *The Law in the Fourth Gospel: Moses and Jesus, Judaism and Christianity according to John.* NovTSup 42 (Leiden: E. J. Brill, 1975) 64–71, rightly points out that vv. 18-24 cannot be regarded as a trial. All "trials" (Jesus by "the Jews" and "the Jews" by Jesus) have taken place during the public ministry. See also Brown, *Death of the Messiah* 1:423–26.

[24] See Francis J. Moloney, *The Johannine Son of Man.* BibScRel 14 (2nd ed. Rome: LAS, 1978) 181–85.

[25] See Bernard, *St John* 2:600–601.

[26] The aorist is, therefore, complexive. See BDF 171 § 332. One does not have to read the aorist ἐδίδαξα in this way. It may simply be the appropriate tense to

2. Nevertheless, "I have spoken openly to the world . . . I have said nothing in secret" (v. 20a,c). Although the teaching (διδαχή) directed by Jesus to "the Jews" has ended, the word of Jesus (λελάληκα) has been proclaimed in the world. The Fourth Gospel's rich use of ὁ κόσμος can never be simply equated with "the Jews." The author uses it for the creation (see 1:10; 17:5, 24; 21:25) or, very positively, for the object of God's saving love (see 1:29; 3:16; 4:42; 6:51; 8:12; 9:5). It can also refer to those who reject the person and teaching of Jesus (see 1:10; 7:7; 12:31; 14:17, 22, 27, 30; 15:18-19; 16:8, 20, 33; 17:6, 9, 14-16).[27] It is "the world" that is the object of God's saving love that is in question in 18:20a. This is indicated by the use of the perfect tense for the verb λελάληκα. A word has been let loose in the world that is παρρεσίᾳ. Jesus' historical presence as teacher and as the proclaimer of the word has come to an end (12:36b: ἐκρύβη) but his word, spoken in the past, was never hidden (18:20c: ἐν κρυπτῷ ἐλάλησα οὐδέν). The perfect tense, placed in close proximity to the aorist ἐδίδαξα, indicates that although the teaching to "the Jews" has come to an end the word of Jesus is still available. Something began in the past, and its consequences are still abroad![28]

Jesus has answered the question of his teaching. He is no longer prepared to teach "the Jews" who are now interrogating him. They have al-

---

associate with πάντοτε, but the Johannine account of Jesus' encounters with "the Jews" in chs. 5–12 suggests my reading of 18:20b. Rightly, Bultmann, *John* 646, comments: "In the present situation the statement of Jesus no longer signifies an indirect appeal for decision or for faith; rather it affirms, 'You have already decided!' It is too late for discussion; the confrontation with Judaism is at an end." See also Dauer, *Passionsgeschichte* 247–49.

[27] On this, see N.-H. Kassem, "A Grammatical and Contextual Inventory of the Use of *kosmos* in the Johannine Corpus with Some Implications for a Johannine Cosmic Theology," *NTS* 19 (1972–73) 81–91. Unacceptable, therefore, is the claim of Barrett (*St John* 528), citing Fenton, that "the world" is represented by "the Jews" in this passage. If "the Jews" were intended here, why use the heavily loaded expression κόσμος? There must be more to it.

[28] See BDF 175–76, §§ 340-341, at 175: "The perfect combines in itself, so to speak, the present and the aorist in that it denotes the *continuance* of *completed* action." Brown, *John* 2:825, sees the difficulty: "The tense is perfect while the subsequent verbs ('taught'; 'I said') are in the aorist." But he avoids the problem, through reference to J. H. Moulton, by claiming that the strange syntax "points to this as an example of a verb in the perfect tense functioning in an aorist sense."

ready been taught, but they have definitively rejected that teaching.[29] Nevertheless, the word of Jesus is alive in the world. The perfect tense of the verb in Jesus' words: "I *have spoken* openly to the world" (v. 20a) made this clear to the original readers of this gospel, familiar with the nuance of the use of the Greek tenses. The "foreignness" of this world calls for interpretation so that this important Johannine message may not be lost. If the physical presence of Jesus "in the synagogues and in the temple" (v. 20b) is no longer available (12:36b), where is this word to be found, spoken so openly to the world (v. 20a.c)? "The Jews" must no longer expect a word from Jesus (v. 21a); they are to ask those who have heard him (τοὺς ἀκηκοότας) what he said (ἐλάλησα) to them. During the ministry of Jesus the word was spoken (ἐλάλησα: complexive aorist) to "those who have heard." They are in possession of the word to the world, spoken once by the person and through the deeds of Jesus, but still at large in the world. Anyone, including "the Jews," who wishes to hear that word must ask them (v. 21b). They know (οἴδασιν) what Jesus said (v. 21c).

Who are τοὺς ἀκηκοότας, now the custodians of the word, and the ones to whom one must go to discover the word Jesus has spoken to the world? According to many commentators Jesus' reply simply insists that his accusers "take testimony in the legal manner."[30] But the readers surely understand that they are the followers of Jesus (see v. 15a), the μαθηταί who have learned at the school of Jesus.[31] Jesus is no longer available to speak his own word. He has given it to followers and disciples, who know what he said. Among the many commentators only Sir Edwyn Hoskyns has seen this: "The author insists that the teaching of Jesus must be known through attention to His disciples, who by the guidance of the Spirit preserve and interpret his words (cf. ii.22, xiv.25, xvi.4sqq)."[32]

---

[29] The experience of the Johannine community that has been expelled from the synagogue because of their belief that Jesus was the Messiah (see 9:22; 12:42; 16:2) lies behind this exposition.

[30] Barrett, *St John* 528. See also Brown, *John* 2:826; Lindars, *John* 550.

[31] For the importance of this feature of a μαθητής see Karl H. Rengstorf, "μανθάνω κτλ.," *TDNT* 4 (1967) 444–50.

[32] Edwyn C. Hoskyns (ed. Francis N. Davey) *The Fourth Gospel* (2nd ed. London: Faber & Faber, 1947) 514. He also rightly points out: "The questions of the high priest concerning the disciples of Jesus and his teaching, and our Lord's answer were pertinent and appropriate at the time when the gospel was written" (p. 514). Hoskyns does not, however, see the dramatic contrast between Jesus' instructions and the frame of Peter's denials. This would also have been "appropriate at the time when the gospel was written" (see especially 15:18–16:3). See also Schnackenburg, *St. John* 3:237–38; Ernst Haenchen, *John.* 2 vols. Hermeneia (Philadelphia: Fortress, 1984) 2:169.

Ignace de la Potterie has shown that the Fourth Gospel distinguishes carefully between two verbs used to express knowledge.[33] He has claimed, on good grounds, that γινώσκειν refers to the acquisition of experiential knowledge, which one gains through time and effort. Εἰδέναι (οἶδα) on the other hand, does not mean "to come to know," but simply to know facts with assurance. However careful one must be in applying this distinction across the gospel, it applies here. Those who have heard Jesus certainly "know" the facts (οἴδασιν), and one must go to the disciples to learn these facts. However, such knowledge says nothing of their success or failure as authentic followers of Jesus. It says nothing of them as true believers whose "knowledge" is matched by the quality of their love for Jesus, his Father and their brethren.[34] The high priest's questioning Jesus about his disciples and his teaching has now been answered. The two belong together. Anyone who wishes to hear the teaching of Jesus will find it among his disciples.

A slap greets the response of Jesus to his opponents. Jesus has told them where they must go if they hope to hear his teaching (v. 22), but the slap, and the haughty words that accompany it, are signs of rejection. The Johannine Passion narrative is marked by two slaps that indicate the rejection of what was said in the immediately previous context. Here the one of the ὑπηρέται, given out of loyalty to the high priest, refuses to accept the promise of Jesus (18:22). Later in the narrative the Roman soldiers will proclaim Jesus as "the King of the Jews," and slap him, making a mockery of the truth they themselves have ironically proclaimed (see 19:3).

Jesus' response to the rejection returns the significance of the events to his level. If Jesus has spoken evilly (εἰ κακῶς ἐλάλησα) he asks his assailant to bear witness. If he has spoken well (εἰ δὲ καλῶς), the officer must explain his action (v. 23). Jesus is using technical language. Κακῶς λαλεῖν is used in the LXX with reference to blasphemy (see Exod 22:7; Lev 19:14; 20:9; Isa 8:21; 1 Macc 7:42). If the slap results from blasphemy, witnesses must be brought. But if this is not the case, and Jesus is proclaiming what is right (καλῶς), a truthfulness that opposes blasphemy, then the officer stands condemned by his action.[35] The tradition of Jesus' guiltlessness, found in both the synoptics (see Mark 15:14; Matt 27:4, 19,

---

[33] Ignace de la Potterie, "οἶδα et γινώσκω, les deux modes de la connaissance dans le quatrième évangile," *Bib* 40 (1959) 709–25.

[34] At this stage of the narrative, especially after chs. 13–17, the reader is well aware that the believer's commitment to these relationships is an all-important criterion.

[35] See Brown, *Death of the Messiah* 1:415–16.

24; Luke 23:13-16, 22) and in the Johannine trial before Pilate (see John 18:38; 19:4, 6), is carried farther here. Not only is Jesus guiltless; he has revealed the truth. But the slap indicates that Jesus' revelation of the truth is definitively rejected.[36] The narrator removes Jesus from the scene. He is bound and led to the house of Caiaphas (v. 24). There is no report of what takes place before Caiaphas. Jesus will next appear in v. 28, led from the house of Caiaphas to the Praetorium.[37]

This brief report of Jesus' so-called "Jewish trial" depicts neither a trial nor an interrogation. Although Christian tradition, through association with the synoptic stories, has regarded John 18:19-24 as a "Jewish trial" there is nothing in it that smacks of a trial. There is no accusation, only questions about his teaching and his disciples (v. 19). Jesus does not call up witnesses in his defense; he answers the questions asked. Despite Jesus' disappearance from the scene, the revelation of God made known through his διδαχή is still available. It is to be found in the testimony of the μαθηταί, the followers of Jesus who form the Johannine church. The unfolding story of the Johannine gospel, the subject of the reader's interest, reflects acceptance of this truth. The reader of this story of Jesus is asking those who have heard Jesus speak. The existence of the written and spoken text of the gospel is the fulfillment of the words of Jesus during his Jewish interrogation. Those who have heard him are now passing on what he said through this narrative. The gospel is proof of the truth of Jesus' words. The reader is being told what the Johannine Christians remember and understand of what Jesus said (see 2:22; 12:16). But what of Peter? While Jesus directs the reader anxious to know his "teaching" away from himself toward the witness of "those who have heard him," the disciples, the reader also recalls that one of them has just denied his role as a disciple of Jesus (v. 17).

THE DISCIPLE IN JOHN 18:25-27

The discipleship theme has been present throughout the narrative, even during the interrogation of Jesus where, although absent, he pointed to his disciples as "those who have heard me." Simon Peter and another disciple appeared in vv. 15-18, but that scene closed with

---

[36] On this see Ignace de la Potterie, *The Hour of Jesus. The Passion and the Resurrection of Jesus according to John.* Translated by Gregory Murray (Slough: St Paul Publications; New York: Alba House, 1989) 72–74. See also Bernard, *St John* 2:601; Schnackenburg, *St. John* 3:239; Brown, *Death of the Messiah* 1:413.

[37] The Johannine treatment of the hearings before Jewish authorities is thus markedly different from that of the synoptics. See the chart illustrating these differences in Brown, *John* 2:830–31.

Peter's rejection of his role as a disciple of Jesus. The term "disciple" was present in v. 19 as Jesus was questioned about "his disciples and his teaching." In v. 21 the disciples became "those who have heard me." They know what Jesus has said. But the language and the central character from vv. 15-18 return as the narrator resumes his presentation of Peter's denials. The other disciple has disappeared, but Simon Peter, still "with them" at the fire (see v. 19), is again asked whether he is a disciple of Jesus (ἐκ τῶν μαθητῶν αὐτοῦ). He repeats his first denial: οὐκ εἰμί (v. 25). The almost exact repetition, in v. 25, of what was done and said in Peter's first denial in v. 17 creates a tight frame around Jesus' directions that those who wish to know his teaching must go to those who have heard him (vv. 20-21).

Scholars sometimes complain that there are no changes of time mentioned throughout these alternating scenes.[38] There is no difficulty involved. By not interspersing the narrative with such expressions as the customary μέτα ταῦτα or other such indications of a succession in time the author creates the impression that all these events are happening contemporaneously.[39] As Jesus points to the disciples as the ones who have heard him, and custodians of his word, one of them—indeed, the leading disciple—is with the powers of darkness (v. 18: μετ' αὐτῶν), denying his association with Jesus.

The final denial again looks back to the Gethsemane scene. On several occasions during vv. 12-27 the immediately previous scene of vv. 1-11 provides essential background to the denials of Peter or the witness of Jesus.[40] Particularly important is Peter's reversal of Jesus' words in the garden (see vv. 5, 8: ἐγώ εἰμι), as he rejects his discipleship with the words οὐκ εἰμί (v. 17). But there are further links. Peter has associated with the ὑπηρέται who came to Jesus with their lanterns and torches (v. 3), and who took him and bound him (v. 12), as they arrange their further false light in the courtyard (v. 18). The ὑπηρέται are still present, as one of them rejects Jesus' words with a slap (v. 22). A further contact with the themes present in the garden scene now appears, linking Peter's final denial with the scene in Gethsemane. There Peter was

---

[38] See Quast, *Peter and the Beloved Disciple* 75, 85. For example, Bernard, *St John* 2:602–603, postulates about an hour between Peter's first (vv. 15-18) and second and third (vv. 25-27) denials, on the basis of the synoptics.

[39] See Fowler, *Let the Reader Understand* 143–44: "Intercalation is narrative sleight of hand, a crafty manipulation of the discourse level that creates the illusion that two episodes are taking place simultaneously."

[40] Stibbe, *John as Storyteller* 96–97, argues attractively that 18:1-27 can be read "as a single act of the passion drama." See also Lang, *Johannes und die Synoptiker* 111–14.

the only active disciple, drawing his sword and cutting off Malchus' right ear (v. 10). A blood relative of Malchus who saw Peter in action in the garden now lays a charge that cannot be denied (v. 26), but Peter insists that he has no association with Jesus (v. 27a).[41] The third denial is not only an attempt on the part of Peter to dissociate himself from Jesus. His denial implies that he was never in the garden, a place known to Judas the betrayer because "Jesus often met there with his disciples" (v. 2). Peter, who has gradually drawn closer to the darkness represented by the ὑπηρέται, lyingly denies any link with Gethsemane, Jesus, and his disciples, who often met there.

The report of Peter's threefold denial concludes: "and at that moment the cock crowed" (v. 27b). The reader recalls the words of Jesus reported in 13:38: "Very truly, I tell you, before the cock crows, you will have denied me three times." But the point of this conclusion to the account of Peter's denials is not an ominous reminder to Peter or, as Lindars claims, "the sense of personal danger."[42] On the contrary, it is a firm indication to the reader that the promises of Jesus are fulfilled. What Jesus said will happen (13:38) does happen (18:27). This is crucial for the reader's broader appreciation of the author's careful arrangement of the series of events reported in vv. 15-27. Jesus has indicated that his word is abroad in the world. It can be found among those who heard him, those who know what he said (vv. 19-24). But one of them is denying that he had anything to do with Jesus (vv. 15-18, 25-27). Nevertheless the reader is confident that, as with the cock crow, what Jesus has said will happen . . . will happen.[43] However badly Peter may perform, Jesus' teaching can be received from those who, like Peter, have heard him.

The Christian community is the place where the word of Jesus can be found, but the members of the Christian community are capable of being disloyal to their responsibilities. Here the reader finds a coherent theology of the Church as the custodian of the word of Jesus, but a custodian that at times is capable of denying its association with Jesus. Despite such human fragility the promises of Jesus come true. Those

[41] For a discussion of the historicity of this connection see Quast, *Peter and the Beloved Disciple* 86–87. The charge that Peter had drawn a weapon and assaulted one of the high priest's household was, in fact, more serious than being a disciple of Jesus. See Bernard, *St John* 2:603.

[42] Lindars, *John* 552.

[43] Against Bultmann, *John* 648, who claims that the cock-crow: "in itself . . . has no particular significance for him (the evangelist)." Parenthesis mine. For a better appreciation of this episode as belonging to Jesus' prophecy see Schnackenburg, *St. John* 3:240.

who have heard Jesus, those who know what he said, may be capable of betraying and denying him, but Jesus' promises come true. The crowing of the cock immediately after Peter's final denial is proof of that fact. Betrayers and deniers that the disciples of Jesus may be (vv. 15-18, vv. 25-27), the community of Christian believers remains the place where the word of Jesus can be found (v. 21).

The intended readers of this narrative, an early Christian community under the threat of death because of their belief in Jesus of Nazareth as the Christ (see 16:2), identified with this point of view. It was not only the disciple of Jesus *in the story* who was the custodian of the word of Jesus but capable of denying it, but also the disciple of Jesus who was *the reader of the story*. The Johannine community, faced with their own fears and disloyalties, saw their experience in the experience of Peter. But what of the other disciple? He was also present in the courtyard but is never again mentioned during these hearings. The reader suspects, but cannot be sure, that this may be the Beloved Disciple. One of the disciples has lost his way, but have all the disciples?[44] The reader can only proceed farther into the narrative to discover the whole truth about the disciples of Jesus. At the cross of Jesus the reader will encounter the Beloved Disciple, and at 20:2, as the Easter light begins to dawn, the identification of "the other disciple" with "the one whom Jesus loved" will associate "the other disciple" of 18:15 with the Beloved Disciple of 13:23 and 20:2.[45]

CONCLUSION

It is beyond the limitations of this study to follow the reader farther into the narrative in any detailed fashion, but a few concluding re-

---

[44] Kragerud, *Der Lieblingsjünger* 74–81, argues strongly for an ecclesiological and symbolic understanding of the Beloved Disciple in 18:15-16. He claims that there is a close link between 18:15-16 and 10:1-5 (especially the entering through the θύρα into the αὐλή [see 10:1-2; 18:16]), and that the evangelist wished to present the Beloved Disciple as the symbol of the good shepherd, the true Christian leader, superior to the recognized shepherd, Peter. Similarly, without reference to John 10, see Haenchen, *John* 2:167–68. Stibbe, *John as Storyteller* 100–105, without reference to Kragerud, has recently proposed a close link between 18:1-27 and 10:1-21. See also Staley, "Subversive Narrator," 87–88.

[45] Although the reader is now approaching the climax of the Johannine story of Jesus, the adage of Shlomith Rimmon-Kenan holds true: "Narrative texts implicitly promise the reader the great prize of understanding—later" (Shlomith Rimmon-Kenan, *Narrative Fiction: Contemporary Poetics*. New Accents [London: Methuen, 1983] 125).

marks will indicate that the ecclesiological reading of John 18:15-27 points in the right direction. The Johannine story of Jesus' crucifixion is more about what Jesus does for the believer than what happened to Jesus.[46] At the heart of that section of the narrative the mother of Jesus is given to the Beloved Disciple and the Beloved Disciple to the mother of Jesus (19:25-27). The hour of Jesus has come (see 12:23; 13:1; 17:1), and because of that hour (see 19:27: ἀπ᾽ ἐκείνης τῆς ὥρας) the disciple and the mother become one. Whatever one makes of this scene, a new "communion" has been established.[47]

The Johannine Passion account has been carefully shaped. At the center of the story lies the trial before Pilate. There Jesus is ironically proclaimed and crowned as king (18:28–19:16). At its beginning (18:1-11) and at its end (19:38-42) Jesus is again in a garden. Flanking the trial before Pilate are two scenes that tell the reader about the Church (18:12-27; 19:17-37).[48] Schematically, the Johannine Passion narrative unfolds as follows:

18:1-11:	*Jesus in a garden:* with his enemies.
18:12-27:	The Jewish interrogation. *The Johannine Church*
18:28–19:16:	The trial before Pilate: Jesus as King.
19:17-37:	The crucifixion. *The Johannine Church*
19:38-42:	*Jesus in a garden:* with his friends.

In the story of Peter's denials and Jesus' witness the reader learns of the one who has heard the word of Jesus and is the custodian of that

---

[46] See Brown, *John* 2:912: "The principal episodes of the crucifixion are concerned with the gifts that the enthroned king gives to those who accept his kingdom. . . . The Johannine crucifixion scene is, in a certain way, less concerned with the fate of Jesus than with the significance of that fate for his followers."

[47] See Hoskyns, *Fourth Gospel* 530: "The Church proceeds from the sacrifice of the Son of God, and the union of the Beloved Disciple and the Mother of the Lord prefigures and foreshadows the charity of the *Ecclesia* of God." For a quite different "symbolic reading" see Bultmann, *John* 671–73. Against these interpretations see Barrett, *St John* 552; F. F. Bruce, *The Gospel of John* (Basingstoke: Pickering & Inglis, 1983) 371–72. For Stibbe, *John as Storyteller* 154–67, the scene comes from a genuine reminiscence of Lazarus, the Beloved Disciple. In its present literary context it provides the solution for the Johannine community's experience of social dislocation created by family disruption (see John 9). A "familistic image which enhanced the sense of religious belonging" is established in 19:25-27. For more detail on the interpretation of 19:25-27 see Moloney, *The Gospel of John* 503–504.

[48] I am avoiding the term "chiasm," as such a spatial, visual pattern may be more a part of the modern critic's trade than the reader's experience. On this

word but always capable of betraying this responsibility (18:15-24). At the cross, a more positive note is sounded. The Church will not be divided (19:23-24). United in the oneness of belief and love characterized by the Mother of Jesus and the Beloved Disciple (19:25-27), the Church is gifted with the Spirit of Jesus and nourished by the blood and water that flow from his side (19:28-37).[49]

But for the Johannine community this could not be the end of the story. Peter failed to accept his responsibility as one who heard the word of Jesus and the Beloved Disciple emerged as the one to whom the mother of Jesus was given at the hour of the cross. But what of Peter? He will run with the Beloved Disciple to the empty tomb (20:3-10), but it is only of the other disciple, now clearly identified as the one whom Jesus loved (see v. 2), that the narrator will comment: "he saw and believed" (v. 9). Nothing will be said of the faith of Peter at the empty tomb. There can be little doubt that the Beloved Disciple provides the model for discipleship in the Johannine church, but Peter is still the primate. Throughout the gospel he holds pride of place. He confesses that Jesus alone has the words of eternal life, that he is the Holy One of God (see 6:68-69). At the supper table he lies in the position of honor, at the right side of Jesus, able to beckon across the Beloved Disciple who is on the left, leaning on the breast of Jesus (13:22-24). When the Beloved Disciple arrives at the empty tomb he stands back to allow Peter the honor of entering the tomb first (see 20:5-7). There is enough evidence in the Johannine narrative to inform the reader that Simon Peter has a position of primacy in the hierarchy of Jesus' disciples.[50]

However, the appendix added to the narrative by the same Johannine school that produced the gospel proper wished to say more.[51] There was recognition that Peter was not only the first of the disciples

---

see the remarks of Fowler, *Let the Reader Understand* 151–52. In a way applicable to several places in the Fourth Gospel, however, Fowler comments: "A 'reader' always experiences one episode after another in temporal sequence, with the readerly work of prospection and retrospection enabling her to tie discrete and sometimes distantly removed episodes together" (p. 152). For a reading of John 1–4 along these lines see Francis J. Moloney, *Belief in the Word. Reading John 1–4* (Minneapolis: Fortress, 1993). See the summary there on pp. 192–99.

[49] For a more detailed analysis of John 18:1–19:42 supporting the brief reflections of this conclusion see Moloney, *The Gospel of John* 481–515.

[50] On this see Raymond E. Brown, Karl P. Donfried, and John Reumann, eds., *Peter in the New Testament. A Collaborative Assessment by Protestant and Roman Catholic Scholars* (Minneapolis: Augsburg, 1973) 129–47.

[51] Not all would accept that John 21 is an appendix. It is, however, a majority opinion to which I subscribe. See, for some recent contrary opinion, Paul S. Minear, "The Original Function of John 21," *JBL* 102 (1983) 85–98; Jeffrey L. Staley,

in terms of honor; he also had the ecclesial responsibility of being pastor to the sheep of Jesus' flock (see 21:15-19 in light of 10:14-18).[52] The ecclesial significance I have attempted to uncover behind Peter's threefold betrayal of Jesus continues into the later scene added by the community to its story. It shows how this pastoral role was possible for the disciple who three times denied his association with Jesus.[53] Peter must three times profess his love for Jesus. It is only on the basis of a positive response to Jesus' thrice-repeated question, "Do you love me?" that he can be told: "Feed my lambs" (21:15). . . . "Tend my sheep" (v. 16). . . . "Feed my sheep" (v. 17).

Christian, and especially Roman Catholic tradition often looks to Petrine texts in the New Testament to understand its leadership and mission. John 18:15-27 is *never* one of those texts. But the story of Peter's denials, set as a frame around the witness of Jesus, also addresses the issue of a Church that claims to hear and to know the word of Jesus (see v. 21). This passage indicates that the Church succeeds only because the design of God, worked out in and through Jesus, will not be thwarted (vv. 21, 27), despite the denials of those who know what Jesus has said (vv. 17, 25, 27). The disciple whom Jesus loved and the shepherd whose profession of love negates his fear-filled denials are always part of "those who have heard him." They know what he said.

The Print's First Kiss: A Rhetorical Investigation of the Implied Reader in the Fourth Gospel. SBLDS 82 (Atlanta: Scholars, 1988) 50–73; Fernando F. Segovia, "The Journey(s) of the Word of God: A Reading of the Plot of the Fourth Gospel," *Sem* 53 (1991) 22–54. For an exhaustive survey of current literature and a statement of my position see my *Glory not Dishonor. Reading John 13–21* (Minneapolis: Fortress, 1998) 182–92.

[52] See above, n. 44, for Kragerud's suggested link between 10:1-5 and 18:15-16. His reading is overly symbolic (see also *Der Lieblingsjünger* 25–26), but the danger that Peter's denials could risk his reputation as the shepherd of the flock needs to be avoided. Thus we have 21:15-19. See Moloney, *The Gospel of John* 554–62.

[53] On John 21 as a reflection of the ongoing development of the Johannine school see Barrett, *St John* 576–88; Brown, *John* 2:1077–84. On the post-Easter Church writing its own story into the denials of Peter see Haenchen, *John* 2:170–74.

CHAPTER 7

THE GOSPEL OF JOHN:
A STORY OF TWO PARACLETES

FOR BARBARA M. STEAD, R.S.M. IN MEMORIAM

In the Fourth Gospel the expression "the Spirit," received from both Jewish and early Christian traditions, is an all-embracing term. The Paraclete is singled out as a distinct "character" who will be associated with a later "time" in Jesus' promise of 14:16: ἄλλον παράκλητον δώσει ὑμῖν. This same "character" is mentioned on four further occasions in Jesus' last discourse: 14:25-26; 15:26-27; 16:7-11, 12-15. Who is this character who will appear later, and what is this character's relationship to Jesus? The major part of this reflection is dedicated to a detailed reading of the first Paraclete saying (John 14:15-17) within its immediate literary context. I will then use my exegesis of this passage to make a suggestion concerning the relationship between Jesus and the Paraclete. This suggestion has further theological implications that I will touch upon by way of conclusion.

THE CONTEXT

There is widespread disagreement among scholars concerning the internal articulation of John 14:1-31.[1] I propose a threefold division of the

[1] Fernando F. Segovia, *The Farewell of the Word. The Johannine Call to Abide* (Minneapolis: Fortress, 1991) 64–65 nn. 6-13, lists thirty scholars who have divided the material into two to nine major sections. See also A. Niccaci, "Esame letterario di Gv 14," *Euntes Docete* 31 (1978) 209–14; Secondo Migliasso, *La presenza dell'Assente. Saggio di analisi letterario-strutturale e di sintesi teologica di Gv. 13,31–14,32* (Rome: Pontificia Universitas Gregoriana, 1979) 64–73.

material. The imperative "believe" in 14:1 dominates vv. 1-14. Belief is explicitly mentioned in vv. 1, 10, 11, and 12, and Jesus' words throughout this section are related to the content and consequences of belief in Jesus. The recommendation to "love" appears in v. 15 for the first time in 14:1-31. It reappears in vv. 21, 23, and 24, and the section is framed by statement and restatement of the same point, at first positively: "If you love me, you will keep my commandments" (v. 15), and then negatively: "Whoever does not love me does not keep my words" (v. 24a). The section that runs from vv. 25-31 is dominated by the theme of communication by means of the word: "speaking" (v. 25: λελάληκα), "teaching" (v. 26b: διδάξει), "saying" (v. 26c: εἶπον), "saying" (v. 28: εἶπον), "telling" (v. 29: εἴρηκα), and "speaking" (v. 30: λαλήσω).

Verses 1-6 are highlighted by the theme of Jesus' departure (see vv. 2, 3a, 4), the theme of faith (see v. 1), and words of encouragement (see vv. 1-4, 6). Jesus' words in v. 1, μὴ ταρασσέσθω ὑμῶν ἡ καρδία, set the mood. The same association of themes is again found as the discourse closes in vv. 27b-31: departure (see vv. 28, 31), faith (see v. 29), and encouragement (see vv. 27b-29, 31). Jesus repeats his instruction to his disciples: μὴ ταρασσέσθω ὑμῶν ἡ καρδία in v. 27b.[2] When one notices the steady rhythm of Jesus' command to love him, through the keeping of his commandments and his word, across the central section of the discourse (vv. 15-24) in vv. 15, 21, 23, and 24, a threefold division emerges: vv. 1-14, vv. 15-24, and vv. 25-31.[3] The following scheme indicates the major elements that form this division:[4]

---

[2] This obvious repetition in vv. 1 and 27b is often accepted as indicating an inclusion between v. 1 and v. 27b. See, for example, Rudolf Bultmann, *The Gospel of John: A Commentary.* Translated by G. R. Beasley-Murray (Oxford: Blackwell, 1971) 599; Johannes Schneider, "Die Abschiedsreden Jesu: Ein Beitrag zur Frage der Komposition von Johannes 13:31–17:26," in *Gott und die Götter: Festgabe für Erich Fascher zum 60. Geburtstag* (Berlin: Evangelische Verlagsanstalt, 1958) 106. Rather than finding an inclusion here, I am regarding both v. 1 and v. 27b as statements of encouragement, introducing subsections (vv. 1-6 and vv. 27b-31) dealing with Jesus' departure.

[3] This macro-structure follows that proposed by (among others) Johannes Beutler, *Habt keine Angst. Die erste Johanneische Abschiedsrede (Joh 14).* SBS 116 (Stuttgart: Katholisches Bibelwerk, 1984) 21–22, 51–53, 87–88; Yves Simoens, *La gloire d'aimer. Structures stylistiques et interprétatives dans le Discours de la Cène (Jn 13–17).* AnBib 90 (Rome: Biblical Institute Press, 1981) 107–12; D. François Tolmie, *Jesus' Farewell to the Disciples. John 13:1–17:26 in Narratological Perspective.* BibIntS 12 (Leiden: E. J. Brill, 1993) 29–30.

[4] See Simoens, *La gloire d'aimer* 105–29. For further detail, especially the articulation of the subdivisions within this tripartite structure, see Francis J.

(a) Verses 1-14: *Jesus speaks encouragingly of his departure:* encouragement (vv. 1, 3, 6, 12-14), departure (vv. 2, 3, 4, 5), belief (vv. 1 [twice], 11 [twice], 12).

Verses 1-6: ταρασσέσθω ὑμῶν ἡ καρδία *opens the first subsection of the discourse, dealing with Jesus' departure (vv. 2, 3a, 4), the need for belief (v. 1), and encouragement (vv. 1, 3, 6).*

(b) Verses 15-24: *Jesus instructs on the fruits of belief and love:* love (vv. 15, 21 [three times], 23 [twice], 24). Love is manifested in keeping Jesus' commandments and his word (vv. 15, 21, 23, 24).

(c) Verses 25-31: *Jesus speaks encouragingly of his departure:* encouragement (vv. 25, 27, 30), departure (vv. 25, 28, 29, 31), belief (v. 29).

Verse 27b begins the closing subsection of this part of the discourse and opens with Jesus' words, μὴ ταρασσέσθω ὑμῶν ἡ καρδία. *The words beginning the opening section of the discourse (vv. 1-6) are repeated verbatim. The themes dealt with in vv. 27b-31 (departure, encouragement, and belief) also link vv. 1-6 and vv. 27b-31.*

The impression created over the latter stages of Jesus' public ministry, that his departure will be through the experience of death, is reinforced. Jesus commands his disciples to avoid all consternation. His words recall the use of Psalms 42–43, already found in 11:33, 35, 38; 12:27, 13:21, and point the reader forward to the Passion.[5] His promise that he will not leave his disciples "orphans" (v. 18: ὀρφανούς) indicates that he is about to leave them through death.[6] The first section of the discourse concludes with the affirmation, "the ruler of this world is coming" (v. 30), and the reader recalls that Jesus has already explained that this ruler will be cast out as Jesus is lifted up on a cross (see 12:31-33). After a narrative that spoke openly of a gift of self in love within the context of betrayal, denial, and death (13:1-38), the discourse proper of 14:1–16:33 opens with Jesus' teaching his disciples the *fact* of his imminent departure through death, (14:1-31) and the *consequence* of the departure for those who love and believe: the gift of a peace that "the world" can never give (v. 27a).

Moloney, *The Gospel of John.* SP 4 (Collegeville: The Liturgical Press, 1998) 393, 401, 409. They differ from those proposed by Simoens.

[5] See Johannes Beutler, "Psalm 42/43 im Johannesevangelium," *NTS* 25 (1978–79) 33–57. On 14:1-9, 27 see pp. 46–54. See also G. R. Beasley-Murray, *John.* WBC 36 (Waco: Word Books, 1987) 249.

[6] On John 14 as an example of the Jewish testament form, as a hero leaves his disciples through death, see Beutler, *Habt keine Angst* 15–19.

An Exegesis of John 14:12-14, 15-24

Given that vv. 1-14 form a major division, the double "amen" and the introduction of the theme of the future "greater works" of the disciples marks vv. 12-14 as the closing subsection of vv. 1-14. The centerpiece of vv. 15-24, which opens and closes with the theme of love (see vv. 15, 23-24), has three subsections: vv. 15-17 deal with the other Paraclete, vv. 18-21 affirm the ongoing presence of the departed Jesus, and vv. 22-24 instruct the reader on love and loyalty.[7] The following exegetical section of this study will focus on the immediate literary context of 14:15-17, the closing verses of the first division (vv. 12-14), and the three subsections of vv. 15-24, beginning with the first Paraclete saying (vv. 15-17).

1. Verses 12-14:
To Believe, and to do the Works of the Father

The theme of belief and "the works" introduced in v. 11 leads the reader into vv. 12-14).[8] The double "amen" also links what has gone before with what follows. Belief in Jesus will enable the believer (ὁ πιστεύων) to do the works of Jesus, and to excel the works of Jesus (v. 12ab). The issue close to the surface throughout vv. 1-15, Jesus' departure, motivates the increased greatness of the works of the believer (v. 12c). The absence of Jesus created by his departure will not lead to the end of the works of the Father by which Jesus has made God known (see 5:41; 7:18; 8:50, 54). The return of Jesus to the Father (see 13:1; 14:2, 6) will lead to disciples' doing greater works. They are exhorted to ask *in the name of Jesus* so that works will continue to be done. The greatness of the works lies in their being done *in his name*, after his departure. Jesus affirms *that* his works, and even greater works, will continue in the life

---

[7] For more detail see Francis J. Moloney, *Glory not Dishonor. Reading John 13–21* (Minneapolis: Fortress, 1998) 30–32.

[8] Verse 14 is omitted by some manuscripts. Despite the clumsy αἰτήσητέ με, and its repetition, it should be retained. See Bruce M. Metzger, *A Textual Commentary on the Greek New Testament*. (2nd ed. Stuttgart: United Bible Societies, 1994) 208; Donald A. Carson, *The Gospel according to John* (Grand Rapids: Eerdmans, 1991) 497–98. For Jürgen Becker, *Das Evangelium nach Johannes*. 2 vols. ÖTK 4/1–2 (Gütersloh: Gerd Mohn; Würzburg: Echter, 1979–81) 2:465, vv. 14-15 are clumsy Johannine paraenesis, and disturb the link between v. 13 and v. 16. This ignores the important relationship between v. 15 and v. 24, which separates vv. 15-24 from vv. 12-14. See Andreas Dettwiler, *Die Gegenwart des Erhöhten. Eine Exegetische Studie zu den johanneischen Abschiedsreden (John 13,31–16,33) unter besonderer Berücksichtigung ihres Relecture-Charakters*. FRLANT 169 (Göttingen: Vandenhoeck & Ruprecht, 1995) 125–26.

of the believers after his departure. There will be a difference between the works of Jesus, done during his ministry, and the works of the disciples after Jesus' departure. Jesus' departure opens a new era when the works of the disciples surpass those of Jesus.[9] Jesus will be present in his absence, as the disciples do the works that he is doing (v. 12: ἃ ἐγὼ ποιῶ), and *he* will do (vv. 13-14: ἐγὼ ποιήσω) what the disciples request *in his name*.[10] The reader wonders *how* this will take place.[11] There is a logic to Jesus' exhortation. He has done the works of the Father during his time with the disciples (see v. 9) because of his oneness with the Father (vv. 10-11). He is now departing to the house of the Father (v. 2), and he will come again (v. 3). There will be an in-between time during which the disciples must ask in Jesus' name, and he will continue the works of the Father among them.[12] *The ongoing presence of the absent Jesus will be found in the worshiping community*. Its members will associate themselves with the departed Jesus, asking in his name. Jesus, here presented as a Paraclete, doing whatever is asked in his name (vv. 13a, 14), glorifies the Father in the Son (v. 13b). The glory of God, once seen in the deeds of Jesus (see 2:11; 5:41; 7:18; 8:50, 54; 11:4, 40), will be seen in the deeds of worshiping disciples, deeds done as a result of their asking in the name of Jesus (vv. 13-14).[13] *The time after Jesus' departure, and*

[9] See Christian Dietzfelbinger, "Die grösseren Werke (Joh 14.12f.)," *NTS* 35 (1989) 27–32.

[10] See Rudolf Schnackenburg, *The Gospel according to St John*. 3 vols. HTCNT IV/1–3 (New York: Crossroad, 1968–82) 3:72; David E. Aune, *The Cultic Setting of Realized Eschatology in Early Christianity*. NovTSup 28 (Leiden: E. J. Brill, 1972) 104–105.

[11] Becker, *Johannes* 2:464–65, rightly claims that vv. 12-13 present Jesus as a Paraclete and thus prepare the way for the "other Paraclete" of v. 16. On vv. 12-14 as a preparation for vv. 15-27 see Segovia, *The Farewell of the Word* 90–93.

[12] Asking ἐν τῷ ὀνόματι probably reflects the practice of the earliest communities who called upon the name of Jesus in prayer. This practice, which is not a repetition of the practice of the magical cults, reflected a prayer in union with Jesus, accordance with his will, and acceptance of his mission. See Wilhelm Heitmüller, *"Im Namen Jesu." Eine sprach- u. religionsgeschichtliche Untersuchung zum Neuen Testament, speziell zur altchristlichen Taufe*. FRLANT 2 (Göttingen: Vandenhoeck & Ruprecht, 1903) 53–65, 77–80, 264–65; Hans Bietenhard, "ὄνομα κτλ.," *TDNT* 5 (1968) 258–61.

[13] There is no need to have recourse to the subsequent missionary successes of early Christianity to explain the "greater works." See, for example, Walter Bauer, *Das Johannesevangelium erklärt*. HKNT 6 (Tübingen: J. C. B. Mohr [Paul Siebeck], 1933) 181; Edwyn C. Hoskyns (Francis N. Davey, ed.), *The Fourth Gospel* (London: Faber & Faber, 1947) 457; Miguel Rodriguez Ruiz, *Der Missionsgedanke des*

Jesus' Paraclete-role during that time, have already paved the way for the introduction of "another Paraclete" in v. 16.

2. Verses 15-17: The "Other Paraclete"

While vv. 12-14 demanded faith and dependence, v. 15 asks for love, and the theme of love holds vv. 15-24 together. The disciple who loves Jesus shows this union by holding fast to his commandments (v. 15).[14] Jesus has received a commandment from the Father, to make God known. The way Jesus loves (see 10:14-18) and the way Jesus speaks (see 12:49-50) reveal this life-giving commandment. On the evening before his death Jesus exhorts his disciples to match his love (13:34-35; 14:15a) by holding fast (τηρήσετε) to his revealing word (v. 15b).[15] Jesus will pray, asking his Father to send "another Paraclete" (ἄλλον παρά-κλητον) to be with them forever. Jesus' description of his ongoing presence to the believers in vv. 12-14, and especially in v. 13, indicates that *he performs the role of a Paraclete* (see also 1 John 2:1). But there will be "another Paraclete." This Paraclete will not be lifted up in death to reveal the love of God in a consummate act of love for the disciples (see 12:32-33; 13:1), but will remain with the disciples εἰς τὸν αἰῶνα (v. 16).[16]

Johannesevangeliums. Ein Beitrag zur johanneischen Soteriologie und Ekklesiologie. FB 55 (Würzburg: Echter, 1987) 171–84.

[14] The future τηρήσετε, following Vaticanus, rather than the imperative (Bezae, Koridethi) or the subjunctive (𝔓66, Sinaiticus), makes the best sense. See C. K. Barrett, *The Gospel According to St John* (2nd ed. London: S.P.C.K., 1978) 461.

[15] This section (vv. 15-24) is marked by Jesus' demand that the disciple keep the "word," "words," and "commandments" (see vv. 15, 21, 23, 24). There is widespread agreement that these expressions all ask for faith in the revelation of God in and through the word of Jesus. See Segovia, *The Farewell of the Word* 94–95. Xavier Léon-Dufour, *Lecture de l'évangile selon Jean.* 3 vols. Parole de Dieu (Paris: Seuil, 1988–93) 3:112–16, has shown the close link that exists between the demands of Jesus and the demands of the Covenant, especially as they are found in Deuteronomy (see Deut 5:10; 6:5-6; 7:9; 10:12-13; 11:13, 22). See also Beutler, *Habt keine Angst* 55–83.

[16] There is a voluminous discussion of the background for the term παράκλητος, and of the possible source from which the Fourth Evangelist may have taken the Paraclete material. For a survey see Raymond E. Brown, "The Paraclete in the Fourth Gospel," *NTS* 13 (1966–67) 113–32; Gary M. Burge, *The Anointed Community. The Holy Spirit in the Johannine Tradition* (Grand Rapids: Eerdmans, 1987) 3–45; Ignace de la Potterie, *La Vérité dans Saint Jean.* 2 vols. AnBib 73 (Rome: Biblical Institute Press, 1977) 1:330–41; Dettwiler, *Gegenwart* 181–89. The primary meaning of the Greek word is forensic: "legal assistant,

The Paraclete is the S̲p̲i̲r̲i̲t̲ ̲o̲f̲ ̲t̲r̲u̲t̲h̲ (τὸ πνεῦμα τῆς ἀληθείας), "the Spirit who communicates truth,"[17] the ongoing presence of the revelation of God in the world, which "the world" is unable to recognize. One cannot live in "the world of Jesus" if one thinks it can be determined by the realities of "this world." Jesus' *origin* with the Father has always been the stumbling block (see 1:35-51; 3:1-21, 31-36; 4:10-15; 5:19-30, 36-38, 43-44; 6:41-51; 7:25-31, 40-44; 8:12-20, 21-29; 9:24-34; 10:31-39). His *return* to the Father continues "the world's" inability to recognize the ongoing presence of the revelation of God (v. 17a).

The disciples are part of the "world of Jesus." Because of this the Spirit of truth *already dwells with them* (v. 17cα: παρ᾽ ὑμῖν μένει), and there will be another Paraclete who *will be in them* (v. 17cβ: ἐν ὑμῖν ἔσται). Is the Paraclete with them *now* as well as *in the future*, or does the present refer to Jesus and the future refer to the "other Paraclete"? The interplay between Jesus as Paraclete (see v. 13) and the gift of another Paraclete (see v. 16) continues. Jesus is the gift of the truth (see 1:17), the way who is the truth (see 14:6) who dwells with them (παρ᾽ ὑμῖν μένει). His departure to the

---

advocate" (LSJ, 1313, s.v.). This meaning is also found, transliterated, in Hebrew and Aramaic documents. On this see the discussions of Nils Johansson, *Parakletoi. Vorstellungen von Fürsprechern für die Menschen vor Gott in der alttestamentlichen Religion, im Spätjudentum und Urchristentum* (Lund: Gleerup, 1940), who looks to the widespread Jewish idea of an intercessor, and Otto Betz, *Der Paraklet. Fürsprecher im häretischen Spätjudentum, im Johannesevangelium und in neu gefundenen gnostischen Schriften*. AGSU 2 (Leiden: E. J. Brill, 1963) 36–116, who uses Qumran to point to an angelic being (Michael) behind the interceding Paraclete. See also Frédéric Manns, *L'Evangile de Jean à la lumière du Judaïsme*. SBFA 33 (Jerusalem: Franciscan Printing Press, 1991) 360–73. Such views are generally regarded as not best responding to the *overall* Johannine use of the term. De la Potterie, *La Verité* 1:336–39, argues for the forensic nature of the Paraclete sayings by setting them within the Fourth Gospel understood as a trial between Jesus and "the world." Bauer (*Johannesevangelium* 182–83) and others suggest that the Johannine expression is best linked with the use of παρακαλεῖν and παράκλησις in early Christianity and with uses of παρακαλῶν in LXX Greek (see Job 16:2, but not elsewhere) for the concept of consolation (see Isa 40:1). This position has been thoroughly developed by Ulrich B. Müller, "Die Parakletenvorstellung im Johannesevangelium," *ZTK* 71 (1974) 31–77. For Müller, "Die Parakletenvorstellung," 43–52, the earliest Johannine concept was "the Spirit of truth," and this notion was then associated with the Paraclete as the guide, comforter, and teacher. The originally separate traditions of "Holy Spirit" and "Paraclete" have been joined in the Fourth Gospel (see 14:16-17, 26).

[17] Barrett, *St John* 463. The identification of the Paraclete with the Spirit links what may originally have been two traditions. The link had probably been made before the gospel came into existence.

Father will not bring that revealing presence to an end. It will be in them (ἐν ὑμῖν ἔσται).[18] The Paraclete, a new character in the narrative, is the on-going presence of the truth as "the Spirit who communicates truth." These first words on the Paraclete introduce the figure as the ongoing presence of the revelation of God to those who love Jesus and keep his commandments (see v. 15). The presence of the Paraclete will ensure that the ongoing revelation of the truth will continue among disciples of Jesus.[19] Despite the absence of the physical Jesus his revealing mission is not coming to an end; it is moving toward a new era when the role of the *former Paraclete,* Jesus, will be taken over by *another Paraclete,* the Spirit of truth. The reader recalls the narrator's comment as Jesus promised the gift of living water during the celebration of Tabernacles: "Now he said this about the Spirit, which those who believed in him were to receive; for as yet the Spirit had not been given, because Jesus was not yet glorified" (7:39*). But Jesus' glorification is also the time of his departure: "Jesus knew that the hour had come to depart out of this world to the Father" (13:1). The moment of glorification and departure is at hand (see 11:4, 51-53; 12:23, 32-33; 13:1, 31-32), and Jesus' gift of the Spirit is associated with it. *That* such a gift will take place is now an established part of the narrative; *how* it will happen is yet to be discovered.[20]

3. Verses 18-21:
The Revelation of the Oneness of Jesus and the Father

Jesus' departure (see vv. 2-3, 4-5, 18) will not leave the disciples, known to the reader as "children" (see 1:12; 11:52: τέκνα τοῦ θεοῦ), or-

---

[18] Copyists and scholars have attempted to smooth out the two uses of the present tense (γινώσκετε . . . μένει) and the final future (ἔσται). Manns, *L'Evangile* 352, claims that it represents a rabbinic practice, where both verbs simultaneously mean present and future. See the discussion in J. E. Morgan-Wynne, "A Note on John 14.17b," *BZ* 23 (1979) 93–96. Morgan-Wynne correctly insists: "The future ἔσται points to the post-cross era" (96). Copyists have made the μένει future (it only requires a change of accent [μενεῖ]), while some scholars who rightly accept the present tense argue that it has a future meaning. See, for example, Beasley-Murray, *John* 243.

[19] Many scholars (see, for example, Schnackenburg, *St. John* 3:76; Manns, *L'Evangile* 352) explain the tenses as a reflection of the later experience of the Johannine community, experiencing the Spirit and confident of the future presence of the Spirit. Schnackenburg distinguishes between the prepositions to make this point: παρ' ὑμῖν refers to the present experience of the community and ἐν ὑμῖν stresses the disciples' future knowledge of the Spirit's "inner presence."

[20] There is a *temporal* distance between Jesus and the Paraclete that must be maintained, despite Gail R. O'Day's claims ("'I Have Overcome the World'

phans (ὀρφανούς). This situation should follow the death of a parent, and Jesus' departure is associated with his death, yet it leads to his coming. The departure and the return coalesce (v. 18)! Jesus' physical departure will not be the end of his presence. This theme dominates vv. 18-21. Jesus' departure ends all "sight" of the revelation of the truth for "the world." As he warned "the Jews": "The light is with you for a little longer (ἔτι μικρόν). Walk while you have the light, so that the darkness may not overtake you" (12:35ab). That "little while" (14:19a: ἔτι μικρόν) is now coming to an end for "the world," as Jesus will depart definitively from its midst,[21] but the disciples, who believe in Jesus (see vv. 1, 11, 12), love him, and hold fast to his commandments (v. 15), are promised the sight of the departed Jesus and a life that will flow from his life beyond the departure of his death (v. 19).

When will this be? Most scholars opt for the resurrection while others refer to different forms of a life-giving presence of the risen Christ among the believers.[22] This offends against the narrative, as two characters who have been distinguished (v. 16), and who belong to a time sequence of "now" and "afterwards," are combined. The distinction between the physical Jesus, a Paraclete (v. 13) who is departing, and the "other Paraclete," who will be given (see v. 16), must be maintained. They are two different characters in the narrative, however closely their roles may be linked. The reader is aware that Jesus' departure will be through death (see 12:32-33), and that the other Paraclete is a gift of the departed Jesus (v. 16). Although Jesus is going away (v. 18a), he is coming to his disciples (v. 18b: ἔρχομαι) and they will see him (v. 19b: θεωρεῖτε). The death and departure of Jesus will lead to his life with the Father (v. 19cβ), and life for the disciples (v. 19cγ). Because he still lives, one consequence of his departure from the world is his life-giving presence to the disciples (v. 19b: ὅτι ἐγὼ ζῶ καὶ ὑμεῖς ζήσετε).[23] The departure of Jesus and the gift of the Paraclete, the Spirit

---

(John 16:33: Narrative Time in John 13–17," *Sem* 53 [1991] 160–61) that the Paraclete is not time-bound. Jesus departs before the gift of the Spirit.

[21] The use of ἔτι μικρόν in 12:35, warning "the Jews," as well as the more positive use of the expression with the disciples in 13:33, is involved in 14:19. It still contains an "oppressive element" denied by Schnackenburg, *St. John* 3:77–78.

[22] For a survey see Aune, *Cultic Setting* 128–29. See also Migliasso, *La presenza dell'Assente* 207–26; he unites the going, the coming, and the life-giving presence of the absent Jesus to the redemptive event of the cross.

[23] This "life" is linked to the gift of the Paraclete. See Müller, "Die Parakletenvorstellung," 51. On the disciples as "successor-agents" of the working of Jesus and bearers of the presence of the Father and the Son see D. Bruce Woll, "The

of truth, necessitate a distinction between Jesus and the Spirit, but what the Spirit *does* for the disciples is the prolongation and perfection of what Jesus *does* for them. In the Spirit-Paraclete the absence of the physical Jesus is overcome.[24] How is this possible? There can be no notion of the departed Jesus' return in any physical form. *It is in the community's "experience of the presence of the exalted Jesus in the midst of the worshiping community" that the absent one is present to those who love him and keep his commandments.*[25] Jesus' departure is not leaving them orphans (v. 18), because he comes to them in a gift of a living presence (v. 19); but Jesus is leaving his disciples, and this affirmation must be taken seriously. It no doubt reflected the experience of the Johannine readers, for whom the fleshly Jesus of Nazareth was no longer present (see 20:29).[26] But the experience of the living Jesus, exalted and thus no longer available in and through the physical Jesus, continues in and through the permanent presence of the Spirit-Paraclete. In the worshiping community, and especially in baptism and Eucharist, those who love and believe experience *the presence of the absent one.*[27]

Jesus promises a knowledge that will be granted to the believer on the day of his departure (ἐν ἐκείνῃ τῇ ἡμέρᾳ), the time of his coming and his gift of new life (v. 20). I am taking the traditional eschatological ex-

---

Departure of 'the Way': the First Farewell Discourse in the Gospel of John," *JBL* 99 (1980) 231–39.

[24] The Greek Fathers, especially Cyril of Alexandria, identified Jesus with the Paraclete. See Anthony Casurella, *The Johannine Paraclete in the Church Fathers. A Study in the History of Exegesis.* BGBE 25 (Tübingen: J. C. B. Mohr [Paul Siebeck], 1983) 43–45, 143–44. This position is nowadays generally rejected. See, for example, Hoskyns, *Fourth Gospel* 458–60. I am arguing for a position between that of the Fathers, who *identified* Jesus and the Paraclete, and most contemporary scholarship, which argues that *Jesus returns* in the post-resurrection period. One must distinguish yet associate Jesus, the former Paraclete (v. 13), and "the other Paraclete" (vv. 16-17). See Becker, *Johannes* 2:464–67); Jean Zumstein, "Mémoire et relecture pascale dans l'évangile de Jean," in Daniel Marguerat and Jean Zumstein, eds., *Le mémoire et le temps. Mélanges offerts a Pierre Bonnard* (Genève: Labor et Fides, 1991) 165.

[25] Aune, *Cultic Setting* 126–33. For the quotation see 133.

[26] See Müller, "Die Parakletenvorstellung," 40–43. See also Felix Porsch, "Der 'andere Paraklet,'" *BK* 37 (1982) 134.

[27] See Aune, *Cultic Setting* 16–18, 112–14. Francis J. Moloney, *Belief in the Word. Reading John 1–4* (Minneapolis: Fortress, 1993) 109–14 (on John 3:3-5); idem, *Signs and Shadows. Reading John 5–12* (Minneapolis: Fortress, 1996) 55–59 (on John 6:51-58); idem, *The Gospel of John* 505–10 (on John 19:34-37). See also the essay, "When Is John Talking about Sacraments?" in this volume, pp. 109–30.

pression ἐν ἐκείνῃ τῇ ἡμέρᾳ as referring to Jesus' "hour" and departure, producing what Brown rightly describes as "the period of Christian existence made possible by 'the hour.'"[28] Most read it as indicating the return of Jesus at his resurrection. This knowledge, a fruit of the presence of the Spirit, is the revelation of the oneness that exists between the Father and the Son, and the mutual oneness that exists between Jesus and the believer. The oneness between the Father and the Son has been at the heart of much of Jesus' teaching, and the basis of his authority (see, for example, 5:19-30), but the introduction of the believer into that oneness is new. The resolution of the search for knowledge and union with God has been promised to those who believe in Jesus (see vv. 1, 11, 12), who love him and keep his commandments (v. 15). They will not be left orphans through the departure of Jesus (v. 18), but granted life (v. 19), a knowledge of God, God's Son, and themselves (v. 20). The departure of Jesus unleashes something hitherto unknown and unspoken among his disciples. *It will happen, however, as a consequence of the departure of Jesus, and not as a result of Jesus' return at the resurrection.*

As v. 21 opens Jesus shifts from the intimacy of the second-person address to disciples to the wider audience of the gospel's readership: "They who have my commandments." All potential recipients of the promise of v. 20 are told that oneness with God is to be understood in terms of love. The reader is aware that Jesus' departure to the Father will be highlighted by his love for his own (13:1), having read how this will shortly take place in the midst of the disciples' ignorance, betrayal, and denial (13:1-38). But disciples must transform their response to the revelation of God in Jesus by a commitment to loving Jesus and holding fast to his commandments. They are now called to a parallel life of love in the in-between time after the departure of Jesus (13:34-35), enlivened by the gift of the Paraclete (14:16). The Paraclete will communicate life to the disciples that flows from the departed but living Jesus (v. 19). This love will lead to their being loved by the Father and by Jesus (v. 21b) and to the ongoing revelation of Jesus (ἐμφανίζειν αὐτῷ ἑαυτόν; see Exod 33:13, 18; Wis 1:2; 17:4) even after his departure (v. 21c).[29] Jesus' departure is not a departure in the sense in which "the world" would understand the experience of death. On the contrary, *as a consequence of the gift of the Paraclete, the Spirit of truth (vv. 15-16), it leads to the intimacy of being loved by both the Father and Jesus*

[28] Raymond E. Brown, *The Gospel According to John*. 2 vols. AB 29, 29a (New York: Doubleday, 1966–70) 2:640. See also Ernst Haenchen, *John*. 2 vols. Hermeneia (Philadelphia: Fortress, 1984) 2:126–27.

[29] As Barrett, *St John* 465, points out, ἐμφανίζειν, a *hapax*, "is an appropriate word since it is used of theophanies."

*and the ongoing revelation of God in and through Jesus as disciples experience
the presence of the absent one in their worship.*

4. Verses 22-24:
Loving Jesus and Keeping His Word

The theme of loving Jesus and holding fast to his commandments
opened the first subsection of vv. 15-24 in v. 15. Judas' question, asking
further clarification on the privilege of a revelation to the disciples that
will not be given to "the world" (v. 22), enables this subsection of the discourse to round off vv. 15-24 with the same themes (vv. 23-24). As with
earlier questions (see vv. 5, 8), Judas asks for information already obvious to the reader.[30] Jesus' revelation of himself, which is the sight of
God's glory (see 1:14, 2:11; 11:4, 40), can only be given to those who are
open to his word. Judas wonders about a revelation that will startle the
world (see 7:3-4). From the beginning of the story the author has instructed the reader that the sight of the revelation of God in Jesus is the
consequence of belief (see 1:9-13, 19-51; 2:1–4:54). The present discourse,
uttered on the eve of Jesus' consummate act of love for his own (see
13:1), has opened with a strong insistence on the need for belief (see 14:1,
11, 12), but has made a further demand on the disciples. Disciples are not
only to believe in the word of Jesus, but also to love him (see 14:15, 21,
23-24). The departed Jesus will manifest himself to the disciples because
they believe in his words and love him. He will not manifest himself to
"the world" because it refuses both belief and love. The reader knows of
the hostility, rejection, and increasing threat of a violent end that marked
the public life of Jesus, but during that period of time he was physically
present. Such a situation will no longer exist in the in-between time after
the departure of Jesus. The absent Jesus will only be present to those
who, gifted with the Spirit, believe and love.

Jesus reaffirms the positive results of a disciple's loving him and
keeping his word: the Father of Jesus *will love* that disciple and both
Father and Son *will come* and *will set up* their abode in him or her (v. 23).
As with vv. 18-21, the question arises: when will this "coming" take
place? In v. 23 the departure is coupled with the promise of the coming
of the Father and the Son to make their home (μονήν) with the disciple
who loves Jesus and keeps his word. But unlike vv. 18-21, which promised the experience of the presence of the absent Jesus after his departure (see v. 18: ἔρχομαι πρὸς ὑμᾶς), in v. 23 every verb is in the future:
the Father and Son *will love*, they *will come*, and they *will establish* a

---

[30] On "Judas, not Iscariot," see Schnackenburg, *St. John* 3:80–81.

dwelling place (see v. 23: πρὸς αὐτὸν ἐλευσόμεθα). The temporal setting of the meal must be kept in mind. Jesus opened his discourse speaking of an in-between time between his departure and the promise of his future coming (vv. 2-3). This period will be filled by the presence of the Paraclete (vv. 15-17) and the life-giving presence of the departed and exalted Lord in the worshiping community (vv. 18-21). There are two details in v. 23 that point the reader toward the end of the in-between time. The use of the present tense in v. 18 (ἔρχομαι) and the future tense in v. 23 (ἐλευσόμεθα) in such proximate contexts indicates that the author is suggesting different possibilities for the "coming" in vv. 18-21 and v. 23.[31] Second, the resumption of an image from vv. 2-3, where μονή was used, suggests the definitive and permanent presence of the Father and the Son, establishing their μονήν with the one who loves Jesus and holds fast to his word (v. 23).[32] The departed Jesus comes to those who love and believe as they experience the presence of the absent one (vv. 18-21), and they can also look forward to a final coming when Jesus and the Father will set up their dwelling with them (v. 23). I am rejecting the widespread interpretation of v. 23 as "in terms of the mystical abiding of God with the believer."[33] The almost universal agreement that vv. 18-24 refer to the *present* coming of Jesus (and the Father) to the believer *does away with the need for the "other Paraclete."*[34] The person who does not love Jesus and does not keep his words is rejecting the words of the Father, who sent Jesus. It is not the sent one who is being rejected, but the one who sent him (v. 24). The promise of the dwelling of the Father and the Son is in the future, but rejection by the one who does not love Jesus or keep his commandments (μὴ ἀγαπῶν . . . οὐ τηρεῖ) is an action that takes place in the present. This is a rejection of the ongoing revelation of God that took place in the

---

[31] The ἔρχομαι in v. 18 cannot be put down to the use of the present with a future meaning, unlike the use of πάλιν ἔρχομαι in v. 3 where a future meaning is likely within the general context and after πάλιν.

[32] Here I depart from Aune, *Cultic Setting* 130–31, who associates the μονή of v. 23 (where οἰκία does not appear) with the use of οἰκία and μονή in v. 2, claiming that they both refer to "an individual believer who is the locus for the pneumatic dwelling of the Father and the Son."

[33] Barrett, *St John* 466.

[34] See, for a similar assessment, Udo Schnelle, "Johannes als Geisttheologe," *NovT* 40 (1998) 19–20. Schnelle (p. 20 n. 9) sees Wilhelm Heitmüller, *Das Johannes-Evangelium*. SNT 4 (3rd ed. Göttingen: Vandenhoeck & Ruprecht, 1920) 152, as the founder of this point of view in modern exegesis. Heitmüller seems to return to the Greek Fathers: "im Geist kommt Jesu selbst" [in the Spirit Jesus himself comes].

words and works of Jesus and is continued in the Spirit-filled community. The passage restates a theme that has appeared repeatedly during Jesus' public ministry (see 3:34; 5:23-24; 8:18, 28, 38, 47; 12:49). In a short time Jesus will be physically absent, but the revelation of God continues in and through the Spirit-filled community of disciples, enlivened by the presence of the absent one.[35] It can be rejected by those who refuse to love Jesus and keep his commandments, but such rejection is nothing less than a rejection of God (v. 24).

The theme of Jesus' departure is present across vv. 1-14, especially in vv. 1-6. It is a fundamental presupposition for all that is said in vv. 15-24. The situation of the disciples after Jesus' departure (see vv. 18-19) is dealt with. While some of Jesus' instructions are based upon the reader's knowledge and experience of the story of his public ministry (see vv. 16-17, 19, 24), they increasingly look forward to the inevitable end of the gospel, known to the reader as Jesus' glorification and the revelation of the glory of God (see 11:4; 12:23; 13:31-32), the moment in the future when the Spirit will be given to the believer (see 7:37-39). This feature of the story has led to the insinuation of a theme that has not been present earlier in the story: love (vv. 15, 21, 23-24: "love me") and loyalty (vv. 15, 21, 23-24: "keep my word/words/commandments"). The association of belief, love, and loyalty leads to a new promise: disciples who, in the presence of the Paraclete, love Jesus and keep his commandments in the in-between time will come to know God and will be loved by God and Jesus. Because the exalted Jesus lives, gifted by the Spirit-Paraclete (see vv. 16-17), they will experience the life-giving presence of the absent one (see v. 19). They will be privy to the life of love that unites the Father and the Son (vv. 20-21), until the Father and the Son finally come to establish their dwelling with them (v. 23).

Some Consequences

There are exegetical, theological, and hermeneutical consequences to this sharp distinction between Jesus and the Paraclete.

The remaining Paraclete sayings

My thesis is that the Paraclete is a distinct character who will play a major role in the ongoing story of those who subsequently read this account of the life, teaching, death, and resurrection of Jesus. They are

---

[35] See Aune, *Cultic Setting* 103–105.

sharply aware of the absence of the physical Jesus (20:29).[36] Once this absence is taken as an essential starting point for the interpretation of the Paraclete sayings many of the so-called tensions surrounding the interpretation of the other Paraclete sayings are eased.[37]

Opening the final section of 14:1-31, vv. 25-26 return to the figure of the other Paraclete, introduced at the beginning of the central section of the discourse. Jesus' words in vv. 25-31 repeat the encouragement he gave to his disciples, despite his imminent departure, in vv. 1-14. If vv. 15-17 introduced a new character and told of his never-failing presence to the members of a believing community, vv. 25-26 tell them that he will continue the revealing role of Jesus. The words and commandments of Jesus, so central to vv. 15-24, will not be forgotten. The Paraclete will remind them of the teachings of Jesus *despite his absence*, and will go on teaching them all things. The former Paraclete must be "lifted up" and glorified so that the Spirit may be given (see 7:37-39; 19:30). This will not happen to the other Paraclete, who will remain forever to ensure the ongoing revelation of God initiated by Jesus (14:25-26).

John 15:26-27, regarded by many commentators as an intrusive editorial addition to the original text, is entirely appropriate. Jesus tells the disciples that the Paraclete will be sent from the Father by Jesus into the hatred they will experience *during the time of his absence*. They will be hated, persecuted, thrown out of synagogues, and even slain by people claiming to offer service to God (15:18–16:3). The departed Jesus will send the Paraclete from the Father to ensure ongoing witness to Jesus in the lives of disciples who must go on witnessing to the absent Jesus (15:26-27). The Paraclete not only continues the revealing task of Jesus (see 14:25-26), but empowers suffering disciples so that they might steadfastly continue their witness to the absent Jesus (15:26-27).

The judging and revealing task of the Paraclete, described in 16:7-11, 12-15, continues these critical functions of the historical Jesus *during the period of his absence*. The presence of Jesus has unfailingly produced a κρίσις (see 3:19; 5:24, 27; 12:31), and the other Paraclete continues that critical and divisive presence of the revelation of God during the period of Jesus' absence (16:7-11). The definitive revelation of God that took place in Jesus continues in the presence of the other Paraclete

---

[36] For a study of 20:1-31 as a narrative directed to a community needing encouragement, faced by the absence of Jesus, see Francis J. Moloney, *Glory not Dishonor. Reading John 13–21* (Minneapolis: Fortress, 1998) 153–81.

[37] See also Schnelle, "Johannes als Geisttheologe," 18–22.

(vv. 12-15). Many claim that the risen Jesus has returned to the community in some form and is present in a way *paralleling* the presence of the Paraclete. What, then, is the meaning of 16:7: "It is to your advantage that I go away, for if I do not go away, the Paraclete will not come to you; but if I go, I will send him to you"? The narrative makes sense. Jesus is *absent*, but the other Paraclete continues some of his functions and adds others not called for while Jesus, the former Paraclete, was present. Many of the difficulties experienced by contemporary Johannine scholars stem from their inability to admit that the departure of Jesus through "the hour" is definitive. He is present after the resurrection, but only in and through the gift of "the other Paraclete."

Johannine Eschatology

Theologically the Fourth Gospel's eschatology can be seen as more at home with mainstream New Testament thought than is sometimes suggested. As with the bulk of early Christian understandings of time, based on a traditional Jewish eschatological model, there is a period of ambiguity following the death and departure of the historical Jesus. Part of this ambiguity results from the fact that a period marked by the absence of Jesus lay before the early Christians. The Fourth Evangelist is not the first to suggest that this absence will be filled by the presence of the Spirit, even though the incorporation of the Paraclete material makes this gospel's understanding of the in-between time unique. For all the attention devoted to the Johannine realized eschatology, the Johannine community is conscious of living an in-between time, and it awaits the parousia as did other communities in the early Church and all subsequent Christian communities. Like all human communities, the Christians who produced and first read or listened to the Fourth Gospel had to grapple with the reality of the death of their friends and associates. The regular references to an end-time on the lips of Jesus (see 5:28-29; 6:39, 40, 44, 57), the story of Lazarus (11:1-44), and Jesus' self-revelation as the resurrection and the life both here and hereafter (11:25-26) all have their proper place in this gospel. The dedication of this essay to a dear friend, too soon and too painfully departed, was a sharp reminder to me that a gospel that only preaches "life now" fails to address the most fundamental of all human experiences: death.[38]

---

[38] Dr. Barbara M. Stead, R.S.M., returned to the one who sent her on 29 April 1998, after a short and painful illness. She was my longstanding friend and an outstanding colleague at Australian Catholic University. "The grass withers, the flower fades; but the word of our God will stand forever" (Isa 40:8).

Joachim Jeremias' attempt to resolve the hefty debate of the 1950s over the eschatology of Jesus of Nazareth as a *sich realisierende Eschatologie* is also applicable to the Fourth Gospel.[39]

The role of the Johannine story in the in-between-time

Finally, again in light of this distinction between the present Paraclete and the absent Jesus, I would like to suggest a hermeneutical key for the interpretation of the Fourth Gospel. Classically the gospel can be divided into two major blocks. One deals with the public ministry, prefaced by a Prologue (1:1–12:50), and the other is devoted to Jesus' departure, his glorification, and the glorification of the Father (13:1–20:31).[40] Major statements, one from the narrator (12:43) and the other from Jesus (20:29), at the end of each of these sections provide a key for the understanding of the gospel. As the story of Jesus' public ministry comes to an end the narrator comments on the failure of "the Jews" to accept Jesus: "They loved the δόξαν τῶν ἀνθρώπων rather than the δόξαν τοῦ θεοῦ" (12:43). For those who do not judge by human criteria (see 7:24; 8:15) the story of Jesus Christ makes known the glory of God (see 2:11; 11:4, 40).

"The Jews" were unable to accept that the glory of God, once revealed on Sinai and transmitted to the people of God through Moses and the Law, could be seen in the revelation of God in and through the presence of Jesus among them (see 1:16-17).[41] As they comment in their trial of the man born blind, "we are disciples of Moses. We know that God has spoken to Moses, but as for this man, we do not know where he comes from" (9:28b-29). Before the resurrection of Lazarus Jesus comments: "Did I not tell you that if you believed, you would see the glory of God?" (11:40). In his prayer to the Father he then remarks, "I have said this for the sake of the crowd standing here, so that they may believe that you sent me" (11:42b). The Johannine story of Jesus proclaims that Jesus of Nazareth is the definitive revelation of the glory of God (see 1:51; 3:13-14, etc.)

[39] Joachim Jeremias, *The Parables of Jesus* (London: SCM, 1963) 230: "an eschatology that is in process of realization."

[40] See the classic statement of this position in C. H. Dodd, *The Interpretation of the Fourth Gospel* (Cambridge: Cambridge University Press, 1953) 289–443. For the hermeneutical implications of the overall structure and argument of the gospel and the role of the Paraclete see also Schnelle, "Johannes als Geisttheologe," 18–19, 30–31.

[41] For this interpretation of 1:16-17 see Moloney, *Belief in the Word* 45–51; idem, *The Gospel of John* 39–41, 45–47.

But for the members of the Johannine community who take this text in hand or listen to its public proclamation Jesus of Nazareth is no longer present. Like contemporary Christians they are living in the in-between-time and experiencing the *absence of Jesus*. Jesus' final words in the gospel address this situation. After the climactic confession of faith from Thomas who, like Mary Magdalene, longed to touch and cling to the physical Jesus,[42] Jesus announces: "You have believed because you saw me. Blessed are those who have not seen and yet believe" (20:29). The Fourth Gospel addresses Christians, challenged to believe despite the physical absence of Jesus Christ. The *story* has been written so that they might go on believing that Jesus is the Christ, the Son of God, and have life in his name *despite his absence* (20:30-31). This tale of two Paracletes is sacred γραφή, as yet unread by the two disciples at the tomb, characters *in the story*, but written so that *readers of the story*, who do not see, might believe (see John 20:9, 30-31).[43] Enlightened, taught, strengthened, and supported by the presence of the *other* Paraclete, they are to find the δόξαν τοῦ θεοῦ (12:43) in the *story* of the absent Jesus (20:29), the *former* Paraclete.

---

[42] On this see Dorothy A. Lee, "Partnership in Easter Faith: The Role of Mary Magdalene and Thomas in John 20," *JSNT* 58 (1995) 37–49.

[43] See especially Andreas Obermann, *Die christologische Erfüllung der Schrift im Johannesevangelium. Eine Untersuchung zur johanneischen Hermeneutik anhand der Schriftzitate*. WUNT 2nd ser. 83 (Tübingen: J. C. B. Mohr [Paul Siebeck] 1996), especially 409–22. See also Moloney, *The Gospel of John* 520–24, 542–45.

CHAPTER 8

"GOD SO LOVED THE WORLD."
THE JESUS OF JOHN'S GOSPEL

FOR VIRGINIA ANNE MOLONEY: *IN MEMORIAM*

Like every piece of literature, ancient or modern, the Gospel of John was produced by its own circumstances, has its own internal narrative structure and literary techniques, and addresses its own readership.[1] A correct reading of the Fourth Gospel demands recognition of three worlds: the world behind the text, the world in the text, and the world in front of the text. There are a number of contexts that have shaped the Jesus-story of the Fourth Gospel, and, as our literary colleagues are busy telling us, text without context is pretext.[2] In plain terms, the Jesus of John's gospel is not a videotaped presentation of the historical Jesus, who lived and died some seventy years before this gospel saw the light of day. Yet, however much the emerging theological perspectives of the Christian community in which and for which this story was produced may have influenced the gospel's portrait of Jesus, there is a link with the fundamental historical event of the death of Jesus.

---

[1] There are many publications dealing with this issue. See, for example, Francis J. Moloney, *The Living Voice of the Gospel. The Gospels Today* (Melbourne: Collins Dove, 1986).

[2] See my essay, "Narrative Criticism of the Gospels," in this volume, pp. 85–105.

This is one of the few historical events that even the most cynical of contemporary critics must accept took place, however oddly they might like to explain it.[3] But although this gospel takes for granted the inevitable *fact* of the death of Jesus, it has a unique interpretation of the *meaning* of that event.

After decades of attempts on the part of the critics to make better sense of the narrative by rearrangements, and then by tracing a variety of hands and strata in the gospel, contemporary literary approaches are reaffirming the integrity of the traditional narrative structure.[4] This may be comforting to those who have been annoyed by the somewhat archeological approach to the text by historical critics, but it must be remembered that a Christian storyteller, writing in the social, religious, and political maelstrom of the last decade of the first Christian century, would tell a story that responded to the literary practices of that time and place. The story of the Fourth Gospel is strongly conditioned by the Jesus-tradition that informs it, but this does not lessen the fact that *the point of view* of a first-century author plays a large part in the way this story is shaped and the way in which this literary shape influences the portrait of Jesus that emerges from its pages.

The hermeneutical question must be posed. If so much of the interpretation of this ancient text is determined by its *origins,* what is it that leads us to look to this text for direction and inspiration at the turn of the millennium? I will respond briefly to that question in my conclusion. I am dedicating this essay to the memory of my sister-in-law, Virginia Anne Moloney, who left us on 9 October 1997 after a remarkable life and an equally remarkable death by pancreatic cancer. I trust that my brief conclusions to this study will indicate the suitability of the dedication.

1. WHAT DOES THE JOHANNINE JESUS CLAIM TO BE DOING?

On three occasions during the gospel Jesus addresses this question. Toward the end of his first foray into Samaria, a non-Jewish world, his disciples bring provisions and the Samaritan woman returns to her village, leaving her water container behind. She will be back, but the dis-

---

[3] On this issue see the contrasting positions of Raymond E. Brown, *The Death of the Messiah. From Gethsemane to the Grave.* ABRL (New York: Doubleday, 1994), and John Dominic Crossan, *Who Killed Jesus? Exposing the Roots of Anti-Semitism in the Gospel Story of the Death of Jesus* (San Francisco: HarperCollins, 1994).

[4] For a survey see Francis J. Moloney, *The Gospel of John.* SP 4 (Collegeville: The Liturgical Press, 1998) 11–20.

ciples are shocked that Jesus should be speaking to a Samaritan woman. The situation worsens when he refuses to take any of their food (John 4:27-28). They suspect that he has even eaten with her (see v. 33). The narrator's earlier comment on the relationship between Jews and Samaritans is still operative in the narrative: "Jews do not share things in common with Samaritans" (John 4:9c).[5] Playing upon their perplexity, Jesus transcends their concerns, thus explaining why he was with the Samaritan woman and why he has no need of food: "My food is to do the will of him who sent me and to complete his work" (v. 34). Two important expressions appear for the first time in the gospel: Jesus is on a mission to do the will of God, and this means that he must bring to perfection (τελειώσω) a certain "work," a task that forms part of God's design: "his work" (αὐτοῦ τὸ ἔργον).[6]

As the ministry progresses Jesus defends his mission against "the Jews" who have decided that he must be slain because he offends Sabbath law. He tells them, "The works that the Father has given me to complete, the very works that I am doing, testify on my behalf that the Father has sent me" (5:36). God's design, that Jesus bring to perfection the work of the Father, made visible in the works of Jesus, legitimates Jesus' words and actions in the face of all contrary suggestions and accusations.[7]

At the conclusion of Jesus' final encounter with his disciples, as he goes to the cross, looking back across the ministry, he tells the Father: "I glorified you on earth by finishing the work that you gave me to do" (17:4). The expressions found across the public ministry reappear: "bringing to perfection/finishing" (τελειώσας) "the work" (τὸ ἔργον). One of the features of Jesus' final prayer is its wandering in and out of the time-sequence of the narrative. Having made the claim that the work has been accomplished in 17:4, Jesus goes on to explain how he has done this:

> I have made your name known to those whom you gave me from the world. They were yours, and you gave them to me, and they have kept your word. Now they know that everything you have given me is from

---

[5] The verb συνκράομαι is generally translated as "to have dealings with." David Daube, *The New Testament and Rabbinic Judaism* (London: Athlone, 1956) 373–82, has argued for the translation adopted here. See also C. K. Barrett, *The Gospel According to St John* (2nd ed. London: S.P.C.K.; Philadelphia: Westminster, 1978) 232–33.

[6] On this passage see Francis J. Moloney, *Belief in the Word. Reading John 1–4* (Minneapolis: Fortress, 1993) 134–68. On 4:34 see pp. 160–62.

[7] On this passage see Francis J. Moloney, *Signs and Shadows. Reading John 5–12* (Minneapolis: Fortress, 1996) 19–27.

you; for the words that you gave to me I have given to them, and they have received them and know in truth that I came from you; and they have believed that you sent me (vv. 6-8).

But this assessment of the disciples is somewhat flattering, and events lie ahead that are even more a part of Jesus' perfection of the work of the Father than his having made known the name of God to his disciples. They will misunderstand him, deny him, and betray him, but he will love them "to the end" (13:1: εἰς τέλος).[8] That is yet to come in the narrative.

However one handles the critical problem that arises from the "timing" of 17:4, the author's point of view is made clear in 4:34, 5:36, and 17:4: Jesus regards his life as determined by the will of the one who sent him. His task is to bring to perfection the work of the Father. What is already becoming evident is that, despite the remarkable things that are said about Jesus in the Fourth Gospel, his life, death, and resurrection function as once-and-for-all moments in the realization of God's design for the human story. The gospel may be about Jesus, but Jesus is about God's business. To use theological language, Johannine christology is not an end in itself. It is in service of the author's major concern: theology.[9]

This becomes even more obvious when another text from John 17 is added, one that articulates what it means to do the will of the Father: "to give eternal life to all whom you have given him. And this is eternal life, that they may know you, the only true God, and Jesus Christ whom you have sent" (17:2b-3).[10] An equation is emerging. Jesus claims to be:

- doing the will of the Father who sent him (see 4:34),
- bringing to perfection the work of God (see 4:34; 5:36; 17:4),
- by enabling eternal life for all who come to know the one true God (17:2-3),
- through Jesus, the sent one (17:2-3).

[8] See Francis J. Moloney, "A Sacramental Reading of John 13:1-31," *CBQ* 53 (1991) 237–56.

[9] This is the central claim of my article, "Johannine Theology," in *NJBC* 1417–26. See p. 1420: "Despite appearances, John really is not a story about Jesus, but a story about what God has done in Jesus."

[10] John 17:3 is often regarded as secondary and thus is given little importance by critics. There are many indications that 17:3 has been added to an already existing prayer. See Moloney, *The Gospel of John* 464. But this does not make the explanation of what "eternal life" means for the gospel as we have it in its final form any less important. Indeed, the opposite is the case.

But this equation hides a number of issues unknown to us at this stage of our reflection. We must locate these unknowns within the Johannine story. Most important is the question: if Jesus does the will of God and brings to perfection the task God has given him, enabling eternal life by making God known, what sort of God does Jesus make known? Again to state the question in more theological terms, if the christology of the Fourth Gospel is determined by its theology, what is said about the God of the Johannine Jesus?

2. WHAT SORT OF GOD IS THE FATHER OF JESUS?

As one would imagine in an early Christian world, there is never any attempt to describe or define God, although some have claimed that 1 John 4:8, 16 ("God is love") makes such an attempt. In the Fourth Gospel God is in relationship, and God acts. The relationship that exists between God and Jesus is articulated in the Prologue (1:1-18) and taken for granted from that point in the narrative: "And the Word became flesh and lived among us, the fullness of a gift that is truth. We have gazed upon his glory, glory as of the only Son from the Father. . . . No one has ever seen God; the only Son, who is turned toward the Father, he has told God's story" (1:14, 18*).[11] The relationship between the Father and the Son is fundamental to Jesus' unique role in the human story: making God known. Toward the end of the gospel Jesus asks the father that believers be swept into the relationship with God that he has had from all time:

> Father, I desire that those also, whom you have given me, may be with me where I am, to see my glory, which you have given me because you loved me before the foundation of the world. . . . I made your name known to them, and I will make it known, so that the love with which you have loved me may be in them, and I in them (17:24, 26).

The love that has existed from all time between God and the Word, between the Father and the Son, has burst into the human story. Jesus has made it known so that others might be swept into that same relationship.

The gospel always speaks of an acting God, and the most consistent expression used to speak of the action of God is that God "sends." There are two verbs used for the sending action of God (πέμπω and ἀποστέλλω), and many have argued for a nuance of meaning between

---

[11] For the exegetical basis of this translation of John 1:14, 18 see Moloney, *Belief in the Word* 40–51.

them.[12] I doubt if this distinction can be maintained, and for our purposes it is important simply to be aware that God "sent" John the Baptist (1:6: ἀπεσταλμένος παρὰ θεοῦ) to bear witness to the light, and that Jesus is, above all, the "sent one" of God, the "sent one" of the Father. In the first section of this essay I have already used two passages that link Jesus' being the sent one of the Father with his mandate to do the will of the Father, to bring to perfection his "work": "My food is to do the will of *him who sent me* and to complete his work" (4:34); "the very works that I am doing testify on my behalf that *the Father has sent me*" (5:36). But again God's sending action does not cease with the Witness (1:6) and Jesus (4:34; 5:36, and *passim*). Toward the end of the gospel Jesus prays that the disciples be caught up into the sending action of God: "As you have sent me into the world, so I have sent them into the world" (17:18). The ultimate responsibility of the Father for the mission of the Christian disciple is rendered by the "as" (καθὼς) . . . "so also" (κἀγὼ).

But there is a further action of God that determines even more radically the Johannine presentation of the person and actions of God. It is provided by the title of this paper: "For God so loved the world that he gave his only Son, so that everyone who believes in him may not perish but may have eternal life" (3:16). It is God's love for the world that determines the sending of the Son, so that the world might have eternal life. But we have already seen the author's definition of eternal life in the prayer of Jesus in 17:3: "this is eternal life, that they may know you, the only true God." Further elements in the equation are being added. The task of Jesus is to make God known and to create the possibility of eternal life, but our only access to Jesus' revelation of a God whom no one has ever seen (see 1:18) is through Jesus' words and actions.

The Fourth Gospel makes clear that God has a relationship with the Son, and has sent the Son so that others may enter that same relationship and continue the mission of Jesus. Above all, the motivation for the sending of the Son is God's love for the world. Little wonder that an elder from the Johannine community of early Christians, in a period that slightly postdates the gospel, could twice affirm: "God is love" (1 John 4:8, 16). While this might sound like a definition of God, it would never pass the strict criteria of a modern description of a definition. To describe God as "love" tells us very little about the essence of God. It goes no further than the gospel's affirmation: "God so loved the world" (3:16). As one of the many post-Vatican II posters once announced: "God is not a noun, but a verb." Those of us versed in the

---

[12] See, for example, Karl H. Rengstorf, ἀποστέλλω, *TDNT* 1 (1964) 404–406.

finer points of development of the ancient Hebrew name of God, YHWH, are aware how true the poster's claims are for the God of the Hebrew Bible,[13] but the same must be said for the God of the Fourth Gospel. The God of the Johannine Jesus cannot be known in the divine essence, or in the divine being, but only through divine actions: relating, sending, and loving. The task of Jesus is to make known a God who can only be approached as the one who loved the world so much as to send the only Son of God. The task of Jesus is *to make love known.*

3. HOW DOES JESUS MAKE KNOWN A GOD OF LOVE?

There are two ways in which Jesus makes God known: by his words and in his actions. It would require more space than we have at our disposal to analyze the *words* of Jesus throughout this gospel, and especially the magisterial discourses of John 5, 6, 7–8, 10:1-14; 14:1–16:33, and the prayer of 17:1-26.[14] For the purposes of this reflection I would like to focus attention on the crucial *action* of Jesus' life: his death. The Fourth Gospel is unique in the New Testament in presenting the death of Jesus as his most significant achievement, the moment when he brings to perfection the task given him by the Father, the one who sent him, glorifying God and achieving his own glory.

A brief glance sideways at two other New Testament witnesses will serve as contrast. The Gospel of Mark has often been described as a Passion narrative with a long introduction. Jesus marches courageously to Jerusalem, prophesying his oncoming death (see Mark 8:31; 9:31; 10:32-34). He is arrested, tried, and hammered to a cross from which he cries: "My God, my God, why have you forsaken me?" (15:34). But that is not his only cry from the cross. The narrator recalls that, at the moment of his death, "Jesus gave a loud cry and breathed his last" (15.37). It is not until after he has been ignominiously done to death that things begin to happen. The curtain of the Temple is rent from top to bottom, a Gentile confesses that he was a Son of God (15:38-39), and women discover God's messenger and hear the Easter proclamation at an empty tomb (16:1-8). God's immediate intervention in the events of

---

[13] The sacred, indeed unpronounceable, name of the God of Israel is a form of the Hebrew verb "to be." God is, always will be, and is the cause of all that is and always will be. For a challenging presentation of a number of effects a shift of perspective from "God as a noun" to "God as a verb" would have, see Mary Daly, *Beyond God the Father: Toward a Philosophy of Women's Liberation* (Boston: Beacon, 1973) 33–40.

[14] I can only refer an interested reader to my more extensive work on the Fourth Gospel for this, especially *The Gospel of John.*

the story indicates that Jesus' cry from the cross has not been in vain: he has not been abandoned by his God.

In the famous hymn found in the second chapter of Paul's letter to the Philippians (Phil 2:6-11) the Apostle to the Gentiles traces Jesus' career. He did not regard his equality with God as something to be grasped jealously to himself, but he emptied himself, taking on the form of a slave, born into the human condition (see Phil 2:6-7). At the center of the hymn he comes to his lowest moment: "he humbled himself and became obedient to the point of death—even death on a cross" (v. 8). It is as a *consequence* of this humility and humiliation that God highly exalted him and gave him the name that is above every name, that every knee should bend and every tongue confess Jesus as Lord (vv. 9-11). For both Mark and Paul the experience of the cross is the *lowest moment* in Jesus' human experience, and his exaltation is the *consequence* of this unconditional commitment to the will of God.

This is not the case in the Fourth Gospel. From its earliest pages Jesus begins to speak of his oncoming death as a "lifting up," an exaltation.

> "Just as Moses lifted up the serpent in the wilderness, so must the Son of Man be lifted up, that whoever believes in him may have eternal life" (3:14).

> "When you have lifted up the Son of Man, then you will realize that I am he" (8:28).

> "And I, when I am lifted up from the earth, will draw all people to myself." He said this to indicate the kind of death he was to die (12:32-33).

It is fascinating that the verb Paul used in Phil 2:9 to speak of God's exaltation of Jesus *because of* his readiness to humble himself unto death, even death on a cross (ὑψωθῆναι) is used in the Fourth Gospel to speak of Jesus' being exalted *upon the cross*. In its Pauline context it only has one meaning: God's exaltation into glory of God's obedient crucified one. In the Fourth Gospel the verb has two meanings. It means both the physical act of "lifting up" on a stake, as is obvious from the use of the verb in the parallel description of Moses' lifting up the serpent in the desert (3:14: "Just as [καὶ καθώς] . . . so [οὕτως]"), but it also retains the meaning of "exaltation."[15] The crucifixion of Jesus is at one and the same time both the physical lifting up of Jesus from the ground on a cross and his exaltation.[16]

---

[15] For this possibility see Walter Bauer, William F. Arndt, F. Wilbur Gingrich, and Frederick W. Danker, *A Greek-English Lexicon of the New Testament and Other Early Christian Literature* (2nd ed. Chicago: University of Chicago Press, 1979) 850–51, s.v. ὑψόω.

[16] See Moloney, *Belief in the Word* 117–18.

Other elements in the gospel begin to gather more meaning. As Jesus and his disciples accompany the mother of Jesus to a wedding at Cana his mother points out that they have no wine. Jesus replies, "Woman, what concern is that to you and to me? My hour has not yet come" (2:4). Despite the rebuke, the mother of Jesus has limitless faith in the efficacy of Jesus' word, and she tells the attendants, "Do whatever he tells you" (2:5). The miracle that follows is a symbol of the messianic fullness promised by the prophets: an abundance of wine, happiness, and good things (see Isa 25:6-8; 54:4-8; 62:4-5). The best will be kept till last (see 2:10). The "hour" of Jesus will be associated with a final messianic gesture, of which the marriage feast is an anticipatory sign.[17] At the celebration of the Feast of Tabernacles, Jesus' brothers insist that he go up to the feast to manifest himself by means of his wonderful miracles. Jesus replies, "My time has not yet come, but your time is always here. . . . Go to the festival yourselves. I am not going to *this* festival, for my time has not yet fully come" (7:6, 8). The "hour" of Jesus will not take place at *this* feast, but it will come at *another* feast. On another occasion during this same celebration of Tabernacles, as Jesus points to his unique unity with the Father, his opponents attempt to arrest him, but they are not able to do so "because his hour had not yet come" (7:30). Still in the Temple precincts, he accuses his opponents of not being able to know God because they do not know him, "but no one arrested him, because his hour had not yet come" (8:20). In the end they take up stones and drive him out of the Temple (8:59). Not only will "the hour" be associated with the messianic event (2:1-12), but it points forward to a later feast of the Jews (7:6-8) when those who would violently lay hands upon him will have their way (7:30; 8:20, 59).[18] Until that time, however, his hour has not yet come.

In 11:55 the narrator announces, "Now the Passover of the Jews was near." The temporal aspect of a narrative that has moved rapidly through at least a two-year cycle of the festive celebrations of Israel: Pentecost, Passover, Tabernacles, and Dedication, almost comes to a stop. While John 1:1–11:54 covers two years, 11:55–20:31 fills only a few days.[19] On the first of these days some Greeks come to see Jesus. Jesus announces: "The hour has come for the Son of Man to be glorified"

---

[17] Ibid. 77–92.

[18] On the dense and complex encounters between Jesus and "the Jews" in the Temple on the occasion of the celebration of Tabernacles (John 7–8) see Moloney, *Signs and Shadows* 65–116.

[19] On the use of "time" in narrative see the fundamental work of Gérard Genette, *Narrative Discourse: An Essay in Method.* Translated by Jane E. Lewin; foreword by Jonathan Culler (Ithaca, N.Y.: Cornell University Press, 1980) 33–85.

(12:23). The hour of Jesus is also the moment of his glorification, and Jesus' words to his disciples on the reason for Lazarus' illness can be recalled: "This illness does not lead to death; rather it is for God's glory, so that the Son of God may be glorified through it" (11:4). The raising of Lazarus triggers the coming of the Greeks, "the Jews'" decision that he must die (11:49-50), and Jesus' proclamation that "the hour" has come for his glorification.[20] The theme of the hour dominates the final days. It marks the beginning and the end of Jesus' final night with the disciples. As it opens the narrator comments: "Now before the festival of the Passover, Jesus knew that his hour had come to depart from this world and go to the Father. Having loved his own who were in the world, he loved them to the end" (13:1). As he closes the evening with his prayer, Jesus prays, "Father, the hour has come; glorify your Son so that the Son may glorify you" (17:1). At the cross Jesus consigns his mother to the Beloved Disciple and the Beloved Disciple to his mother, and the narrator comments: "And because of that hour he took her into his own home" (19:27*). A new family of God is founded by the exalted and crucified Jesus "because of that hour."[21]

There is another theme that points to the cross for its consummation: the gathering of the children of God who are scattered abroad. Although hinted at earlier in the narrative, it is first explicitly stated within the context of Jesus' discourse on the Good Shepherd who lays down his life for his sheep. In a discourse shot through with images that have their roots in the traditions and symbols of Israel[22] Jesus announces, "I have other sheep that do not belong to this fold. I must bring them also, and they will listen to my voice. So there will be one flock, one shepherd" (10:16). Hard on the heels of this discourse the raising of Lazarus leads Caiaphas to instruct his faltering colleagues: "You know nothing at all! You do not understand that it is better for you to have one man die for the people than to have the whole nation destroyed" (11:49b-50). To this the narrator adds, "He did not say this on his own, but being high priest that year he prophesied that Jesus

---

[20] See Moloney, *Signs and Shadows* 178–95.

[21] Most translations render 19:27 "from that hour," but the Greek ἀπ᾽ ἐκείνης τῆς ὥρας is open to two meanings: a temporal "from that hour" or a causal "because of that hour." Both are involved in 19:27, given the theological and dramatic significance of "the hour" in the gospel story as a whole. For the use of ἀπό with the genitive for a causal meaning see BDF 113 §210.

[22] See Johannes Beutler, "Der alttestamentlich-jüdische Hintergrund der Hirtenrede in Johannes 10," in Johannes Beutler and Robert T. Fortna, eds., *The Shepherd Discourse of John 10 and its Context.* SNTSMS 67 (Cambridge: Cambridge University Press, 1991) 18–32.

was about to die for the nation, and not for the nation only, but to gather into one the dispersed children of God" (11:51-52). The raising of Lazarus remains a problem for the leaders of "the Jews," and they plot steadily to put both Jesus *and* Lazarus to death "since it was on account of him that many of the Jews were deserting and were believing in Jesus" (12:11). The entrance of Jesus into Jerusalem generates even further anxiety, as they comment: "You see, you can do nothing. Look, the world has gone after him!" (12:19), and in fulfillment of those words some Greeks ask to see Jesus. This news not only enables Jesus to announce the advent of the hour of his glorification (12:23), but he explains further: "unless a grain of wheat falls into the earth and dies, it remains just a single grain; but if it dies, it bears much fruit" (12:24), and then, "Now is the judgment of this world; now the ruler of this world will be driven out. And I, when I am lifted up from the earth, will draw all people to myself" (12:31-32). The narrator adds: "He said this to indicate the kind of death he was to die" (12:33).[23]

This theme of "gathering" so intensely developed over the final episodes of the public ministry is resolved in the gift of mother to disciple and disciple to mother at the cross (19:25-27). Only then can Jesus call out in death, "It is consummated" (19:30a*: τετέλεσται). Jesus has brought to perfection the task (τὸ τέλος) given him by the Father. The hour has come and a new family of God has begun at the foot of the cross. It is upon this family that he pours down the Spirit (19:30b: παρέδωκεν τὸ πνεῦμα) and gifts them with the blood and water that flow from his side (19:34-35).[24]

4. HOW CAN A CRUCIFIXION MAKE GOD KNOWN?

We now have all the parts of the equation. The solution is apparent, but it must be formally drawn. The Johannine reinterpretation of the death of Jesus claims that Jesus brought to perfection the task given to him by his Father (see 4:34; 5:36; 17:4) in his death on the cross: "It is consummated" (19:30). The themes of "lifting up," "the hour," "the gathering," and the glorification of Jesus all play their part, but they are subordinated to the major concern of the storyteller: Jesus' death on the cross reveals the glory of God (see 11:4; 13:31-32; 17:1-5). Jesus' final discourse is framed by two affirmations of his love for "his own."

---

[23] On the "gathering" in 11:50–12:33 see Moloney, *Signs and Shadows* 200–201.

[24] For the exegetical arguments that support positions taken above in the interpretation of the Johannine Passion narrative see Francis J. Moloney, *Glory Not Dishonor. Reading John 13–21* (Minneapolis: Fortress, 1998) 127–52.

It begins with a comment from the narrator: "Having loved his own who were in the world, he loved them to the end" (13:1). The Greek behind the English "to the end" (εἰς τέλος) is another of those double-meaning words so often found in this subtle gospel. It can mean "to the end" in a chronological sense, i.e., until his very last breath, or "to the end" in a qualitative sense, i.e., in a most consummate fashion. As so often in the interpretation of the Fourth Gospel, one must not choose one against the other. Both meanings blend as the narrator tells the reader that the death of Jesus is also the time and the place where Jesus reveals his unconditional love for his own. In the final words of the prayer that closes the evening with the disciples Jesus prays, "I made your name known to them, and I will make it known, so that the love with which you have loved me may be in them, and I in them" (17:26). The author believes passionately that God is love, and that the love of Jesus for his own has made God known so that they might be swept into the oneness of love that unites the Father and the Son. But how is this possible? The answer is very simple, and its truthfulness is part of our own experience: "No one has greater love than this, to lay down one's life for one's friends. You are my friends" (15:13-14a).[25]

The God of Jesus is a God who loved the world so much as to send God's only son so that everyone could have eternal life. Jesus did not come to judge the world, but to offer it life (see 3:16-17). This life is possible because Jesus has made God known (see 17:3). If you wish to know and understand the God of Jesus, then gaze upon the lifted up, pierced Son of Man. This is not a homily, but a development of the very last words of the Johannine Passion narrative: "They will look on the one whom they have pierced" (19:37). The Johannine storyteller says to the reader: If you wish to know how much God loves you, gaze upon the pierced one. Therein lies the revelation of a God of love. Of course a first-century Church did not imagine the later practice of the veneration of an icon of the cross. They gazed upon the pierced one in their self-giving love for one another, living the example Jesus had given them (see 13:15), known as his disciples by their obedience to the new commandment Jesus had given them: that they love one another as he had loved them (see 13:34-35; 15:12, 17), that is, εἰς τέλος, to the

---

[25] Hartwig Thyen, "'Niemand hat grössere Liebe als die, dass er sein Leben für seine Freunde hingibt' (Joh 15:13). Das johanneische Verständnis des Kreuzestodes Jesu," in Carl Andresen and Günter Klein, eds., *Theologia Crucis, Signum Crucis. Festschrift für Erich Dinkler zum 70. Geburtstag* (Tübingen: J.C.B. Mohr [Paul Siebeck], 1979) 467–81, has shown the link between John 15:13 and the Johannine understanding of the cross.

end.[26] They gazed upon the pierced one as they crossed the road from the security of their former ways to enter the kingdom by being born again by water and the spirit (see 3:3-5; 19:34), by recognizing the broken body of Jesus and the spilt blood in the fragments that were gathered at the table of the Lord (see 6:1-15, 51c-58; 19:34), but that is another story. It is a story that needs to be told and lived, and it is told elsewhere in this volume.[27]

5. CONCLUSION

What has this understanding of a God who is made known in the loving self-gift of Jesus to do with me? The Johannine theology of the cross is a proclamation of God's love and the foundation of a Christian community of believers and lovers. For many reasons an understanding of the cross as a place where Jesus reveals God's glory, and is himself glorified in the foundation of a believing and loving community "because of that hour" has not played a great part in Christian spirituality. Yet in the day-to-day life of so many Christians it is an understanding of the cross that underpins much of what we do and how we do it. The christology of the cross that I have outlined must be relevant to a Christianity of today, and it is. What we have shared explains a Christian life that lives and believes in the revelation of love that shines forth from the steady, day-to-day commitment to the messiness of life. As Gerard Manley Hopkins put it:

. . . sheer plod makes plough down sillion
Shine . . .

But it is not only Jesus of Nazareth whose death can be understood as the supreme moment of his life, the time and the place where he makes known a God of love and is himself glorified. Glory and pain, love and suffering, self-gift in the moment of self-loss entwine in the death of all those who have taken to heart the words of Jesus: "No one has greater love than this, to lay down one's life for one's friends. You are my friends" (John 15:13-14a). As I began, I mentioned Virginia. On 17 July 1998, just nine months after her death, her only daughter

---

[26] On the relationship between 13:15 (the example) and 13:34-35 (the new commandment) see Moloney, *Glory Not Dishonor* 25–26.

[27] For some reflections on these passages and their place in the Christian experience of the Johannine community see my essay, "When is John Talking About Sacraments?" in this volume, pp. 109–30.

Nicole gave birth to what would have been Virginia's first grandchild: a little girl named Grace Virginia.

There is more to those last lines of Gerard Manley Hopkins's "The Windhover," subtitled "To Christ our Lord."[28] Quoted in full they catch magnificently the heart of both Johannine christology and Johannine Christianity:

No wonder of it: sheer plod makes plough down sillion
Shine, and blue-bleak embers, ah my dear,
Fall, gall themselves, and gash gold-vermillion.

---

[28] Cited from W. H. Gardner, ed., *Gerard Manley Hopkins. A Selection of His Poems and Prose.* The Penguin Poets (Harmondsworth: Penguin Books, 1953) 30.

PART 3

THE NEW TESTAMENT AND CONTEMPORARY CULTURE

CHAPTER 9

JESUS CHRIST: THE QUESTION TO CULTURES

Central to Christian belief is the claim, classically stated by the Fourth Evangelist, that in Jesus of Nazareth the divine has entered the human story: "The Word became flesh and lived among us" (John 1:14). Such a belief necessarily involves Jesus' embracing "culture," defined at the Second Vatican Council as: "all those things which go to the refining and developing of humanity's diverse mental and physical endowments" (*GS* 53). Culture, thus validly perceived as a reality that is part of humankind's universal progress, is incarnated in a variety of particular "cultures." For example, Jesus of Nazareth lived out the major part of his life within the confines of the Galilean culture of Roman-occupied first-century Judaism.[1] The problem of the harmony and tension between "culture" as the dream of every woman and man and "the cultures" within which this dream is lived out is longstanding (see *GS* 56). The following essay attempts to outline the New Testament's understanding of Jesus within his culture, in the hope that such an outline will offer a valid paradigm for a contemporary Christian response to culture and the cultures.

---

[1] See Gerd Theissen, *The Shadow of the Galilean. The Quest of the Historical Jesus in Narrative Form.* Translated by John Bowden (Philadelphia: Fortress; London: SCM, 1987).

1. INTRODUCTION: METHODOLOGICAL CONSIDERATIONS

A reflection on the life, person, and teaching of Jesus of Nazareth must look to the gospels for its information. With the Gospel of Mark (written about 70 C.E.) a new literary form entered world literature: a narrative form that communicates faith in the saving purpose of God the Father of Jesus by telling the story of the life, teaching, death, and resurrection of his Son: the εὐαγγέλιον.[2] By communicating their faith in Jesus of Nazareth as the Christ and the Son of God (see Mark 1:1; 9:7; 15:39) and their understanding of the demands of Christian discipleship through "telling the story of Jesus" (see, for example, Mark 8:22–10:52) the evangelists never intended to pass on to future generations the brute facts of history. From the vantage point of their own faith experience and commitment to Jesus, risen and alive in his Church (see John 2:22 and 12:16), they faced the crises and problems any community professing faith in a Christ crucified (see, for example 1 Cor 1:22-25) would necessarily encounter. To do this they went back to the traditions about Jesus that were alive among them: oral traditions, traditions living in their liturgical celebrations, perhaps even some written documents we no longer have. From these sources they wrote their particular "story of Jesus."

Despite some destructive scholarship from a small minority of scholars[3] there is widespread agreement that through the careful use of the gospels we are able to reach back and rediscover a reliable portrait of Jesus, his teaching, his work, his death and resurrection. The wedge

---

[2] The verbal form of this word, εὐαγγελίζομαι, is common enough in Greek literature, and it had been used generally to indicate a joyous proclamation. However, its use in the Christian tradition to refer to Jesus' life, a use initiated by Mark, is unique. On this see Gerhard Friedrich, "εὐαγγελίζομαι κτλ.," *TDNT* 2 (1964) 707–37, and Willi Marxsen, *Mark the Evangelist. Studies on the Redaction History of the Gospel.* Translated by James Boyce, et al. (Nashville and New York: Abingdon, 1969) 117–50.

[3] Fanciful opinions on the personality and life-style of Jesus of Nazareth have always been abroad. For the classic survey see Albert Schweitzer, *The Quest of the Historical Jesus. A Critical Study of its Progress from Reimarus to Wrede.* Translated by William Montgomery (3rd ed. London: A. & C. Black, 1954; New York: Macmillan, 1955). The greatest proponent of a radical skepticism in the modern era has been Rudolf Bultmann. His approach to this question is readily available in his *Jesus and the Word.* Translated by Louise Pettibone Smith and Erminie Huntress Lantero (New York and London: C. Scribner's Sons, 1958). A contemporary presentation of the Bultmannian position can be found in Helmut Koester, *Introduction to the New Testament. Foundations and Facets* (Philadelphia: Fortress, 1982) 2:73–86.

earlier scholarship had driven between the historical Jesus and the Church's preaching of him (the *kerygma*) has been removed. As James M. Robinson has written: "It is simply because Germany's leading exegetes have correctly understood the demythologized meaning of the New Testament *kerygma* that they have looked through the *kerygma* not directly to a principle inherent in human nature, but rather to Jesus as the event in which transcendence becomes possible."[4] In a study of Jesus' affirmation—yet transformation of—culture it is precisely his impact on humanity as a transcendent event that interests us most. Our other major New Testament witness, Paul, had contact with the living tradition about Jesus of Nazareth. Paul understood and proclaimed the significance of Jesus' life and teaching through the prism of his death and resurrection. The inclusion of the Pauline literature in the New Testament by the early Church has properly recognized in these writings an authentic understanding of the mystery of Jesus Christ.[5]

I will trace the New Testament's presentation of Jesus' attitude to his culture and the cultures in three steps. Jesus affirmed God's creation but, second, he demanded that all those who would follow him should surpass the "human way" in choosing "the ways of God" (see Mark

---

[4] James M. Robinson, *A New Quest of the Historical Jesus and Other Essays* (Philadelphia: Fortress, 1983) 84–85. These "leading exegetes," all Bultmann's students, are: Ernst Käsemann, Günther Bornkamm, Ernst Fuchs, and Hans Conzelmann, who have challenged their master's skepticism. For a survey of this issue see Norman Perrin, *The Kingdom of God in the Teaching of Jesus* (London: SCM, 1963) 119–29, and Raymond E. Brown and P. Joseph Cahill, *Biblical Tendencies Today: An Introduction to the Post-Bultmannians*. Corpus Papers (Washington and Cleveland: Corpus Books, 1969).

[5] I am taking a position in a long debate concerning Paul's being such a creative theologian that he proclaimed a religion of his own rather than authentically interpreting the Jesus-phenomenon. This position, which claims that while Jesus preached the kingdom Paul preached the Christ, was classically formulated by Adolf von Harnack in 1900: "The Gospel as Jesus proclaimed it has to do with the Father only and not with the Son" (*What is Christianity?* Translated by Thomas Bailey Saunders. Introduction by Rudolf Bultmann [New York: Harper & Row, 1957] 144). For an older study supporting the (majority) position that I have taken see F. F. Bruce, *Paul: Apostle of the Free Spirit* (Exeter: Paternoster Press, 1977) 95–125. See also the support from a more "existentialist" perspective in Robinson, *A New Quest* 111–25. Most recently Richard B. Hays has argued that Paul's theological language is grounded in a narrative substructure and that the narrative is the story of Jesus. See his *The Faith of Jesus Christ. An Investigation of the Narrative Substructure of Galatians 3:1–4:11*. SBLDS 56 (Chico: Scholars, 1983).

8:33). Finally, Jesus' challenge to culture and the cultures can be gleaned from the New Testament's criticism of sin.

2. JESUS AND THE PROMOTION OF VALUES LINKED WITH THE DESIGN OF CREATION

A Christian view of culture and human history, which are intimately linked (see *GS* 57–59), looks to creation and the role of a creating God. At the center of the life and teaching of Jesus of Nazareth stand his convictions about the reigning presence of God as creator and Sovereign. This is most evident in his teaching through the parables of the kingdom.[6]

The Parables and the Kingdom

The notion of God as sovereign over the whole of creation, and especially in the divine role at the center of God's human creation, was found in the Old Testament (see, for example, Pss 22:28; 45:6; 103:19; 145:11-13; Dan 4:3, 34; 1 Chr 17:14; 29:11). The creator God made all things perfectly (see especially Gen 1:1–2:4). As creator, however, YHWH also saves, judges, and loves a people with whom he has forged a covenant.[7] Thus the Old Testament notion of God as Sovereign also carried with it the idea of an end-time, a "day of the Lord" that would spell the end of human history and the final manifestation of God's rule (see, for example, Isa 2:2-4, 24-27; 24:21-23; 32:22; 52:7-10; Micah 2:12-13; 4:1-7; Obadiah 21; Zechariah 9–14).[8]

---

[6] One of the features of modern gospel criticism has been research into the parables of Jesus. For a survey with copious bibliographical material see Warren S. Kissinger, *The Parables of Jesus. A History of Interpretation and Bibliography.* ATLA Bibliography Series 4 (Metuchen, N.J.: Scarecrow Press, 1979). Since then see Bernard Brandon Scott, *Hear Then the Parable. A Commentary on the Parables of Jesus* (Minneapolis: Fortress, 1989).

[7] See Gerhard von Rad, *Old Testament Theology.* Translated by D. M. G. Stalker. 2 vols. (New York: Harper; Edinburgh: Oliver and Boyd, 1962–65) 1:136–65 for Israel's use of its creation myth as a part of its theology of salvation.

[8] Since the days of Johannes Weiss this is the aspect of the "kingdom of God" that has most fascinated scholars. Only in recent years, and especially in contemporary parable research, has the dominance of the "end-time" concept begun to be seriously questioned. For an excellent survey see Norman Perrin, *Jesus and the Language of the Kingdom. Symbol and Metaphor in New Testament Interpretation* (Philadelphia: Fortress, 1976). For an extensive and balanced presentation of Jesus' teaching on the Kingdom as both incipiently present and yet to come see John P. Meier, *A Marginal Jew. Rethinking the Historical Jesus. Volume Two: Mentor, Message, and Miracles.* ABRL (New York: Doubleday, 1993) 237–506.

Jesus used the term to refer to a future decisive intervention of God into the affairs of men and women, where the false values of the world would be reversed and the values of God established (see, for example, Matt 5:3-12//Luke 6:20-23). He used the traditional symbols, such as the "messianic banquet," to express this idea (see especially Matt 8:11; the same symbolism may be behind John 2:1-11). He also spoke of a final blessed state into which the redeemed would "enter," which they would "inherit" or "receive" at some point in the future (see, for example, Mark 9:47; 10:14-15, 23-25; Matt 5:20; 7:21; 21:31). Such a usage can be explained in terms of Israel's idea of God as sovereign, and especially in terms of the apocalyptic use of the expression "Kingdom of God" which, although rare, is to be found in the Judaism of the time of Jesus.[9] Such background, however, cannot explain the person and teaching of Jesus. There is something new and startling in both his person and his teaching that defies the categories provided by the world and culture in which he lived. It is clearest in all its radical nature in Jesus' insistence that *in his person and activity* God's decisive intervention was already present: "But if it is by the finger of God that I cast out the demons, then the kingdom of God has come to you (Luke 11:20//Matt 12:28)."[10] While there are other isolated sayings of Jesus that are similarly significant in this regard (see especially Matt 11:12-14 and Luke 17:20-21), contemporary parable study is showing with increasing clarity that in Jesus of Nazareth the ways of God were being reestablished.

The parables of Jesus forced his listeners to wonder about what he was doing, and consequently about who he was. They had no great difficulty with Jesus' proclamation of God as sovereign. Their problem arose from his surprising immediacy with a God who was strange to their accepted "theologies," who reigned in an unexpected way:

> Which one of you, having a hundred sheep and losing one of them, does not leave the ninety-nine in the wilderness and go after the one that is lost until he finds it? (Luke 15:4).

The question was asked seriously: what man would leave ninety-nine sheep in the wilderness to seek out a lost one? Similarly, what father had the depth of strength, love, and internal freedom to create a similar freedom for his two sons? Who would allow each of his sons to go down his own way, making his own mistakes, and still, at the end of the parable, be waiting out in the dark searching for his second lost

[9] For a brief survey of the evidence see Perrin, *The Kingdom of God* 161–85.

[10] On the originality, authenticity, and meaning of this saying see Meier, *A Marginal Jew* 2:404–23.

son? And who would finally say to this son: "Son, you are always with me, and all that is mine is yours" (Luke 15:31)? Shepherds and fathers, as we know them, do not behave in this way.[11] Jesus taught that the Kingdom of God demanded the overturning of all prior values, closed options, set judgments, and established conclusions. Amos Wilder writes of the "clash of worlds" in Jesus' teaching.[12] Jesus of Nazareth's person and teaching asked that God's world become our world. Humankind was being asked to let the God and Father of Jesus be its God.

Jesus thus created a problem for his contemporaries. He spoke, through astonishing parables, in a way that questioned the substructure of their religion and culture: their understanding of God and God's presence to God's people. They would have been able to comprehend and even accept Jesus as the authoritative messenger of the final intervention of the Kingdom of God, but they could not accept the immediacy with God that enabled Jesus to tell his parables with authority as he announced that in his presence God was already reigning among them.

> They (the parables) are stories which shatter the deep structure of our accepted world and therefore render clear and evident to us the relativity of the story itself. They remove our defenses and make us vulnerable to God. It is only in such experiences that God can touch us, and only in such moments does the kingdom of God arrive.[13]

However, Jesus the teller of parables was also the one who lived the parables. The parabler *is* the parable of God. The immediacy with God created by the Jesus-*Abba* relationship made Jesus the one who knew the Father better than anyone else ever had.[14] His lifestyle, therefore,

---

[11] While the evangelist has certainly constructed Luke 15 for his own theological purposes, the parables themselves reach back to the teaching of Jesus. On this see I. Howard Marshall, *The Gospel of Luke. A Commentary on the Greek Text*. The New International Greek Testament Commentary (Exeter: Paternoster Press, 1978) 597–613; Eduard Schweizer, *Luke: A Challenge to Present Theology* (Atlanta: John Knox, 1982) 80–81.

[12] Amos N. Wilder, "Semeia, An Experimental Journal for Biblical Criticism: An Introduction," *Semeia* 1 (1974) 15.

[13] John Dominic Crossan, *The Dark Interval. Towards a Theology of Story* (Niles, Ill.: Argus Communications, 1975) 121–22.

[14] On this see Edward Schillebeeckx, *Jesus: An Experiment in Christology*. Translated by Hubert Hoskins (New York: Seabury; London: Collins, 1979) 256–71; idem, *Jesus in Our Western Culture: Mysticism, Ethics and Politics* (London: SCM, 1987) 15–22.

"told the story of God" (see John 1:18). One could single out so many of his actions that are also parables: his gathering of followers, his commitment to a life of forgiveness for sinners and sharing his table with them, offering them a genuine experience of "salvation," his perseverance along this way despite the tension this created between himself and both the political and religious authorities of his time, the expression of this tension in his symbolic "destruction" of the Temple, his supper with his disciples, his death on a cross. In these "actions" Jesus, the teller of parables, became the parable of God. He revealed a different God, and proclaimed that in his presence God's decisive intervention was taking place. In Jesus of Nazareth God was truly God, and he dared to call God *Abba*.[15]

The Restoration of God's Creation

The opening pages of the Gospel of Mark provide a striking synthesis of the early Church's understanding of Jesus' restoration of God's order. After a prologue to the gospel (Mark 1:1-13) Jesus breaks into the story (1:14), announcing the kingdom of God: "The time is fulfilled, and the kingdom of God has come near; repent, and believe in the good news" (1:15). Into the "disorder" of the world as it had come to be accepted he brings:

- a discipleship founded entirely on his person and his promise (vv. 16-20),
- a new authority that routs the authority of unclean spirits (vv. 21-28),
- a power over prejudice and sickness that enables him to touch a woman and cure her through his touch (vv. 29-31),
- an authority over law and legal uncleanliness that enables him to touch and cure a leper (vv. 40-45).

The section is also marked by two summaries. One stresses Jesus' power over evil and his concern for the broken (vv. 32-34). The other already indicates that he has not come to spread his own kingdom, but that he is responding to an authority greater than himself (vv. 35-39). Mark's message is that God's ways and God's victory over all the

---

[15] Current parable research asks the christological question: who is this man who could tell such stories? See especially John Dominic Crossan, *In Parables. The Challenge of the Historical Jesus* (New York: Harper & Row, 1973), and idem, "The Servant Parables of Jesus," *Semeia* 1 (1974) 17–62. See also John R. Donahue, "Jesus as the Parable of God in the Gospel of Mark," *Int* 32 (1978) 369–86, and Perrin, *Jesus and the Language of the Kingdom* 194–205.

disorders of broken humanity have entered history in the person and preaching of Jesus of Nazareth. It is equally important to notice that in Mark 2:1–3:6 there are continual conflicts between Jesus and a variety of opponents. While Jesus' authority over the disorders of the world seems unquestioned in the first part of Mark's narrative (1:16-45), the evangelist is quick to show that men and women were free to make their own decision, to accept or refuse the reigning presence of God as Sovereign in Jesus of Nazareth—and that many decided to refuse.[16]

A further important aspect of Jesus' dedication to the promotion of the values of God's original creation is his forgiveness of sins. Perhaps the episode where this is most clearly demonstrated is the curing of the paralyptic at Capernaum (Mark 2:1-12). The man is lowered through the roof by his friends.

> When Jesus saw their faith, he said to the paralytic, "Son, your sins are forgiven." Now some of the scribes were sitting there, questioning in their hearts, "Why does this fellow speak in this way? It is blasphemy! Who can forgive sins but God alone?" (vv. 5-7).

Jesus, linking the paralysis to sin, claims to be able to forgive sins; thus he would also be able to cure the man's illness. However, only God or a messianic representative could claim to forgive sin. Here is the key to a ministry of healing: Jesus heals because he forgives sins. The rest of the Markan account leads to conflict. Against opposition, Jesus claims to be one who can forgive sin. Behind the account lies an important feature of the life and teaching of Jesus: the restoration of God's order. He promoted the values of God's creation by healing the brokenness of the human heart as well as the human body. For Jesus, the two were intimately linked.[17]

---

[16] I have been telling Mark's story of Jesus, but I am convinced that this narrative reaches back not to events that happened in this way and in this order but to an evocation of the pre-Easter experience of what James M. Robinson called "Jesus as the event in which transcendence becomes possible" (*A New Quest of the Historical Jesus* 85).

[17] I have dwelt briefly on this one episode because it is so clear. However, it has been shown conclusively by Joachim Jeremias, *The Parables of Jesus* (London: SCM, 1963) 124–46 that one of the major aspects of Jesus' ministry was belief that he was bringing God's mercy and healing to sinners. See further the study of Pierre Grelot, "Jésus devant le monde du mal," in *Foi et Culture à la lumière de la Bible. Actes de la session plénière 1979 de la Commission Biblique Pontificale* (Turin: Elle di Cie, 1981) 131–201. On his curing of "the broken" see especially pp. 159–63.

Jesus' attitude to the Law of Moses is a further indication of his mission to restore things to their original order.[18] A superficial reading of the gospels could leave the impression that Jesus deliberately broke the Law on two issues: the Sabbath observance (see Mark 2:23-28; John 5:1-9; 9:1-7) and the food laws (see Mark 7:17-19//Matt 15:17-18). A consideration of the literary function of these passages in their respective gospels and a reconstruction of the events behind them that led to the conflicts exclude the possibility that he deliberately flouted the Law of Moses or exposed himself to charges of having transgressed it.[19] The religious authorities of Judaism clearly had a part to play in Jesus' being consigned to death, and the gospel stories indicate a mounting antagonism with such authorities.[20] It is obvious that Jesus' teaching would not have accommodated the Sadducees or the Zealots, but there are some aspects of his mission that would have brought him close to the Pharisees. Above all they would have shared his desire to make a sense of God part of the routine activities of daily life.

However, Jesus cannot be fitted into the scheme of the Pharisees. Although he may not have flouted the Law he would not fit into a Pharisaic "legalistic" scheme of behavior. He would not fast (Mark 2:18), nor would he submit himself to the ritual washings (Mark 7:2). These "performances" were, for Jesus, human traditions (Mark 7:3). Unlike the Pharisees, he allowed himself unlimited social contact and shared his table with all who looked to him in hope, even those judged by the Pharisees as immoral: the tax-collectors, the prostitutes, and the sinners (Mark 2:13-17; Luke 8:1-3; 19:1-10 etc.).[21] Essential to Pharisaic teaching was the unending teaching tradition that passed from Moses

[18] This is a much-discussed issue. For two recent monographs on the question see Klaus Berger, *Die Gesetzesauslegung Jesu; ihr historischer Hintergrund im Judentum und im Alten Testament.* WMANT 40 (Neukirchen: Neukirchener Verlag, 1972); Robert J. Banks, *Jesus and the Law in the Synoptic Tradition.* SNTSMS 28 (Cambridge, Cambridge University Press, 1975). For what follows see Anthony Ernest Harvey, *Jesus and the Constraints of History.* The Bampton Lectures 1980 (London: Duckworth, 1982) 36–65.

[19] See Harvey, *Constraints* 36–41.

[20] The gospels as we now have them are marked by a great number of "controversy stories" that have their origins *(Sitze im Leben)* in both the life of Jesus and the conflicts between early Christians and their Jewish neighbors. Rudolf Bultmann, *The History of the Synoptic Tradition.* Translated by John Marsh (Rev. ed. New York: Harper & Row; Oxford: Blackwell, 1968) 12–27 lists twenty-six such sayings.

[21] On this see Joachim Jeremias, *Jerusalem In the Time of Jesus* (London: SCM, 1969) 310–12. See also Theissen, *The Shadow of the Galilean* 97–108.

to each generation. Jesus broke through this Mosaic dependency by claiming that the authority of his teaching flowed not from an authentic line of tradition back to Moses but from his own word and person, from his own immediacy with God.[22]

Critical study provides us with the portrait of a teacher and prophet bringing comfort to the afflicted and affliction to the comfortable. From his immediacy with God, whom he called *Abba*, he challenged the Temple authorities and the political leaders of his day. He did not flout the Law or deliberately risk legal procedure through a program to "take on the Law." Nevertheless, in the fashion of a prophet he went beyond the Law, which suffered from the constraints of a given religion, history, and culture. Living under the urgency of his response to his Father, he could ask for the incredible from his disciples: "Follow me, and let the dead bury their own dead!" (Matt 8:22).[23] All prophets, however, looked beyond themselves for the criteria they used to call God's people to conversion. Jesus' teaching on the kingdom and his parables pointed to the restoration of God's original purpose: to let God be God.

The teaching of Jesus on other issues is consistent with this. When faced with the question of divorce he looks to the way things were "from the beginning of creation" (Mark 10:6//Matt 19:8).[24] Similarly, his teaching concerning women ultimately reaches back to the reestablishment of the wholeness God gave to both male and female (see, for example, Mark 5:21-43).[25] Although Matt 5:17-48 has a long literary history, its conclusion provides an excellent summary of Jesus' challenge that God be allowed to be God in the world and in the life-style of his followers: "Be perfect, therefore, as your heavenly Father is perfect" (5:48). Such an imperative to reach beyond ourselves in response

---

[22] Also important for this element in the person and teaching of Jesus is the authenticity of the basic teaching style now found in the "antitheses" in Matt 5:21-48. Current scholarship believes that Matthew reflects an authentic teaching pattern of Jesus even though the present shape of the antitheses is Matthean. For a discussion of this issue see John P. Meier, *Law and History in Matthew's Gospel. A Redactional Study of Mt. 5:17-48*. AnBib 71 (Rome: Biblical Institute Press, 1976) 125–61.

[23] This saying, which is offensive in all cultures, has been the subject of a study by Martin Hengel, *The Charismatic Leader and His Followers*. Translated by James Greig. Studies of the New Testament and Its World (New York: Crossroad; Edinburgh: T & T Clark, 1981).

[24] See my essay, "Matthew 19:3-12 and Celibacy. A Redactional and Form-Critical Study" in this volume, pp. 35–52.

[25] See my study, "Jesus and Women" in this volume, pp. 3–34.

to the challenge of Jesus can never be totally worked out within the context of any particular culture or cultures.

Some fifty years ago H. Richard Niebuhr surveyed the many contemporary attempts to "define" Christ.[26] His penetrating survey concludes with remarks that demolish all such attempts, and match the conclusions of my own analysis:

> The power and attraction Jesus Christ exercises over men never comes from him alone, but from him as Son of the Father. It comes from him in his Sonship in a double way, as man living to God and God living with men. Belief in him and loyalty to his cause involves men in the double movement from world to God and from God to world. Even when theologies fail to do justice to this fact, Christians living with Christ in their cultures are aware of it. For they are forever being challenged to abandon all things for the sake of God; and forever being sent back to the world to teach and practice all the things that have been commanded them.[27]

A Pauline Synthesis

One senses from a reading of the gospel accounts that in Jesus God again becomes God to creation. This has been thematized in the Pauline notion of the new creation. Although the term "new creation" appears only twice in the letters of Paul (2 Cor 5:17 and Gal 6:15) the theme lies at the heart of a great deal of his christology and anthropology.[28] Like Jesus, and correctly interpreting Jesus' person and message, Paul worked within the Jewish framework of "this age" and "the age to come." The present age was governed by the powers of evil; the age to come, the result of the direct intervention of God, would be marked by a never-ending era of glory. The experience of Jesus of Nazareth and the subsequent Christian experience of life in the Spirit (Gal 4:1-7; Rom 8:9-17) changed this view of things.

Paul taught that the old age had passed away and that the new age had dawned in Jesus Christ (see 2 Cor 5:17). However, it was more than evident to Paul that a total change, the change described by the Jewish scheme, was not at hand. Indeed, he had problems in several of

---

[26] H. Richard Niebuhr, *Christ and Culture* (New York: Harper & Row, 1951) 11–29. He discusses scholarly attempts to define Jesus in terms of one overarching principle: his morality, his love, his hope, his faith, or his humility.

[27] Ibid. 29.

[28] See Jerome Murphy-O'Connor, *Becoming Human Together. The Pastoral Anthropology of St. Paul.* Good News Studies 2 (Wilmington: Michael Glazier, 1982) 33–138, and Wolfgang Trilling, *A Conversation with Paul.* Translated by John Bowden (London: SCM, 1986) 31–50.

his churches (especially at Corinth) with converts who believed that they now lived the "risen life" completely. Paul had no illusion about the evil of this world, its gods, and its rulers (see 1 Cor 10:11; Gal 1:4; 2 Cor 4:4), yet it was "doomed to perish" (1 Cor 2:6). There were evil powers in this world but they could not hope to rival in any final way the power of God and the decisive intervention of God in this world in the person of Jesus Christ (see, among many other passages, the lyrical confession of faith in this truth found in Rom 8:31-39). The evil was doomed because now there was life in its midst (see Rom 8:20-21).

Paul links this theology with a "new creation" through the use of his scheme of an old Adam and a new Adam, which he received from current Jewish speculation.[29] Reading the Genesis story, Paul can speak of Adam as the agent through whom humankind's two great evils, sin and death, entered the world (see Rom 3:9-18), and because all have sinned, all have fallen short of the original glory of God (Rom 3:23). All must die because all are sinners, and such is the fate of all (Rome 5:12)—up till the time of Christ. In continuity with current Jewish speculation Paul understands Adam as a collective reality already containing within himself condemned humanity, but the disorder created "in Adam" has been set right "in Christ." Jesus Christ becomes the one who begins the new creation, the new humanity that belongs to him.

> But in fact Christ has been raised from the dead, the first fruits of those who have fallen asleep. For since death came through a human being, the resurrection of the dead has also come through a human being; for as all die in Adam, so all will be made alive in Christ (1 Cor 15:20-22).

Perhaps the clearest contrast between the two Adams is found in Rom 5:12, 18-19:

> Therefore, just as sin came into the world through one man, and death came through sin, and so death spread to all because all have sinned . . . therefore just as one man's trespass led to condemnation for all, so one man's act of righteousness leads to justification and life for all. For just as by the one man's disobedience the many were made sinners, so by the one man's obedience the many will be made righteous.

Nevertheless, Paul is not arguing that the Adam-Christ parallel is a parallel between equals. Jesus' free gift of himself was not merely to re-

---

[29] For an analysis of the background to the Pauline use of this scheme see Robin Scroggs, *The Last Adam. A Study in Pauline Anthropology* (Philadelphia: Fortress; Oxford: Blackwell, 1966) 1–58. See also James D. G. Dunn, *Christology in the Making* (Philadelphia: Westminster; London: SCM, 1980) 101–27.

gain the paradise lost by Adam. Here Paul differs from his Jewish contemporaries. It is the life, death, and resurrection of Jesus of Nazareth
that make the difference. Paul is not "speculating." He is building a
theology of a new and all-surpassing Adam on the basis of the life and
teaching, and especially on the death and resurrection, of Jesus. It is
not a question of the restoration of things as they were at the beginning, but of a newness far in excess of the old. That means the break-
through and dawn of the End, the *eschaton*. However, such a conviction
came to Paul from his understanding of the life, death, and resurrection of Jesus as the "free gift" of God, and equally as Jesus' "free gift"
of himself, and this is what makes the difference:

> But the free gift is not like the trespass. For if the many died through the
> one man's trespass, much more surely have the grace of God and the free
> gift in the grace of the one man, Jesus Christ, abounded for the many. And
> the free gift is not like the effect of the one man's sin. For the judgment
> following one trespass brought condemnation, but the free gift following
> many trespasses brings justification (Rom 5:15-16).

Jesus' pointing to the original intent of creation has been repeated by
Paul in his theological use of the Adam-Christ scheme. The Adam side
of the scheme tells of humanity's falling from right relationship with
God. The story of Christ is the story of a human response that accepts
God's offer of right relationship. In this way Paul not only continues
the theme of the restoration of the values of creation; in the "free gift"
of God in the life, death, and resurrection of Jesus Christ he claims that
the original gift has been surpassed.

Paul is developing an idea also present in the gospels. He questions
those who settle for what is purely natural and normal in the accepted
religious and cultural dogmas of his time (see, for example, Gal 3:27-
28).[30] He challenges them to go farther. Paul's gospel tells of the inter-
twining of both the story of Adam and the story of Christ, and it issues
a challenge: "You have been part of the Adam story; your human history

---

[30] See Trilling, *Conversation* 49–50: "Paul wishes grace and peace from the
Lord Jesus Christ, 'who gave himself for our sins' (Gal 1:4), and in the utterly
personal formulation of faith 'in the Son of God who loved me and gave himself for me' (Gal 2:20). What is at work in his life becomes manifest in the sur-
render of this life (see also 1 Cor 8:11; Rom 14:15). Here Paul has a deep insight
and has made a decision statement about the 'words and works' of Jesus, as
they can also be read out of the Gospels. One thinks of Jesus' encounter with
the 'woman who was a sinner,' his action towards 'tax collectors and sinners,'
his concern for the sick, the weary and the heavy laden, of many of his words
and his silent journey to death."

is marked by its consequences. Do you wish to let the Christ story and its (more powerful) consequences be the final story told in your life and in your world?"[31]

3. JESUS AND THE SURPASSING OF "NATURAL ATTITUDES"

New Testament Christianity refuses to allow Jesus to be "controlled" by the cultural and religious absolutes of its own time. The unanimous attitude of the various authors of the New Testament reflects the life and teaching of Jesus. The Christian belief that his life was crowned by death and resurrection is "foolishness" (see 1 Cor 1:18-25). It questions attempts to answer all the needs and dreams of women and men in terms of religion, history, and culture. While Jesus affirmed and reestablished God's creation, New Testament Christianity is frankly counter-cultural. Jesus and his message cannot be completely "inculturated." The Corinthians may have been making a reasonable attempt to adapt to the surrounding intellectual and cultural milieu, but Paul challenged that in the light of his "apocalyptic" gospel.[32] The Galatians wanted to opt for an "inculturation" that was both out of date and inapplicable to them in their return to the Jewish Law, and that position was similarly condemned by the Pauline gospel.[33] Mark, at the beginning of a gospel-telling tradition, starkly raised the cross over against any attempt to have the Son of God come down from his place of execution (see Mark 15:25-32).[34]

The Challenge of the Life and Teaching of Jesus

Although each gospel has its own christology[35] there is consistency in the presentation of Jesus as one who cannot be contained by the

[31] Brendan J. Byrne, *Reckoning with Romans. A Contemporary Reading of Paul's Gospel.* Good News Studies 18 (Wilmington: Michael Glazier, 1986) 224. On the Adam-Christ question see Byrne's excellent treatment in ibid. 111–20.

[32] See Johann Christiaan Beker, *Paul the Apostle. The Triumph of God in Life and Thought* (Philadelphia: Fortress, 1980) 135–81, especially 163–76.

[33] See Hans Dieter Betz, *Galatians: A Commentary on Paul's Letter to the Churches in Galatia.* Hermeneia (Philadelphia: Fortress, 1979) 28–33.

[34] On this see Donald Senior, *The Passion of Jesus in the Gospel of Mark.* The Passion Series 2 (Wilmington: Michael Glazier, 1984) 117–21.

[35] For a brief summary of the christologies of the synoptic gospels see Jack Dean Kingsbury, *Jesus Christ in Matthew, Mark and Luke.* Proclamation Commentaries (Philadelphia: Fortress, 1981) and for a brief study of Johannine christology see Francis J. Moloney, *The Word Became Flesh.* Theology Today Series 14 (Dublin and Cork: Mercier Press, 1977).

categories his contemporaries used to understand him. Two examples will have to suffice.

In Mark 8:27-33 this gospel reaches a crucial stage in the development of its christology. In light of what has happened in the narrative thus far, as the messianic nature of Jesus' words and behavior have continually raised the question of who Jesus might be (see 1:27; 2:7, 12; 4:41; 5:15-17, 42; 6:2-3, 14-17, 51-52; 7:5-8, 37; 8:14-21), Jesus himself asks the question that has been hovering over the story: "Who do people say that I am?" (8:27). There are five answers to this question: three given by others, one given by Peter in the name of the disciples, and one provided by Jesus himself. It is generally held (8:27, see also 6:14-15) that Jesus is either John the Baptist come back from the dead, or one of the prophets fulfilling the promise made to Moses in Deut 18:18, or Elijah *redivivus,* another messianic precursor expected by current Jewish messianic speculations (see already Mal 4:5-6). These categories were part of the cultural and religious heritage of Israel at the time of Jesus, living under foreign domination and thus awaiting the coming of a Messiah.[36] Read in the context of the life of Jesus, Peter's confession: "You are the Messiah" (v. 29) must be judged as belonging to the same order: "the Messiah" was a central part of Israel's religious and political hopes.[37] Jesus does not refuse Peter's confession, but he asks for silence, as his dream stretches beyond what Israel's heritage provided (v. 30). Jesus was to be a suffering Son of Man because of his unconditional obedience to the ways of God, but would be vindicated as that same God entered his life and had the final word: resurrection. "He said all this quite openly" (vv. 31-32). The hopes and expectations of culture and history, indeed of all that would appear "right" to the natural order of things, have been questioned and surpassed.[38]

---

[36] On this issue see Henri Cazelles, *Le Messie de la Bible. Christologie de l'Ancien Testament,* Série Jésus et Jésus Christ 7 (Paris: Desclée, 1978) 191–212; Pierre Grelot, *L'espérance Juive à L'Heure de Jésus.* Série Jésus et Jésus Christ 6 (Paris: Desclée 1978); Jacob Neusner, *Messiah in Context. Israel's History and Destiny in Formative Judaism.* Foundations of Judaism 2 (Philadelphia: Fortress, 1984).

[37] As Cazelles, Grelot, and Neusner (see previous note) all point out, albeit from their different perspectives, one must be aware that in the time of Jesus there was no single messianic idea: "My own impression is that to claim there was ('the') messianic idea in Judaism is to produce a picture we cannot reduplicate in any single and distinctive group and its definitive system of thought and life" (Neusner, *Messiah in Context* xxi). See also the concluding remarks of Grelot, *L'espérance Juive* 259–78.

[38] This is not the place to expand on the Son of Man question, so central to the interpretation of this passage. The never-ending attempts on the part of modern scholarship to grasp the full significance of Jesus' use of the term indicate how

Although the subject is handled differently by each evangelist, the parallel scenes in Matthew (16:13-23) and Luke (9:18-22) make the same point. Faced with the expectations of his contemporaries, Jesus surpasses their hopes and attitudes. The opening narrative of the Fourth Gospel, although later in the development of the tradition, repeats this message. Against a background of "days" the first narrative section of the Fourth Gospel (John 1:19-51) prepares for the revelation of the glory of Jesus in the Cana miracle (2:1-11). The background for the narrative was the traditional series of days of preparation of God's people for God's decisive intervention among them at Sinai (see 1:29, 35, 43; 2:1).[39] Against this background the evangelist has aroused his readers' interest in two central issues: an understanding of who Jesus is and the response of faith that is required from those who will commit themselves to his ways. John the Baptist, the greatest of all "witnesses" to Jesus (see 1:6-8, 15), responds to the messianic expectations of the religious authorities from Jerusalem by pointing away from himself (1:19-23) toward the one who will come after him (vv. 24-28).[40] He makes it clear why his place in God's design is "lesser" (see also 3:25-30): Jesus is the Lamb *of God*, he "was" before the Baptist (see 1:1.15), he is full of the Holy Spirit, and he baptizes with that Holy Spirit. In short, Jesus is the Son of God (vv. 29-34). The Baptist's confession of Jesus is correct, and he places himself in a subordinate position. Even though the "preparation" of the future disciples has begun, Jesus himself has not yet appeared on the scene in any active way. This is changed as we move into the final two "days" (vv. 35-51). Two dis-

---

puzzling his self-designation was, and still is. For recent work on the issue see Morna D. Hooker, "Is the Son of Man Problem Really Insoluble?" in Ernest Best and Robert McLean Wilson, eds., *Text and Interpretation. Studies in the New Testament Presented to Matthew Black* (Cambridge: Cambridge University Press, 1979) 155–68; Maurice Casey, *Son of Man. The Interpretation and Influence of Daniel 7* (London: S.P.C.K., 1979); Barnabas Lindars, *Jesus Son of Man. A Fresh Examination of the Son of Man Sayings in the Light of Recent Research* (London: S.P.C.K., 1983). See my own reflections in Francis J. Moloney, "The End of the Son of Man?" *DRev* 98 (1980) 280–90, and idem, "The Reinterpretation of Psalm viii and the Son of Man Debate," *NTS* 27 (1980–81) 656–72. See now the excellent summary by Morna D. Hooker, *The Gospel According to St Mark*. Black's New Testament Commentaries (London: A. & C. Black, 1991) 88–93.

[39] For the details of this case and for references to the relevant Jewish and secondary material see Francis J. Moloney, *Belief in the Word. Reading John 1–4* (Minneapolis: Fortress, 1993) 53–60.

[40] See Morna D. Hooker, "John the Baptist and the Johannine Prologue," *NTS* 16 (1969–70) 354–58.

ciples of the Baptist, having been told that Jesus was the Lamb of God, "follow" him (vv. 35-37). They are asked a question of major importance—"What are you looking for?"—but they trivialize it, asking where Jesus is staying (v. 38). Again Jesus takes the initiative by issuing an important challenge (in Johannine terms): "Come and see" (v. 39). This experience leads them to confess that Jesus is the Christ as they attempt to bring Simon to him. Jesus "names" Simon with a new name: "Cephas (which is translated Peter)" (vv. 41-42).

The initiatives of Jesus are decisive and challenging, but one senses that they are preparatory. The disciples' confessions of faith are in terms they can control and understand. This is made particularly clear in the evangelist's use of the expression "we have found" (v. 41; see also v. 45). Faithful to Christian tradition, this gospel places the initiative for God's ways in the world on the side of God and God's Sent One. It is never the result of something "we" succeed in doing (see also 9:24, 29, 31). Thus far the disciples (as also the religious authorities from Jerusalem: vv. 19-25) have either raised questions or made confessions about the identity of Jesus in terms that were comprehensible to their religious and cultural heritage. The encounter between Jesus and Nathanael on the fourth "day" brings this process to a climax. In 1:43-51 the evangelist describes Nathanael's journey of faith in some detail. Jesus finds Philip, a compatriot of Andrew and Peter, who also follows him. Philip finds Nathanael, and a further confession of faith, again understandable in terms of first-century Jewish messianic expectations, is made by Philip: "*We have found* him about whom Moses in the law and also the prophets wrote, Jesus son of Joseph from Nazareth" (v. 45). In light of Nathanael's subsequent skepticism Philip invites him also to make that important Johannine journey: "Come and see" (v. 46). However, it is Jesus who "sees" Nathanael first, describes him, and then tells him: "I saw you under the fig tree before Philip called you" (v. 48). For Nathanael this is an incredible statement. It would have been impossible for Jesus to have known that Philip called him, or to know that he was under the fig tree, yet he does. He thus confesses his faith in Jesus: "Rabbi, you are the Son of God! You are the King of Israel!" With Nathanael's confession we come to the culmination of a series of messianic confessions (or queries) that has been mounting throughout all these first "days."

But even Nathanael's confession is an expression of first-century Jewish messianic expectations. While "Rabbi" is a term of honor and "the King of Israel" is messianic (see, for example 3:2 and 6:15 where the expressions are misunderstandings of Jesus), so also the title "the Son of God" is to be understood as a Jewish title accorded to the expected Messiah, based on the use of such a term in 2 Sam 7:14 and Ps 2:7

to refer to the King of Israel.[41] While the Baptist was able to point away from himself and toward Jesus as "Lamb *of God*," full of the Spirit of God, and "Son *of God*" in the fullest meaning of that last title, this is not the case with the first disciples. One can only understand "who" Jesus is for the Fourth Evangelist in terms of his *origins*. For the Baptist, Jesus is "of God," but for these first disciples he is "of Joseph" (v. 45), "from Nazareth" (v. 46), "of Israel" (v. 49). Such faith has its roots in the natural, historically conditioned expectations of Israel. Jesus is not happy with the faith of Nathanael, based on the slight event of the fig tree. Jesus' words conclude these "days" of preparation with a correction of Nathanael's faith and a promise of greater sight for all who will come to see with the eyes of true faith:

> "Do you believe because I told you that I saw you under the fig tree? You will see greater things than these." And he said to him, "Very truly, I tell you, you will see heaven opened and the angels of God ascending and descending upon the Son of Man" (1:51).

True "sight" must go beyond the signs of Jesus (see especially 2:23-25). The true believer will see that in Jesus of Nazareth, the Son of Man—a man among men and women—the heavenly and the earthly are one.[42] Using language that comes from the apocalyptic tradition (heavens opening and angels appearing) and recalling the story of Jacob's dream of the ladder connecting heaven and earth at Bethel (see especially Gen 28:12), these days of preparation call the reader to recognize that there is no earthly, culturally, or historically conditioned religious category that can contain the mystery of Jesus of Nazareth. Many have tried throughout these days of preparation (1:19-51), but true faith cannot be contained within such limits.[43]

---

[41] For a full discussion, with analysis of the Jewish material, see Brendan J. Byrne, *"Sons of God—Seed of Abraham." A Study of the Sonship of God of All Christians in Paul Against the Jewish Background.* AnBib 83 (Rome: Biblical Institute Press, 1979) 9–78. See also Hans-Joachim Kraus, *Theology of the Psalms.* Translated by Keith Crim (Minneapolis: Augsburg, 1986) 112–15.

[42] For a study of this passage see Moloney, *Belief in the Word* 60–76. The literary-theological "pattern" I traced in John 1:19-51 is found throughout the gospel (see, for example, 2:1–4:54; 6:25-71; 9:1-41 etc.). For some general indications see M. Baron, "La progression des confessions de foi dans les dialogues de S. Jean," *BVC* 82 (1968) 32–44.

[43] On this theme through the Fourth Gospel see Marinus de Jonge, "Jewish Expectations about the 'Messiah' according to the Fourth Gospel," *NTS* 19 (1972–73) 246–70, also available in idem, *Jesus: Stranger from Heaven and Son of God.* SBL Sources for Biblical Study (Missoula: Scholars, 1977) 77–116. See also

The Challenge of the Death and Resurrection of Jesus

Paul uses very little of the life and teaching of Jesus (Gal 4:4; 1 Cor 11:23-26; 1 Cor 15:3-7 contain the only parts of Jesus' story that he tells). His teaching is dominated by the impact the death and resurrection of Jesus had made on him (see Gal 1:13-16; Phil 3:4-11). But so are the gospel stories! The narratives of the life of Jesus are written in light of the fact that Jesus of Nazareth was nailed to a cross, was buried, but has been raised (see 1 Cor 15:3).[44] However, it is to Paul that we will turn for a synthesis of the early Church's conviction that the death and resurrection of Jesus of Nazareth constituted an action of God in the life of a man that surpassed all natural attitudes and understanding.[45]

The death of Jesus is never presented in the New Testament purely in terms of something that happened to Jesus. Paul indicates that Jesus' death was intimately linked with the purposes of God and is thus the hallmark of the "obedience" of the new Adam, contrasted with the "disobedience" of the first Adam (see Rom 5:12-21). Again Paul repeats what is central to the narratives of the gospels, perhaps best summed up in the prayer of Jesus in Gethsemane: "Abba, Father, for you all things are possible; remove this cup from me; yet, not what I want, but what you want" (Mark 14:36). Even though Paul did not tell Jesus' story, he would have been aware that it was the quality of Jesus' life that led to his death. Mark 14:36 summarizes not only Jesus' attitude to his death but also his attitude to his life.

Niebuhr, *Christ and Culture* 196–206 for a treatment of the Fourth Gospel as a model of the "transformation of culture." Despite exegetical difficulties (e.g., John's sacramental teaching, his understanding of "the world," his defense of a given culture over against Judaism, the second-century background of the gospel, etc.) Niebuhr is correct when he claims: "In general John's interest is directed toward the spiritual transformation of man's life in the world" (p. 204). A closer attention to the Johannine narrative structure could have produced even more aggressive claims.

[44] For a work showing how each evangelist's story of the end of Jesus' life illuminates his telling of the whole story see Frank J. Matera, *Passion Narratives and Gospel Theologies. Interpreting the Synoptics Through Their Passion Stories* (New York: Paulist, 1986).

[45] For what follows see the synthesis by Trilling, *Conversation* 51–65. Here I must disagree with the remark of Niebuhr, *Christ and Culture* 85, who uses Paul as an example of an early Christian attempt to identify Christ and culture: "Jesus was for them [i.e., Paul and the Ebionites] not only the promised Messiah but the Messiah of the promise, as this was understood by their society." I disagree with the closing remark.

Because the event of the cross flows from a radical obedience of the Son of the Father what happens on the cross is an indication of the Father's relationship to a world at present dominated by sin and division.[46] Linked with this obedience of the Son to the Father is another central element in the Pauline understanding of the death of Jesus: salvation. Some Jewish literature at the time of Paul saw the death of a just person or a martyr as in some way "atoning" for the nation (see, for example, 4 Macc 6:27-29; 17:22; 18:4). While traces of this can be found in Paul (see, for example, Rom 3:25, Gal 3:13; 2 Cor 5:21), it does not play an important part in his understanding of the salvation God offers the world through the cross of God's son. Some of these passages may have come to Paul from his churches, and were thus pre-Pauline.[47] Paul looks to the horror of the reality of the physical experience of the death of Jesus on a cross as a condemned criminal. How can such an event make sense of the sin and division that stand at the heart of both society and each individual (see especially 1 Cor 1:23-24)? From a life deeply committed to Judaism (Gal 1:13-14; Phil 3:5-6), Paul understood that "cursed is everyone who hangs on a tree" (Gal 3:13; see Deut 21:22-23), and he believed that blessing came from the exact performance of the Law. This changed when "God, who had set me apart before I was born and called me through his grace, was pleased to reveal his Son to me" (Gal 1:15-16). His previous view was turned upside down: the curse became the blessing and the blessing, while not becoming a curse, fell little short of it (Gal 3:10; Rom 7:7). It both informed humankind about the reality of sin and actually provoked sin (see Rom 5:20; 7:5, 7-13). Now it was the cross that was the power of God and the wisdom of God (1 Cor 1:24). The Law was unable to do anything to save lost humankind except drive it further into its misery by informing it of the reality of sin while offering no genuine escape from that sin (see especially Rom 7:7-24).

The language of the cross expresses the helplessness that God was prepared to embrace in this love for humankind. The cross embodies the evil and cruelty of the world in an inescapable way. It reveals the mercilessness of the world and its dominant powers when left to their own devices, without the love of God. This is "the offense of the cross (Gal 5:11)."[48] The absolutes of "this world" and its value systems are

---

[46] See Murphy-O'Connor, *Becoming Human Together* 70–86.

[47] See Ernst Käsemann, "The Saving Significance of the Death of Jesus in Paul," in *Perspectives on Paul*. Translated by Margaret Kohl (Philadelphia: Fortress; London: SCM, 1971) 42–44.

[48] On the grim reality of the cross and the processes of crucifixion see the study by Martin Hengel, *Crucifixion in the Ancient World and the Folly of the Message of the Cross*. Translated by John Bowden (London: SCM, 1977).

questioned at the most radical level. Paul can only know a Christ crucified: "For I decided to know nothing among you except Jesus Christ,
and him crucified" (1 Cor 2:2). The harshness revealed in the cross is
still part of the human story, and Paul thus calls the members of his
churches to recognize that to lapse into the ways of old would be to become "enemies of the cross of Christ" (Phil 3:18; Gal 6:12). Our "old
self" has been crucified with Christ in the experience of the death of
baptism (see Rom 6:3-6; Gal 2:19), but the symbol of the cross, which
Paul raises up over against the "old world," has its roots in the bloody
reality of the experience of Jesus. Ultimately, however, that cross was
empty. Salvation comes from the death of Jesus because this death is
swallowed up in the victory of the resurrection (see 1 Cor 15:54-57).

As with the bloody event of the cross, Paul's theology of the resurrection of Jesus starts from a firm conviction. The events indicated that
the one who was believed to be crucified, dead, and buried was now
alive and had shown himself (1 Cor 15:3-7). In fact, Paul provides us
with our earliest evidence of the beginnings of Easter faith.[49] As the
Adam-Christ reversal served Paul in his treatment of Christ's over-
coming of sin and death in Rom 5:12-21, so also in his theology of the
resurrection the same image reappears:

> But in fact Christ has been raised from the dead, the first fruits of those
> who have fallen asleep. For since death came through a human being, the
> resurrection of the dead has also come through a human being; for as all
> die in Adam, so all will be made alive in Christ (1 Cor 15:20-22).

Just as Adam's death is the root cause of death for all, so Christ's resurrection is the root cause of life for all. For Paul the resurrection of
Jesus was not something that happened to Jesus in the past. It is the establishment of a new order of life, because a new power has been set
free in the relationship that exists between the human being and God.
Thus the resurrection of Jesus and the resurrection of all, although not
the same thing, run side by side.

The difference is important, however. Only Jesus Christ has been definitively raised from the dead, while the believer lives and dies in the
hope of the resurrection. The message of Paul is that such hope is not in
vain. Just as the alienation that sin has created between humankind and

---

[49] There is a large literature on this issue. For balanced and fully-documented
surveys of the contemporary discussion see John Kloppenborg, "An Analysis of
the Pre-Pauline Formula in 1 Cor 15:3b-5 in Light of Some Recent Literature,"
CBQ 40 (1978) 351–67, and Jerome Murphy-O'Connor, "Tradition and Redaction in 1 Cor 15:3-7," *CBQ* 43 (1981) 582–89.

God has been overcome by the death of Jesus, so also the hold of death itself has been similarly overcome by the resurrection of Jesus. The resurrection of Jesus has set free the Spirit of God (see Rom 8:11) in the world. It is a life-giving power experienced *now:* "The last Adam became a life-giving spirit (1 Cor 15:45)." Paul's own life story has been dominated by a readiness to abandon all his natural honors and successes so that he might "know Christ and the power of his resurrection" (Phil 3:10). It is also a guarantee (2 Cor 1:22; 5:5; Eph 1:14) that just as God has raised Christ from the dead, so also God will raise the faithful from the dead (1 Cor 15:23, 50-55). Thus the resurrection is the ultimate reason for the Christian life lived as a manifestation of the love, the power, and the faithfulness of God. This, of course, could lead us to a reflection on the Christian response which, called to manifest the love, power and faithfulness of God, similarly transforms natural attitudes.[50]

Our theme, the death and resurrection of Jesus as the surpassing of natural attitudes, has been lucidly summarized by Paul himself:

> . . . we ourselves, who have the first fruits of the Spirit, groan inwardly while we wait for adoption, the redemption of our bodies. For in hope we were saved. Now hope that is seen is not hope. For who hopes for what is seen? But if we hope for what we do not see, we wait for it with patience (Rom 8:23-25).

In a world that has always sought to control its own destiny, a problem already faced by the sacred writers in the biblical story of human origins in Genesis 1–11, such an attitude leaves us uncomfortable. It is not "natural" in the established use of that word.[51] Saint Leo the Great challenges us to recognize in the event of Jesus of Nazareth a renewed and transformed Christian view of what is "natural."

> O human, rouse yourself! Learn to know the dignity of your nature. Remember that image of God in which you were created, which, though defaced in Adam, is now restored in Christ. Use this visible creation as it

---

[50] See further Francis J. Moloney, *A Life of Promise. Poverty, Chastity, Obedience* (London: Darton, Longman and Todd, 1984).

[51] On this see Morna D. Hooker, *Pauline Pieces* (London: Epworth, 1979) 95: "It is natural for men to expect God to reveal himself in glory, wisdom and power. Paul himself uses all those terms to describe God's activity; but he reminds us that in the divine pattern these ideas may well all be turned on their heads, so that men fail to see God at work. It is all too easy to look for future glory in the heavens and ignore the glory under one's feet, but if God reveals himself supremely in the degradation of the Cross, then there is no human situation in which he may not be found."

should be used, as you use the earth, sky, sea, air, springs and rivers; and whatever is beautiful and wonderful in them acknowledge to the praise and glory of God.[52]

3. THE CRITICISM OF SIN

While the life, teaching, death, and resurrection of Jesus are presented in the New Testament as a powerful "re-creation" of the original design of God and a call to look beyond the dictates of the "natural," there is a darker side to the message. The New Testament also presents the possibility of the refusal of the dream of Jesus: sin. Sin can be described as the denial of Jesus' affirmation of creation and his challenge to look beyond the absolutes produced by the human spirit, however noble they might be. We have traced Jesus' complete identification with the ways and the will of God through a human life lived out unto death in radical obedience to God, whom Jesus called *Abba*. His call to others to "follow" him meant that he summoned disciples to go down the same way of obedience.[53] Although it is impossible to describe a complete "ethic" of Jesus, his criticism of sin is patent. Sin was nothing less than the refusal of the ways of God the life and teaching, death and resurrection of Jesus have made known. This message is repeated in the Pauline insistence that no human creation, be it the Law or human wit and wisdom, can come between the believer and the gracious gift of God's saving love.

Jesus and Sin

In the teaching of Jesus his insistence on doing the will of God is directed at specific situations. In the antitheses of the Sermon on the Mount (Matt 5:21-48) Jesus moves from the general to the particular. While the Law (see Exod 20:13 and Deut 5:17) said "'You shall not murder'; and 'whoever murders shall be liable to judgment,'" Jesus' demand is more radical: "if you are angry with a brother or sister, you will be liable to judgment; and if you insult a brother or sister, you will be liable to the council; and if you say, 'You fool,' you will be liable to the hell of fire" (Matt 5:22-26). The movement in the teaching of Jesus is from the external act of killing to the internal attitude of being angry. So it is also with adultery. While the Law of Moses (see Exod 20:14 and Deut 5:18) prohibits adultery, Jesus teaches: "everyone who looks at a

---

[52] Pope St. Leo the Great, *Sermon on the Nativity* VII, 6; PL 54, 220–21.
[53] See Moloney, *A Life of Promise* 119–63.

woman so that she shall become desirous has already committed adultery with her in his heart" (Matt 5:28*).[54] Jesus moves away from the specific act of adultery. After all, a person may refrain from physical adultery but be adulterous in attitude. The radical obedience to the ways of God demanded by Jesus asks that we be concerned with an attitude toward and an understanding of women that produces adultery.

The same pattern is found with another great acquisition of Mosaic Law: the *lex talionis:* "eye for eye, tooth for tooth" (see Exod 21:24; Lev 24:20; Deut 19:21). In ancient Israel this law had put an end to the practice of the vendetta. It limited retaliation only to the offended party. Jesus redirects this in three ways. He asks for nonresistance (Matt 5:39), for the avoidance of lawsuits (5:40), and for acceptance of impressment into military service (5:41).[55] This is not a new legalism, but a radical shift of emphasis from external act to internal attitude. What is at stake is not how one performs but how one relates to God. The basis of the new imperative is: "Be perfect, therefore, as your heavenly Father is perfect" (5:48). The new criterion for right and wrong is one's relationship to God, the Father of Jesus, now the Father of all those who claim to be followers of God's son (see Luke 11:2-13). Sin is a refusal to allow God to be Father. Jesus' own relationship to the Father in the endearing use of the term *Abba* was already an indication of the quality of the love of God that stood behind the mystery of Jesus of Nazareth.

Jesus' command to love (see Matt 5:43-48) has thus rightly been seen as the essence of Christian morality. It both reflects how the ways of God were reflected in the quality of the life and teaching of Jesus and stands at the heart of his preaching.[56] The ways of God are now available in the

---

[54] For this translation see Klaus Haacker, "Der Rechtssatz Jesu zum Thema Ehebruch (Mt 5:28)," *BZ* 21 (1977) 113–16.

[55] This is the background for the request that the follower of Jesus accept impressment not merely for one mile but for two. It is probably a reference to the Roman practice of forcing someone to carry the baggage. Not only are they to accept the task, but they are to go two miles instead of one. On this see Marie-Joseph Lagrange, *Evangile selon Saint Matthieu.* EB (Paris: Gabalda, 1927) 113–14.

[56] On the Matthean material see Luise Schottroff, Reginald H. Fuller, Christoph Burchard and M. Jack Suggs, *Essays on the Love Commandment.* Translated by Reginald H. and Ilse Fuller (Philadelphia: Fortress, 1978). On the overall theme see Victor P. Furnish, *The Love Command in the New Testament* (Nashville: Abingdon; London: SCM, 1973). The most thorough New Testament presentation of the love command is found in John 13:1–17:26. On this see Yves Simoens, *La gloire d'aimer. Structures stylistiques et interprétatives dans le Discours de la Cène (Jn 13–17).* AnBib 90 (Rome: Biblical Institute Press, 1981); Francis J. Moloney, *Glory not Dishonor. Reading John 13–21* (Minneapolis: Fortress, 1998) 1–126.

way of Jesus. The Christian is called to allow God to be God in a radical obedience that matches the obedience of Jesus of Nazareth. To compromise these values for anything less is to compromise God, to succumb to the power of sin, making of some created reality a new god. This is vain and sinful, noble as some of those creations may be. The teaching of Jesus calls into question all tendencies to make absolutes of any particular history, any particular culture, and any particular religion.

Paul and Sin

Paul applies what we have seen in the teaching and person of Jesus. He is at one with the earliest Christian tradition in understanding that there is but one saving gospel: faith in a Christ crucified whom God has raised (see Gal 1:6-9; Rom 1:16-17). His dramatic experience of conversion had taught him that crucifixion, once regarded as a curse (Gal 3:13), was now God's assumption of the lostness of humanity (1 Cor 1:22-24). What he once saw as his glory, the observation of the Law (Phil 3:6), could not deliver him from the body of death (see Rom 7:21-24). Out of this context *anything* that claimed to be able to take the place of the saving act of God's gift in Jesus Christ could only merit Paul's scorn. Such was the case with the Law.[57] As a follower of Jesus Christ, Paul had discovered that right relationship with God, for which he had struggled for so long under the Law, was now available to him through the "free gift" of God in Jesus Christ. To attempt to save oneself by observance of a humanly-made Law was to lose Christ and to lose the gift of God (see Gal 5:4). Certainly the Law revealed sin (Gal 3:22; Rom 7:7), but it was only temporary (Gal 3:19-25). A true people of God had to be delivered from a possible absolutization of something that was the product of history, culture, and religion (Gal 2:19; 3:13; 4:5, 8-10, 21-31; 5:1, 18). No one can serve two masters. For Paul serving Christ meant freedom from the rule of the Law: "For freedom Christ has set us free. Stand firm, therefore, and do not submit again to a yoke of slavery" (Gal 5:1).

In the "new creation" established through the free gift of God in the death and resurrection of Jesus Christ salvation depends entirely on readiness to lay oneself open in total faith and obedience, thus to enter

---

[57] On this see Joseph A. Fitzmyer, "Paul and the Law," in idem, *To Advance the Gospel* (New York: Crossroad, 1981) 186–201; E. P. Sanders, *Paul, the Law, and the Jewish People* (Philadelphia: Fortress, 1983); Hans Hübner, *Law in Paul's Thought*. Translated by James C. G. Greig; edited by John Riches (Edinburgh: T & T Clark, 1984); Brendan J. Byrne, *Reckoning with Romans* 134–47. Niebuhr, *Christ and Culture* 166, puts it well: "It is not exactly an ethics of death, but it is an ethics for the dying." On this whole issue see 159–67.

into the obedience of Jesus Christ, to die with him, to rise with him, to walk in newness of life (see Rom 6:1-4). Only in this way is the Christian in a position to receive the offer of the "free gift" of a new relationship with God, which only God can establish.

> Because life flows from righteousness (that is, from the renewed relationship with God), there is an intrinsic link between human obedience and God's future for the world. God pursues his purpose and exercises his righteousness through the bodily obedience of human beings, which continues in the Spirit the obedience of Christ.[58]

It is now clear that the Law was not at the center of Paul's thought and teaching.[59] It forms part of his argument in the "great letters" (see especially Gal 2:16–6:13 and Rom 2:12–8:7) because it was the basis of a significant attempt to gain salvation by means of one's own abilities (see Gal 2:21). At Corinth Paul faced a similar attempt that had a different basis. He had to deal with a group that had a taste for a particular form of Hellenistic Jewish wisdom speculation, which they regarded as the vehicle of salvation.[60] The danger in Corinth was as acute as the danger in Galatia and elsewhere. That is why the early chapters of 1 Corinthians (1–4) insist that salvation does not depend on one's own wit, cleverness, ability, or intellect. Indeed, the search for cleverness could empty the cross of all meaning (1:17):

> God chose what is low and despised in the world, things that are not, to reduce to nothing things that are, so that no one might boast in the presence of God. He is the source of your life in Christ Jesus, who became for us wisdom from God, and righteousness and sanctification and redemption (1 Cor 1:29-30).

The object of scorn is no longer the Law, but the argument is the same. It is the crucified and risen Christ who is the power of God and the wisdom of God (see 1 Cor 1:22-24). Paul, in an authentic understand-

---

[58] Byrne, *Reckoning with Romans* 222.

[59] See Fitzmyer, "Paul and the Law," 186–87. See also the important more general reflection by Krister Stendahl, "The Apostle Paul and the Introspective Conscience of the West," in idem, *Paul Among Jews and Gentiles, and Other Essays* (Philadelphia: Fortress, 1976) 78–96.

[60] See Richard J. Horsley, "Wisdom of Word and Words of Wisdom in Corinth," *CBQ* 39 (1977) 224–39. Horsley has rightly pointed to the Corinthians' identifiable Hellenistic Jewish use of eloquence in language directed toward the heavenly Sophia. Paul combats this with his message of God's power revealed in the eschatological events of the crucifixion of Christ and the parousia.

ing of Jesus' criticism of sin, insists that to sin is to make our own creations into gods. He demands, like Jesus, that we let God be God, allowing God to save us through the death and resurrection of God's Son (see Gal 3:10-14).

4. CONCLUSION

These reflections on Jesus of Nazareth as he is communicated to us through the documents of the New Testament all point to a single and simple conclusion. God's saving intervention in the person of Jesus of Nazareth became part of a religious practice, a culture, and a history, but that culture, history, and religion were assumed and transformed by his life, teaching, death, and resurrection. While his contemporaries could in some way understand who he was and what it was he was asking of them, his story ended with the enigma of death and resurrection. Such a "life story" broke through the expectations and limitations their religion, culture, and history would have preferred to impose on him.

Who Jesus Christ is, and what he asks from all who claim to be responding to his call to "follow" (see Mark 1:16-20) cannot be "controlled" or "contained" by *any* religion, *any* culture, or *any* history. The life and teaching, death and resurrection of Jesus of Nazareth stand as a challenge to the absolutization of any particular culture, religion, or history. God the Father of Jesus is God, and creation is part of God's design. However, the beauties of creation can never exhaust the promises of God revealed in Jesus of Nazareth. He calls us to transform our particular cultures by defying sin, which makes our ways and our absolutes the shapers of our destiny. Jesus' followers will strive—against all the tendencies of human culture and history to settle for what has been achieved—to transform their particular cultures as Jesus strove to transform his. As his life story tells us, it will cost no less than everything (see Mark 8:34-35; John 12:24-26; 15:13).

━━10━━
CHAPTER

THE EUCHARIST AS JESUS' PRESENCE
TO THE BROKEN

It can be said, without too much fear of error, that major periods of the history of the Church's life and liturgical practice have been marked by their own eucharistic practice.[1] There have been many factors that have led to the predominant view of Eucharist in the particular eucharistic tradition to which each of us belongs.[2] This is not the place to discuss those issues. I merely wish to indicate one important feature of a widespread view of Eucharist that this study will investigate—and

---

[1] For a study of the historical development of the theology and celebration of the Eucharist see Louis Bouyer, *Eucharist. Theology and Spirituality of the Eucharistic Prayer* (Notre Dame: University of Notre Dame Press, 1968). For a briefer survey see Johannes H. Emminghaus, *The Eucharist: Essence, Form, Celebration.* Translated by Matthew J. O'Connell (Collegeville: The Liturgical Press, 1978; new rev. edition edited by Theodor Maas-Ewerd and translated by Linda M. Maloney, 1997) 39–98.

[2] Traditional Anglo-Irish Catholicism in Australia (and the United States) had its uniqueness: the absolute necessity of Sunday Mass, silence in front of the tabernacle, women's wearing hats in church and gloves when they received the Eucharist, the absolute necessity for confession before communion, and so on. Newly arrived traditions (European, Arab, and Asian) have shown how "local" such firmly entrenched practices are. African-American celebrations in the U. S. are a fine example of the way culture shapes celebration.

question: the Eucharist as an encounter with the Lord to which only those whom we consider worthy are invited.[3]

Eucharist is denied to Roman Catholics whose marriages (often the second after a failed relationship) are not in accord with Catholic teaching; those struggling with the Church's teaching on birth control often have difficulties in approaching the eucharistic table, and the issue of intercommunion with non-Roman Catholic Christians hinges on someone's being considered not fully prepared for the reception of the eucharistic Lord in our tradition.[4] The list could go on. Such a practice reflects a eucharistic theology that rightfully has its own history and tradition in the Western Church, but there is nowadays widespread feeling, and even some action on the part of a group of German bishops,[5] asking that this tradition be rethought. As the bishops from the Northern Rhine made clear, it is methodologically unsound to go ahead, either theologically or pastorally, on the basis of "widespread feeling."[6] In this important contemporary debate within the Roman Catholic tradition, which also has its parallels in the Christian churches

---

[3] This tradition has been expressed juridically in Canons 915-916 of the 1983 revision of *The Code of Canon Law* and firmly restated by John Paul II in *Familiaris Consortio* 84 (November 1981). He states that "the church reaffirms her practice, *which is based upon sacred scripture,* of not admitting to eucharistic communion divorced persons who have remarried." The words I have italicized bear further investigation.

[4] I am well aware that there is much more to the ecumenical question, especially as regards ecclesiology and the theology of ministry, particularly the latter. An uncritical "intercommunion" without regard for one's theology of ministry can lead to serious ecumenical problems. For that reason I chose the expression "not fully prepared," as this vague phrase can cover a multitude of difficulties.

[5] In 1993–94 the bishops from the Northern Rhine Province of Germany conducted conversations with the Congregation for the Doctrine of the Faith on this issue. See the full documentation, and some commentary on it, in Kevin T. Kelly, *Divorce and Second Marriage. Facing the Challenge* (new and expanded ed. Kansas City; Sheed & Ward, 1997) 90–141.

[6] More than one pastor has told me that at the level of practice people traditionally excluded from the Eucharist are now simply admitted, without further ado. This is not sufficient. Ultimately such pastoral practice is based on one's "feeling" about the issue. No matter how finely tuned a particular pastor may be to the ways of the Spirit in the Church, the biblical and theological motivations for or against such practice must be considered. It is in the light of all these factors that the magisterium should eventually teach. For the theological principles undergirding the approach of the German bishops see Kelly, *Divorce* 98–117.

of other traditions, does the New Testament offer a more solid basis upon which one might place one's feet in order to raise a questioning finger to this predominant tradition?[7]

Although it is one of the most difficult aspects of the theological and pastoral task, it is essential to the Roman Catholic Church that it be enlightened from the two sources of its faith: Scripture and tradition (*Dei Verbum* 7–10).[8] The relationship of Scripture and tradition has never been easy to either define or practice, but it calls for interaction and mutuality: "Sacred tradition and sacred scripture, then, are bound closely together, and communicate one with the other. Flowing from the same divine well-spring, both of them *merge, in a sense,* and move towards the same goal" (*Dei Verbum* 9).[9] The Council has taught that Scripture and tradition need one another even though neither is totally at ease with the other. Tradition alone is insufficient,[10] but Scripture

[7] Such a need in any critical approach to a tradition has been well described by Rosemary Radford Ruether, *Sexism and God-Talk: Toward a Feminist Theology* (Boston: Beacon, 1983) 18: "To look back to some original base of meaning and truth before corruption is to know that truth is more basic than falsehood. . . . One cannot wield the lever of criticism without a place to stand."

[8] See especially *Dei Verbum* 10: ". . . in the supremely wise arrangement of God, sacred tradition, sacred scripture and the magisterium of the church are so connected and associated that one of them cannot stand without the others. Working together, each in its own way under the action of the one holy Spirit, they all contribute effectively to the salvation of souls."

[9] Emphasis supplied. As the stressed words in my citation of the text of *Dei Verbum* 9 indicate, the fact of the mutuality is affirmed, but what precisely is meant by "merge, in a sense" *(in unum quodammodo coalescunt)*? This formula was deliberately left vague, but it leads to difficulties in understanding how Scripture and tradition relate to one another. As Rudolf Schnackenburg, "Die Funktion der Exegese in Theologie und Kirche," in idem, *Maßstab des Glaubens: Fragen heutiger Christen im Licht des Neuen Testaments* (Freiburg: Herder, 1978) 20 has commented: "Das war ein Kompromissformulierung, die den Weg zum ökumenischen Dialog offenhalten sollte, aber ihn eher verfehlte. Theologisch bedarf der Satz noch weiterer Klärung" [This was a compromise formula intended to keep open the way for ecumenical dialogue, but in that regard it missed the mark. The phrase requires further theological clarification]. This valuable essay runs from pp. 11–36. For a fuller critical discussion see Joseph Ratzinger, "The Transmission of Divine Revelation," in Herbert Vorgrimler, ed., *Commentary on the Documents of Vatican II.* 5 vols. Translated by Lalit Adolphus, Kevin Smyth, and Richard Strachan (London: Burns and Oates; New York: Herder and Herder, 1967–69) 3:190–96.

[10] As Alessandro Manzoni's "storyteller" so wisely commented: "E sapete che le tradizioni, chi non le aiuta, da sè dicon sempre troppo poco" [And you

alone can also lead us into a "blind alley."[11] While the exact nature of the relationship between them remains the subject of theological debate, experience teaches that while the tradition keeps the Scriptures alive in the Church, Scripture keeps the traditions honest.[12]

In the reflection that follows I would like to question an aspect of our current "traditions" by looking at some of the foundational eucharistic passages in the Scriptures.[13] Over the years, as I have pondered these texts, it came as a surprise to me that while I understood Eucharist as the place of encounter between Jesus and the worthy, the Word of God seemed to argue that it is a place of encounter between Jesus and the broken. No doubt there are many pastoral and theological arguments that could and should be raised both for and against the issue addressed here.[14] These reflections are limited to a brief analysis of some

---

know that traditions alone, unless you help them, always say too little]. See Fausto Ghisalberti, ed., *I Promessi Sposi: Storia Milanese del Secolo XVII* (Milan: Ulrico Hoepli, 1973) 553.

[11] I take this expression from an earlier groundbreaking study from the Protestant tradition: Ernst Käsemann, "Blind Alleys in the 'Jesus of History' Controversy," in idem, *New Testament Questions of Today* (London: SCM, 1969) 23–65. Important contributions on the limitations of *sola scriptura* have been made by other Protestant scholars. See Peter Stuhlmacher, *Schriftauslegung auf dem Wege zur biblischen Theologie* (Göttingen: Vandenhoeck & Ruprecht, 1975). One of the essays from this work has been published in English in idem, *Historical Criticism and Theological Interpretation of Scripture: Toward a Hermeneutics of Consent.* Translated by Roy A. Harrisville (Philadelphia: Fortress, 1977). See also James Barr, *The Scope and Authority of the Bible.* Explorations in Theology 7 (Philadelphia: Westminster; London: SCM, 1980).

[12] On this see Francis J. Moloney, "'The Living Voice of the Gospel' (*Dei Verbum* 8). Some Reflections on the Dynamism of the Christian Tradition," *Sal* 48 (1986) 225–54. A simpler version of this study can be found in my *The Living Voice of the Gospel: The Gospels Today* (Melbourne: Collins Dove, 1986) 223–43. See also Francis J. Moloney, "Whither Catholic Biblical Studies?" *ACR* 66 (1989) 83–93.

[13] This study looks primarily to the theological and religious message of the present structure of the gospels and of 1 Cor 11:17-34. For the classic study of the history of the eucharistic words and their eventual incorporation into the New Testament documents see Joachim Jeremias, *The Eucharistic Words of Jesus.* Translated by Norman Perrin from the German 3rd ed. (London: SCM, 1966).

[14] Since the original publication of this article (1989) I have written a book that offers a more complete study of both the biblical texts and some of the theological and pastoral issues involved. See Francis J. Moloney, *A Body Broken for a Broken People. Eucharist in the New Testament.* (rev. ed. Peabody, Mass.: Hendrickson, 1997).

key gospel passages and 1 Cor 11:17-43,[15] which, it appears to me, question a significant tradition and practice in the Christian churches.[16] Such a "questioning" of traditional practices through a careful use of the Scriptures is a delicate but necessary task in a human institution that always runs the risk of distorting its traditions.[17] This study in no way pretends to solve the questions it raises, but I suspect that, as always, "the word of God is living and active, sharper than any two-edged sword, piercing until it divides soul from spirit, joints from marrow; it is able to discern the thoughts and intentions of the heart" (Heb 4:12).

THE GOSPEL OF MARK

There are important eucharistic teachings in Mark's two bread stories (Mark 6:31-44; 8:1-10),[18] but I will base my reflections on the major eucharistic text in this gospel, the Markan version of the last meal Jesus shared with his disciples (14:17-31).[19] One of the features of Markan

[15] As Matt 26:20-35 largely repeats Mark 14:17-31 I will not devote a separate section to that text. I will merely mention its place in my argument as I conclude the analysis of the Markan material. For a study of the Matthean eucharistic passages see Moloney, *A Body Broken* 57–83.

[16] This is one of the tasks of the theologian who, through all his or her questioning, stands by the teaching and practice demanded by the magisterium.

[17] Joseph Ratzinger, in his commentary on the conciliar document on Divine Revelation (*Dei Verbum* 9) is critical of the Council's lack of clarity on this issue. See Joseph Ratzinger, "The Transmission of Divine Revelation," in Vorgrimler, ed., *Commentary on the Documents of Vatican II* 3:192–93: "We shall have to acknowledge the truth of the criticism that there is, in fact, no explicit mention of the possibility of a distorting tradition and of the place of Scripture as an element within the Church that is also critical of tradition, which means that a most important side of the problem, as shown by the history of the Church— and perhaps the real crux of the *ecclesia semper reformanda*—has been overlooked. . . . That this opportunity has been missed can only be regarded as an unfortunate omission." In a later article in the same volume ("Sacred Scripture in the Life of the Church"), commenting on *Dei Verbum* 23, he writes: "A reference to the ecclesial nature of exegesis, on the one hand, and to its methodological correctness on the other, again expresses the inner tension of Church exegesis, which can no longer be removed, *but must be simply accepted as tension*" (p. 268; emphasis supplied).

[18] See further Moloney, *A Body Broken* 37–44. See also Robert M. Fowler, *Loaves and Fishes: The Function of the Feeding Stories in the Gospel of Mark.* SBLDS 54 (Chico: Scholars, 1981) 132–47.

[19] Not all would see the section in 14:17-31 as a unit. Many would break the passage at either v. 26 or v. 27, divorcing vv. 26-31 (or vv. 27-31) from vv. 17-25 (26). See below, n. 21, and Moloney, *A Body Broken* 44–54.

style is a tendency to "frame" stories. Very often the author singles out an important narrative and frames it with another. A well-known example of this is the frame of Jairus' summoning Jesus to come to his daughter (5:21-24) and the actual raising of Jairus' daughter (vv. 35-43) around the cure of the woman with the flow of blood (vv. 25-34). Another is the frame of Jesus' cursing of the fig tree (11:12-14) and the sight of the withered tree (vv. 20-21) around the story of Jesus' ending all business and cultic practices in the Temple in Jerusalem (vv. 15-19). The list could be expanded (see also 3:20-35; 6:7-30; 14:1-11, 54-72), as it is a structure dear to Mark.[20]

Sections of Mark's Gospel that are "framed" in this way must be interpreted as a whole. The sections that form the "frame" serve to explain the section framed, and vice-versa. Once this is noticed, Mark 14:17-31 must be read as the description of Jesus' final meal with his disciples (14:22-25), framed by stories of their betrayal of him, their denial and flight (vv. 17-21 and vv. 26-31).[21] In 14:17-21 the evangelist

---

[20] On this see John R. Donahue, *Are You the Christ? The Trial Narrative in the Gospel of Mark*. SBLDS 10 (Missoula: Scholars, 1973) 57–63. Further literature is offered there. It is often asked whether an author such as Mark could have used such skillful techniques. Donahue's response to this question is: "The present work moves in opposition to the above views by studying what Mark actually did, not what he could or could not have done" (p. 3). See also Howard Clark Kee, *Community of the New Age: Studies in Mark's Gospel* (Philadelphia: Westminster, 1977) 50–76.

[21] For this structure see Rudolf Pesch, *Das Markusevangelium*. 2 vols. HTKNT II/1–2 (Freiburg: Herder, 1976–77) 2:345–46; Klemens Stock, *Boten aus dem Mit-Ihm-Sein. Das Verhältnis zwischen Jesus und den Zwölf nach Markus*. AnBib 70 (Rome: Biblical Institute Press, 1975) 167. Michael Fitzpatrick, O.F.M., who left us too soon after a long struggle with cancer, had long pointed out that this particular "frame" forms part of a much wider literary pattern used throughout 14:1-72. There is a deliberate situating of Jesus' story between narratives that tell of the failure of one or all of the disciples (14:1-2: Plot [failure]; vv. 3-9: Anointing; vv. 10-11: Judas [disciples' failure]; vv. 12-16: Preparation for the Supper; vv. 17-21: Prediction of Judas' betrayal [disciples' failure]; vv. 22-25: The Supper; vv. 26-31: Prediction of the denial of Peter and the failure of all the disciples [disciples' failure]; vv. 32-42: Gethsemane; vv. 43-62: Arrest [disciples' failure]; vv. 53-65: Jewish trial; vv. 66-72: Peter's denial [disciples' failure]). Although vv. 1-2 do not mention disciples, the "chief priests'" need to arrest Jesus "by stealth" is closely linked with vv. 10-11, where Judas looks for an opportunity to betray Jesus to the "chief priests." Some scholars separate vv. 26-31 from the supper because of "and they went out" in v. 26. See, for example, Ernst Lohmeyer, *Das Evangelium des Markus*. Meyers Kommentar (Göttingen: Vandenhoeck & Ruprecht, 1967) 310; Vincent Taylor, *The Gospel According to*

goes to considerable trouble to indicate that Judas, who will betray Jesus, belongs to the inner circle of his friends. We read that Jesus "came with the twelve," a group specially appointed in 3:14 "to be with him" in a unique way (v. 17). The setting for Jesus' prediction of his betrayal is the meal table, a sacred place among friends. The tragedy is heightened by the idea that someone who shares table-fellowship will betray Jesus. In the prediction Jesus further explains that the betrayer will be "one who is eating with me" (v. 18). The intimacy is heightened even further by the words of Jesus: "It is one of the twelve, one who is dipping bread into the bowl with me." Jesus is to be betrayed by a person who has shared the most intimate of experiences with him.[22]

A similar attention to the closeness that exists between Jesus and his future betrayers is found in the other section of the frame devoted to the rest of the disciples (14:26-31), where he predicts that they "will all fall away" (v. 27). He uses the image of the shepherd and his sheep (v. 27), and his predictions lead to expressions of love and devotion. Peter swears an unfailing loyalty, better than all the others who may fall away (v. 29), and even claims that he is prepared to lay down his life for his master (v. 31). But Peter is not alone in swearing loyalty and love. The storyteller further comments: "And all of them said the same." There can be no mistaking Mark's desire to communicate to his readers a sense of foreboding, as Jesus' most intimate circle of associates will prove to be those who betray, deny, and abandon him. In the center of this frame, and shedding light on the passage, is the Markan version of Jesus' last meal with the disciples, who will betray, deny, and abandon him (14:22-26).

The theme of table fellowship with the betrayers opens the passage: "While *they* were eating, he took a loaf of bread, and after blessing it he broke it, *gave it to them* . . ." (v. 22). This theme is continued in the sharing

---

St Mark (London: Macmillan, 1966) 548; Lamar Williamson, *Mark.* Interpretation (Atlanta: John Knox, 1983) 257. Others separate vv. 27-31, linking v. 26 to vv. 22-25, as they see in the singing of the hymn (v. 26) a reference to the use of the second half of the Hallel psalms as the conclusion to table-fellowship. See, for example, William L. Lane, *Commentary on the Gospel of Mark.* The New International Commentary on the NT (Grand Rapids: Eerdmans, 1974) 509–10.

[22] On this passage see Vernon K. Robbins, "Last Meal: Preparation, Betrayal, and Absence," in Werner Kelber, ed., *The Passion in Mark. Studies on Mark 14–16* (Philadelphia: Fortress, 1976) 21–40, at 29–34. Robbins' study is typical of much contemporary Markan scholarship, marked by a "corrective christology" approach. For a critical survey of this approach see Jack Dean Kingsbury, *The Christology of Mark's Gospel* (Philadelphia: Fortress, 1983) 25–45.

of the cup, where the same recipients are again specified: "Then he took the cup, and after giving thanks *he gave it to them,* and *all of them drank from it."* (v. 23). The words over the bread and the cup point to the cross: a body given and blood poured out (vv. 22 and 24), but they also point to something beyond the day of crucifixion. The blood is to be a covenant (v. 24), and Jesus comments that he will not "again drink of the fruit of the vine until that day when I drink it new in the kingdom of God" (v. 25). The word "until" rings out a message of trust and hope that looks well beyond the events of Good Friday.[23]

There is to be a body given and blood poured out that will set up a new covenant that reaches beyond the cross into the definitive establishment of the Kingdom. A covenant with whom? The readers of this passage—both the original Markan community and all subsequent Christian communities—are aware that the body broken and the blood poured out have indeed set up a new covenant, and that they form a part of that Kingdom, *thanks to the betrayers* who were the first recipients of that bread and that cup.[24] Mark has given us an account of

[23] Vernon K. Robbins, "Last Meal," argues that the "until" points beyond the Markan community into the parousia: "With this saying, Jesus refers to his approaching absence from the community and the reunion which will occur with his return as Son of Man" (p. 37). It appears to me that the eating of the bread and the drinking from the cup still practiced within the Markan community itself (the fixed formulae of Mark 6:41-42; 8:7-8; 14:22-25 indicate such a practice) meant more than waiting for the final arrival of "the absent one." The "kingdom of God" referred to in v. 25 must be in some way linked with the "new temple," founded on the rejected cornerstone (see 12:10-11; 14:58; 15:29-30, 37-38), the Markan community itself, where Jesus was "present" in the midst of failure. See Donald Juel, *Messiah and Temple: The Trial of Jesus in the Gospel of Mark.* SBLDS 31 (Missoula: Scholars, 1977).

[24] Robbins, "Last Meal," 21–40 misses this point, for both structural and theological reasons. He argues that the key to the interpretation of the Markan supper is the correction of false understandings of Jesus engendered in the narrative among Pharisees, Herodians, and disciples by the eating scenes of chs. 2–8. It is especially directed against those "false prophets" who use meals to proclaim the "presence" of Jesus (see chs. 6–8). Thus 14:12-25 is a proclamation of the suffering and crucified Jesus' "absence" from the Markan community. I am suggesting that the message is one of the "presence" of the crucified Jesus to a failing community. See, for example, David M. Stanley, *The Call to Discipleship: The Spiritual Exercises with the Gospel of St. Mark. The Way* Supplement 43/44 (London: *The Way,* 1982) 153: "A 'new covenant' (Luke 22:20; see Jer 31:31) is being struck with the future community of faith, represented in this scene by the Twelve." For the theme of the Markan post-resurrection discipleship see Ermenegildo Manicardi, *Il cammino di Gesù nel Vangelo di Marco: Schema narrativo e tema cristologico.* AnBib 96 (Rome: Biblical Institute Press, 1981) 171–93.

Jesus' gift of himself unto death so that he could set up a new and last-ing kingdom with the characters in the story who frame the narrative of the meal. The meal Jesus shared was not a meal for the worthy ones. It was a meal for those who were closest to Jesus but who, faced with the challenge to love him even unto death, betrayed and abandoned their Master. As the Markan Church looked back over its own experi-ence it knew that Jesus had given himself, and now believed that he continued to give himself, to disciples who failed. For this reason, when they came to tell the story of the beginning of Jesus' presence to them at the meal, they told the story in this striking way: a gift of self in love to those who had failed him most. Jesus loves his failing disciples with a love that is in no way matched by the love they bear him.[25]

The Markan message has been reproduced in the Gospel of Mat-thew. No doubt the Matthean community also sensed, from their own experience of the presence of the Lord in the midst of their failure (see Matt 1:23 and 28:16-20),[26] the truth of Mark's point of view. Thus their evangelist made only slight stylistic changes to the basic Markan mes-sage of betrayal/meal/betrayal we have already examined (see Matt 26:20-35).[27]

The Gospel of Luke

Luke presents an account of the disciples' last meal with Jesus that is strikingly different from that of Mark and Matthew. Indeed, he was probably not depending on Mark for this part of his story, but drew it

---

[25] Although this message is particularly clear through the Markan structure of 14:17-31 it stands behind the whole of 14:1-72, where Jesus' story is so strongly related to a story of disciples who fail. Indeed, a closer look at the structure suggested above in n. 21 shows that the narrative of the supper stands at the very center of 14:1-72. Five episodes precede it and five follow; 14:22-25, therefore, acts as the major statement of Mark's presentation of Jesus' gift of himself to his failing disciples.

[26] Matthew's theology is strongly marked by a sense of a discipleship that knows the answers but fails in faith (see, for example 28:17). It is equally marked by a well-developed idea of Jesus as the Emmanuel, God-with-us (1:23 and 28:20). On this see Moloney, *The Living Voice of the Gospel* 136–43.

[27] See, for example, the analysis of John P. Meier, *Matthew*. New Testament Message 3 (Wilmington: Michael Glazier, 1980) 315–22. Commenting on the Matthean version of the supper, Robbins, "Last Meal," 22, writes that "the verbal agreement indicates direct copying." See, however, my analysis of the slight but significant Matthean additions to the Markan story in *A Body Bro-ken* 77–81.

from different sources.[28] Given this fact, it is impressive that the account of the meal in Luke 22:14-23 makes the point of Jesus' gift of himself to his betrayers even more powerfully. He juxtaposes the breaking of the bread and the sharing of the cup with an immediate indication of the presence of the betrayer at the table. It is enough simply to see (and hear) the text to sense the power of the argument:

> Then he took a loaf of bread, and when he had given thanks, he broke it and gave it to them saying, "This is my body, which is given for you. Do this in remembrance of me." And he did the same with the cup after supper, saying, "This cup that is poured out for you is the new covenant in my blood. But see, the one who betrays me is with me, and his hand is on the table."[29]

Luke explicitly states, over both the bread and the cup, that they are "for you" (vv. 19-20). For whom? For those fragile disciples—and even the betrayer—who share the table. The rest of Luke's supper scene is dominated by references to the fragility of the disciples in the light of the immensity of their tasks (vv. 24-38).

However, I would like briefly to survey another famous Lukan eucharistic text: the Emmaus story (24:13-35). The theme of a "journey" is important across the Gospel of Luke and the Acts of the Apostles, the two-volume work of the author known to us as Luke.[30] Throughout the gospel a journey leads to Jerusalem, where the paschal events take place (see especially Luke 9:51). At the beginning of Acts the first Christian community is still in Jerusalem. The Spirit is given to the community there, and it is from Jerusalem that a second journey begins, reaching out to the ends of the earth. The city of Jerusalem is the center of God's history. Jesus journeyed there, and from there returned to his Father. The early Church was founded in that city, the Holy Spirit was given there, and from there a mission began which would extend to the ends of the earth (see Luke 24:46-49; Acts 1:8). The city of Jerusalem acts as a fulcrum around which God's salvation history swivels.[31]

---

[28] For a detailed analysis see Joseph A. Fitzmyer, *The Gospel According to Luke X–XXIV.* 2 vols. AB 28, 28A (New York: Doubleday, 1981–85) 2:1385–1406.

[29] Luke 22:19-21. There is a notorious textual difficulty with this passage. I have cited a longer reading, but some witnesses do not reproduce the word over the cup. In defense of the longer reading see Joachim Jeremias, *The Eucharistic Words of Jesus* 139–59. For a survey see Fitzmyer, *Luke* 2:1387–89. Even if we were to accept the shorter reading the point I am making would remain true.

[30] On this theme through the Gospel of Luke see Moloney, *The Living Voice of the Gospel* 67–92.

[31] For detail see Richard J. Dillon, *From Eye-Witnesses to Ministers of the Word.* AnBib 82 (Rome: Biblical Institute Press, 1978) 89–91.

Given this crucial point for the correct understanding of Luke-Acts, the opening remarks of the journey to Emmaus are an indication of the situation of the two disciples. We are told that, in the midst of the paschal events, they were going to Emmaus, "about seven miles [*away*] *from Jerusalem*" (24:13: ἀπὸ Ἰερουσαλήμ).[32] They are walking away from Jerusalem, the central point of God's story. They are walking away from God's design of the journey of the Son of God from Nazareth to Jerusalem, and of the Christian community from Jerusalem to the ends of the earth. This impression is further reinforced once one begins to notice the details of the account itself. In their sadness and disappointment the disciples do not recognize Jesus (vv. 15-17). They tell him of their expectations: "we had hoped that he was the one to redeem Israel" (v. 21). Jesus' way of responding to the design of God (see vv. 25-27) has not fulfilled their expectations of the one who would redeem Israel. In fact, they know everything that one might expect a believer to know about Jesus, including the very words of the Easter proclamation. They know of his life: "Jesus of Nazareth, . . . a prophet mighty in deed and word" (v. 19).[33] They know of his death: "our chief priests and leaders handed him over to be condemned to death and crucified him" (v. 20). They know of the events at the tomb: "it is now the third day" (v. 21), and women have been at the tomb "early this morning, [but] they did not find his body" (v. 23). They have even heard the Easter proclamation: there has been a vision of angels who said "that he was alive" (v. 23). The two disciples know everything, "but they did not see him," (v. 24) and thus they have had enough. They continue their walk away from Jerusalem.[34]

---

[32] None of the major commentators sees the importance of Luke's deliberate insertion of ἀπὸ Ἰερουσαλήμ. See, for example, I. Howard Marshall, *The Gospel of Luke. A Commentary on the Greek Text*. The New International Greek Testament Commentary (Grand Rapids: Eerdmans, 1978) 892–93; Eduard Schweizer, *The Good News According to Luke*. Translated by David E. Green (Atlanta: John Knox, 1984) 370. There is a hint of it in Schweizer's passing parallel between the disciples' departure (vv. 13-14) and return (vv. 33-35) on p. 368. Fitzmyer, *Luke* 2:1562 argues that Emmaus is mentioned because it is "in the vicinity of Jerusalem" and thus there is no journey away from Jerusalem. Similarly see Dillon, *From Eye-Witnesses* 85–86.

[33] For an excellent study of the Lukan christology involved in the disciples' description of Jesus see Dillon, *From Eye-Witnesses* 111–45.

[34] Their knowledge of the "brute facts" of the resurrection story is widely recognized. For a suggestive analysis of what this means for Lukan thought see Dillon, *From Eye-Witnesses* 55–56; 110–11.

It is with these failed disciples who have abandoned God's journey that Jesus journeys and with whom he joins in Eucharist. We read of a long liturgy of the word reflecting the practice of the Lukan Church as Jesus "interpreted to them the things about himself in all the scriptures" (v. 27). At the meal they recognized him in the breaking of the bread (vv. 30-31). Jesus followed, joined, and journeyed with these failing disciples as they walked away from God's design. He has come to meet them, to make himself known to them and to draw them back to the journey of God through opening the word of God to them and through the breaking of the bread.[35] Touched in their failure, the failed disciples react immediately by turning back in their journey: "That same hour they got up and returned to Jerusalem" (v. 33).[36] Once they arrive back at the place they should never have abandoned, they find that Easter faith is already alive. They are told: "The Lord has risen indeed, and he has appeared to Simon!" (v. 34).[37] They have come back home, but only because the Lord has reached out to them in their brokenness and made himself known to them in the breaking of the bread:

[35] For a fully documented discussion of the eucharistic character of 24:30 see Jacques Dupont, "The Meal at Emmaus," in Jean Delorme, et al., *The Eucharist in the New Testament: A Symposium.* Translated by E. M. Stewart (Baltimore: Helicon; London: Geoffrey Chapman, 1965) 115–21. See also Dillon, *From Eye-Witnesses* 149–55. Dillon has further pointed out that in both Luke and Acts "breaking of the bread" is associated with instruction concerning Jesus' person and mission.

[36] The fact that they "return to Jerusalem" in v. 33 further enhances the importance of their traveling "away from Jerusalem" in v. 13. Many scholars have seen the theological importance of this "return." For details of this scholarship see Dillon, *From Eye-Witnesses* 92–94. Dillon finds himself in difficulty here. He has not appreciated the importance of the going "away from Jerusalem" in v. 13 (see above, n. 30) and thus can only be "tentatively affirmative" (p. 93) to these suggestions.

[37] Perhaps the use of the name "Simon" in 24:34 is important for our argument. Once Simon becomes a disciple of Jesus he is called "Peter" (see 5:8 in the light of 4:38). In speaking of his denials Jesus again calls him "Simon" (22:31), and thus it is to the failed Simon that the risen Lord has appeared. Most scholars see this return to "Simon" as merely an indication of the traditional nature of 24:34 (see 1 Cor 15:4). See, for example, Fitzmyer, *Luke* 2:1569: "a stereotyped formula for appearances." I would suggest that there may be a more subtle Lukan point at stake. For a similar suggestion along these lines see Dillon, *From Eye-Witnesses* 100 n. 88. See also Robert C. Tannehill, *The Narrative Unity of Luke-Acts: A Literary Interpretation.* Foundation and Facets (Philadelphia: Fortress, 1986) 292–93.

Here . . . we find Jesus eating with outcasts, but this time the outcasts are two of his own disciples who have abandoned their journey of faith, fled Jerusalem, and embarked on their own journey. Jesus crosses the boundaries of disloyalty and breaks the bread of reconciliation with these disciples. Strengthened by the risen Jesus, Cleopas and his companion hasten back to Jerusalem and rejoin the journey of discipleship.[38]

Like Mark, and Matthew who has repeated Mark's story, the evangelist Luke has no hesitation in setting the eucharistic presence of the Lord in the midst of the broken disciples. His widespread use of "table settings" for Jesus' teaching, and the parable of the great supper (Luke 14:16-24), convey the same message, but an analysis of this material would take us beyond the limitations of this study.[39] From the material we have studied we can confidently claim that through his special version of the last meal and his addition of the Emmaus journey Luke has taken the early Church's understanding of the Eucharist as Jesus' presence to the broken to even greater depths.[40]

---

[38] Robert J. Karris, "God's Boundary-Breaking Mercy," *The Bible Today* 24 (1986) 27–28. See also Donald Senior and Carroll Stuhmueller, *The Biblical Foundations for Mission* (Maryknoll, N.Y.: Orbis, 1983) 266–67.

[39] For a fuller study of the Lukan eucharistic material see Moloney, *A Body Broken* 84–112. See also the analysis of Luke 14:16-24 in John R. Donahue, *The Gospel in Parable* (Philadelphia: Fortress, 1988) 140–46. Donahue concludes: "Within Christian communities, some of the most violent debates continue to rage over inclusiveness, often centered on the celebration of the Lord's Supper. Yet when Luke's Jesus told a parable about eating bread in the kingdom of God, he shattered his hearers' expectations of who would be the proper table companions. Can his parabolic word continue to challenge our expectations?" (p. 146).

[40] There is a growing sensitivity among scholars to Luke's special interest in the "lost ones." This has always been noticed as central to the three parables in Luke 15, but the theme is now seen as all-pervasive. See especially Donahue, *The Gospel in Parable* 126–93. With particular reference to the way in which the Emmaus story embodies a theme that runs through the whole gospel see Dillon, *From Eye-Witnesses* 240–49. Interestingly (for our purposes) Dillon entitles this section of his study: "Guest and host of the unworthy." More generally see Richard J. Cassidy, *Jesus, Politics and Society: A Study of Luke's Gospel* (Maryknoll, N.Y.: Orbis, 1980); J. Massyngbaerde Ford, *My Enemy is My Guest: Jesus and Violence in Luke* (Maryknoll, N.Y.: Orbis, 1984); Robert F. O'Toole, *The Unity of Luke's Theology: An Analysis of Luke-Acts.* Good News Studies 9 (Wilmington: Michael Glazier, 1984) 109–48; Robert J. Karris, *Luke, Artist and Theologian: Luke's Passion Account as Literature* (New York: Paulist, 1985) 23–78.

THE FOURTH GOSPEL

Given the limitations of this study, I must again be selective in my choice of eucharistic texts from the Fourth Gospel. There is a uniquely Johannine presentation of eucharistic theology in John 6:51c-58,[41] and the flow of blood and water from the pierced side of Jesus in 19:34 also continues this theme.[42] However, in 13:1-38 it appears to me that the theme of Jesus' presence to the broken disciples, which we have traced through Mark, Matthew, and Luke, reaches its profoundest expression.[43] The Fourth Evangelist opens the last discourse of Jesus with a memorable chapter on the footwashing and the gift of the morsel (13:1-38). This passage can be divided, using literary criteria, into three major sections. There is a section dealing with the footwashing and its aftermath (vv. 1-17), a central statement that touches the meaning of the whole chapter (vv. 18-20), and a final section dealing with the gift of the morsel and its aftermath (vv. 21-38).

As vv. 1-17 open, the major theme is immediately struck through the explicit reference to the fullness of Jesus' knowledge and the perfection of his love: "Now before the festival of the Passover, Jesus knew that his hour had come to depart from this world and go to the Father. Having loved his own who were in the world, he loved them to the end" (v. 1). Immediately the theme of the betrayal of Judas is sounded (v. 2). However, knowing all these things, and aware of the ways of God from whom he came and to whom he is about to return, Jesus girds himself for the footwashing and washes the feet of the disciples (vv. 4-5). His encounter with Peter, who objects to the footwashing, only serves to show Peter's ignorance in contrast to the knowledge of Jesus: a knowledge, in this case, of who is about to betray him (vv. 6-11). Taking his garments, he instructs his ignorant and failing disciples about the great gift he has given them through this gesture of love:

---

[41] On this see Francis J. Moloney, "John 6 and the Celebration of the Eucharist," *DRev* 93 (1975) 243–51; idem, "The Function of Prolepsis in the Interpretation of John 6," in R. Alan Culpepper, ed., *Critical Readings of John 6*. BibIntS 22 (Leiden: E. J. Brill, 1998) 129–48.

[42] See my essay, "When is John Talking about Sacraments?," in this volume, pp. 109–30.

[43] For what follows see my more detailed study, "A Sacramental Reading of John 13:1-38," *CBQ* 53 (1991) 237–56. Particularly important for me in this study was the pathbreaking work of Yves Simoens, *La gloire d'aimer: Structures stylistiques et interprétatives dans la Discours de la Cène*. AnBib 90 (Rome: Biblical Institute Press, 1981) 81–104.

"I have set you an example, that you also should do as I have done to you. Very truly, I tell you, servants are not greater than their master, nor are messengers greater than the one who sent them. If you know these things, you are blessed if you do them" (vv. 15-17).

This first section of 13:1-38 (vv. 1-17) has been dominated by several themes. Jesus shows his love for his disciples in his gift of himself for them in the footwashing and in the gift of the example to them. It is also highlighted by the theme of Jesus' knowledge: of the ways of God (v. 3), and of all that is about to happen (v. 11). This series of gracious gifts of Jesus to his disciples is contrasted to the themes of the betrayer (vv. 2, 10-11) and the ignorance of the disciples (vv. 6-10). Leaving aside vv. 18-20, which, as I have already mentioned, should be regarded as the central section of 13:1-38, we come to the final section, vv. 21-38, devoted to the gift of the eucharistic morsel and the gift of the new commandment. Here many of the themes of vv. 1-17 return. There is the repeated reference to the betrayer (vv. 21-26a), the return of the theme of the ignorance of the disciples (vv. 26b-29), the exit of Judas for the betrayal (v. 30), and the prophecy of the denial of Peter (vv. 36-38). However, set within this context of ignorance, betrayal, and denial we find the gift of the eucharistic morsel to his failing disciples; indeed, it is even given to Judas (vv. 26-27).[44] Once the betrayer has departed, Jesus tells his disciples of a further gift he offers to them: "I give you a new commandment, that you love one another. Just as I have loved you, you also should love one another" (v. 34). Repeating the argument of vv. 1-17 in vv. 21-38, we find Jesus' love for his disciples in the gift of the eucharistic morsel, and the gift of the new commandment of love, set in the midst of the ignorance of the disciples, the denial of Peter, and the betrayal of Judas. To failing disciples Jesus has insisted: "I have set you an example, that you also should do as I have done to you" (v. 15), and "I give you a new commandment, that you love one another . . . as I have loved you" (v. 34).

It is at the heart of this context of unconditional love given to failing disciples that we situate the centerpiece: vv. 18-20:

"I am not speaking of all of you; I know whom I have chosen. But it is to fulfill the scripture, 'The one who ate my bread has lifted his heel against me.' I tell you this now, before it occurs, so that when it does occur, you may believe that I AM. Very truly, I say to you, whoever receives one

---

[44] For further detailed explanation of these circumstances concerning the morsel see Francis J. Moloney, *Glory not Dishonor. Reading John 13–21* (Minneapolis: Fortress, 1998) 20–23.

whom I send receives me; and whoever receives me receives him who sent me."

The Fourth Evangelist has deliberately set vv. 18-20, the central piece of 13:1-38, between two flanking passages (vv. 1-17 and vv. 21-38). As we have seen, these passages state and restate the theme of the greatness of the love of God as it has been revealed in Jesus' gift of himself in the footwashing and the Eucharist, in the midst of ignorance, denial, and betrayal. In vv. 18-19 these themes return, but more succinctly. In v. 18 Jesus speaks of the fact that he has no illusions about the very ones whom he has chosen: "I know whom I have chosen." In fact, one of the chosen will become the betrayer who has shared in the eucharistic morsel, and another will deny him: "The one who ate my bread has lifted his heel against me." Despite all this he speaks of his intention to send forth his disciples: "Whoever receives one whom I send receives me; and whoever receives me receives him who sent me" (v. 20). John 13:1-38 is marked by the extraordinary love of God, revealed in Jesus, who gives himself in the footwashing and the eucharistic morsel. In the midst of betrayal and failure his commitment to his disciples does not lessen, despite their lack of commitment to him. He knows whom he has chosen; he is aware that one who shares his table will betray him, another will deny him, and all the others are unable to understand him, yet he loves them and sends them out to proclaim both himself and his Father, betrayers, deniers, and ignorant though they may be. The ultimate significance of this message is now summed up in the central statement of the whole of 13:1-38: "I tell you this now, before it occurs, so that when it does occur, you may believe that I AM" (v. 19*).

This is a remarkable statement. Jesus loves his own so much that he chooses them (v. 18a) and sends them out as his presence (v. 20). Yet these very loved ones are responsible for his death on a cross (v. 18b). It is precisely in this unconditional gift of himself to people who do not love him that he reveals who he is. The Fourth Evangelist uses the expression "I am," a phrase with a long history in the literature of Israel, to refer to the living presence of a God who is made known among the people, and applies it to the person of Jesus.[45] Jesus informs his dis-

---

[45] See, among many studies written on the use of "I am" in the Fourth Gospel, the work of Philip B. Harner, *The "I am" of the Fourth Gospel.* Facet Books, Biblical Series 26 (Philadelphia: Fortress, 1970), and the summary by Raymond E. Brown, *The Gospel According to John.* 2 vols. AB 29, 29a (New York: Doubleday, 1966–70) 1:533–38.

ciples—and John's readers—that when love reveals itself in such an extraordinary fashion, loving "to the end" (13:1) those who do not love him, we can begin to understand the God whom Jesus has come to make known to us. When these things happen, when his disciples have betrayed, denied, and abandoned him and he is "lifted up" on the cross (see 3:13; 8:28; 12:32), his disciples of all times will know that he is the very revelation of God: "I tell you this now, before it occurs, so that when it does occur, you may believe that I Am."

The eucharistic elements in John 13 are not the main features of the chapter. However, the use of the eucharistic morsel is central to the overall and larger message of Jesus, who gives himself in love to disciples who do not love him in anything like the same way. Indeed, he has even given himself to Judas! The Fourth Evangelist would not have been able to tell his story in this way if his own community, and their celebration of the Eucharist, had not provided him with an understanding of the presence of Jesus in the Eucharist that repeats and deepens what we have discovered in Mark, Matthew, and Luke: the Eucharist celebrates and proclaims the presence of Jesus to the broken.

1 Corinthians 11:27-28

1 Corinthians 11:27-28, lifted from its historical and literary context within Paul's argument in 1 Corinthians, reads very strongly: "Whoever, therefore, eats the bread or drinks the cup of the Lord in an unworthy manner will be answerable for the body and blood of the Lord. Examine yourselves, and only then eat of the bread and drink of the cup" (1 Cor 11:27-28). The passage has been read in the traditional moral and dogmatic theology manuals as a biblical word *against* the presence of the broken at the eucharistic table.[46] However, such a reading

---

[46] It is extremely interesting to consult the best of these manuals. See, for example, Patres Societatis Iesu, facultatum theologicarum in Hispania professores [I. K. de Aldama, F. A. P. Solá Severino Gonzales, and J. F. Sagüés], *Sacrae Theologiae Summa*. Biblioteca de Auctores Cristianos II/73 (Madrid: La Editorial Catolica, 1953) 280–81. The author of this section (I. K. de Aldama) is modest in his claims, and is well aware of difficulties created by reading the passage within the overall context. However, the traditional argument is made. A similar care is shown by Henry Davis, *Moral and Pastoral Theology*. 4 vols. Heythrop Series 11 (7th rev. ed. London and New York: Sheed and Ward, 1958) 3:101–102. After indicating the usual norms on the need for holiness in approaching the Eucharist the author concludes: "The obligation of confessing conscious unforgiven mortal sin before celebrating Mass or receiving Holy Communion is probably an obligation of Ecclesiastical law (p. 101)." In a note

is only possible when it is entirely divorced from its original Pauline literary and theological context.[47] The Greek expression translated "whoever, therefore, eats" (ὥστε ὃς ἂν ἐσθίῃ) demands that the passage be interpreted in the light of what Paul has just written. It cannot be properly understood apart from that context. Throughout 1 Corinthians Paul addresses problems that have arisen in the community at Corinth. There are divisions among the brethren (1:11), immorality (5:1–6:20), problems concerning sexual relations in marriage (7:1-9), divorce (7:10-16), changes in social and sexual status (7:17-40), food laws (8:1-13), and overconfidence in oneself over against the scruples of the weak (10:1–11:1). Through chs. 11–14 Paul addresses a series of problems that were arising within the Corinthians' liturgical assemblies: dress (11:1-16), the Lord's Supper (vv. 17-34), and the use and abuse of the gifts of the Spirit (chs. 12–14). Paul finally looks to the problem of the resurrection of the body, also apparently causing difficulties in this charismatic early Christian community (see 15:1-2). In each one of these cases Paul discusses the real problems of a church's enthusiastic beginnings.

Paul's discussion of the Corinthians' problematic participation in the Lord's Supper is approached in the following fashion. He first attacks the nature of the Corinthians' abuse of the eucharistic table in 11:17-22. This is then followed by the Pauline version of the eucharistic words (vv. 23-26), followed by his more theological conclusions and recommendations (vv. 27-34). Our traditional reading of vv. 27-28 devotes no attention to Paul's overall argument, especially the details of the Corinthians' behavior indicated in vv. 17-22. It thus uses the warning to distance "sinners," in our understanding of that term, from the eucharistic celebration. Such an approach to the passage is faulty, as we must read this important text in Paul's terms. What was the "unworthy manner" mentioned in v. 27? Why must one "examine oneself" (v. 28)? The wider context of the passage we are considering provides the solution to these questions. It is found in Paul's attack on the Corinthian abuses in vv. 17-22. He expresses his displeasure over the divisions between "those who have" and "those who have not" that have developed: "I hear that there are divisions among you" (v. 18). These divisions are described as follows:

Davis refers explicitly to 1 Cor 11:28, concluding that it "does not clearly prove the existence of a divine precept" (p. 101 n. 1).

[47] For a fuller study of 1 Corinthians 10–11 see Moloney, *A Body Broken* 151–77. For a contemporary study of the Pauline context see Xavier Léon-Dufour, *Le Partage du pain eucharistique selon le Nouveau Testament* (Paris: Editions du Seuil, 1982) 236–65.

". . . when the time comes to eat, each of you goes ahead with your own supper, and one goes hungry and another becomes drunk. What! Do you not have homes to eat and drink in? Or do you show contempt for the church of God and humiliate those who have nothing? What should I say to you? Should I commend you? In this matter I do not commend you!" (vv. 21-22).

The Lord's supper was supposed to be a common meal, but Paul has heard that this has become impossible at Corinth because such divisions between the wealthy and the humble have arisen that no one is concerned about the other.[48] It would be better for the Corinthians to eat in their own houses rather than pretend a unity their behavior belies. Such behavior, in addition to humiliating the "have nots," shows that they hold true community in contempt.[49] This is the "unworthy manner" of participating in the Eucharist chastised by Paul in v. 27, and the reason for the request that one should "examine oneself" expressed in v. 28. The situation has been well summarized by C. K. Barrett:

> The rich man's actions are not controlled by love; they therefore amount to contempt not only of the poor, but also of God, who has called into his Church not many wise, not many mighty, not many noble born (1:26). God has accepted the poor man, as he has accepted the man who is weak in faith and conscience (8:9-13; 10:29f.; Rom 14:1, 3f., 10, 13, 15:1, 7); the stronger (whether in human resources or in faith) must accept him too. It is by failure here that the Corinthians profane the sacramental aspect of the supper—not by liturgical error, or by undervaluing it, but by prefixing it to an unbrotherly act.[50]

Although Paul may be seen as simply insisting on good order at the eucharistic meals his complaint has a more profound motivation. It is this motivation that leads him now to insert his version of the eucharistic words of Jesus. As Paul reports them in 1 Corinthians (11:23-26) they are highlighted by the command, repeated over both the bread

[48] Scholars discuss whether the division was created by the wealthier people *not sharing* or *not waiting* for the less privileged. The discussion hinges on the meaning of προλαμβάνει ("takes before others have theirs" or "going ahead with eating"?) in v. 21. The idea of "waiting" is supported by the imperative "wait for one another" (ἀλλήλους ἐκδέχεσθε) in v. 33. Whichever meaning one takes, the basic social point is the same: the poor were disadvantaged. See C. K. Barrett, *The First Epistle to the Corinthians.* Black's New Testament Commentaries (London: A. and C. Black, 1971) 262–76.

[49] On this see Jerome Murphy-O'Connor, *1 Corinthians.* New Testament Message 10 (Wilmington: Michael Glazier, 1979) 110–11.

[50] Barrett, *The First Epistle to the Corinthians* 263–64.

and the wine, to perform the action of breaking the bread and sharing the cup "in remembrance of me" (vv. 24 and 25).[51] While this twice-repeated command may have its origins in the earliest liturgies, it is not only a liturgical instruction. It is also an important challenge to a deeper appreciation of the eucharistic nature of the Christian life.

To celebrate Eucharist is to commit oneself to a discipleship that "re-members" Jesus, not only in the breaking of the ritual bread and sharing the ritual cup but also in "imitation" of Jesus, in the ongoing breaking of one's own body and spilling of one's own blood "in remembrance" of Jesus.[52] As Peter Henrici has written:

> When Jesus thus enjoins on his disciples the task of doing "this" in his re-membrance, all his activity is meant—not only his symbolic gesture at the Last Supper (which can and should be ritually repeated) but also his whole sacrificial attitude of delivering himself up to mankind in obedi-ence to the Father.[53]

For this reason, Paul adds, "you proclaim the Lord's death until he comes" (v. 26). It is in the broken body and the spilt blood of a Church of disciples who live the Eucharist they celebrate that the Lord's death is proclaimed in the world until he comes again.[54]

> Thanks to this clarification made through the liturgy, the whole Christian life becomes an act of worship and proclamation: it "proclaims the death of the Lord until he comes again"—that is, it makes clear the meaning

[51] The Lukan version of the eucharistic words has the same command (see Luke 22:19).

[52] For more detail on this perspective see Hans Kosmala, "Das tut zu meinem Gedächtnis," *NovT* 4 (1960) 81–94, and Peter Henrici, "'Do this in remembrance of me': The sacrifice of Christ and the sacrifice of the faithful," *Communio* 12 (1985) 146–57. See also Jeremias, *The Eucharistic Words of Jesus* 237–55, and the comprehensive study by Fritz Chenderlin, *"Do this as my memorial": the semantic and conceptual background and value of Anamnesis in 1 Corinthians 11:24-25.* AnBib 99 (Rome: Biblical Institute Press, 1982).

[53] Henrici, "'Do this in remembrance of me,'" 148–49. For a similar position from a dogmatic theologian see Karl Rahner, *The Practice of Faith: A Handbook of Contemporary Spirituality,* edited by Karl Lehmann and Albert Raffelt (New York: Crossroad, 1984) 175–79. See, for example, p. 175: "We can only receive the grace of Eucharist insofar as we personally also realize the sacrifice con-tained in it."

[54] For further consideration of this argument, with bibliography, see John D. Laurance, "The Eucharist as the Imitation of Christ," *TS* 47 (1986) 286–96. Es-pecially useful is the survey of contemporary discussions on 291–94.

and the source of the eschatological tension that gives shape to the Christian life (cf. 1 Cor 7 and the letters to the Thessalonians).[55]

Paul's call for unity in 1 Cor 11:17-22 is a summons motivated by the need for the Corinthian community "to remember," to practice at the level of life what they proclaim at the level of ritual (vv. 23-26). To continue in their present practice would be to eat the bread and drink the cup "unworthily" (v. 27). Thus they must examine themselves carefully on these issues before approaching the eucharistic meal (v. 28). This brief reading of 1 Corinthians 11:27-28 within the context of 11:17-34 warns us against its traditional use as a Pauline imperative giving the subsequent Church authority to separate the broken from the eucharistic table.[56] As our analysis suggests, this is a serious distortion, and even a denial of Paul's original teaching.

In v. 29 Paul warns the Corinthians: "all who eat and drink without discerning the body eat and drink judgment against themselves." There is a division over the interpretation of the expression "the body" in this passage. A traditional Catholic interpretation has seen it as not discerning the eucharistic presence,[57] while the favored Protestant interpretation has been to see it as a reference to "the body of Christ," the community as "church."[58] Both interpretations are probably involved. "Not to discern the body" is to fail to recognize the Lord's presence in

[55] Henrici, "'Do this in remembrance of me,'" 155. See also Laurance, "The Eucharist as Imitation of Christ," 289: "Not only do truly Christian actions contain Christ in his saving events but . . . they do so because those same events somehow include in themselves the reality of all Christian living in this world."

[56] There are still contemporary writers who continue with this uncritical use of 1 Cor 11:27-28, without any reference to its literary and theological context. See, for example, E. Diederich, "Reflections on Post-Conciliar Shifts in Eucharistic Faith and Practice," *Communio* 12 (1985) 234.

[57] See, for example, Antonio Piolanti, *The Holy Eucharist* (New York: Desclée, 1961) 45–46; Pierre Benoit, "The Accounts of the Institution and What they Imply," in Delorme, et al., *The Eucharist in the New Testament* 93. A contemporary Catholic scholar, Jerome Murphy-O'Connor, *1 Corinthians* 114, comments: "It is sometimes said that what Paul demands here is that participants distinguish the eucharist from common food, but this does not fit the context, and betrays a preoccupation with the doctrine of the real presence characteristic of a much later era."

[58] See the discussion in Barrett, *The First Epistle to the Corinthians* 273–75. See also Günther Bornkamm, "Lord's Supper and Church in Paul," in idem, *Early Christian Experience*. Translated by Paul L. Hammer (New York: Harper & Row; London: SCM, 1969) 148–52.

the Eucharist in the sense of the Lord who died for us (see v. 24: "This is my body that is ὑπὲρ ὑμῶν [for you])." This means that by ignoring the context of the whole community in their eucharistic meals the Corinthians are proclaiming the presence of the Lord in a way that runs counter to that very "rhythm" of the offering of Christ they claim to be "remembering" in their celebration.[59] As we have seen, the Christian is called to repeat the self-gift of Christ in memory both in cult and in life. Not to celebrate Eucharist in this way is to "eat and drink judgment" upon oneself (v. 29). By not recognizing the sacrificed "body" of Jesus in the Eucharist they offend against the "body" that is the Church, called to repeat that sacrifice in its own life.[60]

I trust that this analysis of the context of the Pauline teaching on the Eucharist that surrounds 1 Cor 11:27-28 shows that the passage was originally written to accuse the Corinthian community of their sinfulness in celebrating their eucharistic meals in such a way that some were excluded.[61] This "lack of discerning" (see v. 29) should warn us lest we, in our arrogance, merit the same accusation as we exclude the broken from our eucharistic table.

CONCLUSION

As I opened these reflections I spoke of the necessarily critical function the Word of God must cultivate over against the tradition. Exercising this critical function is becoming increasingly more difficult in the contemporary Roman Catholic Church. This is one crucial area where we need to ask whether or not the theology and practice of the Church is at one with the Gospel message we proclaim. It is here that I believe we must go quietly forward, raising the critical question, asking the in-

---

[59] Rahner has appreciated this in his use of 1 Cor 11:29. See *The Practice of Faith* 178: "The meaning of 1 Corinthians 11:29 will always remain true: by sins against the love of neighbor we eat and drink judgment for ourselves in the Lord's Supper."

[60] For these reflections I am in debt to a personal communication from Brendan Byrne, S.J.

[61] See, for example, the comments of Hans Conzelmann, *Der erste Brief an die Korinther*. Meyers Kommentar (Göttingen: Vandenhoeck & Ruprecht, 1969) 238: "Man isst unangemessen, wenn man das Mahl des Herrn als 'eigenes mahl' behandelt" [One eats inappropriately if one treats the Lord's Supper as "one's own meal"]. See also William F. Orr and James A. Walther, *I Corinthians*. AB 32 (New York: Doubleday, 1976) 274: "Judgment comes because they do not discriminate the divine nature of this fellowship and are guilty of splitting it apart and mistreating its humbler members."

stitution why it was instituted in the first place. Pope John Paul II has written of this difficult task within a community:

> The attitude of solidarity does not contradict the attitude of opposition; opposition is not inconsistent with solidarity. The one who voices his opposition to the general or particular rules or regulations of the community does not thereby reject his membership; he does not withdraw his readiness to act and work for the common good. . . . In order for opposition to be constructive, the structure, and beyond it the system of communities of a given society must be such as to allow the opposition that emerges from the soil of solidarity not only to *express* itself within the framework of the given community but also to *operate* for its benefit. The structure of a human community is correct only if it admits not just the presence of a justified opposition but also that practical effectiveness required by the common good and the right of participation.[62]

At the heart of a community that calls itself Christian is found the call to the authentic celebration of Eucharist and the living of eucharistic lives. This study indicates that part of the message of the New Testament is a message of the Lord's eucharistic presence to the broken. The New Testament, however, also indicates that the earliest communities felt that there were situations in which they had the right, and even the duty, to exclude certain members from the community and its life (see especially 1 Corinthians 5 and Heb 6:1-8).[63] There can be no

---

[62] Karol Wojtyla, *The Acting Person*. Analecta Husserliana X (Dordrecht: D. Reidel, 1979) 286–87; emphasis in original. The Pope was writing of the philosophical notion of human community, but his argument holds good for the "common good" advocated and promoted by the institution of the Church as a community.

[63] For further reflection on these texts, and their consequences, see Moloney, *A Body Broken* 192–98. For some indications of the theological process that inevitably led to some form of "exclusion" in early Christian communities see James D. G. Dunn, *Unity and Diversity in the New Testament. An Inquiry into the Character of Earliest Christianity* (Philadelphia: Westminster; London: SCM, 1977). See especially 262–63, 306–307, 378–79. For a survey of the contemporary discussion of sociological processes behind this practice see Derek Tidball, *An Introduction to the Sociology of the New Testament* (Exeter: Paternoster Press, 1983) 104–22. It is sometimes suggested that Matt 5:23-24 (reconciling oneself with one's brother before offering sacrifice) is pertinent to this discussion. The text is not eucharistic. The passage may well be dominical, and presupposes the sacrificial system in Jerusalem, not the Christian Eucharist (see W. D. Davies and Dale C. Alison, *A Critical and Exegetical Commentary on the Gospel According to Saint Matthew*. 3 vols. ICC [Edinburgh: T & T Clark, 1988] 1:516–18; W. F. Albright and C. S. Mann, *Matthew*. AB 26 [New York: Doubleday, 1971] 62).

selective reading of the New Testament to argue for a "free for all" admission to the eucharistic table. This study must not be understood in such a way, but I trust that it has also indicated that John Paul II's claim that not admitting divorced persons who have been remarried "is based upon sacred scripture" (*Familiaris Consortio* 84) needs some modification.[64]

Nevertheless, before we can come fully to understand and make vital the Gospel message of the Eucharist as God's saving action in the lives of the many broken people who look to God for just that we must come to grips with the brokenness of our own Church and all its structures, and the deep brokenness of the lives of each and all of us who make up that Church.[65] It is, as Paul has said, a question of correctly "discerning the body of the Lord" (see 1 Cor 11:29). Here we are at the heart of our problem. The Church itself, in all its traditions and structures, must come to a deeper realization that it was well described at Vatican II: "The church . . . clasping sinners to its bosom, at once holy and always in need of purification, follows constantly the path of penance and renewal" (*Lumen Gentium* 8). While such an affirmation is relatively easy to state in principle, it is very difficult to put into practice. To render this teaching part of the day-to-day life of the Church would mean questioning traditions that developed in an era when the Church's understanding of itself was more in terms of the perfect society rather than a

---

Indeed, the message of Matt 5:23-24 is further indication of the centrality of the case I have argued. As John P. Meier, *The Vision of Matthew* (New York: Paulist, 1979) 245 remarks: "In a sense, Jesus' basic teaching on the union of the love of God and love of neighbor is summed up in this parable. An alienated brother alienates us from God, no matter how splendid be the liturgy we perform." See also Eduard Schweizer, *The Good News According to Matthew.* Translated by David E. Green (Atlanta: John Knox, 1975) 119.

[64] The genuine holiness and search for God in the lives of many people whom we traditionally exclude from the Eucharist is well known. What is urgently required, if the biblical argument pursued in this study has any importance, is a new set of criteria concerning admission to the Eucharist, certainly not a "free for all" approach to this central mystery of the Christian life. The major criterion should be, I would suggest, the quality of a person's "communion" with the Church at many other levels, which is sacramentalized in that Church's eucharistic celebrations. See Moloney, *A Body Broken* 178–201.

[65] The present difficulties, in the Catholic Church, over the proper exercising of a critical role—voicing "opposition to the general or particular rules or regulations of the community"—are an indication of that particular institution's "brokenness." They also indicate a deepening rift in the "communion" needed for genuine Eucharistic celebrations, as Paul has indicated (see 1 Cor 11:17-34).

pilgrimage of sinners. In concrete terms: does our present practice of Eucharist indicate a Church "clasping sinners to its bosom?"

As we proclaim the gospels we come to realize that it is not only to the failing and broken disciples of the gospel stories that Jesus comes in his eucharistic presence. He comes to the failing and broken disciples of all places and times. He comes to his fragile yet grace-filled Church in all its brokenness: "at once holy and always in need of purification" (*Lumen Gentium* 8). However, it is easy to raise a questioning finger to "the institution" and feel that we have done our job. We are touching here a basic injustice of which we are all guilty. We all have a tendency, in this matter, to preach one message and live another. To frequent the Eucharist full of self-righteousness and worthiness is to leave no space for the presence of a eucharistic Lord who seeks me out in my brokenness, challenging me to go on taking the risky and difficult task of the Christian life in imitation of him.

CHAPTER 11

LIFE, HEALING, AND THE BIBLE: A CHRISTIAN CHALLENGE

For many Christians, no matter what their training and background, the Bible is a book that can range from the inspirational to the irrelevant. But on both extremities, and across the many shades of opinion that lie between them, the biblical text is too often read in a dangerously uncritical fashion. An English translation, especially the Authorized Version of 1611, might be taken as the inspired text and then interpreted according to the canons of *contemporary* poetry, history, philosophy, or wise aphorisms.[1] The uniqueness of an ancient literature written in Hebrew, Aramaic, and Greek disappears. The problem is quite serious in Roman Catholic circles. The bishops at the Second Vatican Council launched a new era among Catholics, asking that believers from all walks of life look to the word of God as we have it in the Bible for their nourishment and inspiration (see *Dei Verbum* 25–26). In the thirty years that have elapsed since the close of the Council, Catholic biblical scholarship has blossomed, but much still remains to be done to bring the Bible more directly into the lives of Catholics.[2] This phenomenon is more complex than it may at first appear. Many of

---

[1] On the well-deserved respect for the Authorized Version as literature see David Lyle Jeffrey, ed., *A Dictionary of Biblical Tradition in English Literature* (Grand Rapids: Eerdmans, 1992) 875–77. As Jeffrey remarks: "It was stylistically beautiful, its language often still unsurpassed" (876).

[2] On this see Francis J. Moloney, "Whither Catholic Biblical Studies?" *ACR* 65 (1988) 83–93; idem, "Catholic Biblical Scholarship—Fifty Years On," *ACR* 70 (1993) 275–88.

the changes in thought, liturgy, and understanding of what Catholicism is, readily embraced or violently opposed by various contemporary faces of Catholicism, flow from the "subversive" presence of the results of modern biblical criticism. Indeed, there are small but powerful and vocal groups who claim that it is harmful to "the understanding and the faith of ordinary intelligent and educated Catholics."[3] As the Professor of Theology in a university that seeks "the integration of the truth attained through faith with knowledge gained by human endeavour"[4] I am challenged to build bridges between the critical study of the Bible and the understanding of human experience in all its manifestations.

I will limit my reflections to the consideration of four related issues. First, I will make some remarks on how to approach the Bible when faced with contemporary problems undreamt of by the authors of the books that make up the Bible. To exemplify my case I will focus on some of the delicate issues emerging in contemporary health care to test whether one can establish a relationship between an ancient text, regarded by Christians as inspired and normative, and modern problems. From there it is but a short step to the second part of this article: a reflection on the centrality of life. Third, what are we to make of the crucial Christian belief that this life is not the only life? Finally, as a further exercise in hermeneutics, and by way of a conclusion, I will devote some brief attention to the ongoing significance of the healing miracles of Jesus.

1. READING OLD TEXTS IN A NEW WORLD

It may appear obvious that one should not "plunder" texts from antiquity to find solutions to twentieth- and twenty-first-century health problems. God is made known to us in a variety of ways, not only through the words of the Bible. The positive achievements of modern science, medicine, and technology can form part of the gradual unfolding of God's design. Yet the Bible, the traditional "Word of God," must be a reference point in all Christian discussions. From the beginning of the modern era, with the accompanying emergence of a critical reading of the Bible, the sacred book of Judaism and Christianity has struggled to be interpreted on its own terms.[5]

---

[3] Bartholomew A. Santamaria, "Problems of Modern Biblical Scholarship," *AD2000* 5/3 (April 1992) 2. See also pp. 14–15.

[4] *Australian Catholic University Mission Statement.* I was the Foundation Professor of Theology at Australian Catholic University from 1994–1998.

[5] For a fine survey of the difficulties the post-Enlightenment and emerging modern era created for the interpretation of the New Testament see William

For Christians difficulties sometimes arise from advances in science, medicine, technology, and the subsequent human control over and manipulation of God's creation. In this delicate intersection between the gifts of God's creation and the developing skills of human beings it is possible both to use and to abuse biblical material. I would like to give two examples that are regularly, but wrongly, used in such discussions: the reference to human procreation in John 1:13 and the condemnation of unnatural sins in Rom 1:26-27.

The NRSV translation of John 1:12-13 reads: "he gave power to become children of God, who were born, not of blood or of the will of the flesh or of the will of man, but of God." To understand this text correctly one must ask questions of the world that produced it. This passage was originally written and read in a world that understood the conception of a child in three ways. In the first place there was the purely physiological belief that a woman fell pregnant from the coagulation of the woman's blood, which sometimes occurred when it was mingled with the male seed.[6] But children of God are not born "of blood." Then there was the frailty of the human flesh that must express itself sexually and may consequently produce a child. But children of God are not born "of the will of the flesh." Finally, and most nobly, there were those situations where human beings act as human beings and decide on the birth of a child. But children of God are not born "of the will of a human being." This famous text says nothing normative for Christians about conception, but a great deal that is fundamental for Christianity about the initiative of God. Children of God come from divine intervention in their lives, and not from any imaginable form of human generation. They are born "of God." For the author of the Fourth Gospel this statement is fundamentally *theological,* and was never intended to be *physiological.* The reader is being instructed that divine filiation does not come from human activity or success, but from the gift of God.[7]

In Rom 1:26-27 St. Paul wrote: "Their women exchanged natural intercourse for unnatural, and in the same way also the men, giving up natural intercourse with women, were consumed with passion for one

Baird, *History of New Testament Research. Volume One: From Deism to Tübingen* (Minneapolis: Fortress, 1992)

[6] As John Henry Bernard, *A Critical and Exegetical Commentary on the Gospel according to St John.* 2 vols. ICC (Edinburgh: T & T Clark, 1928) 1:18, explains, the unusual plural "not from bloods" (Greek οὐκ ἐξ αἱμάτων) is to be understood as the mixing of the female and the male "bloods."

[7] For a detailed study of this passage see Francis J. Moloney, *Belief in the Word. Reading John 1–4* (Minneapolis: Fortress, 1993) 38–41.

another. Men committed shameless acts with men and received in their own persons the due penalty for their error" (NRSV). Can this text, written by a Jew in the middle of the first century, be taken as a biblical judgment on AIDS victims? Unfortunately, the letter to the Romans is sometimes used in this way. But there was no AIDS problem in the first century! The background to Paul's words is not specifically Christian. It reflects standard Jewish abhorrence of the sexual mores of the surrounding Greco-Roman world, and his point is to be understood as an indication of what happened when God "gave up" the pagans (see 1:24, 26, 28). Because they worship false gods, the creation of their own hands, God leaves them to "stew in their own juice."[8] Joining all those who abhor Greco-Roman morality, Paul points to certain patterns of behavior as an indication that those who practice it have lost contact with a God who establishes right order, and they must suffer the mess of the consequences of this. As with any application of the Johannine Prologue to understanding God's design for human intercourse, to use the letter to the Romans as a quarry for a word that provides a biblical, and thus authoritative, condemnation for specific modern vices is to neglect the main point of Paul's argument. He wished to focus his reader's attention on the fundamental importance of a right relationship with God as the foundation for right relationships between human beings.[9] It simply could not have been his concern to provide later preachers with texts to condemn AIDS victims, and should never be used as such.

These two examples, which could be multiplied, are instructive. Succinctly, and using the language of contemporary literary criticism, one could say that the theological message that must be traced *in the text*, speaking to the Christian world *in front of the text*, cannot properly be understood unless one comes to grips with the world *behind the text*.[10] This is always the case when one is dealing with a text that comes from the past but is regarded as "canonical," or in some way normative for the reader or the community to which that reader belongs. Our

---

[8] See John A. T. Robinson, *Wrestling with Romans* (London: SCM, 1979) 18–20.

[9] On this see Brendan Byrne, *Reckoning with Romans. A Contemporary Reading of Paul's Gospel.* Good News Studies 18 (Wilmington: Michael Glazier, 1986) 57–60.

[10] For more detail on these three "worlds" (behind, in, and in front of the text) see Francis J. Moloney, *Beginning the Good News. A Narrative Approach.* Biblical Studies 1 (Homebush: St. Paul Publications, 1992) 19–42. For a more detailed study see Sandra M. Schneiders, *The Revelatory Text. Interpreting the New Testament as Sacred Scripture* (2nd ed. Collegeville: The Liturgical Press, 1999).

use of biblical material in discussions of complicated questions of life, death, and healing must accept that the application of a text from the past, no matter how normative it might be, calls for a process of interpretation. Hermeneutics, an increasingly important science in its own right, addresses the problem. Without surveying this important branch of contemporary thought[11] we may simply say that biblical texts *must* be used in all Christian discussion of life and healing, *but only* after the necessary work has been done to create a "horizon" where three worlds meet:

1. There is a *world behind the text*. Sometimes this world is very obvious to the reader and sometimes it can be subtly hidden. An example of the obvious world behind a text is the command of YHWH to exterminate all those who have opposed Israel: armies, women, children, cities, villages, and crops (see the ideal of a sacred war in Numbers 31). Here one senses the traditional practices of Near Eastern armies in the first half of the millennium before Christ.[12] No matter how "theologically" the authors of the biblical books that report such activities may interpret these words as an activity of YHWH, they are foreign to our sense of justice. But an author can gaze into the night sky of Jerusalem and cry out: "When I look at your heavens, the work of your fingers, the moon and the stars that you have established; what are human beings that you are mindful of them, mortals that you care for them?" (Ps 8:3-4 NRSV).[13] The prayer retains its value, and there is a world behind this prayer that is also part of our contemporary experience: the wonder of the sky at night, the sense of a God who is the unique source of all creation, and the sense of belonging to a people chosen by a God whose loving care is made known in the beauty of the cosmos. The contemporary reader's awareness of this "world behind the text" inevitably enlightens an understanding of the text, and such knowledge

---

[11] See Anthony C. Thiselton, *New Horizons in Hermeneutics. The Theory and Practice of Transforming Biblical Reading* (London: Harper Collins, 1992), for a fine study of the use of contemporary hermeneutical theory in biblical interpretation.

[12] On this see the foundational study of Gerhard von Rad, *Holy War in Ancient Israel.* Introduction by E. W. Conrad (Sheffield: JSOT Press, 1989).

[13] This is one of several places where the inclusive translation of the Hebrew in the NRSV obscures an important play on words in the original: "What is man *(mah enosh)* that you should think of him, the son of man *(ben adam)* that you should visit him?" For the theological and christological importance of this play on "Man/Son of Man" in the Hebrew, and later Jewish and Christian use of Psalm 8, see Francis J. Moloney, "The Reinterpretation of Psalm VIII and the Son of Man Debate," *NTS* 27 (1980–81) 656–72.

may not render reflection on ancient practices irrelevant for the contemporary world. As John L. McKenzie wrote of Israel's holy wars, "Modern readers find the Israelite concept of the holy war a primitive type of morality; this it is, but it is doubtfully more primitive than the modern concept of war."[14] The contemporary reader can respond to Psalm 8 in terms of her or his own experience of God, creation, and a sense of being cared for. Necessarily tied to a place, a time, and a culture, the world behind the text brings its uniqueness, its limitations, and its richness. Every biblical text has its origins in the lived experiences of an individual, a community, or even a nation. It is thus rightly said that biblical texts can be compared to windows through which one can gaze to see what lies on the other side.

2. The world *in the text*. Full respect must be given to the literary and theological structure of the whole document within which certain passages appear. Every text creates its own "world"; it has its own social, geographical, and historical setting, its use of literary form, time, characters, point of view, focus, and so on. Each part of a text can only be understood properly as part of the world that is created by the text as a whole. To return to images once again, it can also be said that biblical texts are like large portraits that tell their own story, and must be read and interpreted in terms of that story, not manipulated to fit the story of the reader.

3. The world *in front of the text*. The reader and the interpreter of the text bring themselves to the text. This must be recognized and appreciated as we read.[15] However difficult a text might be, the reader strives "even if unconsciously, to fit everything together in a consistent pattern."[16] Thus biblical texts are also mirrors insofar as readers find something of themselves reflected in the text. As David Tracy has written: "The classic text's real disclosure is its claim to attention on the ground that an event of understanding proper to finite human beings has here found expression."[17] The Bible can claim, on these grounds, to be a classic. The perennial value of the biblical text arises from the fact that it continues to speak relevantly to the human predicament. The two-thousand-year-long existence of a reading community, the many

---

[14] John L. McKenzie, *Dictionary of the Bible* (Milwaukee: Bruce, 1965) 921.

[15] For a most helpful study of this see Tony Kelly, "The Historical Jesus and Human Subjectivity: A Response to John Meier," *Pac* 4 (1991) 202–28.

[16] Wolfgang Iser, *The Implied Reader: Patterns of Communication in Prose Fiction from Bunyan to Beckett* (Baltimore: Johns Hopkins University Press, 1978) 283.

[17] David Tracy, *The Analogical Imagination. Christian Theology and the Culture of Pluralism* (New York: Crossroad, 1981) 102.

communities that use the Bible as one of their major sources for that reading, are existential proof of this claim. To continue the images I have used earlier, a text can be compared to a mirror in which a reader finds her or his own face.

The Bible, as one of the great classic texts of all time, must be approached as window, portrait, and mirror.[18] Genuine interpretation of the Bible must attempt to create a "horizon" that respects all three elements generated by the world behind, within, and in front of the text. This should not discourage, but lead to a great sense of humility in interpretation. As a contemporary literary critic has written: "The meaning of a text is inexhaustible because no context can provide all the keys to all its possibilities."[19]

2. INTERPRETING THE TEXT

In light of these criteria much traditional, and a certain amount of contemporary use of biblical texts in discussions of life, death, and healing is somewhat misplaced. I have already mentioned John 1:13 and Rom 1:26-27. The list could be extended. It is, for example, unacceptable to use Ps 139:13: "For it was you who formed my inward parts; you knit me together in my mother's womb," or Jer 1:4: "Before I formed you in the womb I knew you," to develop a biblical theology of the divine presence in the act of human conception. I have no doubt, theologically, that God is present, but only as divine love is incarnated in the loving self-gift of the parents. But this is not what the texts are claiming.[20] It is more fruitful to allow these texts to say what they have always meant. Both of them reflect the Hebrew Wisdom tradition of the presence of every single individual in the design of God from before all time. We are because we have our origins in the design of God.

Even more outrageous is an attack on a recent book dealing with the beginnings of the human person: In the course of a passionately negative

---

[18] For this image see Murray Krieger, *A Window to Criticism: Shakespeare's Sonnets and Modern Poetics* (Princeton, N. J.: Princeton University Press, 1974) 3–70. To my knowledge it was first applied to the New Testament literature by Norman R. Petersen, *Literary Criticism for New Testament Critics*. Guides to Biblical Scholarship NT Series (Philadelphia: Fortress, 1978) 24–48.

[19] Edgar V. McKnight, *Postmodern Use of the Bible: The Emergence of Reader-Oriented Criticism* (Nashville: Abingdon, 1988) 241.

[20] For further reflection on this see Francis J. Moloney, "Biblical Reflections on Marriage," *Compass* 28 (1994) 10–16.

review of Dr. Norman M. Ford's study, *When Did I Begin?* Dr. Daniel C. Overduin wrote: "I find ample evidence in the Holy Scriptures supporting my view: the human conceptus is an individual; it has genetic, organic and personal individuality."[21] Such claims are not a use, but an abuse of biblical material. Biblical anthropology has no knowledge of the physiology of "the human conceptus" or the philosophical discussions that surround a "genetic, organic and personal individuality." These few examples should indicate that within the Christian community that looks to the Bible as its canonical and authoritative "book" the way one interprets that book is critical to much of the community's thought, life, and practice. Yet "hermeneutics" is not something that should be left to the biblical scholars and theologians. Christians are assessing life through the filter of their traditions every day, as we are all involved in the difficult task of relating the givenness of our past to the exciting reality of our present.

Every time we use an ancient text to address a modern problem we are dealing with the balance of three worlds. It can and must be done, but we need to be aware of how to work and act responsibly. We have a responsibility to the creation within which we live, to society at large, to one another, and to the Christian tradition to which we belong. Our serious attention to our world and one another and our careful listening to what Christian tradition teaches should guide us as we open the Bible to deepen our understanding of life, health, and healing. If I may borrow a phrase that sums up all I have said about the importance of a proper hermeneutic for the use of the Bible in contemporary discussions: a text without context is pretext.[22] But even when we are armed with this more critical approach, the question remains: is the Bible still relevant in this world of high technology and sophistication? Critical biblical scholarship has taught me that one cannot "quarry" material from the Bible to find answers to questions that would never have crossed the minds of the authors of the biblical books, yet I have an equally strong conviction that this "Word of God" retains its fundamental importance in a Christian approach to the mission of both the Church and society to all human beings, of whatever race or creed, of whatever social or economic status. Central to every page of the Bible is a concern for life.

---

[21] Daniel C. Overduin, "Further Reflections on 'When Did I Begin?'" *AD2000* 2/3 (1989) 16. The book under discussion was Norman M. Ford, *When Did I Begin? Conception of the Human Individual in History, Philosophy and Science* (Cambridge: Cambridge University Press, 1988).

[22] This is a favorite expression of my colleague, Dr. Mark Coleridge.

3. THE CENTRALITY OF LIFE IN THE BIBLE

The biblical tradition, from Genesis to Revelation, affirms that the most important element in any human being is life itself.[23] There are differences between the Old Testament and the New Testament views of life, largely created by the novelty of the christology of the New Testament, but the Hebrew religion lies behind both traditions, and they can be seen as representing a common concept of life. What makes the biblical view of life, both in the Old Testament and in the New Testament, so peculiar is its contrast with the ideas reflected in the cultures, the religions, and the literature that surrounded Israel.

Although this is something of a caricature, it can be broadly claimed that most cultures that surrounded Israel viewed life either naturalistically or dualistically. Some clarification of terms is called for here. A naturalistic understanding of life sees all the elements that make up a human being, the way we think, love, hope, eat, and so on, as flowing from our physical makeup. It is the flesh and blood and concrete reality of the material elements in the human being that form everything we are and do. We are determined by our natural instincts. On the other hand, a dualistic understanding of life recognizes that there are certain things that cannot be the product of our bodily functions. There is something more than "doing what comes naturally" in the makeup of the human being. The problem with this system, however, is that it starts from the correct observation of something "spiritual" in the human being only to conclude that we must *separate* the higher activities of the mind and the baser actions of the body. What is spiritual is superior, and is untouched by the baser instincts of human nature. It is this division between "the flesh" and "the spirit" that has led theoreticians to call all such systems "dualistic," whether they are speaking of the idol worship of the ancient world, the more subtle religions of the Greek myths, or the even more subtle phenomenon of second-century Gnosticism.

In light of these predominant understandings of the human being the biblical tradition seems to come from a world of its own. The Hebrew understanding of the human being, which flows into the earliest Church's understanding, is that human life is an essential oneness. Obviously a religion based on a fundamental belief in an all-creating, one and only God, YHWH, cannot allow that nature alone determines life, health, and death, but neither can there be higher or lower principles

---

[23] For what follows see Otto A. Piper, "Life," in *The Interpreter's Dictionary of the Bible.* 6 vols. (New York and Nashville: Abingdon, 1962) 3:124–30.

that exist uncomfortably side by side in the human being. Hebrew theology determines Hebrew anthropology. There is differentiation in the various functions of the active human being according to the goals to be served. Who we are and what we are points to something beyond the physical but never denies the intrinsic value of what we are. What does this theory mean in practice? This is an important question because the authors of the Bible did not start from the theory to arrive at the practice, but started from an astute observation of human beings in action and from there worked out the theory that eventually undergirded the biblical understanding of life.

Life has a common origin in all human beings. It is the gift of God who breathes life into the human being (see Gen 2:7), but there are important differences between human beings. There are the different nations, the two sexes, and a rich variety of individuals. These principles are already well established in the saga of Genesis 1–11: man and woman, nations across the face of the earth, people of different caliber and even of different color in the descendants of Japheth and the descendants of Ham (see Gen 10:1-32). Nobody is simply "a human being," as every single individual forms part of a rich diversity. The biblical view is above and beyond both the self-interested individual and a vague, anonymous collectivity of human beings. Who we are and what we are as individuals and as a community depends on the spontaneous and responsible participation of each one of us as individual human beings and as members of a larger community with its own collective responsibilities. The Bible emphasizes that the human being is free to make of life what he or she pleases. To apply what this means to a concrete situation: I can become a good man, a good woman, I can play an essential role in creating a happy community. But I am also free to do the exact opposite, deliberately deciding to create division and pain around myself by the selfish pursuit of my individual hopes and desires. Such a direction is universally regarded by the Bible as sinful; the story of David's strengths and weaknesses is an eloquent example (see 1 Sam 16:1–2 Sam 24:25). More subtle, but equally founded on this view of the human predicament, is the gospel teaching on the strengths and weaknesses of the disciples of Jesus. The biblical understanding of the human being and its performance in response to an all-creating God and Lord of a chosen people is very black and white. At least in the Old Testament there is little space for the various shades of indifference that enable most of us to balance the living of our lives somewhere between an outright "yes" and an outright "no" to the God who gave us life, situated us in *God's* world and within the human community. It has been rightly said that most Christians live quasi-agnostic lives because they lack the courage to be saints—but they also lack the courage to be apostates.

1. Life as the Gift of God

There is much that could be said in detail.[24] Some fundamental notions need to be mentioned here. As far as the Hebrew mind is concerned God is the creator of life, who places "spirit" (*ruaḥ:* see Gen 25:8, 17; 35:29; 49:33; Job 3:11; 10:18; 11:20) and "breath" (*nephesh:* see Gen 2:7; Job 11:20; Jer 15:9; Isa 53:12) into created "flesh" (*baṣar:* see Gen 2:23; Deut 5:26; Ps 56:4; Isa 31:3). All three elements blend and work together to form a live human being. Life is entirely the result of the action of God, and everything that is living has its origins in God's initiative. Because of that the individual's life is God's property. No man or woman has the right to destroy his or her own life or to kill other people (see Exod 20:13; Deut 5:17). The death penalty in Israel (see Lev 20:10; Deut 12:23), like the flood that destroys "every living thing that was on the face of the ground" (Gen 7:23), denotes God's total abhorrence of certain crimes. In the Old Testament life is valued as the supreme earthly good, surpassed only by God's grace or mercy (Ps 63:3). Thus "life" and "happiness" have become synonymous (see, for example, Gen 15:15; Exod 20:12; Judg 8:32; Ps 91:16).

Such a view led to difficulties in understanding hardship and death. The former is generally explained by relating it to the individual's or the nation's loss of YHWH's favor. A certain theological perspective marks many books of the Old Testament, especially the historical books; it is based on the simple premise that God looks after the good and punishes the bad.[25] A joyful life and a peaceful death or a trouble-filled life culminating in a sad or tragic death are indications of the presence and absence of God's blessings. In a very direct and simple fashion the author of the book of Exodus can state, without explanation:

> "I the LORD your God am a jealous God, punishing children for the iniquity of parents, to the third and the fourth generations of those who reject me, but showing steadfast love to the thousandth generation of those who love me and keep my commandments" (Exod 20:5-6; see also Deut 5:9-10).

[24] For a fuller discussion see Walther Eichrodt, *Theology of the Old Testament.* 2 vols. Translated by J. A. Baker (Philadelphia: Westminster; London: SCM, 1961–67) 2:131–50.

[25] This theological point of view is called deuteronomistic. It is spelled out in the book of Deuteronomy and runs through all the historical books (Joshua, Judges, 1–2 Samuel, 1–2 Kings). See Anthony F. Campbell, *The Study Companion to Old Testament Literature. An Approach to the Writings of Pre-Exilic and Exilic Israel* (2nd ed. Collegeville: The Liturgical Press, 1992) 139–251.

How does one explain the misfortune of an early death, or a death by accident? If these things happen, says the older biblical tradition, then it must be a penalty for sin (see, for example, Job 8:13; 15:32; 22:16; Pss 9:18; 31:18; Prov 10:27; Jer 2:19). One thing is clear—and theologically correct: God cannot be blamed. God gives life and the blessed person will live it for a long time, thus showing a closeness to God. A long life and a happy old age are the supreme goods (Prov 3:16), and thus people wish one another a long life (see Dan 2:4; 3:9). Death, the departure into the nothingness of *sheol*, the sequel to old age, is accepted without sentimentality as the end willed by God (see, for example, 2 Sam 14:14; Ps 89:48). The idea of an afterlife, so important to the New Testament and to all Christian religions, was originally unknown in ancient Israel. It is here that the Old Testament appears to lay too much importance on the joys of "this life," although it must be said that there is no tragedy about death at the end of a well-lived long life. Nevertheless, Israel's political independence was eventually lost, and the rich and sinful foreigners with their strange gods prospered while the pious Israelites suffered and died. The later Old Testament authors struggled with the great mystery of suffering and early death, as do most of our contemporaries: why do the wicked prosper, and the good go sadly to their graves? These questions led the later Old Testament writers to develop two quite revolutionary ideas: the possibility of an afterlife (see, for example, Dan 12:2-3; Wis 3:1-9; 2 Macc 7:7-29) and an understanding of true wealth being found in a spirit of radical openness to the strange ways of God in the spirituality of the ʿanawim (see, for example, Pss 22:24-26; 40:17; 69:33; 86:1-2, 12-13; 109:22, 30-31; Zeph 3:11-13).[26]

All that has been said of the Old Testament must be presupposed of the New, but there are important developments. God is the living God (Matt 16:16; 26:63; John 6:68-69; Acts 14:15; Rom 9:26), possessing life and immortality (John 5:26; 1 Tim 6:16). God has entered our history of flesh and blood through the incarnation of God's Son, Jesus Christ (John 1:14), the way, the truth, and the life (John 14:6). God is sovereign over life and death (see, for example, Luke 12:20; 2 Cor 1:9; James 4:15) and the life and death of Jesus are a visible revelation of the sovereignty of God: "I am the good shepherd. I know my own and my own know me, just as the Father knows me and I know the Father. And I lay down my life for the sheep. . . . For this reason the Father loves me, because I lay down my life in order to take it up again. . . . I have received this command from my Father" (John 10:14-15, 17-18). The gift

---

[26] See Francis J. Moloney, *A Life of Promise. Poverty, Chastity, Obedience* (Homebush: St. Paul Publications, 1985) 18–23.

of self in death does not in any way lessen the gospel's understanding of God's love and compassion (see John 3:16-17; 1 John 4:8, 16).[27]

As in the Old Testament, human life is the life of flesh and blood. It involves the human being in its totality, its unity, and its concrete situation (see Matt 16:17; 1 Cor 15:50; Eph 6:12). There is no sense of a person being in two parts, the good and the bad, and there is even less understanding of life as a response to our physical capacities. Indeed, such an attitude is condemned by Paul as worshiping false gods and leading to a state of moral depravity: "they exchanged the truth about God for a lie and worshiped and served the creature rather than the Creator" (Rom 1:25; see 1:18-32). But once again the event of Jesus of Nazareth and the Church's subsequent reflection on its significance add a radically new dimension to the continuation of a traditional Hebrew anthropology. Jesus is regarded as the bringer of true life (see John 14:6; 2 Tim 1:10). His story informed the early Church that true life only came through his self-gift to the Father as a revelation of both the Father's and his own love for creation. This leads to the important new distinction between the human being's *actual physical life* and *a true life*. The developing understanding of a life that transcends "this life," which already had its beginnings in the last era of the Old Testament literature, continues to be strongly associated with the way one lives *now* (see, among many passages, John 3:19-21), but it looks beyond the concrete situation within which one works out one's personal and communitarian history for its ultimate significance. It is this crucial distinction that we will need to investigate in our final reflection: this life is not the only life.

2. New Creation, True Life

Across the New Testament there is a consistent assertion that adherence to the message of Jesus introduces the believer into a new creation (see 2 Cor 5:17; Gal 6:15), into a new and regenerated life (see John 3:3-8; 1 Pet 1:3). Paul especially remodels the Jewish apocalyptic image of an end-time (the *Endzeit*) that would be the restoration of the glory of the time of Adam (the *Urzeit*).[28] Paul's concept of the new

---

[27] This Christian view of the death and resurrection of Jesus lies behind an understanding of the death and resurrection of all human beings that rejects the suggestion that it is "compassionate" to terminate the life of a suffering human being.

[28] For an influential study of Paul that has shown the centrality of this notion to his theology and christology see Johan Christiaan Beker, *Paul the Apostle. The Triumph of God in Life and Thought* (Philadelphia: Fortress, 1980). See also Brendan

creation is closely linked with his belief that the obedient death and glorious resurrection of Jesus have let loose a new power in world history. The glory of the end-time is already with us even though the time of Adam, marked by sin and disobedience, is also still present. We live in an overlap time when we are free to choose between the death that was introduced into history by the disobedience of Adam and the much more powerful free gift of the new life that has entered our story through Jesus Christ (see especially Rom 5:12-20).[29] The language used by the New Testament shows that a sinful person, closed to the ways revealed by the life, teaching, death, and resurrection of Jesus, is "dead" (Luke 15:24, 32; Rev 3:1; Matt 8:22), while a follower of Christ has passed from death into life (John 5:24; Eph 2:1; Col 2:13; 1 John 3:14). *True life is not an extension of our present "normal" life.* By the work of Christ the human being is freed from the inhibitions that had made it impossible to practice unrestricted love. True life is possible even now, if we no longer restlessly seek to create our own ultimate satisfaction. Life, happiness, and satisfaction can only be found by "entering" the kingdom of heaven (see Mark 9:47; 10:14-15, 23-25; Matt 5:20; 7:21; 21:31).

One of the great difficulties of the Old Testament understanding of life has been overcome: the meaning of suffering and death. The "life" brought into the world by the suffering and death of Jesus of Nazareth, which established him as the Christ and the Son of God (see Rom 1:3-5), points all who wonder about these mysteries to a "life" that can already be initiated during our human story but looks to life everlasting through personal resurrection. The basis of personal resurrection, for the New Testament authors, is the resurrection of Jesus. The Christian understanding of resurrection is not that it is a compensation for the miseries of life, but rather that it is the continuation and perfection of the true life that disciples of Jesus already begin during their earthly journey: "If Christ has not been raised, your faith is futile and you are still in your sins. Then those also who have died in Christ have perished. If for this life only we have hoped in Christ, we are of all people most to be pitied" (1 Cor 15:17-19).

This view, present in a variety of ways across most of the books of the New Testament, explains the seeming paradox that the new life is sometimes spoken of as a present possession (see Matt 10:39; 16:25;

Byrne, *Reckoning with Romans. A Contemporary Reading of Paul's Gospel.* Good News Studies 18 (Wilmington: Michael Glazier, 1986) 20–25.

[29] See Brendan J. Byrne, "Life after Death. Some Scripture Evidence Reconsidered," *ACR* 58 (1982) 386–403.

Luke 17:33) and sometimes as a future good (see, for example, Mark 9:43, 45; 10:30; Matt 7:14; 18:8-9; 19:16; Luke 18:30; Rev 2:10; 3:1; 11:11). Early Christian belief, however, saw no contradiction in this view. Physical death is the end of the human story (Matt 10:28; Rom 7:24), but through physical death the believer rises to be alive in the resurrection (see especially 1 Cor 15:35-57).[30]

The central event of the Christian story, the death and resurrection of Jesus of Nazareth, is also the crucial element in an understanding of "life" in the New Testament. Indeed, both Paul and the Fourth Evangelist developed the use of the theme of "life" for unique expressions of both christology, where Jesus becomes "life" (see, for example, Rom 8:29; Col 1:18; 2:13; John 14:6), and Christianity, as all life is transformed into the possibility of "new life" both now and hereafter. Paul works on the basis of a "new creation" (2 Cor 5:17; Gal 6:15). The original life-giving creative act of God had been thwarted by Adam, and sin and death entered the human story (see Rom 5:12), but Jesus' radical acceptance of the ways of God, which led to his death and resurrection, instituted a new situation where "life" is now a possibility. Where once there was sin, now there is a superabundance of grace (see Rom 5:12-21). For John, Jesus comes as the unique revelation of the one and only God (see John 1:18). The acceptance of this revelation brings life, while refusal brings death (see, for example, John 3:11-21, 31-36). As Jesus is lifted up on the cross he calls out that he has brought to perfection the task his Father gave him (see John 4:34; 13:1; 17:4; 19:30). From that point on we can gaze upon a God who reveals divine love for us through the gift of God's Son (see 19:37). Life is

---

[30] There is a longstanding problem concerning the nature of "the body" in its physical state and in its risen state. Is there a sameness, a continuity, yet a difference, or is the risen body something quite different from the mortal body? Paul attempts to resolve this question in 1 Corinthians 15. He speaks of a corruptible mortal body and an incorruptible risen body, but one is a continuation of the other: "The body is taken seriously because it shares the world's destiny; it is as important to the new creation as it is to the old" (Dorothy A. Lee, "Freedom, spirituality and the body. Anti-dualism in 1 Corinthians," in Maryanne P. Confoy, Dorothy A. Lee, and Joan Nowotny, eds., *Freedom & Entrapment. Women Thinking Theology* [North Blackburn, Vic.: Dove, 1995] 54). On the question of "the body" in Paul see Brendan Byrne, "Sinning against One's Own Body: Paul's Understanding of the Sexual Relationship in 1 Corinthians 6:18," *CBQ* 45 (1983) 608–16, especially 608–12. For a more comprehensive survey of scholarly discussion see Robert Jewett, *Paul's Anthropological Terms. A Study of their Use in Conflict Sayings.* AGJU 10 (Leiden: E. J. Brill, 1971) 200–250.

there for the taking, both now (see, for example, 5:24-26) and forever (see, for example, 5:27-29).[31]

Both Paul and the Fourth Evangelist have only developed, however skillfully and subtly, the basic understanding of "life" that comes to them from the Christian tradition. When it comes to the issue of "life" there is a deep sense of unity across the biblical tradition. God is the giver of life, and we have life insofar as we respond to this gift as God-given. Once we take life into our own hands, leaving the life-giver out of consideration, the deepest meaning of "life" is at risk. It is Jesus Christ, the way, the truth, and the life (see John 14:6) who injects something startlingly new into this thinking. We do live in a new creation, where this life will merge into the new and everlasting life if we are prepared to put on Jesus, to live as he lived. The enigma of this message, however, is that to live one must die to self, and in the end die in the flesh: "The death he died, he died to sin, once for all; but the life he lives, he lives to God. So also you must consider yourselves dead to sin and alive to God in Christ Jesus" (Rom 6:10-11).

The world *behind* the text of the Bible and the world *within* the text of the Bible cannot be uncritically appropriated to answer every question that arises from our contemporary medical and health-care worlds *in front of* the text of the Bible. Nevertheless, the Bible retains its fundamental importance in any attempt on the part of Christians to understand and articulate their tradition on life and healing and their mission to the broken of body and spirit. At the heart of the Bible lies one of the basic concerns of all human beings: the centrality of life, our care for our own life and the lives of others. But we must face a seeming contradiction. Does the Bible not also ask: is this life the only life?

4. This Life is Not the Only Life

In any biblical introduction to the question of "life" this theme needs to be stressed. Often contemporary debates about medical ethics proceed as if physical death had no place in God's design. Life is central because it is a gift of God. There is little need for me to develop this theme any further, but the theme of a life that flows from death also needs to be understood. "Life" is more than "this life." However crucial life's joys and pleasures are to the modern mind and the contemporary value

---

[31] On these questions see the syntheses of C. K. Barrett, *Paul. An Introduction to His Thought*. Outstanding Christian Thinkers Series (London: Geoffrey Chapman, 1994) 105–119, and C. H. Dodd, *The Interpretation of the Fourth Gospel* (Cambridge: Cambridge University Press, 1953) 144–50, 201–12.

system, the Bible looks beyond them. According to the Bible there is a perfection of the life the human being lives while on earth. Belief in life on the other side of death may be of even more importance for the theological discussion of health care than insistence on the sacredness of "this life." Indeed, it can be said that the theme of life on the other side of death is more important, because when it is based on the death and resurrection of Jesus it is the uniquely Christian contribution to the discussion. Whatever might be the case concerning what is "more" or "less" important, the theological commitment of Christianity to a life that extends beyond the limitations of this life is seldom heard in contemporary health-care discussions.

The defense of the centrality of human life on this side of death can smack of an earlier Old Testament understanding, where the only life one had was the one lived here on earth. A typical example of this way of thinking can be found at the beginning and end of the book of Job. The hero of the book is described as a righteous man, and the clearest indications of his being blessed by God are his many wealthy sons, his beautiful daughters, and his many servants and animals (see Job 1:1-3). However, Job is tested. He loses all his possessions and then suffers a painful disease. The agony of Job comes from his inability to understand why this has happened to him. He has never offended God; why is God withdrawing the divine blessing? Through all his trials, during which his so-called friends suggest that he must have offended God in some way, Job never turns away from God. Because of the loyal, God-directed "patience of Job," in the end the blessings return: "And the LORD restored the fortunes of Job when he had prayed for his friends; and the LORD gave Job twice as much as he had before" (Job 42:10).

The major part of the Old Testament saw this life as the end of things. But this view of life was only possible in a world where Israel was its own master. Once the nation became a mere vassal to other powers, when the men were sold into slavery, the women taken into the tents of the conquering armies, and the crops used to fill foreign bellies, the joys and pleasures of "this life" could not be seen as the fruits of God's blessing. Thus by the early second century B.C.E. an idea of a life after death enters Jewish thought. This is found in the three most recent books of the Old Testament, the books of Daniel, Maccabees, and Wisdom.[32] It was necessitated by the reality of suffering and especially the

---

[32] First and Second Maccabees and Wisdom are considered apocryphal by the Protestant tradition, which only regards works preserved in Hebrew as canonical, while the Roman Catholic tradition, which calls these books "deuterocanonical," accepted works from the Septuagint into its Bible of inspired literature.

reality of martyrdom for the nation and for the faith of Israel. Some of these ideas are very physical: the body of the risen martyr still has all its elements (see 2 Macc 14:46). Others are more spiritual, in instances where the dualism of Hellenistic thought has already begun to penetrate into Judaism. The book of Wisdom begins to speak about "the souls of the just" (see Wis 14:1-2). The sufferings and turbulence of the second century B.C.E. produced an aggressive affirmation that if one lived, loved, and died for YHWH there would be a commensurate reward after death (see Dan 12:2-3).

Jesus certainly adhered to this understanding of life and death, as one can see from his discussion with the Sadducees, who still defended the traditional view that there was no life after death (see Mark 12:18-27). Jesus' own resurrection is an event that radically altered all subsequent thinking about life and death. It was perceived by the early Church as taking place after his death, but also as transforming all subsequent history and not just Jesus' personal destiny.[33] The action of God in raising Jesus from death to a new and glorious life made him "the firstborn from among the dead" (cf. 1 Cor 15:20). Many more would follow him through this new birth into a new life. Could it not sometimes be said of a certain fanaticism to protect and prolong life at all costs that the Old Testament understanding of God's blessings being available only to "this life" still predominates? According to the whole of the Bible (both Old and New Testaments) life as we live it in the world is certainly central, but it still has a certain relative status vis-à-vis the greater biblical idea of the universal sovereignty of God, which transcends life and death. God has revealed sovereignty over death in the resurrection of Jesus, but Jesus is the firstborn of many from the dead. If Jesus is the "firstborn" from among the dead, then we are promised that we will be among the myriads of others who will be "born from death." Belief in the God of Jesus tells us that "life" is larger than "this life."

In the midst of our deep commitment to the values and even the sacredness of the life God has given us to live in its fullness and to care for we must always be prepared to bow before the mystery of the greater gift of the life that transcends all death. If life now is to be understood as a great gift of God, how much more so is the life that is ours on the other side of physical death, where God becomes the unquestioned Lord of creation.

---

[33] On this see the fine study of Peter Selby, *Look for the Living. The Corporate Nature of Resurrection Faith* (Philadelphia: Fortress; London: SCM, 1976).

5. THE HEALING MIRACLES OF JESUS

Jesus certainly cared for "life now." We can point to the many stories of miracles in the gospels, where Jesus cured the sick and healed the broken. Does this miraculous ministry of Jesus not say something about the care of the sick? There is no doubt that Jesus' ministry was marked by a great concern for those whose bodies were broken with illness or whose spirits were broken by sin.[34] The healing miracles reflect this concern. There should be no doubt that Jesus was a doer of wonderful things. Even the Jewish historian Josephus tells us: "He was a doer of wonderful deeds, a teacher of people who receive the truth with pleasure."[35]

Working within the worldview of his time Jesus, by driving out demons and healing, is indicating that sickness is not simply a bodily ailment but a manifestation of the power of evil in the world. Whatever modern science and medicine might make of these phenomena— for example, that demon possession was epilepsy, that what Jesus brought was more psychological than physical—is irrelevant to what Jesus thought he was doing. One view involves modern knowledge and science, the other looks at sickness and brokenness more theologically. For Jesus, sickness and brokenness were concrete evidence of the presence of evil. Deeply immersed in his own Hebrew traditions, Jesus understood the presence of evil in the world as the result of powers other than God. From the sagas of Genesis 1–11 onward Israel argued that God's creation was good (see Gen 1:1–2:4a). The presence of evil came from the use and abuse of the God-given gift of freedom (see Gen 2:4b–3:24).[36] Exercising his own freedom in a radical and responsible openness to the God of Israel, whom he called *Abba* (see Mark 14:36),

[34] For a synthesis see Raymond E. Brown, *An Introduction to New Testament Christology* (New York: Paulist, 1994) 60–67. For more detail see Ben Witherington III, *The Christology of Jesus* (Minneapolis: Fortress, 1990) 145–77, and the exhaustive study by John P. Meier, *A Marginal Jew. Rethinking the Historical Jesus.* 2 vols. ABRL (New York: Doubleday, 1991–93) 2:509–1038.

[35] Josephus, *Ant.* 18.3.3. For a well-documented study of Josephus' witness to Jesus see Meier, *A Marginal Jew* 1:56–88.

[36] For the ongoing importance of this issue see the question posed by the disciples to Jesus when they see the man born blind in John 9:1-2: "Rabbi, who sinned, this man or his parents, that he was born blind?" (v. 2). Behind the question lies the conviction that God could not be held responsible for the evil of physical blindness. For a review of the question, and further reference to rabbinic discussion, see Francis J. Moloney, *The Johannine Son of Man.* BibScRel 14 (2nd ed. Rome: LAS, 1978) 145–46.

Jesus could not allow this evil to continue its sway. He did not work miracles as a modern doctor heals sickness. He was not simply a person who saw his mission as that of a healer. The reality of sickness and his powerful healings point beyond the immediately visible to a deeper reality.

Nowhere has this been more clearly represented than in the very first day of Jesus' ministry as it is reported in the Gospel of Mark. Announced by John the Baptist (Mark 1:1-8), Jesus is baptized and further announced as God's Son by a voice from heaven and by the sign of the dove (vv. 9-11). He withdraws into the wilderness, overcomes Satan (vv. 12-13), and suddenly bursts upon the scene with the first words he utters in the gospel story: "The time is fulfilled, and the kingdom of God has come near; repent, and believe in the good news" (v. 15). But the presence of the kingdom in the person of Jesus is not mere words. He calls disciples, who immediately follow him (vv. 16-20), and he has them accompany him as he systematically overcomes the evils of demon possession (vv. 21-28), the sickness of Peter's mother-in-law (vv. 29-31), and the evil of leprosy (vv. 40-45). But these are only a few of his miracles. The author lets the reader know that Jesus' presence inevitably conquered all evil. The narrator comments: "And he cured many who were sick with various diseases, and cast out many demons" (v. 34), and again: "And he went throughout Galilee, proclaiming the message in their synagogues and casting out demons" (v. 39). Whatever one might make of the historicity of these events, gathered by the evangelist Mark into the first day of Jesus' ministry, this story reflects an enduring memory in the early Church. The powers of evil are hopelessly outmatched by the goodness and power of the reign of God, present in the person of Jesus of Nazareth. Here we have a dramatic portrayal of the significance of Jesus' healing miracles.[37]

No doubt many contemporary skeptics are not prepared to accept Jesus' view of sickness as evil and his presence as the goodness that comes into our story with the arrival of the reign of God. They are all the poorer for such skepticism. Human brokenness is not only the result of some physical or emotional malfunction. We have all been both the agents and the recipients of deeds and decisions that have brought about suffering. The human situation is still afflicted by the incredible sufferings that result from institutionalized injustice and violence. Anyone committed to a biblical faith should accept Jesus' view. If we

---

[37] See Morna D. Hooker, *The Gospel According to Mark.* Black's New Testament Commentaries (London: A. & C. Black, 1991) 31–75. See also Donald H. Juel, *A Master of Surprise. Mark Interpreted* (Philadelphia: Fortress, 1994) 33–43.

believe that when God accomplishes the divine plan not only will there be "salvation of souls" but a blessing extended to the whole universe, so that what was destructive will end and there will be no more suffering and tears, disasters and death, we should recognize that such things represent an alienation from God. They are evil. This does not necessarily mean that the person subject to sickness and brokenness is evil or has committed evil, but that the very existence of such factors indicates the incompleteness of God's plan. There is a necessary tension between the beauty of what has been given in creation, and perfected through human involvement in its further development, and the ongoing presence of the many manifestations of evil that can never be definitively eliminated. Faced with the AIDS virus, optional euthanasia, family breakdown, abandoned and abused children, genocide, the return of an irrational nationalism with its concomitant mass slaughter and widespread dislocation, disease, and starvation, we hardly need to be taught that greater human sophistication has not lessened the burden of human sinfulness. Only miracles can bring such evils to an end.

The gospel accounts of Jesus' care for and healing of the broken are a dramatization, based on events from Jesus' ministry, of a basic biblical understanding of God and the world. It is crucial, however, that the healing miracles be understood for what they are. They are never ends in themselves. Jesus does not heal simply to heal. They are signs of the inbreaking of the reign of God. As such they necessarily point beyond the human situation, so seriously damaged by the presence of evil, physically present in demon possession and illness, to the gift of God's reign, which transcends all human values.[38]

6. CONCLUSION

Anyone involved in the healing ministries, and we are many, from those in the professional medical world to pastors, teachers, parents, lovers, must recognize that *we are involved in a divine work*. There is a presence of God in the mystery of life that we are privileged to touch. A Christian understanding of health care must attend to both the wholeness and the holiness of life. We are all involved in this ministry, and we should be aware that we are continuing Jesus' ministry. Life is the greatest of all God's gifts, and we minister to God in maintaining this gift with our skills. What is it, however, that we are doing in and through this ministry? Are we continuing to work miracles? Each day we are

[38] See Hooker, *Mark* 71–75.

witnesses to the fact that we are working miracles. But as with the miracle-working ministry of Jesus, our miraculous ministry opposes evil with all the forces available to us: spiritual, intellectual, scientific, and medical. We have worked hard to equip ourselves for this ministry, and we continue to work hard both in the performance of our daily tasks and in our commitment to keep abreast of all the wonders of modern medical science and a deepening understanding of the gifted-ness of being human. The natural sciences must not be divorced from reflection on the Christian tradition, which is the bedrock upon which so much that is good in our culture is founded. We Christians have a gift to give, and the world we live in looks to us trustingly for that gift. As part of our Christian response we cooperate in a privileged way with the ongoing creating and healing work of God.

In the end, however, the task is to point beyond the treasure of the good things of this life to the Lord of all life, made known to us through the life and teaching, death and resurrection of Jesus of Nazareth: "as all die in Adam, so all will be made alive in Christ. But each in his own order: Christ the first fruits, then at his coming those who belong to Christ. Then comes the end, when he hands over the kingdom to God the Father, after he has destroyed every ruler and every authority and power" (1 Cor 15:22-24). Every day the healing ministry meets with the reality of suffering and death. It is part of the Christian tradition that it be fought and overcome in all its forms, but Christians must also recognize that beyond all attempts to conquer sickness and death lies the greater mystery of a creating, loving God who is Christianity's final hope and destiny.

CHAPTER 12

ADVENTURE WITH NICODEMUS: AN EXERCISE IN HERMENEUTICS

Some remarkably gifted and hard-working scholars gave so much to see that historical-critical scholarship would have its rightful place in Catholic biblical scholarship. It is understandable that these veritable founders of critical scholarship within the Catholic tradition are skeptical about some current practices.[1] But the Bible's being the "book of the Church" does not permit its interpreters to ignore newer methods of interpretation. The relentless application of the criterion of *objectivity* is dissipating as it is more widely accepted that something of the interpreter is inscribed in every interpretation. Indeed, it is generally recognized that there has never been an objective reading of any text. The patristic and reformation tradition focused on *the world in the text*, but unashamedly read their own worlds and their own texts into it. The form critics focused on *the world behind the text*, but their reconstructions of that world are now seen to have been influenced by their

---

[1] Some of the world's finest biblical scholars, now advancing in years but still teaching and publishing in an exemplary fashion, remain skeptical about the value and future of some recent developments in biblical scholarship. My own career owes much to these giants. Modern methods attempt to handle the hermeneutical questions more vigorously: why were the New Testament documents written, how have they maintained their readership over two thousand years, and are they still relevant in contemporary Christian communities? On this, see Ulrich Luz, "Kann die Bibel heute noch Grundlage für die Kirche sein?" *NTS* 44 (1998) 317–39.

own worlds. The redaction critics claimed to have returned, in a more scientific fashion, to *the world in the text*, but their dependence upon form-critical conclusions concerning *the world behind the text*[2] and the risk that they rendered the evangelists in their own image[3] makes their work open to the criticism leveled against both form criticism and patristic-medieval exegesis.

1. HISTORY, HERSTORY, AND MYSTORY

Following the larger world of literary criticism, contemporary biblical scholars are focusing more and more on *the world in front of the text*. But this shift of focus presents its own problems. There are many worlds in front of the text. It is not possible, within the limits of this essay, to address the applications of contemporary literary criticism to today's biblical criticism, and what follows is a caricature. The emergence of narrative critical and reader-response criticism in the late 1980s initiated a process in which more and more attention was given to the multiplicity of readers and cultures, and to an increasingly sophisticated critique of a fragile text.[4] In an attempt to devote greater attention to *the world in the text* narrative critics trace implied authors and readers within a text that maintains its classical status. Many of them claim that the only issue that deserves attention is the text itself, and that questions concerning *the world behind the text* are irrelevant.[5] This detachment of the biblical text from its historical setting and an interest

---

[2] See, for example, Hans Conzelmann, *The Theology of St Luke*. Translated by Geoffrey Buswell (New York: Harper; London: Faber & Faber, 1960) 9: "The analysis of the sources renders the *necessary service* of helping distinguish what comes from the source from what belongs to the author" (emphasis supplied).

[3] See the important critical essay of Morna D. Hooker, "In His Own Image?" in Morna D. Hooker and Colin Hickling, eds., *What About the New Testament? Studies in Honour of Christopher Evans* (London: SCM, 1975) 28–44.

[4] See the essay in this volume, "Narrative Criticism of the Gospels," pp. 85–105.

[5] This practice is still widespread among narrative critics. For example, in a recent fine study of "the Jews" in the Fourth Gospel (Gérald Caron, *Qui sont les "Juifs" de l'évangile de Jean?* Recherches 35 [Québec and Paris: Bellarmin, 1997]), the author argues *from the narrative* that "the Jews" represent a certain form of "Judaism" present among "the crowd," the Pharisees, and the Jewish leaders. Caron rejects any suggestion that this form of "Judaism" needs to be found somewhere in the broader phenomenon of a possible conflict between early Christianity and late-first-century Judaism. Unless some *Sitz im Leben* can be found for the proposed "Judaism" Caron's suggestion remains highly speculative.

in the reader(s) of the text has developed into increasingly subversive readings in which the reader and her or his contexts are the determining factors in interpretation. Even in these more subversive readings the text can be regarded as ideologically offensive, but still part of a normative tradition,[6] or as irrelevant to the multiplicity of post-colonial, feminist, agnostic, postmodern readers.[7] Between these two extremes there is a multiplicity of other readings produced by readers reading "from their place."[8] In his important recent presidential address to the *Studiorum Novi Testamenti Societas* Professor Ulrich Luz takes five pages to describe his *Standortsbestimmung* as a northern European from the classical Protestant tradition. Only after this exercise in self-location can he ask, "Kann die Bibel heute noch Grundlage für die Kirche sein?"[9]

One of the most significant axioms behind these contemporary so-called postmodern methods of reading a biblical text can hardly be challenged: every interpreter inscribes him- or herself in interpretation. On the basis of this axiom a wave of newer scholars suggests that we be honest at all times, admitting that the story I read into my interpretation is my story. Following the lead of the major study by Jeffrey Staley, *Reading with a Passion,* a number of scholars are developing what is known as autobiographical criticism.[10] Feminist scholars have attempted to re-interpret HIS-story as HER-story. Postmodern readings

---

[6] See, for example, Sandra M. Schneiders, *The Revelatory Text. Interpreting the New Testament as Sacred Scripture* (2nd ed. Collegeville: The Liturgical Press, 1999).

[7] See The Bible and Culture Collective, *The Postmodern Bible* (London and New Haven: Yale University Press, 1996), for a systematic presentation of the increasing focus on the readers and their context, leading to a relativizing of the biblical text. See also Stephen D. Moore, *Poststructuralism and the New Testament. Derrida and Foucault at the Foot of the Cross* (Minneapolis: Fortress, 1990), and my review in *Pac* 7 (1994) 360–62.

[8] I take this expression from two important volumes that stress the importance of the sociocultural location of the interpreter in interpretation: Fernando F. Segovia and Mary Ann Tolbert, eds., *Reading from This Place.* 2 vols. (Minneapolis: Fortress, 1995–96). See the review of the first volume by Suzanne Boorer in *Pac* 9 (1996) 217–21.

[9] [Can the Bible still be a basis for the Church?] Luz, "Kann die Bibel?" 316–21.

[10] Autobiographical criticism is not unique to biblical studies, but the first full-scale autobiographical New Testament study comes from Jeffrey L. Staley, *Reading with a Passion. Rhetoric, Autobiography, and the American West in the Gospel of John* (New York: Continuum, 1995). An initial description of this form of criticism and some interesting examples of it can be found in Janice Capel Anderson and Jeffrey L. Staley, eds., *Taking it Personally. Semeia* 72 (1995). For a collection of autobiographical biblical studies see Ingrid Rosa Kitzberger, ed., *The Personal Voice in Biblical Interpretation* (London and New York: Routledge, 1998).

have driven a wedge between a biblical text that is THEIR-story and OUR-story, the product of an intertextuality with little understanding of a time-honored biblical canon. The autobiographical critics argue that the most honest way to interpret a biblical text I still regard as relevant is to read it as MY-story.

One thing is certain: no interpretation can lay claim to ultimate authority. No single interpretation of any text, let alone an ancient canonical text, can claim to have exhausted all possible interpretations. No interpretative context can claim to have understood all the possibilities of an ancient text, especially one that has remained alive in a reading public for two thousand years. Paul Ricoeur has done much to indicate that once the act of interpretation has come to its conclusion there is always a significant "remainder" that lies beyond the limits of the completed interpretation, "the residue of the literal interpretation."[11] However, this same philosopher has also insisted that *many* interpretations are possible, but not *any* interpretation.[12] The acquisitions of one hundred fifty years of modern biblical scholarship must not be pitted one against the other.[13] The contemporary interpreter of the biblical text must create a horizon where the worlds behind, within, and in front of the text meet. The reading of John 3:1-11, 7:50-52, and 19:38-42 that follows attempts to show that there is something of value in all that we have received from one hundred fifty years of critical New Testament scholarship.[14]

[11] Paul Ricoeur, *Interpretation Theory: Discourse and the Surplus of Meaning* (Fort Worth: Texas Christian University Press, 1976) 55. See also idem, *Essays on Biblical Interpretation*, edited by Lewis S. Mudge (London: S.P.C.K., 1981) 73–154. Ricoeur rejects "the absolute claim to self-consciousness" (p. 110) and advocates a "hermeneutics of testimony."

[12] See, for example, Paul Ricoeur, *Hermeneutics and the Human Sciences. Essays on Language, Action, and Interpretation*, edited, translated, and introduced by John B. Thompson (Cambridge: Cambridge University Press, 1981) 210–13. See his conclusion: "If it is true that there is always more than one way of construing a text, it is not true that all interpretations are equal and may be assimilated to so-called 'rules of thumb.' The text is a limited field of possible constructions" (213).

[13] See also Luz, "Kann die Bibel?" 322–34; George T. Montague, *Understanding the Bible. A Basic Introduction to Biblical Interpretation* (New York: Paulist, 1997) 159–80.

[14] The following reading of the Nicodemus passages borrows heavily from my full-scale autobiographical study entitled "An Adventure with Nicodemus," in Ingrid Rosa Kitzberger, ed., *The Personal Voice in Biblical Interpretation*. I am grateful to the editor for permission to use the material in this context. I will not make

2. An Adventure with Nicodemus

1. Are you the teacher of Israel? (John 3:10)

Many years ago I went to the university to do an undergraduate degree, followed by a post-graduate diploma in education, so that I might become a secondary school teacher. There was chalk in my blood, and the urge to be a first-rate teacher was strong. I had been brought up a practicing Catholic, and the social and cultural setting of my life, the 1950–60s in Australia, was steady as a rock. There was no need for the Bible, as I had the pope, the bishop, the priest, and weekly Mass. My belief system came from the family and a Catholic schooling, reinforced by the weekly sermon, the sacraments of the Catholic Church, and various devotions. They were happy days, weeks, months, and years, full of as little study as possible, great friends, sport, movies, and dancing to rock-and-roll music. The Catholic culture of the 1950s gave little space to the Bible.

But the Bible was soon to become *a problem*. The Johannine account of Jesus' meeting with a man who came from the darkness into the light in John 3:1-21, an example of the many who "believed in his name because they saw the signs that he was doing" (2:23), was one passage among many that generated a crisis in my days as a theological student. The healthy crisis persists to this day.[15] Even then I had emerged as a "leader" (cf. John 3:1), and I knew who Jesus was: a teacher from God who had given the Catholic Church an authoritative teaching and a divinely appointed hierarchical structure. I *knew* what was to be known, and I did my best to live accordingly. But the Jesus of the Fourth Gospel used a double-meaning word to insist that I, a reader of the Fourth Gospel, be born again from above (v. 3: ἄνωθεν) if I wished to see the kingdom of God. I was, like Nicodemus, satisfied with only one of the two possible meanings of ἄνωθεν. I had been born again (v. 4: δεύτερον) in the waters of baptism (cf. v. 5: ἐξ ὕδατος), and the Catholic community was the kingdom of God. I had full sight of the kingdom within the structures and sacramental system of the one true Church. But the Johannine Jesus insisted that this was insufficient: I must be born of water *and also of the Spirit* (v. 5: καὶ πνεύματος) if I wished to

---

detailed reference to the scholarship behind the following reading. It can be found in Francis J. Moloney, *Belief in the Word. Reading John 1–4* (Minneapolis: Fortress, 1993); idem, *Signs and Shadows. Reading John 5–12* (Minneapolis: Fortress, 1996); idem, *Glory not Dishonor. Reading John 13–21* (Minneapolis: Fortress, 1998); idem, *The Gospel of John*. SP 4 (Collegeville: The Liturgical Press, 1998).

[15] See Moloney, *Belief in the Word* 106–21; idem, *John* 88–103.

enter the kingdom. The double meaning of ἄνωθεν (v. 3) had been un-packed in v. 5. To "see" (v. 3) and to "enter" (v. 5) the kingdom of God called me to leave my established ways and my closed system of truth (cf. v. 2). The external rite of baptism (ἐξ ὕδατος), retained its impor-tance, but it was to be coupled with another more radical transforma-tion reaching beyond the formality of a water ritual (καὶ πνεύματος). I was okay on the former (v. 3), but had I really "entered" (εἰσελθεῖν) the kingdom (v. 5)?

The "water" rebirth had been part of my experience, although I had no recollection of it. It was something I accepted on the basis of the Roman Catholic Church and my family traditions, something that had been handed down to me by people who, in their own time, had re-ceived it from other generations who believed that it had come from the Lord (cf. 1 Cor 11:23; 15:3). But this same tradition had said little to me about "the Spirit" except some vague notions concerning the third person of the Trinity, called in those days the Holy Ghost. I had been taught that he (male, like everything else associated with God) was a part of the mystery of the Trinity, and that it would be both arrogant and foolish to wonder further about a mystery of religion. I was happy to leave "mystery" alone. "(Un)"fortunately I was able to read on into the Johannine text to find Jesus' clarification of what was meant by being born of the Spirit (cf. vv. 6-8), and I found especially "(un)"help-ful the little parable in John 3:8:

> The wind (τὸ πνεῦμα) blows where it chooses, and you hear the sound of it, but you do not know where it comes from (πόθεν ἔρχεται) or where it goes (ποῦ ὑπάγει). So it is with everyone born of the Spirit (ὁ γεγεννεμένος ἐκ τοῦ πνεύματος).

But why the "(un)," qualifying what one would expect to be quite positive reading experiences?—Because my convictions of the 1950–60s began to crumble when I discovered that to be born of the Spirit meant to be caught up in an experience of life—in all its dimensions—that matched the experience of standing in the wind.

I know when the wind is swirling around me (v. 8a), and I can have the physical experience of its power to penetrate even the warmest of clothing. But, as Jesus' parable so rightly remarks, I have no idea where this wind has its origins, nor do I know where it is going (v. 8b). Jesus adds a disturbing comment to the end of the parable: so it is with every-one who is born of the Spirit (v. 8c). The biblical text tells me that I must experience the Spirit swirling around me in the confusion of *not knowing* where I had come from and where I was going. My true ori-gins and my true destiny, both in terms of my future history and my final resting-place, here and on the other side of death, are shrouded in mystery. Living in this mystery is a fundamental aspect of life in the Kingdom of God. Here was the word that had been used to describe something that I should not bother my head about: mystery! I could only join with Nicodemus and ask "How can these things be?" (v. 9).

But it is Jesus' response to my question that cuts deepest: "Are you a teacher of Israel, and yet you do not understand these things?" (v. 10). Not only are my former certainties questioned by the Johannine Jesus; my very status in the community of faith is at stake. Jesus seems to suggest that I *should have known* all that he was telling me about rebirth in water and the Spirit. My sight of and entry into the kingdom of God depends on my preparedness to let go of what my traditional Catholic culture had given me. I was "the teacher of Israel," but the Johannine Jesus was telling me that I was a fake, that my understanding of life in the kingdom had little to do with the swirling winds of the Spirit leading me from I know not where into a destiny beyond my knowledge and control (v. 8).

I laid claim to be "a teacher of Israel" but I was only at the halfway house, having been born again of water. I was discovering that without the second half of the equation, rebirth in the Spirit, my achievements were irrelevant in the kingdom. My obvious identification with Nicodemus lined me up with the "many who believed in his name because they saw the signs that he was doing" (2:23). This meant that "Jesus would not entrust himself to them (me), because he knew all people and needed no one to testify about anyone (περὶ τοῦ ἀνθρώπου: me); for he himself knew what was in everyone (ἐν τῷ ἀνθρώπῳ: me). Now there was a man (ἄνθρωπος: me) named Nicodemus" (2:24-25; 3:1).[16] I will never forget the anxiety generated by my first serious encounters with the text as I honed the skills of gospel criticism. The product of a community of faith and a culture that articulated that faith in a very clear fashion, I had taken all the right steps to become "a teacher of Israel." But all had been undermined as I gasped, "How can these things be?" (3:9). I had to cope with the now obvious fact that the gospels do not provide a record of the events from the life and teaching, death and resurrection of Jesus. They are narrative proclamations of the belief of the early Church.

This only led to a further problem, as the last sentence is partially correct. The more I acquainted myself with the gospels and scholarly reflection on them, the more I found that they did not record *the belief* of the early Church, but *the beliefs* of the early Church. Not only did the

---

[16] See Moloney, *Belief in the Word* 104–106.

early Christian churches produce a fourfold gospel tradition (and many others that did not make the final selection), but the gospels told the story of Jesus in ways that demonstrated that *different* Christian communities proclaimed *different versions* of the significance of the person and message of Jesus. There is hardly a page in the gospels that does not profoundly question the earlier certainties of my life. I began to come to grips with an idea expressed by the Fathers of the Desert: to go forward it is necessary, momentarily, to lose the balance one had in the previously acquired situation. It is necessary to keep putting one's foot forward and in this way to regain the balance that was briefly lost.[17]

2. Earthly things—heavenly things (John 3:12)

But the Johannine Jesus continues to address my presumption. He makes it clear that my difficulty comes from my being content with those traditions that come to me from culturally conditioned understandings of God, the Christ, the Church, and the Spirit. I should transform (not deny!) these understandings, so he said, in the light of the authentic Christian traditions that had been handed on to me. The Johannine Jesus warned me: "If I have told you about earthly things and you do not believe, how can you believe if I tell you about heavenly things?" (v. 11). I found it hard to imagine that I should have done better, accepting all that Jesus had told Nicodemus in vv. 1-10 as "earthly things" (ἐπίγεια). I thought (and so did many others) that I had done rather well, but the biblical text insisted that I had never fully understood the best and most significant truths of my own Christian tradition.

I began to see that I had unwittingly worked from the comfortable assumption (belief?) that a number of agents in the Catholic Church's hierarchy had access to the secrets of heaven, and I had only accepted uncritically what these agents "revealed" to me. But the Johannine Jesus declares that no one has ever gone up to heaven. There is only one person in the human story who can lay claim to having unveiled the mystery of God, Jesus the Son of Man who, given the cosmology the Fourth Gospel shared with early Gnosticism, had come down from heaven (v. 13). Against all who might lay claim to having ascended to heaven that they might make known the things of God, Jesus states that only the Son of Man has come down from heaven.[18] But it is not

---

[17] See Francis J. Moloney, *A Body Broken for a Broken People. Eucharist in the New Testament* (rev. ed. Peabody, Mass.: Hendrickson, 1997) xv.

[18] For a full discussion of the Jewish and Gnostic background to the "ascent-descent" motif in 3:13 see Francis J. Moloney, *The Johannine Son of Man.* BibScRel 14 (2nd ed. Rome: LAS, 1978) 53–59.

enough to affirm *that* Jesus is the only authentic revelation of God; *how* does this revelation take place? Jesus draws a comparison between the serpent lifted up in the desert, which healed the ailments of all who gazed upon it, and the Son of Man who must be lifted up on a cross to make sense of life, both here and hereafter, for all who accept what he has told of the unseen God (vv. 14-15; cf. 1:18).

Jesus' mini-discourse (vv. 11-21) does not inform me of the *nature* of the Johannine God, but of the way *God acts*. The presence of Jesus in the human story is the result of an act of love (v. 16); God does not condemn, but saves. It is not so much what *God* might do, but how *I* might respond to the mysterious presence of a loving God in my life. I could go on reaching into this mystery by believing in what the Johannine Jesus was telling me, or I could condemn myself to lostness by rejecting it in favor of my long-held and well-established beliefs. I am the one responsible for my own actions, my own present and future, the rightness or wrongness of the way I respond to my world and the people and situations of that world. There is no fixed agenda: just a request to gaze upon the loving gift of God (v. 16), lifted up on a cross. Herein lay the challenge: to recognize in the cross the symbol of the Son of Man lifted up from the earth (cf. 12:32). This event-symbol is presented by other early Christian storytellers as the most horrific of human experiences, only overcome by the action of God in the resurrection.[19] For the Johannine narrative it is the most exquisite way of telling me of the immensity of God's love. "No one has greater love than this, to lay down one's life for one's friends. You are my friends if you do what I command you" (15:13-14). "This is my commandment, that you love one another as I have loved you" (15:12; cf. 13:34-35; 15:17).

Jesus' words to Nicodemus are no longer a threat but a challenge. They might express concern over my ability to understand τὰ ἐπουράνια, but they also challenge me to be responsible for the recognition of love where it can be found, and for the rejection of love made known. The Johannine Jesus concludes his words to Nicodemus (me) by further spelling out that the choice is mine: I can choose light or darkness, goodness or evil. I can walk along the established ways that lead me where I wish to go (cf. John 21:18), but that will leave me in darkness, afraid to come into the light of truth for fear that my sinfulness might be seen. On the other hand, I can live in the Spirit, allowing myself to

---

[19] The Pauline and the Markan understandings of the cross come to mind. On these see Federico Pastor-Ramos, *La Salvación del Hombre en la Muerte y Resurrección de Cristo*. Institución San Jeronimo 24 (Estella: Editorial Verbo Divino, 1991), and Donald Senior, *The Passion of Jesus in the Gospel of Mark*. The Passion Series 2 (Wilmington: Michael Glazier, 1984).

seek the freedom of responding responsibly to the reality of love in my life (cf. v. 8). This is the way that leads into light. Whichever way I decide to go, I judge myself (vv. 19-21).

3. Are you also led astray? (John 7:47)

A new sense of freedom floods into the life of anyone naïve enough to accept the authority of Jesus' words to Nicodemus. I was—and am—such a naïve person, rendered naïve by my belief in the ultimate significance of the God of the Bible and the revelation of that God that Christians hold took place in and through Jesus Christ.[20] But it is one thing to have the principles clear and another to put them into practice. Again, I am able to identify with Nicodemus as he states the truth but falters when "the institution" dares him to exercise his new-found freedom.

During the last day of the celebration of Tabernacles (John 7:37), Temple officers (ὑπηρέται) who had been sent out by the Pharisees "about the middle of the festival" (cf. 7:14) to arrest him (7:32) return to the leaders of "the Jews."[21] The officers have been listening to and observing Jesus for several days, and are now impressed by the authority of his words (cf. v. 46). The Pharisees close ranks, accusing the officers of having been seduced by Jesus, claiming that none of the authorities (μή τις ἐκ τῶν ἀρχόντων) or the Pharisees (ἐκ τῶν Φαρισαίων) believed in him (v. 48). But Nicodemus, one of them (v. 50: εἷς ὢν ἐξ αὐτῶν) had earlier been reduced to silence (3:1-10) and in his silence had been promised the revelation of love and life (3:11-21). He speaks up and makes a lie of their claim (7:51). Nicodemus was from among the Pharisees (3:1: ἐκ τῶν Φαρισαίων), a ruler of "the Jews" (3:1: ἀρχῶν τῶν Ἰουδαίων). I

---

[20] I am aware that sophisticated postmodern biblical criticism tends to ridicule such naïveté. The Johannine view, which I am accepting as having sufficient authority to question everything I stood for in the 1960s, may only be the result of the speculations of a late-first-century pseudo-Gnostic Christian that cry out to be deconstructed. My adherence to a faith tradition and my belonging to a faith community are the reasons for my naïveté. On this see Stanley E. Fish, *Is There a Text in This Class? The Authority of Interpretative Communities* (Cambridge, Mass.: Harvard University Press, 1980) 303–21. See also the *Conclusion* to this essay.

[21] See Moloney, *Signs and Shadows* 84–93; idem, *John* 252–55. Use of the expression "the Jews" (οἱ Ἰουδαῖοι) demands (i) the historical-critical background to the use of the expression, (ii) the way it functions within the Johannine narrative, and (iii) how it should be used in contemporary readings of the Fourth Gospel. For a recent study that performs (ii) and (iii) very well but largely ignores (i) see Caron, *Qui sont les "Juifs"?*

join him again as I look back across my own life story, recalling the times when I tried to stand tall for what I believed to be true. Nicodemus attempts to break ranks and to insist that the opposition to the Jesus of the Fourth Gospel is not as unified as some might like to believe. The only people, insists Nicodemus on the basis of *his own experience* (cf. 3:1-21), who understand Jesus are those who hear his word in faith and recognize his works for what they are: the action of God in God's Son.[22] But abuse and the fear that he (I) might be regarded as one of the fringe dwellers of his (my) social, cultural, and religious context lead to silence. Nicodemus (I) has (have) no word in response to the challenge from the approved hierarchy that has domesticated the approach to God into a system they control (v. 2).

But there is more. As I (he) had come from the darkness into the light to approach Jesus in 3:2, I (he) now skulk (skulks) back into the darkness (cf. 3:2), probably aware that I (he) have (has) blotted my (his) copybook with the powers that be. This situation is further complicated by the fact that I (he) am (is) unable to cope with the challenge of the marginalization the accepted culture might impose upon me (him) if I (he) were to stick to his (my) guns.[23]

4. Nicodemus came, bringing myrrh and aloes (John 19:39)

The story of Nicodemus comes to an end at the tomb of Jesus (19:38-42).[24] Scholarly opinion ranges from a claim that Nicodemus has not progressed beyond the limited faith he displayed in 3:1-11[25] to a suggestion

---

[22] For this interpretation of 7:51 see Severino Pancaro, *The Law in the Fourth Gospel: The Torah and the Gospel. Moses and Jesus, Judaism and Christianity according to John.* NovTSup 42 (Leiden: E. J. Brill, 1975) 149–56. See also idem, "The Metamorphosis of a Legal Principle in the Fourth Gospel. A Closer Look at 7,51," *Bib* 53 (1972) 340–61.

[23] I am deliberately placing my experience in the main text and the *possibility* of Nicodemus' sharing that experience in parentheses because I do not know of Nicodemus' inner response to the rebuff he receives in v. 51. Nothing is said in the Johannine text, but I do know my own experience. What *might* have been the case for a character in the text *is* the case for me, the reader of the text. Is this a valid reading of the text?

[24] See Francis J. Moloney, "The Johannine Passion and the Christian Community," *Sal* 57 (1995) 25–61; idem, *John* 510–13.

[25] See, for example, Paul D. Duke, *Irony in the Fourth Gospel* (Atlanta: John Knox, 1985) 110; David Rensberger, *Johannine Faith and Liberating Community* (Philadelphia: Westminster, 1988) 40; Dennis D. Sylva, "Nicodemus and His Spices," *NTS* 34 (1988) 148–51.

that Nicodemus' reception of the body of Jesus is a hint of the reception of the Eucharist.[26] Neither extreme reflects my adventure with Nicodemus. There is public recognition of Jesus in the association of two previously "hidden disciples" of Jesus (vv. 38-39: Joseph of Arimathea and Nicodemus) with the crucified Jesus.[27] They request the body of Jesus from Pilate, the authority who handed him over to "the Jews" for execution (v. 38; cf. 19:16a), and they bury him with a massive mixture of myrrh and aloes (vv. 40-41). The quantity of fragrant oils suggests that the royal theme that was present in the account of the story from 18:1–19:37 continues (v. 39).

But what of Nicodemus? Is this a sign that he has finally overcome the hesitations and fear of 7:51? Yes, but Nicodemus still has a long way to go. It cannot be said that Nicodemus has achieved the quality of faith of earlier characters in the story: the mother of Jesus (2:5), John the Baptist (3:28-30), the Samaritan villagers (4:42), the royal official (4:50).[28] Nor can it be said that he matches the faith of the Beloved Disciple, who does not see Jesus in the tomb but believes when he sees God's victory over death in the empty burial cloths (19:8). We do not know how Nicodemus might respond to the last words of the risen Jesus in the story: "Blessed are those who have not seen and yet have come to believe" (20:29).[29] The Beloved Disciple believed without seeing, and all Johannine readers are exhorted to become beloved disciples, believing without seeing.[30] Just as Nicodemus at the tomb of Jesus cannot come under the rubric of the Beloved Disciple, neither can I. Neither Nicodemus at the tomb *in the story* nor a Christian reader *of the story* can lay ultimate claims to believing without seeing.

[26] See, for example, Jean-Marie Auwers, "Le Nuit de Nicodème (Jean 3:2; 19:39) ou l'ombre du langage," *RB* 97 (1990) 481–503; B. Hemelsoet, "L'ensevelissement selon Jean," in *Studies in John: Presented to Professor J. N. Sevenster on the Occasion of His Seventieth Birthday.* NovTSup 24 (Leiden: E. J. Brill, 1970) 47–65.

[27] They possibly represent what Raymond E. Brown has called "crypto-Christians" (see *The Community of the Beloved Disciple. The Lives, Loves, and Hates of an Individual Church in New Testament Times* [New York: Paulist, 1979] 71–73).

[28] See Moloney, *Belief in the Word* 192–99.

[29] A further traditional critical question that cannot be bypassed emerges. Does John 21 belong to the narrative design of the original gospel? Unlike most narrative critics I maintain that John 21 was added to an already self-contained narrative that ended at 20:30-31. See Moloney, *John* 562–68.

[30] See Brendan J. Byrne, "The Faith of the Beloved Disciple and the Community in John 20," *JSNT* 23 (1985) 83–97. See also Moloney, *John* 542–44.

My journey with Nicodemus is open-ended. Both Nicodemus and I have come to recognize that God is made known in the loving self-gift of Jesus unto death and thus deserves all honor and even royal respect. But that is not what the Johannine Jesus (cf. 20:29) or the Johannine author (cf. 20:30-31) demands of the readers of this story.[31] Nicodemus and I have come a long way, but more adventures lie ahead. The challenge to live in the Spirit (cf. 3:8), to recognize the revelation of God in loving self-gift (3:13-17), and to walk in the way of that same self-gift (3:19-21; 13:15, 34-35, 15:12, 17; 17:21-26) is still with me in an Australian culture and society where Christian faith and practice are becoming either increasingly irrelevant (except for State occasions and national disasters), or the hope of those who think that some golden era of the past will return. In many ways, although not universally, my own tradition is attempting the restoration of my idealized 1950–60s. Its public face and many of its magisterial pronouncements lack compassion, and they say very little to me. Indeed, they jar when read in conjunction with Mark 10:42-45:

> "You know that among the Gentiles those whom they recognize as their rulers lord it over them, and their great ones are tyrants over them. But it is not so among you; but whoever wants to become great among you must be your servant, and whoever wants to be first among you must be slave of all. For the Son of Man came not to be served but to serve, and to give his life a ransom for many."[32]

Along with Nicodemus, my fellow reader of the biblical text, I cannot go back. At this moment, hopefully only beginning the latter half of my autobiography, I recognize Jesus at the tomb and wonder where my adventure with Nicodemus will lead me. But in the difficulties of this postmodern moment, which may obviously intensify, I journey on, attempting to cross the bridge constructed by the Johannine Jesus' final words: "Blessed are those who have not seen and yet have come to believe" (20:29). In this I am armed with a prayer that comes from another gospel tradition: "I believe; help my unbelief" (Mark 9:24).

---

[31] Particularly helpful in this respect is Jouette M. Bassler, "Mixed Signals: Nicodemus in the Fourth Gospel," *JBL* 108 (1989) 635–46. She argues that Nicodemus is neither "in" nor "out" by the time the reader comes to the end of the story. He is a *tertium quid* whose ambiguity is never resolved. For a summary of scholarly discussion of the role of Nicodemus in the Fourth Gospel see Sylva, "Nicodemus," 150–51 nn. 7 and 12.

[32] See the powerful statement of the same sentiments in the letter of the retiring Bishop of Innsbruck, Reinhold Stecher, "Challenge to the Church," *The Tablet* 20/27 December 1997, 1668–69.

3. CONCLUSION

The above reading of some Johannine passages is obviously a blending (some might say a mishmash) of traditional and more contemporary approaches to the biblical text. I have mixed feelings about this exercise. I can appreciate the concerns of Janice Capel Anderson and Jeffrey Staley, who edited the *Semeia* volume on autobiographical criticism: "We, the editors, have often found ourselves seeking to protect those very authors from themselves, asking them whether they were sure they wanted to divulge the kinds of personal information found in their essays. We were worried that perhaps they had made themselves too open, too vulnerable."[33] My main concern about "vulnerability," however, is not for my personal academic or ecclesiastical career. I am rather more concerned that the establishment of autobiographical criticism might lead to a critical interaction between scholars that does not respond to *what was said or published,* on the basis of certain scholarly (?) criteria, but to *who a scholar might be,* on the basis of who knows what criteria.[34]

Autobiographical criticism lays claim to "point the way toward a more rigorously self-reflective and contextualized biblical criticism."[35] But are we not all aware of the strengths and weaknesses of our various interpretative traditions? As biblical scholars are generally by nature reflective people, we all have an idea where we are coming from and where we are heading (cf. John 3:8!) in biblical scholarship. I fully respect the rights of biblical scholars to use methods that start from the presupposition that the Bible is an oppressive and corrupt text that primarily asks to be subverted by a variety of postmodern readings, although I wonder why they bother. I ask that they respect the rights of the believing biblical scholars to inscribe their stories in interpretations. It is easy to understand why we bother. But is it necessary to develop more and more "methodologies" to make this fact more obvious? I have my doubts, however much I have enjoyed the exercise of sharing my journey with Nicodemus. One of my doctoral students read an early draft of this essay and responded:

---

[33] Janice Capel Anderson and Jeffrey Staley, "Taking it Personally: An Introduction," *Semeia* 72 (1995) 12.

[34] See, for example, Stephen D. Moore, "True Confessions and Weird Obsessions: Autobiographical Interventions in Literary and Biblical Studies," *Semeia* 72 (1995) 30–31. Moore suggests that my commitment to biblical studies was a means to validate "his original decision to become, his daily decision to remain, a priest."

[35] Anderson and Staley, "Taking It Personally," 16.

The experience of reading such a personal encounter with the text, presented not as a personal meditation but a scholarly critique, is disconcerting. There seems to be a clash of genres that leaves the reader dissatisfied. On the one hand there is the profound privilege of sharing another human being's faith journey. This is at the one time humbling, inspiring and a challenge to reflect on one's own journey. On the other hand there is a hesitancy to apply critical analytic skills to such self-disclosure, while being conscious that this is being presented as scholarly discourse. What is the reader to do? How can the biblical scholar read such autobiographical criticism with the distance needed for a scholarly perspective? The nature of this type of writing invites the reader into the text. It calls for involvement as the reader recognizes the reality or at least the possibility of his/her own story. Autobiography invites empathy and evokes human emotions. Does this help the study of and interpretation of the text, or can it, however subtly, manipulate the reader and destroy a healthy objectivity.[36]

She has touched on an important issue when she writes of the "clash of genres," which runs the danger of alienating or at best confusing a reader. What is under scrutiny in autobiographical criticism: a text or the critic's life-experience? Does a reader of this essay respond to the interpretation of John 3, 7, and 19 that results from the insertion of my journey into the interpretative experience, or to my journey, so symptomatic of many who were theologically trained in the Catholic tradition in the years during and just after Vatican II? I also share her refusal to accept that there is no such thing as "objectivity," however mixed up it might be with my own agenda and my own autobiography. Not only have I shaped the text, but the text has shaped me.

As well as these more traditional feelings of discomfort arising from an autobiographical reading there is a further theoretical problem inherent in the use of all biography, whether it be "auto" or not. I recently read a somewhat hagiographical account of the life of one of Australia's great heroes from the Second World War. Sir Edward Weary Dunlop showed remarkable courage and unbelievable skill in looking after the sick and injured among the allies, and even the Japanese, while a prisoner of war on the infamous Burma Railroad, yet as I closed the book I was left wondering about a number of elements in Weary's life and character that had somehow whispered to me between the lines of the written text.[37] Out of respect for the great Australian I will mention only two. I wonder what sort of reputation he had over his latter years as he advocated vigorous surgical intervention

---

[36] I am grateful to Dr. Mary Coloe, P.B.V.M., for allowing me to use this response, which she entitled "Reflections from a Bewildered Bystander."

[37] Sue Ebury, *Weary: The Life of Sir Edward Dunlop* (Ringwood, Vic.: Viking, 1994).

on cancer sufferers, so risky that other practitioners would not dare to operate. Many of those interventions resulted in death on the operating table, and others failed to recuperate. Second, given the reported fact that he did not mince his words and that he became somewhat short-tempered in his later years I wonder if he ever swore at his wife, the love of his young years, as she became increasingly subject to debilitating and disorienting dementia over the last twenty years of her life. Do these things matter? Probably not for us, but they would have no doubt troubled the great man. They do not appear in his biography, just as there is a lot of Frank Moloney's autobiography you do not find in his reading of Nicodemus.

Put theoretically, the reason for my discomfort with the biography of Weary Dunlop and the autobiography of Frank Moloney has been well articulated by Dwight Furrow: "The self, whether we understand it individually or collectively, is a topography of lost and missing pieces cobbled together by a systematically distorted narrative of the remains."[38] I will, however, return to the issue of "systematic distortion" as I close this paper.

Although to the practitioner my use of traditional methods in the above reading will be obvious, I wish to reaffirm the importance of historical-critical questions. Who are "the Jews" in the Fourth Gospel? Does John 21 belong to the Johannine narrative? What is the function of double-meaning words in the narrative (ἄνωθεν, ὑψωθῆναι, πνεῦμα, etc.)? Where do Jesus' words to Nicodemus end and his mini-discourse begin in 3:1-21? The Hebrew and Greek texts of the Bible were written a long time ago, in religious settings very different from our own, in languages (which reflect profound cultural differences) that most contemporary students are not able to read. Unless the critical questions are faced, however skillfully and with however many modern "aids," the text will be lost.

But is that a "loss"? If all that matters is recognition that everything is "intertext," the product of a highly volatile number of possibilities that happened to come together in this way at a particular point in time, then why bother? Why freeze a cultural, historical, and religious moment from the past to generate (and subsequently impose) a normative "canon"? All that matters is the reader. But every potential reader is also "intertext": the product of an infinite number of possibilities that have come together in one particular reading experience. In answer to my own question: yes, to lose the biblical text would be a tragic loss as

---

[38] Dwight Furrow, *Against Theory: Continental and Analytic Challenges to Moral Philosophy* (New York: Routledge, 1995) 192.

we would then be faced with the giddy possibility of spiralling through a never-ending whirlwind of interpretative possibilities, accepted today and discarded tomorrow. No human community, especially one inspired by the Christian tradition, can survive in such a whirlwind.

My autobiographical reading of the Nicodemus story in the Fourth Gospel has not corresponded exactly with the emerging practice of autobiographical readings, at least as we have them in Staley's *Reading with a Passion* and the contributions to the recent *Semeia* volume dedicated to this issue.[39] These initial studies lay claim to "point the way toward a more rigorously self-reflective and contextualized biblical criticism."[40] I heartily accept that agenda, but submit that the process must run in two directions. As should be obvious from my readings of passages from the Fourth Gospel, not only has the exegesis been shaped by my life story, my story has been shaped by the text. This essential interplay between reader and text and text and reader affirms the ongoing importance of text as well as reader.

Without *the text* of the adventures of Nicodemus I would not understand that the Christian tradition was born within Judaism, and that it summoned those who wish to adhere to that tradition to allow the impulse of the Spirit to draw them beyond rituals, accepting the divine origins of their beginning and their end. I would not know that in both past and present times many claim to speak authoritatively of God, but that there is only one who has come from God and has made God known. Jesus of Nazareth, the Son of Man, has been lifted up on a cross to show in his flesh the love of God, so that all who gaze upon this unique revelation of a unique God will have life. In this God's love has been made known, that God sent Jesus, God's Son, not to judge us but to give us life. Thus despite our past and our present public face Christianity is not about judgment, but about life.[41] But we are masters of our own destiny. Johannine realized eschatology is not just a technical term dear to Charles Harold Dodd and Rudolf Bultmann. It speaks to those of us who need to be taught that we are responsible for our

---

[39] See n. 9 above.

[40] Anderson and Staley, "Taking it Personally," 16.

[41] See the important recent pontifical statement on the need for the Catholic Church to "become more fully conscious of the sinfulness of her children, recalling all those times in history when they departed from the spirit of Christ and his Gospel and, instead of offering to the world the witness of a life inspired by the values of faith, indulged in ways of thinking and acting that were truly *forms of counter-witness and scandal*" in John Paul II, *Apostolic Letter Tertio Millenio Adveniente* (Vatican City: Libreria Editrice Vaticana, 1994) §§ 33-36 (pp. 42–48). The citation comes from § 33 (p. 42).

words and deeds. A list of Christian "truth-claims" could go on, but these, selected from my reading of John 3:1-21, will have to suffice.

There must be a multiplicity of possible readings of the biblical text and a multiplicity of interpretations resulting from such readings, but most scholarly readers of the text of the New Testament have been shaped by that particular text. It is a powerful element that has shaped and continues to shape a community and a tradition that recognize Jesus as Son of God, Son of Man, the unique revelation of God in the human story. But there is more. The person of Jesus Christ gives the text authority, not the text itself. Christian tradition pre-existed the text and gave us the βίβλια of the New Testament to grant access for their own and later generations to the person of Jesus Christ. We continue to read the story of Jesus within that tradition.[42] Not only is there a narrative world behind, within, and in front of the text: there is also a Christian tradition that pre-dated the text, generated the text, and continues to give it life within contemporary societies. The relationship between tradition and Scripture, however, is never stable, much less "frozen." The tradition gave birth to and continues to enliven the Scriptures in a Christian community, but the Scriptures perform the prophetic role of keeping the tradition honest when it falls prey to the temptation of absolutizing, through accommodation, any age, culture, or particular religious practice.[43] Not all will accept this view, and I ask, within a postmodern world where *"différance"* is so important, that we Christians be allowed to affirm our "difference."

We must do our best to achieve the impossible. We must work imaginatively within the Christian tradition to create a horizon across the worlds behind the text, in the text, and in front of the text, in an interpretation that respects all three. It will also tell something of the story of the interpreter. My insistence on the need to create a horizon where all "worlds" meet is not new. It was an essential part of Hans-Georg Gadamer's hermeneutic in which true understanding does not take place without a *Horizontverschmelzung,* a fusion of horizons, past and present,[44] further articulated by the reception aesthetics and literary

[42] Parallel affirmations could (and should) be made concerning the place of *Torah, Nebiʾim* and *Kᵉtubim* within the Jewish Tradition. It is beyond the scope of this paper to do so.

[43] For further development of this important point see my study "Jesus Christ: The Question to Cultures," in this volume, pp. 183–209. See also Moloney, *A Body Broken for a Broken People* 7–30, 191–201.

[44] See, for example, Hans-Georg Gadamer, *Truth and Method* (New York: Seabury, 1975) 269–74. See p. 273: "Understanding . . . is always the fusion of these horizons which we *imagine* to exist by themselves" (emphasis supplied).

hermeneutics of Hans Robert Jauss.[45] It has been exquisitely developed by Ricoeur's large-scale *Time and Narrative*.[46] Ricoeur insists that the act of reading produces a "refiguration of time." Indeed, he rightly points out that all attempts, both past and present, to posit different "worlds" in the reading process misunderstand the process. All "worlds" disappear and there remains only the complex relationship between the text and the reader, "the confrontation between the world of the text and the world of the reader at once a stasis and an impetus."[47]

Ricoeur uses the notion of "appropriation," his translation of the German *Aneignung*. The verb *aneignen* means to make one's own what was initially alien. Thus, he rightly comments, "even when we read a philosophical work, it is always a question of entering into an alien work, of divesting oneself of the earlier 'me' in order to receive . . . the self conferred by the work itself."[48] In this playful but challenging process there is no place for the static focus of the interpreter's attention on one of the three "worlds" or the privileging of any one of those worlds. As Ricoeur comments at the close of one of his very few excursuses into biblical scholarship: "repetition means transfiguration."[49]

I was reading Arundhati Roy's Booker Prize-winning novel, *The God of Small Things*, as I was writing this essay. Within that context there was a passage from the narrator that struck me as true, and appropriate for this setting:

> The Great Stories are the ones you have heard and want to hear again. The ones you can enter anywhere and inhabit comfortably. They don't deceive you with thrills and trick endings. They don't surprise you with the unforeseen. They are as familiar as the house you live in. Or the smell of your lover's skin. You know how they end, yet you listen as though you don't. In the way that although you know that one day you will die, you live as though you won't. In the great stories you know who lives, who dies, who finds love, who doesn't. And yet you want to know again.[50]

[45] On this see the impressive study by Ormond Rush, *The Reception of Doctrine: An Appropriation of Hans Robert Jauss' Reception Aesthetics and Literary Hermeneutics*. Tesi Gregoriani 19 (Roma: Editrice Pontificia Università Gregoriana, 1997). On Jauss' use of the "horizon" see pp. 65–124.

[46] Paul Ricoeur, *Time and Narrative*. 3 vols. (Chicago: University of Chicago Press, 1984–88).

[47] Ricoeur, *Time and Narrative* 2:179

[48] Paul Ricoeur, *Hermeneutics and the Human Sciences* 190.

[49] Paul Ricoeur, "The Golden Rule. Exegetical and Theological Perplexities," *NTS* 36 (1990) 397.

[50] Arundhati Roy, *The God of Small Things* (London: Flamingo, 1997) 229.

It is important for Jews and Christians that there be Jewish and Christian communities where both the text *of the Bible* and the interpretation *of the Bible* are treasured. For the Jewish and the Christian tradition the Bible is one of the ways God is made known; it is our Great Story. It is the house we live in . . . the smell of our lover's skin. It has given us the fixed points that support the silken threads upon which the many possible tapestries of Jewish and Christian belief and Jewish and Christian responses to that belief can be woven.[51] We know, and yet we want to know again. Our interpretation of the text is not determined by a dogmatic tradition, itself interpretation of text, but inspired by its beauty and the tradition giving it life. *Mutatis mutandis* a contemporary assessment of the task of the literary critic could be applied to the teacher of the biblical text:

> A great literary critic is like a great musician, who uses his knowledge of music to create beautiful interpretations. These interpretations, although they are called "interpretations *of*," are in fact interpretations *with* the music—they achieve what the art was made for in the first place.[52]

I frankly admit that not only my autobiographical reading of the Johannine text but all my interpretations of text could rightly be described by contemporary theorists like Furrow as a partial cobbling

---

[51] On this process see The Pontifical Biblical Commission, *The Interpretation of the Bible in the Church* (Rome: Libreria Editrice Vaticana, 1993). Despite his claim to speak only for a Northern European Protestant Church, Ulrich Luz's responses to his question on the place of the Bible in a religiously plural society are instructive. In "Kann die Bibel?" 334–39 he formulates eight theses: the Bible (1) keeps religious dialogue open, (2) maintains scholarly and rational discussion, (3) searches for consent (*n.b.* not unanimity), (4) points the way for ecumenical dialogue, (5) maintains the otherness/strangeness ("Fremdheit") of the story of Jesus, (6) shows that religious dialogue transcends the established churches, (7) provides a basis for European (only?) culture, (8) points toward God.

[52] Barend P. van Heusden, *Why Literature? An Inquiry Into the Nature of Literary Semiosis.* Probleme der Semiotik 18 (Tübingen: Stauffenberg, 1997) 235. I am grateful to my colleague at Australian Catholic University, Dr. Dennis Rochford, M.S.C., who drew my attention to this stimulating publication. Ricoeur says something similar: "There is . . . an interesting relation between play and the presentation of a world. The relation is, moreover, absolutely reciprocal: on the one hand, the presentation of the world in a poem is a heuristic function and in this sense 'playful'; but on the other hand all play reveals something true, precisely because it is play. To play, says Gadamer, is to play at something. In entering a game we hand ourselves over, we abandon ourselves to the space of meaning that holds sway over the reader" (*Hermeneutics and the Human Sciences* 187).

together of only some of the pieces. But I am unwilling to accept that this cobbling is driven by a "systematic distortion." Furrow argues that the distortion is generated by "just one more search for the solace of origins, perpetually contested and itself the source of injustice." Jewish and Christian history, and some present experiences, teach that the loss of contact with our origins, our Great Story, is perhaps the most consistent source of injustice in our communities and failure in our mission.[53] My reading of the Nicodemus episodes, however imperfect and partial it might be, attempts to lay bare some elements of present injustices and failures.

The birth, life story, and death of each one of us are more than autobiography. *For me* there is a world beyond the text of "my story" that impinges upon the reading process. I trust that my account of my journey with Nicodemus—only one text among so many in our τὰ βίβλια—shows that this mysterious world does not freeze the Jew and Christian into an irrelevant past. As Ruldolf Bultmann said in 1957: "Ever anew it will make clear who we are and who God is, and the exegete will have to express this in an ever new conceptuality."[54]

---

[53] See, for example, Moloney, *A Body Broken for a Broken People.*

[54] Rudolf Bultmann, "Is Exegesis Without Presuppositions Possible?" in idem, *New Testament and Mythology and Other Basic Writings.* Selected, edited, and translated by Schubert M. Ogden (Philadelphia: Fortress, 1984). The original German appeared in 1957 (*TZ* 13 [1957] 409–17).

SCRIPTURAL INDEX

Index of Ancient Writings

JEWISH WRITINGS

CHRISTIAN WRITINGS

GNOSTIC WRITINGS

AUTHOR INDEX